# Forbidden Fruit

# *Forbidden Fruit*

## Sex & Religion
## *in the* Lives *of*
## American Teenagers

Mark D. Regnerus

OXFORD
UNIVERSITY PRESS
2007

# OXFORD
## UNIVERSITY PRESS

Oxford University Press, Inc., publishes works that further
Oxford University's objective of excellence
in research, scholarship, and education.

Oxford   New York
Auckland   Cape Town   Dar es Salaam   Hong Kong   Karachi
Kuala Lumpur   Madrid   Melbourne   Mexico City   Nairobi
New Delhi   Shanghai   Taipei   Toronto

With offices in
Argentina   Austria   Brazil   Chile   Czech Republic   France   Greece
Guatemala   Hungary   Italy   Japan   Poland   Portugal   Singapore
South Korea   Switzerland   Thailand   Turkey   Ukraine   Vietnam

Published by Oxford University Press, Inc.
198 Madison Avenue, New York, New York 10016

www.oup.com

Oxford is a registered trademark of Oxford University Press

Library of Congress Cataloging-in-Publication Data
Regnerus, Mark.
Forbidden fruit: sex and religion in the lives of American teenagers /
Mark D. Regnerus.
p. cm.
Includes bibliographical references and index.
ISBN-13 978-0-19-532094-7
1. Teenagers—Religious life—United States.   2. Teenagers—United
States—Sexual behavior.   3. Teenagers—United States—Conduct of life.
4. Sex—Religious aspects.   I. Title.
BL625.47.R43 2007
205'.6608350973—dc22      2006021768

1 3 5 7 9 8 6 4 2

Printed in the United States of America
on acid-free paper

*For Deeann*

# ACKNOWLEDGMENTS

No academic is self-made. I am indebted to a wide circle of friends, colleagues, and organizations not only for their assistance on this book project but also with my general intellectual development. I owe Chris Smith a mentorship debt I cannot repay. I can only try to emulate it. He is also great fun to work with. Besides me, Jeremy Uecker has worked the hardest on this manuscript. Without his analytic proficiency, astute information-gathering skills, and general good sense, this manuscript would have been way behind schedule. Jenny Trinitapoli assisted with the structure and analysis of the National Study of Youth and Religion (NSYR) interview data and in numerous conversations about the subject matter. Kenny Steinman, John Wallace, and Michael Emerson read portions of the text and provided helpful and wise feedback. The copyediting skills of Betsy Stokes made this book far more readable. My editor at Oxford, Cynthia Read, has been a pleasure to work with and was enthusiastic about this book at all the right times. Brad Breems started all this way back when (1989–1993) by fostering in me the sociological imagination that had been stimulated by my parents and my brother David.

Many have either helped me to think through analyses of sexual behavior, have written with me on the subject, have been part of my intellectual or professional development, or have simply shared conversations about this material, including Chris Ellison, Bob Hummer, Kraig Beyerlein, Brad Wilcox, Bob Woodberry, Glen Elder, Dave Sikkink, John Bartkowski, Alex Weinreb, Susan Watkins, Monica Gaughan, Byron Johnson, Chris Bachrach, Rob Crosnoe, Mark Warr, Lisa Pearce, Matt Bradshaw, Michael McCullough, Amy Adamczyk, Jacob Felson, Monica Longmore, Melinda Denton, Amy Burdette, Darren Sherkat, Susan Newcomer, Solomon Katz, Kevin Dougherty, Margarita Mooney, Mike Langford, Christy Green, Mike Lindsay, Jim Moody, jimi adams, Rod Stark, Michael Young, Marc Musick,

Guang Guo, Dan Powers, Tom Pullum, Kelly Raley, Chandra Muller, Sherry Rostosky, Brad Smith, and Laura Luchies. A number of students also provided helpful feedback on parts of the text, including Erin Hamilton, Chuck Stokes, Sara Yeatman, Nicole Angotti, Tricia Ryan, Chris Pieper, Elizabeth Swanson, Anita Komanduri, Amy Pieper, Tynisha Wooley, and Sarah Pratt.

I would like to especially express my appreciation to several organizations for providing funding that assisted me in completing this manuscript, including the National Institute of Child Health and Human Development (R03-HD048899-01 for "Race, Religion, and Adolescent Sexual Norms and Conduct"), the Metanexus Institute's Spiritual Transformation Research Program (with the support of the John Templeton Foundation), the University of Texas at Austin, and the National Study of Youth and Religion.

I also benefited from presentations and discussions of the material in this book at a variety of venues, including annual meetings of the American Sociological Association, the Society for the Scientific Study of Religion, and the Population Association of America, and in talks given at the University of Pennsylvania, the University of Kentucky, the Georgia Institute of Technology, the National Institutes of Health, and several at my home institution, the University of Texas at Austin.

I also want to acknowledge the hard work that the Add Health research team at the University of North Carolina at Chapel Hill continues to do, including (but not limited to) Kathie Harris and Dick Udry. The same goes for the NSYR research team, especially Lisa Pearce and Melinda Denton, as well as Chris Smith. Thanks to the Lilly Endowment Inc. and to Chris Coble and Craig Dykstra for funding the NSYR. Thank you also to those NSYR investigators and graduate students who conducted in-person interviews, including Tim Cupery, Kenda Dean, Dan Dehanas, Korie Edwards, Richard Flory, Phil Schwadel, Youn-ok Lee, Norm Peart, Darci Powell, Demetrius Semien, Steve Vaisey, Ria Van Ryn, and Eve Veliz. I am also deeply grateful, in an ongoing manner, to the University of Texas's Population Research Center and its administrative and computing staff.

Finally, without my wife, Deeann, this book truly would not be in print. It has been an honor to walk through half my life with her. My children, Samuel and Elizabeth, continue to provide inspiration and display their own commitment to intellectual curiosity. They constantly push me to wonder anew about child and adolescent development. In conclusion, I wish to honor my father, Carl Regnerus, whom I have continued to miss so much over these past several years. I know he was proud of me. I remain proud of him.

# CONTENTS

# *Forbidden Fruit*

# INTRODUCTION

If there is a developmental trajectory for anything during adolescence, it is sex. Nothing—not smoking, drinking, drug use, nor any form of delinquency—compares to the rapid commencement of paired sexual practices during the latter half of adolescence. In an average day, at least 7,000 American teenagers experience sexual intercourse for the first time.[1] Nearly every human being finds his or her way to it eventually, but few have by age 13 and most have before the age of 20. Some do so unwillingly. Without analyzing any data on adolescent sex, it is obvious that something significant is going on developmentally, biologically, socially, and culturally to make sexual intercourse attractive enough that roughly one-third to one-half of all young Americans try it for the first time—in spite of its physical and emotional risks—within the span of about two to three years (between ages 16 and 18).

Numbers do not help us to properly interpret and understand adolescent sexuality today. Media accounts of teenagers' sexual attitudes, motivations, and behavior do not always clarify matters. One could conclude from several recent news features that today's adolescents are much more into oral sex than ever before (Halpern-Felsher et al. 2005), that abstinence pledgers are more likely to have anal sex than those who don't pledge (Connolly in the *Washington Post*, March 19, 2005), that there is a trend toward bisexuality among high school girls (Irvine on "CBS News," September 16, 2005), or that we have actually overestimated just how sexualized adolescents really are (Brooks in the *New York Times*, April 17, 2005). We are receiving mixed messages, for sure.

The entertainment industry, on the other hand, is largely unconcerned with what real adolescents are doing. Movie and television producers opt to stimulate youthful sexual expression and to glamorize emerging sexuality. Pornographic Web sites feature "just barely legal" teens supposedly bursting with pent-up, "forbidden" sexual desire. Video games come rated by how much sex and violence appear therein. *Donkey Kong* and *Space Invaders* have given way to games like *Playboy: The Mansion* and *Grand Theft Auto*, programmed with hidden sex scenes. "Grinding" to sexually explicit hip hop lyrics is a popular dance form among young Americans. Skin is definitely in. America is becoming "sexier" while the focus of sex is becoming younger.[2]

Even the practice of social science is not exempt from this sea change. The terms that social scientists use to describe adolescent sexuality have undergone an evolution in recent years. "Losing virginity" has been subtly deemed too negative and "coitus" too scientific. Each has been increasingly replaced by the more impartial "first sex" or the positive-sounding "sexual debut." Some even refer to "sexual onset," as if the first experience of intercourse were somehow the beginning of a chronic medical condition (Browning, Leventhal, and Brooks-Gunn 2005).

At the same time, many Americans remain very ambivalent about sex. News reports abound about the high school teacher who pursues a forbidden sexual relationship with her own student and in turn is sentenced to prison "for love," the public officeholder who is caught in a sexual dalliance and forced to resign, the pastor who admits a porn habit and is summarily dismissed by his "sexually pure" church council. Whether punishing or peeping, Americans are a gawking nation when it comes to sex. It captures our attention, our gaze, and sometimes our ire. We remain fixated on punishing the sexually deviant, even as "deviant" sexuality remains a moving target. As a society, we are caught somewhere between understanding sex as sacred and thinking it profane.

Despite all of the mixed messages and confusion, and much to their parents' relief, most youth make it through the teenage years alive and without the sorts of life-altering incidents or conditions that could significantly alter their transition into adulthood (pregnancy, childbearing, rape, a criminal record, etc.). All of which is not to suggest that adolescence ever was—or has become—less stressful. It remains the life stage of greatest and most rapid change. Teenagers have to get along with their parents and adjust to their divorces, battle their own blues, make and keep friendships, build a reputation, try to fit in, concern themselves with grades and college entrance exams, deal with the pressure to look attractive, come to grips with their own emerging sexual feelings, hope for a date, get over being dumped (Eccles 1999; Steinberg and Morris 2001). Some of the turning points of adolescence are inevitable, such as the onset of puberty or one's first menstrual period, the transition from middle school to high school, and reaching the legal driving age. Other turning points are not inevitable but still common, including family relocations, high school graduation, the pursuit of higher education, and—for a considerable majority—the loss of virginity[3] and the commencement of paired sexual activity.

This book is about the last set of these voluntary turning points—the formation of sexual attitudes and motivations, and the initial and subsequent experiences of sexual intercourse and related sexual activities. In particular, I will consider how religion shapes the sexual lives of contemporary American adolescents: what sex means, what adolescents know and expect about sex, and what strategies adolescents use to negotiate the very mixed messages they receive about sex (Martin 2002).

There are numerous ways in which religion *might* affect adolescent sexuality and its practice, including their attitudes, beliefs about, and practices of contraception, masturbation, premarital sexual intercourse, oral sex, homosexuality, bisexuality, and the use of pornography, to name several. Religion might also indirectly shape these things through its effects on friendship choices, dating patterns, parental monitoring, and how adolescents choose to use their time (Wallace and Williams 1997). Yet how religion contributes to sexual values and behaviors *in reality* is not well understood. We should not presume that religion shapes how adolescents understand and express their sexuality simply by observing that some youth are religious. In other words, I want to know how *consequential* religion is among them (Glock and Stark 1965). Does religion matter when adolescents make sexual decisions and take actions? How so? If not, why not? Does Christianity—which is what most American adolescents practice—typically function as little more than a generally assumed cultural background, or does it really motivate the sexual choices of a significant segment of adolescent society? This book takes a solid step in the direction of deciphering the religion-sex association and pursuing explanations for the evidence that emerges from two nationally representative surveys and in-depth interviews with more than 250 adolescents across the country.

## WHY RELIGION?

Evaluating adolescent sexual behavior never goes out of style. It just requires constant updating. Social forces that influence adolescent sexual behavior at one point are often found to have changed when reexamined just 10 years later (Joyner and Laumann 2000). As a result, studies on teenagers and sexuality crop up with regularity to appease parents', educators', and lawmakers' hunger for information.

So why ruin a good social scientific study of adolescent sexual behavior by focusing on religion? Wouldn't I be better off turning my attention toward what scholars suggest *really* matters for adolescent behavior: influences like friendships, peer pressure, body image, educational ambitions, or emotional health? Or perhaps something more sociological, like race or gender? Or the current queen of influences on all things important—social capital?[4]

First, religion and sexuality tap basic drives. Sex concerns the pursuit of an intimate connection with another human being—to be known and to know someone else intensely. Religion concerns the need to make sense and meaning out of life, to connect with something or someone higher and purer than yourself, outside of the realm of the empirical. In short, both religion and sex are *elemental* life pursuits, not mere window dressing but close to the heart of what it means to be human. Perhaps their shared association is why beautiful women are sometimes referred to as "goddesses," why companies like Victoria's Secret dress their models in angelic garb, and why the phrase "forbidden fruit" conjures up images that are both religious and sexual (Yancey 2003).

Second, religion—together with peers, parents, and the media—remains a primary socialization agent of children and adolescents. Though often an understated influence in adolescents' lives, religion as traditionally practiced nevertheless performs a variety of important social functions (independently of its varying particular content): it is both an internal and external social control mechanism; it explicitly and implicitly reinforces collectively held values and beliefs by forbidding some things and encouraging others; it provides social networks to individuals; it encourages trust, caring, and self-sacrifice (Wuthnow 1995); it has enduring faith in the possibility of individual transformation; it galvanizes and organizes moral indignation (Smith 1996); and its practitioners are committed to the next generation. Participation in religious institutions often provides adherents with functional communities (sometimes amid dysfunctional families or communities) and reinforces parental support networks and control. Organized religion establishes norms and reinforces them with its power as a formal institution (Regnerus and Elder 2003). The list could continue. Moreover, since religion often shapes parenting styles, the role of religion in many teenagers' lives may begin at their birth, if not sooner (Bartkowski and Ellison 1995).

Unfortunately, some social scientists ignore religious institutions, organizations, and the power of belief not because they are blind to them (which may be the case for some) but because they remain convinced that religion is epiphenomenal. That is, they believe that religion is *only* about networks of social control, supervised peer groups, and organizational participation. Even when taken seriously, religious influence on human behavior is often mischaracterized and misunderstood in the academic community. Religion in general is often associated with sexual conservatism (if not complete ignorance), repression, prudish behavior, and a tendency toward avoidance, abstinence, and generalized condemnation. But are such associations true?

Third, sex is a sphere of human behavior high in religious applicability. By this, I mean that it is a topic that has more religious relevance—or is more clearly addressed in most religious traditions—than many other topics. Few theologies or religious schemas attempt to sacralize all of life. Much more common is the division of human action into the religiously important (the sacred) and the religiously unimportant (the profane). Some spheres of life, like family and sexuality, are typically seen as more centrally related to religious faith. Other spheres, like employment, leisure activity, and personal finances, are often understood as less central to religious faith.

When roles or norms about what to do in a particular situation compete— for example, to obey your beliefs or to give in to your hormones and a willing partner's expectations—the behavior's religious applicability may affect which roles or norms are adhered to (Wimberley 1989). On the other hand, some classes of actions—like civic participation, sports, and education—employ much less religious applicability, since there are fewer religious teachings or guidelines about them. Failing geometry does not make someone a bad Christian. Quitting the basketball team may invoke guilt, disappointment, and some ostracism, but it is religiously irrelevant.

Sex is simply a sphere of life that has considerable religious import for many Americans. While sexuality falls outside the specific mandate of churches (which is to make Christians, to encourage worship of God, etc.), it does not fall far, since sexuality is tied to the institution of the family, and the family is often closely linked to organized religion (Ellingson 2004). Thus, evaluating the implications of religion for actual sexual decision making makes perfect sense. Remarkably, though, few attempts have been made to determine why exactly religion matters for some adolescents' sexual decision making and not for others' (Hardy and Raffaelli 2003).

## THE PARAMETERS OF THIS STUDY

This book's primary purpose is to take an extended look into the real lives of American teenagers and to document whether religious faith affects—if at all—how they think about sexuality and the practices in which they choose to either engage or refrain. To accomplish this, I employ a variety of research methods and draw on several different data sources on American youth. My primary source is the National Survey of Youth and Religion (hereafter referred to as NSYR), of which I am a project co-investigator. From July 2002 to April

2003, we conducted a national, random-digit-dial telephone survey of a sample of all American household telephone numbers. Eligible households included at least one teenager between the ages of 13 and 17 living in the household for at least six months of the year. In order to randomize responses within households, and so to help attain representativeness of age and gender, we asked to conduct the survey with the teenager in the household who had the most recent birthday. There were 3,370 adolescents who completed the survey, and an accompanying parent interview was conducted with either their mother or father, as they were available (see appendix B for a detailed description of the research methodologies employed in the primary data sources I use).

The second phase of the data collection of the NSYR involved in-depth personal interviews with 267 teenagers from all around the country, drawn from the pool of respondents who had completed the telephone survey. The majority of the in-person interviews were conducted between March 2003 and August 2003, with a final few completed as late as January 2004. The purpose of the interviews was to provide extended follow-up discussions about adolescents' religious, spiritual, family, and social lives. The questionnaire followed closely and expanded upon the topics that were included on the NSYR telephone survey (see appendix B). The interview sample was selected from among the 3,370 adolescents who completed the NSYR telephone survey, and the pool of actual interviewees was drawn taking into account the following demographic characteristics: urban/suburban/rural, region, age, sex, race, household income, religion, and school type. We attempted to achieve a balance in each of these areas. Seventeen different interviewers conducted interviews in 45 U.S. states, each interviewer conducting between 10 and 20 interviews (see Figure I.1). Finally, I draw upon a small number of follow-up interviews with these same youth that were conducted during the summer of 2005, two years after we first spoke with them.

My second source of extensive survey data is the National Longitudinal Study of Adolescent Health. "Add Health," as it is commonly referred to, is arguably the most comprehensive survey of adolescents and young adults ever taken. Designed to help explain the causes of adolescent health and health behavior, Add Health pays particular attention to sexuality, focusing on behaviors, motivations, risk perceptions, and attitudes. Add Health also includes information on the important contexts in an adolescent's life, namely, parents, schools, communities, friends, and romantic partners.

The NSYR and Add Health together comprise the best available nationally representative data to study the influence of religion on the sexual attitudes and practices of America's teenagers. Nevertheless, I occasionally draw on evidence from other national studies, such as the 2002 National Survey of Family Growth, the National Youth Risk Behavior Survey, and Monitoring the Future.[5]

FIGURE I.1. Distribution of NSYR Survey Follow-up Personal Interviewees

While I report simple frequencies in the text, I also make use of multivariate survey analyses (detailed in the appendixes) as well as note the findings of a wide variety of published social scientific studies, including a number of my own.

For parents, youth workers, and educators, this book should prove enlightening and hopefully useful. Providing information for informed decision making is, after all, a key purpose of the social sciences. Nevertheless, this is not a recipe book for successfully reaching, mentoring, or parenting youth. Instead, I offer a thorough, factual portrait of modern adolescence. This is not a book about young adults, although I make occasional reference to them and to Wave III of the Add Health study, which was fielded during the respondents' early adult years. Thus, I make very few claims here about the sexual attitudes and behavior of persons older than 18. From my own and others' studies, young adulthood is a life stage where sex tends to be more prominent than during the teenage years. That is for another book.

## THE SHAPE OF THE BOOK

By now, it should be clear that sex causes considerable ambivalence among Americans, religious or otherwise. We esteem it as sacred, forbid it, police it, yet often treat it as if it were profane. There is no doubt that the issue of sex has religious ramifications. One need only note the headlines about priest sex scandals and homosexual ordination issues to quickly realize that sex matters for organized religion. Chapter 1 will briefly detail how the historical Christian tradition has thought about sex, culled from interpretations of the Hebrew Old Testament and the New Testament and from more recent religious writings and teachings. Following that, I move from ancient wisdom to the most contemporary of thinkers—adolescents themselves. I set the stage for a number of the book's key themes by offering perspectives from six teenagers, each of whom participates (to varying degrees) in organized religion.

In chapter 2, I briefly review and evaluate the various ways in which social scientists have come to understand how religion affects human behavior in general and adolescent sex in particular. In a nutshell, social scientific debate about the *real* influence of religion on human behavior remains intense. Some reasonable conclusions about it are in order, however.

Chapter 3 explores how adolescents learn sex and sexuality. I discuss various parental strategies for the socialization and education of their children about sex and contraception, focusing on distinctions between moral education and information exchange. We learn that religion matters for what parents say about sex and contraception, with whom they discuss it, how often, and with what ease. I also explore—though only briefly—the association between religion and developing homosexual and bisexual identities, attractions, and practices in adolescence.

Chapter 4 traces the development of adolescent heterosexual ethics and norms, including their motivations to avoid or engage in sex. There, I document what types of adolescents are likely to take abstinence pledges, how well they work, and the sexual and familial idealism they portray. I also explore the popular but vaguely defined theme of "emotional readiness" as a barometer of sexual preparedness.

Chapter 5 consummates the study by focusing on actual sexual behavior: teenagers' experience of "first sex," their patterns of heterosexual behavior *after* losing virginity, and some adolescents' regrets about sexual activity. I also document their thoughts about—and differential use of—contraception. Several key stories emerge in this chapter—about race, evangelicalism, and what sociologists call "plausibility structures." Chapter 6 evaluates alternate forms of sex, such as pornography and oral and anal sex. I explore in some detail the preference for replacing vaginal sexual intercourse with forms of sexual expression less threatening to future prospects for material success and conclude that there is evidence of an emerging middle-class sexual morality among some American teenagers.

Chapter 7 returns to "big picture" themes, giving attention to the stated and implicit motivation behind adolescent religious discourse about sexual decision making. Are devout youth really distinguishing themselves in the sphere of sex *because* of their faith, or is religion a pragmatic and strategic tool to help them reach their goals of avoiding pregnancy and retaining virginity until closer to (or at) marriage? I introduce there a typology of religious influence, which should help us to make sense of the ways in which religion actually affects teenagers' sexual behavior. I then conclude with a summary of the book's key findings and contributions, followed by an unscientific postscript—a series of my own reflections about adolescent sex and the social scientific study of it.

## SUMMARIZING ADOLESCENTS' RELIGION

Before I move forward, however, a short introduction to adolescent religiosity is in order. By "religiosity," I am referring to a person's religiousness, as measured several ways, typically in the form of how often they attend religious services, how involved they are in religious activities, how religious they consider themselves to be, and whether they think religion actually matters for their lives and decisions. Since the book is about sex more than it is about religion, I want to steer clear of long descriptions of religious practices, beliefs, and traditions. But a brief overview should help to orient us to what contemporary American teenagers are like when it comes to religion.

Adolescence is the most religiously unstable period of the life course. And how religion affects 13-year-olds may be very different from how it shapes 18-year-olds. Physical, emotional, and moral development occurs at a rapid pace during this period of the lifespan. Such instability provides fodder for some interesting media claims about new religious trends, all the way from spirituality to evangelical revivals and Wicca (e.g., Curran and Estes in the *New York Times*, April 29, 1998; National Public Radio, May 13, 2004; Leland et al. in *Newsweek*, May 8, 2000; Van Biema, Grace, and Mitchell in *Time*, May 31, 1999). Nothing interests media producers and consumers so much as the abnormal, atypical, hypersexual, and paranormal.

So what do social scientists know about the religious lives of adolescents—their beliefs, practices, and affiliations? Most reliable survey research suggests that substantial change happens slowly and that traditional, predictable forms of religion (and sex) are alive and well among American adolescents. To be sure, trends always have their pacesetters, and religious entrepreneurs are adept at attracting a following, but unusual religious practices invariably remain at the cultural margins of American adolescents' religious expression.

According to the NSYR, just over 30 percent of American teenagers identify with a denomination typically considered evangelical (sometimes called conservative) Protestant. By this classification, evangelical Protestant youth outnumber mainline Protestant youth by a ratio of nearly three to one. Slightly more adolescents affiliate with a historically black or African-American denomination[6] (10.7 percent) than with the historically white mainline. The largest single religious denomination in the United States remains Roman Catholicism, claiming about 23 percent of teenagers. Mormon youth comprise just under 3 percent, about twice the number of Jewish adolescents. American youth who are Muslim, Hindu, Buddhist, or another religious tradition together comprise about 3 percent of all American adolescents. About 16 percent of adolescents identify as not religious. Real atheism—adamant conviction that God does not exist—is much rarer than most people think and nearly absent among American teens. Less than one-half of 1 percent report never having believed in God (Smith and Denton 2005).

By and large, most teenagers—even the oldest ones—retain the religious affiliation of their parents (Smith and Denton 2005). And despite the steady flow of immigrants to the United States, the number of Muslims remains small. There are more Mormon adolescents in America than Muslims, Buddhists, and Hindus combined. If the media want to know what is going on religiously with American teenagers, they are likely to get close to the truth by asking an average evangelical Protestant or Catholic 16-year-old. Together, these two groups constitute almost 6 of every 10 American youths.

According to Table I.1, slightly over 40 percent of American adolescents say they attend religious services at least once a week. Roughly the same number attends less frequently. About 18 percent say they never attend at all, but nearly this many attend more than once a week. Although public religious practices *can* be coerced during childhood and adolescence, this is not often the case. The vast majority of adolescents (84 percent, not shown in the table) report that if the decision were up to them, they would still attend their current congregation or congregations (a significant number attend more than one, often due to the religious intermarriage of their parents or stepparents). However, we have not detected considerable enthusiasm about religion among the majority of adolescents, which suggests a generalized religious apathy among many. They can take it or leave it. It's not bothersome, and it doesn't ask too much of them.

About one in every five teenagers, however, says that religion is *extremely* important in shaping how they live their daily lives. These are what I call the "truly devout." Their patterns of behavior are often distinct, even from those (31 percent) who say that religion is "very important." The same can be said

TABLE I.1 Religious Practices and Attitudes of Adolescents (in Percentages)

| | |
|---|---:|
| *Church Attendance* | |
| More than once a week | 16.2 |
| Weekly | 24.3 |
| 1–3 times a month | 18.8 |
| Several times a year | 22.5 |
| Never | 18.1 |
| *Currently Involved in a Youth Group* | 37.6 |
| *Frequency of Private Prayer* | |
| Many times a day | 16.1 |
| About once a day | 21.6 |
| Once–few times a week | 27.1 |
| At most 1–2 times a month | 20.3 |
| Never | 14.7 |
| *Frequency of Personal Scripture Reading* | |
| Many times a day | 2.3 |
| About once a day | 6.3 |
| Once–few times a week | 17.2 |
| At most 1–2 times a month | 33.0 |
| Never | 41.0 |
| *Importance of Religion in Shaping Daily Life* | |
| Extremely important | 19.6 |
| Very important | 31.0 |
| Somewhat important | 31.2 |
| Not very important | 10.8 |
| Not important at all | 7.2 |
| *Spiritual but Not Religious* | |
| Very true | 8.4 |
| Somewhat true | 46.4 |
| Not true at all | 43.0 |

*Source*: National Survey of Youth and Religion

for the 16 percent of youth who attend religious services *more* than once a week, as opposed to once a week (24 percent).

The phrase "spiritual but not religious" has garnered considerable attention lately, though primarily among adults for whom the term is personally appealing. Only about 8 percent of American adolescents (in the NSYR) confidently self-identify as spiritual but not religious. When we asked adolescents in interviews about this phrase, we often drew blank stares. Even most adolescents who fit the label of spiritual but not religious tend toward answers of "I don't know," or "I never heard of that," or "Huh?"

Religious moderation is a common, important theme among them. While being entirely devoid of religion is odd, if allowable, being too religious can be worse, and such extremes should be avoided. This mentality is consonant with the religious individualist approach that is prevalent among contemporary adolescents. As Christian Smith and Melinda Denton (2005) note, most American teenagers have been well socialized to tolerate the religious and the nonreligious alike. Indeed, most nonreligious youth are not *anti*religious. None of the 267 teens with whom we spoke openly attacked organized religion. This group of Americans is simply not as religiously rebellious as many have made them out to be.

Among the majority, then, religion tends to be personal, private, and largely immune to criticism. Asserting only one tradition as true borders on overconfidence, if not overreligiousness. Many youths, extensively socialized into the digital age, find historical religious traditions outdated, open to spontaneous alteration, or simply too challenging to adopt. Many of the adolescents with whom we spoke in person hold low opinions of other people's personal morality, but high views of their own. When asked whether they had been involved recently in anything that was "wrong," adolescents typically reply with a simple answer: no. Most, however, said they *have* opposed their friends' actions at some point. Few could articulate why some things (like murder) may be absolutely wrong. Granted, many adolescents have never been asked such pointed questions about religion and morality (which is too bad). But even beyond this, their generalized inability to discuss morality underscores the thin moral education so many of them receive (Hunter 2000). As Smith and Denton (2005) note about religion—and the same could be said for morality in general—it is like any other language: to learn how to speak it, a person must first listen to "native speakers" and then practice speaking it herself. Few parents, even among the devoutly religious, are native speakers.

In sum, religious *passion* is not the norm among American teenagers. Many youth pray regularly and find it easy to do so. They read the Bible (or the Torah) less regularly than they pray, as the time it takes to read is subject to fierce competition within their busy lives. Most youth are not spiritual seekers, and recent media attention on spirituality has clearly overestimated its popularity among this demographic. Morality matters to adolescents, but they are a tolerant group and typically avoid evaluations of their peers that could be construed as judgmental. People are deemed good or bad because of their actions, not their religion. For this reason, there is little systematic religious bigotry among adolescents. They are well versed in tolerance. Even those we might suspect otherwise, such as evangelicals, tend to give voice to the American language of individualism: "I think my religious views are true, but others may see the world differently, and that's OK." For most, God is more gracious than demanding and serves to help them out when they're in a pinch (Smith and Denton 2005). While this description is not true of all American youth—there are both irreligious and devout minorities on either side of the spectrum—it certainly captures the middle majority.

# *Chapter 1*

## FASHIONING NEW STORIES
## FROM OLD WISDOM

*Marriage should be honored by all, and the marriage
bed kept pure, for God will judge the adulterer and
all the sexually immoral.*

—Hebrews 13:4

A good place to formally begin a book on religion and sex is with what organized religion has had to say about sex, the traditions upon which contemporary youth are able to draw. Religious commentary on sexual behavior is plentiful, yet confusing and seemingly contradictory at points. Yet knowing what religious traditions have said about sex gives us a more intelligent benchmark against which to evaluate what contemporary adolescents both *say* and *do* about their emerging sexuality. And, as I discuss at length in chapter 7, there are a variety of possible say-and-do combinations. Since this study is of Americans, and the vast majority of them are either Protestant or Catholic, I largely confine my report to what these historic traditions have had to say about sexual matters.

### BIBLICAL COMMENTARY ON SEX

Biblical sexuality begins in the Garden of Eden, at the start of it all in Genesis 2 and 3. There, Adam and Eve live naked and unashamed. The serpent—thought by some to be a sexual symbol—comes to tempt Eve to eat the forbidden fruit from the Tree of the Knowledge of Good and Evil. The Hebrew term for *knowledge* can itself imply sexual intercourse (as in Gen. 4:1, where Adam "knew" Eve, after which she conceived a son). She eats the fruit and gives some to Adam, who likewise eats. Subsequently, their eyes are "opened," they are no longer "innocent," and they become aware of their nakedness. Adam defends himself before God by accusing Eve of giving him the forbidden fruit. Such a sexual interpretation of the account of the Fall—though not a widely held one—is nevertheless clearly not without evidence (Bandstra 2004).

    Most biblical references to sex are far less symbolic. Sexual "immorality" or "impurity" is widely and consistently reviled in biblical texts. In at least 11 of its

27 books, the New Testament denounces πορνεια (*porneia*), a Greek word for sexual immorality from which we derive the term *pornography*. Its meaning in historical context, though, had nothing to do with sexual images but rather had to do with behavior. References to lewdness, things that are sexually immoral or "licentious," are found at several points in the Old Testament—especially in the prophecies of Ezekiel—but only sparingly in the New Testament. According to Paul of Tarsus, the well-traveled New Testament missionary who penned 13 letters within the biblical canon, sexual sin is a serious matter, more grave than most transgressions. A person who sins sexually has "sinned against his own body," a reference to defiling or degrading what Christ has purified through his atoning death (1 Cor. 6:18).

Biblical accounts favor monogamous marital sexuality as a gold standard of sorts. But the matter is more complicated than it might first seem. Marriage is defined in the Old Testament, but many aspects of the Old Testament law are no longer practiced by Christians (such as animal sacrifices and a man's responsibility to marry his sister-in-law in the event of his brother's death).[1] Hence, most popular Christian references about sex tend to draw upon the New Testament. Still, the Old Testament commandment "you shall not commit adultery" is often used as a blanket reference to all forms of nonmarital sexual conduct.

In the biblical era, marriage involved both an agreement between a man and his betrothed wife's father or family, and the sexual consummation of the marriage. While formal marriage ceremonies were common, they were not required to validate a marriage. In the earliest set of instructions, God states, "a man will leave his father and mother and be united to his wife, and they will become one flesh," implying sexual consummation as a criterion of marriage (Gen. 2:24). No mention is made yet about permission to marry or virginity conditions.

"Fornication," or sex between unmarried partners, entailed a subsequent relational commitment. The Old Testament also makes reference to the term *concubine*, or a secondary sexual relationship between a married man and an unmarried woman, who in turn enjoyed familial protection but had little household authority. Old Testament Hebrew culture tolerated—but did not actively advocate—the practice of having multiple wives and concubines. Thus the penalty for sexual relations between a man and an unmarried woman—one who was not pledged to be married to another man—tended to be light, involving payment to the woman's family. A woman's virginity was—and, to some extent and in some subcultures, remains—a valued commodity (González-López 2004). While certainly subject to considerable measurement error, only female virginity could ever have been documented (by an intact hymen).

Married women, on the other hand, were always off limits. In the Old Testament law, sexual relations between a man and a married woman were punishable by the death of both partners (Deut. 22). Enforcement of the law, of course, varied widely. How often adulterers escaped the death penalty or went unnoticed is unknown. King David has sexual relations with the married Bathsheba, then orders her husband's death. Yet he escapes capital punishment for his actions. Instead, God is said to have struck down the child produced by their liaison. God even appears to buck his own rules for the sake of making particular points. For example, God tells the prophet Hosea to take as his wife an "adulterous" woman, in order to signify God's anger with his people (Israel), who are "guilty of the vilest adultery in departing from the Lord" (Hos. 1:2). Indeed, Israel's relationship with God is often portrayed using sexual imagery. The prophecies of Jeremiah, Ezekiel, and Isaiah accuse Israel of consorting with "prostitutes"—people of neighboring countries who worship other gods. At the same time, God often perceives Israel—and in the New Testament, the Church—as his "bride."

New Testament writings on sexuality are less fraught with imagery, less concerned with laws and penalties, and much more commonly cited in contemporary Christian writings about sex. They also increasingly recognize the inappropriateness of polygamy and the importance of sexuality within marriage. Jesus makes disparaging references to the popular interpretation of Jewish law that allows a man to divorce his wife for any reason. Instead, Jesus suggests that only sexual unfaithfulness constitutes grounds for divorce. He also criticizes the use of the death penalty for adultery (John 8:7). Thus, the person of Jesus has come to be associated both with forgiveness of sexual sins and a greater emphasis on the "heart" than on external behavior. This shift in perspective is evident when he tells his followers to focus less on adultery per se and more on lust—the mental (or heart's) desire to commit adultery (Matt. 5:28). Lust, he suggests, is equivalent to adultery in God's eyes, since it reveals the sinful condition of a person's will, even if unaccompanied by explicit action. Jesus refers directly to the connection between sexual sin and heart commitment: "What comes out of a man is what makes him 'unclean.' For from within, out of men's hearts, come evil thoughts, [including] sexual immorality... adultery... lewdness" (Mark 7:20–22).

Nevertheless (and, some would say, unfortunately), the words of Jesus are neither extensive nor detailed on sexual matters. Paul of Tarsus is more vocal, often responding in writing to particular sex-related crises in early Christian congregations. If a single biblical passage could characterize the hopes and aspirations of devoutly religious American parents for their adolescent children, it would probably be found in Paul's first letter to the church at Corinth, a Greek city synonymous with sexual permissiveness:

> Flee from sexual immorality. All other sins a man commits are outside his body, but he who sins sexually sins against his own body. Do you not know

that your body is a temple of the Holy Spirit, who is in you, whom you have received from God? You are not your own; you were bought at a price. Therefore honor God with your body. (1 Cor. 6:18–20)

The author of Hebrews (13:4) argues that "marriage should be honored by all, and the marriage bed kept pure, for God will judge the adulterer and all the sexually immoral."[2] Such texts sufficiently warn about the spiritual dangers of sexual immorality yet lack details or practical advice.

Not all biblical references to sex concern immoral practices. Shortly after arguing that the body is a "temple" (i.e., holy), Paul admonishes married couples to consider each other's bodies as belonging to the other and commands husbands and wives to "not deprive each other [of sex] except by mutual consent and for a time.... Then come together again" (1 Cor. 7:5). The Old Testament's Song of Solomon is widely regarded as a sensual read and a model of ideal marital sexuality, though the identities of the lover and the beloved and the exact nature of their relationship is not explicitly disclosed (and it is well documented that King Solomon himself had many wives).

Biblical commentary on masturbation remains unclear. Passages concerning homosexuality (e.g., 1 Thess. 4:3–4; Rom. 1:24; and 1 Cor. 6:9) have been used to condemn masturbation, but the link is suspect. The one account that appears to involve masturbation—or else the contraceptive practice of withdrawal—details God's fatal ire at Onan for "spilling his seed" on the ground rather than attempting to conceive children with the wife of his dead brother (Gen. 38:8–10). However, this is now widely interpreted as a story about God's displeasure with Onan not so much for his particular sexual act but for failing to fulfill his lawful obligation to his brother, a law no longer recognized as valid by most Jews and Western Christians.

Practices like oral sex are not addressed in the Bible at all. Popular Christian writer Lauren Winner (2005: 106) humorously attends to its absence while still advocating against its use outside marriage:

> OK, readers. Does St. Paul say anything explicitly about oral sex? No. Could one make a tortured, literalistic argument that one was having oral sex and not breaking the letter of biblical law? I suppose so. And yet most honest and right-thinking Christians recognize, at least intuitively, that oral sex constitutes sex—that if a husband ... had oral sex with someone other than his wife, he would have committed adultery; and that a single person's having oral sex would constitute a trespass of chastity.

While tomes have been written—and will continue to be published—on the topic of homosexual practice and the Christian tradition, the practice of same-sex sexual behavior by Christians will probably always be more contested than heterosexuality. Biblical justifications for the moral neutrality of homosexual practice often note that Jesus himself had nothing to say about the issue explicitly and that there are not many scriptural passages that directly address the issue. Nevertheless, the biblical record that does exist tends to disparage homosexual practice. While even here scholars have argued that such texts (like 1 Cor. 6:9) may in fact refer to homosexual *abuses* rather than consensual homosexual practice, most American Christians who tolerate or embrace homosexual practice as acceptable tend to do so apart from—rather than via—the biblical record, grounding their response instead in a sense of compassion, social justice, or the perceived need for Christian faith to "get with the times."

So why are most Christian traditions so concerned about sex, since plenty of Old and New Testament characters hardly display sexual fidelity? And why is it so important to them to restrict sex to within heterosexual marriage? While the answers to these questions certainly vary, many Christian traditions formally (though not often practically) articulate that marriage—and, by extension, sex—is essentially a portrait or reflection of God's relationship with his people. It is a New Testament theme that builds on the Old Testament idea of covenant. God promises to love his chosen people, despite their persistent unfaithfulness, and this is made evident in the form of a variety of covenants (with Abraham, Israel, etc.). Paul of Tarsus equates marriage and marital sexuality— "becoming one flesh" (Eph. 5:31)—to the relationship between Jesus Christ and his followers: "This mystery is profound, and I am saying that it [marriage, becoming one flesh] refers to Christ and the church" (Eph. 5:32). In this way, sex points beyond humanity to a divine relationship that hints at the very character of God. Note the sexual double entendre of talk about believers enjoying *union* with Christ and *intimacy* with him.

In turn, Christians are taught to believe that it is their responsibility to reflect God's image and nature by demonstrating the same commitment and intimacy within a covenantal relationship (marriage). Thus, Christians are to restrict sex to marriage not simply because God or Jesus said so—they did— or because Bible stories always honor marital sexuality and disparage other sexual relationships—they do not—but because doing so reflects God's promise-keeping nature. And marital sexuality is thought to reflect God's intentions for human flourishing, which is why many religious conservatives see the institution of marriage as applicable to everyone—not just those of faith. Lest I erroneously suggest that this is how most Christians actually *think* about sex and marriage, I want to stress that these are the tools their traditions offer them. Whether they employ them or instead pay more attention to modern marital and sexual norms is another story, one I will engage further herein.

## MODERN CHRISTIAN SENTIMENT ON SEX

Much more than just the biblical record has shaped contemporary Christian thinking about sex. However, modern Christian commentary on sex is not as well understood or embraced by the average Christian adolescent or adult. The biblical texts and the simpler themes noted above are much easier to recall. Among other modern Christian themes is the "celebration" of sex within marriage: since humans were made in the image and likeness of God, sexual design and feelings are the way God intended them to be and are not necessarily to be stifled. In this light, biblical "rules" about sex are recognized as guidelines for both protecting something of great value *and* encouraging sexual freedom within boundaries, rather than as means to stifle pleasure.

### From Evangelical Protestants

A good deal has been written by popular evangelical authors—or, at least, authors popular among evangelicals—not only about the boundaries for sex, but also about its benefits (Leman 1999; Smedes 1976; Winner 2005). Christians even publish books on sexual technique, though sans any illustrative photographs (Penner and Penner 2003; Wheat and Wheat 1981). Church-sponsored marriage-enhancement workshops and weekend getaways are promoted to enhance, albeit subtly, marital sexual satisfaction between spouses.

Thus evangelical Protestants may be best understood not as "anti-sex" but as concerned with appropriate sexual boundaries—the who and when of sex, not so much the what or how. Still, this mix of celebration and condemnation can be confusing. While marital sexuality is applauded, extramarital sexual activity remains one of the gravest offenses a person of faith can commit. Lauren Winner (2005: 95) laments: "these days most church folk who speak or write about sex bend over backward to insist that *married* sex is great. But somehow the church still manages to convey anxiety and discomfort about sex writ large." Social scientists agree: "Christians who try to affirm the goodness of sex find themselves in organizations that have strong and still operative beliefs about the dangers and immorality of sexual behavior" (Ellingson, Van Haitsma, Laumann, and Tebbe 2004: 311).

Because marriage is so esteemed, and because even most evangelical adults tend to delay marriage well into their 20s, adolescent (and therefore "single") sexuality is a perennial subject of interest and the topic of numerous books, typically on how to resist sexual temptation, or—failing that—how to restore a sense of sexual purity. Most of these books are not educational, like those noted above, but rather assume readers' extensive sexual knowledge and offer help in living what is thought to be a biblical sexual lifestyle.

Evangelical and mainline Protestant organizations have made few statements about fertility and the use of contraception, having somewhat reluctantly approved contraceptive practices early in the twentieth century. Evangelicals tend to only (weakly) contest contraceptive methods that serve as abortifacients, that is, they could operate to expel a fertilized egg rather than only to prevent fertilization (e.g., intrauterine devices, some hormonal methods). And even here, the debate is largely muted by the far noisier contest over abortion, which a majority of evangelicals decry and a majority of mainliners support. A nascent group of evangelicals has recently begun to contest the assumed ethics of contraception in general, but their audience and influence so far is limited.

## From Mormons

While one may equate sexual conservatism with evangelical Protestants, they are hardly the only religious tradition that could be considered so. Nor do they tend to organize their sexual conservatism into structures of accountability, at least not systematically. In this way, Mormons (formally known as the Church of Jesus Christ of Latter-day Saints; LDS) outpace evangelicals in terms of the organization of sexual social control. Among them, chastity is taught in Sunday schools, youth groups, and "seminary" (or daily) classes of religious instruction, along with other core doctrines. Mormons believe that misuse of the powers of procreation is a serious sin, viewed as the misuse of the power to give life. All members over the age of 12 are interviewed periodically by their local congregational leader (a bishop) concerning their temple "worthiness." (The temple is considered the pinnacle of LDS worship.) Temple worthiness is defined by affirmative responses to such questions as whether or not one pays a full tithe, follows the Word of Wisdom (abstaining from tea, coffee, and tobacco), and adheres to the "law of chastity," defined broadly in the LDS faith to encompass *any* sexual contact outside of marriage (including masturbation and oral sex). If adherence to the law of chastity is at issue, the youth will typically have to undergo a repentance process, which is confidentially overseen by a bishop but entails a temporary revocation of temple privileges. So while no explicitly public sanctions are applied, clear incentives remain in order to actively participate in youth temple going and to live up to the church's "gospel standards" for its members. In sum, the practice of worship and spiritual progression (including serving on a mission, marriage, etc.) are linked to these ordinances, and a network accountability system has been institutionalized to ascertain worthiness.

## From Roman Catholics

The Roman Catholic church tends to be more eloquent on matters of sexuality, if less popular than evangelical authors. The centralized and hierarchical nature and extensive resources of the Roman Catholic church allow it to offer clearer instructions about sexual morality (Ellingson, Van Haitsma, Laumann, and Tebbe 2004). Despite his "conservative" reputation, Pope John Paul II actually thought and wrote a good deal about human sexuality, primarily in his first book, *Love and Responsibility*, published in 1960. Then Cardinal Wojtyla, he was considered edgy and was nearly censored for his frank commentary about sexual function and pleasure. He argued that sexual happiness cannot be had by oneself in the free pursuit of relationships but must *depend* upon another person. This is not just because it takes two to tango but rather because sexual fulfillment hinges on two free *persons* (rather than two bodies) "seeking personal and common goods together" (Weigel 1999: 142). Such a radical giving of self and receiving of another person in sexual "communion" is close to the foundation of humanity, he articulated. It is the wonder of the first man, Adam, recognizing the naked Eve as "flesh of my flesh." Intercourse is intended to deepen personal relationships, and desire for it is intended to promote marriage. *Love and Responsibility* and his later collection of philosophical writings, *The Theology of the Body*, emphasize chastity, a term often confused with celibacy. While one could define chastity in terms of rules (such as, no sex outside of marriage), Weigel (1999: 142) refers to John Paul II's description of it as "the integrity of love" and "putting one's emotional center, and, in a sense, one's self, in the custody of another." Lust as the opposite of chastity desires pleasure through the *use* of another human being rather than through mutual self-giving. In a statement that generated considerable media flak, John Paul II suggested that the misuse of sex was even possible *within* marriage. That is, marriage itself does not guarantee sexual chastity.

Talk of sexual abstinence is not only for the unmarried, either. As one Catholic author quipped, "those who never really fast, never really feast" (Wiley 2004: 96). That is, abstinence as a habit should be practiced not only in the virginity of the unmarried but also in the periodic abstinence of married couples practicing "natural family planning" (NFP).

Probably the most famous (or perhaps infamous) doctrine on sexuality to come from the Roman Catholic Church is its forbidding of chemical and mechanical forms of birth control and its preference instead for NFP, based on a woman's fertility cycle. Artificial contraception, the Church argues, demeans women rather than empowers them, because its use encourages men to view women as objects of sexual pleasure. It undermines human dignity, discourages responsibility, and understands children as problems to be avoided rather than as gifts to be valued. However, the most well-known exposition of this doctrine—Pope Paul VI's *Humanae Vitae* (1968)—clearly misfired with millions of Catholics worldwide, and many Catholics still ignore this aspect of church doctrine. A more winsome advocate of NFP than Paul VI, John Paul II argued that the control of fertility encourages humanity's degradation through a utilitarian approach to human relationships, which is something to be resisted in all spheres of life, not just sexuality (Weigel 1999). The "blessing" and responsibility of fertility are ways in which humans are thought to reflect the image of God and to reproduce "the mystery of creation" (Weigel 1999: 337).

Catholic teachings about human sexuality and fertility are not widely practiced by Catholics worldwide, many of whom associate Catholicism with sexual conservatism. Even among the informed, many parishioners ignore the doctrines and many priests overlook them. If so few adult Catholics are even able to articulate their church's teachings on sex, how could one possibly expect their adolescents to know them and to act accordingly? The same could be said for evangelical and mainline Protestants. And even when well understood, religious teachings are not always easy to follow. Sexuality "has a plasticity and variegated logic of its own" that often undermines organizational efforts to control it (Ellingson 2004: 308).

## RELIGION AND SEX IN CONTEMPORARY LIVES: THE STORIES OF SIX ADOLESCENTS

The plasticity of sexuality quickly becomes evident when one moves from talking about historical doctrine to speaking with real people. Indeed, understanding biblical texts and moderns' interpretations of them is only so helpful. It provides a clear sense of what the religious resources about sex are, but conveys nothing of how regular people draw upon them, if at all. Even survey data—of which I will make extensive use—are limited in their ability to convey just how adolescents really think about sex, how they desire its pleasure or fear its pain, how they actually go about making sexual decisions, and how they reconcile their religious faiths with the choices they make.

I want to introduce the key issues and themes in this book by telling short stories about six particular adolescents: Valerie, Ben, Kristin, Jarrod, Justin, and Carla. Each of them is white except Jarrod (who is African American), middle class, and religious (Christian) to some degree. They all reported on the survey that they attended church services at least semiregularly. They are not a random sample of our interview pool, but their stories represent common themes and experiences of religious youth. Their accounts can serve as a baseline of sorts to compare with other adolescents whose stories and remarks will be featured later. Only names and geographical locations (to a similar city or state within the region) have been changed.

### Valerie

We spoke with Valerie in Kansas City. A 15-year-old self-proclaimed Christian, she grew up in a blue-collar Catholic household but now attends a Pentecostal (Assemblies of God) congregation and a small Christian school, each of which she enjoys a great deal. The youngest of four siblings, Valerie still misses her mother, a Jewish convert to Christianity who died of breast cancer when Valerie was five: "it sucks, but I learned to live with it." Her memories of her mother are few but positive: "she was very, she was a good Christian and she was really beautiful, but, I mean, I don't really remember her personality." Her father has not remarried, although he is dating a woman of whom Valerie approves: "[t]his one's really nice. Like, he seems happy." Valerie and her father get along pretty well. It was not always so: a rebellious period early in her teenage years undermined his trust in her, which she is still working to rebuild. Her father is not into organized religion, at least not to the extent that Valerie is. Her father and brothers actually believe "in the same things I do, they just don't act it."

Valerie has close ties with several adults, including a youth pastor and a set of "spiritual parents" at her church. She can talk to them about "certain things" that she cannot with her father. She also enjoys a close relationship with her 21-year-old sister, with whom she shares a measure of religious faith. When asked whom in the world she admires most, she names her sister and her spiritual mother, who is "just a woman of God, she's really cool."

Like many adolescents who attend theologically conservative congregations, Valerie recalls a time in her life when she "made a decision" and "started being different" from her old friends and peers. At first, I wondered if she had been all that different in her past, or if she was feeling pressure to make her past sound worse than it was. After all, she is only 15: "I used to do a lot of stuff my dad didn't know about. [*OK, what kind of stuff?*] Like drugs and hanging out with boys." Later, she remarks that she had "smoked weed every day," a habit she picked up at age 11, drank alcohol, and was regularly overdosing on cold medicine by age 13. She

> hung out with a lot of people who hung out with gangs and they would always talk about it [drinking] and I wanted to know what it was like, so I did it.

[*Why do you think you did those things?*] Probably partly, in the beginning, just to be accepted by other people. Because everyone was doing it, and I was the innocent one. [laughs]

Eventually she lost her virginity in a regrettable episode: "I wasn't dating, but I mean I liked the person and he supposedly liked me." Being arrested for possession of marijuana played a role in bringing matters to a head, primarily by revealing her dad's disappointment in her: "[y]ou look in his [her father's] eyes and it just hurts you because you know that he's, that [disappointment] is inside now." Around that time, her sister introduced her to the youth group at the Assembly of God church. Valerie credits her sister for helping to lift her out of the mess she felt she was in. Her dad also knows about her sexual experience: "[i]t's kind of hard for me to know that my dad knows, and it's like, 'whoa.' But at the same time, it's good just to keep me, like, on track and just to know, like, how my dad felt about it." Her Christian friends know about it too, but most of them encourage her with comments like "that's your past, so it's OK."

Her older sister remains an avowed virgin, which Valerie admires considerably: "that's very unusual these days, and you know, just seeing her never go for just any guy or never going for sex. Like if she could do it, then why couldn't I?" But virtue is not Valerie's only motivation. She reports that a friend of hers who is sexually active will "go to the clinic to see if, like, she's OK [free of STDs, pregnancy], and I never really wanted to go through that. . . . It's kind of scary just to think you have something."

Valerie attempts to avoid filling her mind with particular images and music: "[t]he devil can use anything, and music is a big thing." She listens to Christian rap, worship music, and "just soft stuff." She tries to avoid watching movies with explicit "sexual stuff," and while not attracted to pornography, she suggests that its real danger lies in what it does to people's minds, including her brothers'. In her youth group, Valerie has what she calls an "accountability partner," another girl with whom she is encouraged to be open and honest about temptations. "It helps a lot," she admits. She draws strength from prayer, worship services, and the youth group and its retreats, and she gains inspiration from reading the stories of "martyrs and people who die for, like, their beliefs and stuff, like um, on the other side of the world."

Valerie is clearly better off now at age 15 than she was at 13. Yet negative peer influences are unavoidable: "[m]y cousins all smoke weed and smoke cigarettes and my brothers, so it's, it's in my house. Like, it's really easy for me to do it if I wanted to." But she no longer wants to. All of that, she suggests, is both wrong and behind her: "God made you in a specific way," and substance use "makes you a whole different person." While Valerie confesses to occasional temptation, she conveys a sense of optimism about her future: "my mind's made up. . . . I've learned how to deal with it and not care what other people think." She no longer smokes or drinks and has not had sex again. In fact, boys hold diminishing (though still some) appeal: "I'm not gonna put myself in that situation like other girls do. . . . I'm not gonna go flirt with all the guys and stuff." While "gangbangers" used to appeal to her, she now prefers "pretty boys," young men who "take care of themselves" and are "clean-cut." While she occasionally wishes she were dating, Valerie thinks dating "is a problem" for people her age. In her experience, adolescent romance typically invokes emotional pain, pressure, and depression—the results of a relationship gone "too far" (namely, to sexual intercourse). She notes that even devoutly religious youth are not immune from crossing their own boundaries.

Despite her immersion into a set of Christian institutions (school and church), Valerie's description of her "conversion" from destructive behaviors to positive ones is not peppered with explicitly religious language. And when asked how she decides right from wrong, this Pentecostal adolescent makes quick reference not to a biblically based morality but to her modestly religious father: "[b]asically, how I've seen my dad go through stuff and just the way that other people [whom she admires] react to it [the action]." She is like many adolescents, who may not admit it to their parents but who take cues from them in dealing with difficulties. Even when Valerie speaks about sexuality, religious reasoning is unusual and only comes out when we directly ask about it. Her summary of Christian teachings on sex is as follows: "[y]ou're not to have sex before you marry. Like it's a gift from God to have when you're married and, you know, to enjoy between a wife and a husband."

### Ben

Ben is a likable, confident, and gracious 17-year-old from Pennsylvania with a diverse set of friends ranging from the studious to the troublemaker. His father is Roman Catholic and his mother is Orthodox. Yet unlike many religiously heterogeneous households, in which only one parent is actually active in a congregation, Ben's parents each attend their own congregations. He primarily attends services with his mother, but he is enrolled at a Catholic high school in a nearby Pittsburgh suburb, so in a way he splits his time between the two traditions. A rising senior, he is active in football, track, and wrestling, unlike his bookish parents. The parent-child differences don't stop there. Ben describes his parents as "conservative" and says he doesn't really feel close to them. On his mother: "I don't sit down and have a full-length conversation with her . . . never did really." Conversations with his father aren't much more numerous. Ben thinks his parents are primarily only interested in his safety and behavior, not in anything deeper about him. They are parents more than they are friends, a fact that Ben respects. At the same time, he longs to connect at a deeper level with them, but is not optimistic about it happening.

Ben attends church regularly and affirms that "morals" from church tend to "rub off" on him. When asked about his religious life, he primarily recounts parental requirements to attend church, and he recalls a time when his father would make him and his siblings read the Bible every night. Those days have long since ceased—nobody in the family is very religiously involved—but religious ideas remain: "[i]t kinda gets drilled into your head." He prays regularly, mostly "for forgiveness" for himself and for other people. He doesn't have time to read the Bible, though he is reticent to admit this. The family occasionally jokes around about religion, "but it's never like serious." Ben thinks church involvement is an elective and that all religions are "different interpretations of the same religion." He could be comfortably classified as a moralistic therapeutic deist, to use Smith and Denton's (2005) term.[3] Most of his friends are not religious, but he describes those who are as unique: "the religious ones seem to care more about what they do."

Ben's moral sense appears cobbled together from a variety of sources: religion, "the way I was brought up," and "things that have not really any tie to religion." He says he "always" knows right from wrong, but has trouble with "whether I want to do it [the right thing] or not." I ask how he decides between the two? "Whether or not I'll get caught, I think, or whether or not I'm kind of like [in] the mood . . . if I feel like it."

When asked about sex, Ben tells me that he and his father have had "the talk." "Just once," Ben states succinctly: "he was very, um, conservative, so it was very scientific the way he put everything." His mother attempts to monitor his sexual activity by quizzing his younger sister, who acts as her eyes and ears: "I remember a little while ago, she asked her if I had ever had [sexual intercourse], and then I, I never have, so."

I inquire about what he'd like to accomplish in his life and am met with a standard line about a good job, marriage, etc. Then Ben adds something that no adolescent I interviewed had ever brought up unsolicited: "I would like to, ah, and this kind of sounds funny, like it's weird, 'cause nobody thinks about this, but I would like to, like, you know, stay a virgin 'til I'm married. It's kind of important to me." Considering that Ben doesn't come across as very religious, this was a surprising revelation. Why does he think this is important?

> My dad said it was like kind of a sin to do that and I don't wanna, and it's a pretty big one. And it's in, like, the Bible you know, you shouldn't. It's kind of like, I see sex as, like, a gift from God and it's, like, you know, it feels good for a reason. It's the reason. The purpose of it is to, like, you know,

reproduce and have kids, so I kind of see when the people, like, premarital sex happens and you have a kid, that it's kind of like a punishment. Like, not a punishment. But like, you know, this is what happens when you do stuff like this. So, and nobody ever stays a virgin until they're married. So I kind of want to do that. It's unheard of now. But I think that's kind of respectable, too.

The Roman Catholic influence on his answer is apparent. I press him on how he will maintain his virginity, inquiring about whether he has ever taken a virginity pledge (largely an evangelical Protestant practice). Ben dismisses such an idea: "[n]o, I would never do that. I think that's silly." Has he ever heard of such pledges? "Yeah. But I, I think that's kind of like, that's like, that's like, if you flaunt it. I don't understand it when people flaunt things. It's, you know, people, 'just relax.'"

Ben has had a steady girlfriend for about 20 months and prefers stability and commitment to serial relationships. He will definitely be "the marrying kind" someday: "if you find somebody that you really like, you . . . stick with them as long as possible." He prefers his girlfriend to dress modestly. How far have they gone? "Third base." Having grown up a few years earlier, when the bases might have symbolized something different, I play dumb. Ben spells it out: "[f]irst base is kissing and more than light kissing. Second base would be ah, going underneath clothing. Third base is oral sex." How does he feel about going this far, in light of his position on premarital intercourse?

Um, I don't think it [oral sex] is sex. Like I don't think it's, you know . . . sexual intercourse or anything. It's kind of like a—I don't know how to put that, I don't know how to say it—it's kind of a like, it's like substitution. It's like you're not actually having sex, like you're substituting something else for it.

Ben's frank discussion of substituting oral sex for sexual intercourse is unusual among the adolescents in our study. But that doesn't mean his opinion or approach to sexual activity is rare. It is a common mentality in Ben's school:

Oral sex is more [common]; sex is less. Just 'cause, um, oral sex isn't exactly, like, you know. Sex is like, you know, a big deal. Everybody thinks it's a huge deal. Oral sex less, 'cause there's no, really, consequences, you know. There's STDs, but you know, it's very rare.

Pregnancy is a "huge" deal, Ben indicates: "[t]here's a lot of shows and a lot of stories like, you know, so-and-so had a kid and now he's dropped out of school." In response, the pill is popular. Such complicated problems and possibilities prompt Ben to avoid intercourse, although not for religious reasons.

### Kristin

If Ben could join the club of moralistic therapeutic deists, Kristin could be its poster child. She is 15 years old, a popular cheerleader in her suburban Atlanta high school, consistently on the A/B honor roll, tan, thin, attractive, and largely unreflective about life. Our very long conversation returned again and again to her favorite themes: friends, parties (and the police), boys, drinking, movies, school, and cheerleading.

Kristin feels close to her mother and father and claims she can tell them most anything. Yet her father pays her little attention, and from her account of things, her mother's concern consists primarily in protecting Kristin from the worst of adolescent popular culture. While Ben pines for deeper connections with his parents, Kristin does not. Her parents "make sure that I'm doing what I'm supposed to be doing and make sure I have my head on my shoulders and doing good academically and so I have, like, a great path for when I go out to get a job and go to college." Though at times she finds it annoying, she appreciates their concern. She thinks of herself as a normal teenager and finds in that identity considerable freedom to do whatever she feels like doing. Adolescence, in her eyes, is a time of tolerated experimentation and fun. "Most of the time I go with, like, what I feel." Right and wrong "depends on, like, the situation you're in."

She says she enjoys going to church, though her family does not often attend with her, and she herself doesn't go all that often:

> We never really get to go, just because, like, my brother either has to work, my mom, she has to work sometimes on Sundays. And my dad normally goes with my grandma, and I'm either like at a friend's house. But when I do spend the night at a friend's house, I normally go to either like Bendon River Baptist Church, because that's where most of my friends go to.

She considers herself a religious person: "We're Methodist and you know, I do go to church and stuff like that and I do, like, you know, respect things in the Bible." When Kristin prays, she asks God to help her in cheerleading competitions and with extended family members' health problems. She is affiliated with two evangelical youth organizations, Young Life and, sometimes, Campaigners. Her description of Young Life suggests that it primarily plays a social role for her, while Campaigners is "more serious." Collectively, religious activity helps to "keep my life in order and stuff like that and know what I'm doing . . . keep me straight," but she's not specific about what a "life in order" looks like and what being "straight" amounts to. I suspect that these are words of respect she pays to organized religion, which in Atlanta and the rest of the American South retains a privileged place in the local culture. Kristin wonders aloud why God keeps on forgiving her "if, you know, I keep doing it [sinning]," but she does not dwell upon such questions. She is consummately tolerant of other faiths—or of no faith at all—and takes for granted that "you can't, like, say anything against, like, someone else's religion. Because, like, it's what they believe in. And it's like you have to respect their beliefs." For her, being religious is "not a struggle. Like, it's easy for me to do."

Like Valerie, Kristin is no longer a virgin, having had sex with a former boyfriend, who was a high school senior. But unlike Valerie, she has no real regrets about it and even speaks of the pleasures of sex, something comparatively few adolescent girls talked about. But she nevertheless brought the topic up again when asked whether she had done things that she might think are wrong:

> Well, I have had sex, and I think my mom knows about it, because, like, she jokes around with me about it and stuff like that, like the other night. . . . I started my period, I was like, 'cause I was in, like, such a bad mood, and I was being so mean to her and she was like, "What is wrong with you?" And I was like, "I started my period." And she was like, "Well, I'm glad you started!" And I'm like, "What's that supposed to mean?" [laughs]

Why does she think having sex might be wrong?

> Well, just, like, by what the Bible says, you know, not having sex 'til you're married. But at the same time, like, so many kids have had sex and stuff like that. So . . . like kids make up their own morals, too, and of, like, what is right and wrong, so it's not necessarily like, you know, you're always gonna go by what the Bible says or what your parents say and stuff like that. It's sort of, like, a half-and-half thing, like, you know, you make up your own rules and combine them with what your parents say and mix and match. So . . . I don't know, I mean, it's not like, I've, like I've only had sex with, like, one person. And like, we were, like, together in a relationship for like three months. So it's not as if like I'm, like, a slut or anything. Like with other girls and stuff like that, they go out and like screw many guys 'cause I have friends that are that way, and, like, those are the people my mom don't want me hanging out with and stuff like that . . . 'cause I think she's just afraid that I'll probably go out and, like, turn into them so, but, like, it's not, like I just think, like, it's not necessarily wrong that I had sex, I don't think. [*So why do you think you did it?*] Just because. [laughs]

Kristin and her boyfriend dated for less than four months total and broke up early in the spring semester of his senior year. Despite the depth of sentiment that seemed to accompany their consummated relationship, Kristin reports that the two of them concluded, "we don't want to get too attached to each other because [he's] gonna be leaving for college next year." While she has not dated since the recent break-up, sex now logically accompanies dating, in her mind. When asked what makes dating different from other types of friendships, she responds: "[j]ust like the sexual relationship you have with them. And it's more of, like, you know, a caring factor and, like, trust and stuff like that." What makes it OK to have sex, with whom, and when?

> Well it's appropriate, like, when you're in a relationship with them and, you know, and you have been for a while and you really know that you care about the other person and it's not like if you're just, like, you know, you met the person like a couple weeks ago and then you're gonna go and hook up with them.

Though she describes sex as "something, like, really serious," Kristin also removes herself from any sense of gravity about it: "[y]ou know, you're gonna have sex, and it's not gonna be a big deal." Are certain activities off limits? Not really. "Whatever you guys, like, discuss and whatever you guys got going on [is fine]," she laughs. How does someone know she is ready? "It's just, like, what you feel. Like, you know, it's gotta be your decision. Like you can't, like, no one can pressure you into doing it. Like, it's your decision." Kristin thinks her mother is not too concerned: "mainly she just doesn't want me to go out and like become like a slut or anything."

### Jarrod

Jarrod, a 16-year-old African American from South Carolina, identifies himself as a Baptist and told us over the telephone that religion is an "extremely" important influence in his daily life. In person, however, he says that he doesn't see himself as much of a religious or spiritual person, and he is presently "having a problem with the Christian religion," especially with ministers who "bash" and "judge" people. He was particularly disappointed in his own minister, who has visited his sick father only once in recent memory. He nevertheless affirms that religion remains very important in his life: "[y]ou know, I think that before I, before we do anything, we should think about what would, you know they have the saying 'what would Jesus do,' you know." He wishes he were active in a church youth group, reasoning, "I think it would be pleasing to God a little more, you know." He reads the Bible "at church" and believes in heaven and hell, miracles, angels, and demons, but he doesn't pray a lot.

Jarrod first experienced sexual intercourse with "just a friend." His views on sexual morality could be labeled situational: "[i]t depends on um, the time, the place, and all that. All that's a factor, you know. It all depends. I mean, um, I think it's, I do think it's bad, but I think it's something that most of us can't help, you know. It's chemical, you know, hormones." Jarrod is also uniquely old-fashioned in at least one way: his disdain for *public* expressions of physical affection, as an apparent act of respect for his elders.

When asked about what sorts of sexual behaviors are OK for adolescents, Jarrod responds that it all depends upon where—geographically—you are:

> I think it all depends on the place. If you're by yourself, whatever, you know. But if you're in public, nothing. [*You said whatever, so what do you mean by whatever? 'Cause that's a big range.*] Whatever, like um, whatever. You want me to get that specific? [*If you don't mind.*] . . . Kissing, you know, the whole cuddling thing. You know, sex, maybe even oral sex, you know.

As in other interviews, we asked him about whether adolescents should wait to have sex until they are married, or not: "[y]eah, of course I do, but like I said, [it's] something you just can't help." Concerning emotional readiness, Jarrod responds:

> I don't think teenagers are emotionally ready for it, period. But I think it's just something that happens, you know, physically, that they, physically I think they are ready for it. . . . But emotionally, they're not. [*OK.*] But physically, you know their body's kind of ready for it, you know.

Losing his virginity to a friend was ideal, he thinks: "[m]an, it was cool, you know I mean, I felt like I was physically ready, but like I said, we weren't boyfriend and girlfriend, so it wasn't like I didn't have to be emotionally ready. I mean 'cause there was no feelings attached, really." Were his parents aware of his actions? "No. I don't think, they don't know about that person. But I think they know that I'm having sex. [*How would, or do you think they'd feel?*] Um, I think pops is like, he don't care. But my mama's gonna hurt if she found out." Jarrod relays his brief interactions with his parents about sex: "[l]ike my mama's telling me one thing, and my pop's telling me something else. My pops would be like, 'Just make sure you use protection.' And my mama's like, 'Wait, wait,' you know. But I never really talked to them about it."

Jarrod reports no pressure to have sex, perhaps because the pressure is only felt prior to the "accomplishment" of losing one's virginity. Jarrod acknowledges that his peers, together with his parents and television, do play a role in how he thinks about sex:

> They [his peers] have made me want to try it, made me want to have it, but they never made me [actually do it], you know. They made me want to [do] that, knowing in my mind, you know, we was all like, we was gonna do it, you know, soon. And then one of my boys did it, and then I think I was next, and then my boy did it after me. [*How do you think TV's influenced you, in the way you think about sex?*] Um, porno. Um, and like other movies and whatnot. That's it. [*Like how do you think, I mean how has that affected the way you think?*] Um, it made me want to try it.

When asked about religion, Jarrod articulates a series of disembodied religious statements. That is, although he practices a religion, Jarrod suggests that church teachings about sex are both valid and yet not applicable to him. Does religion matter when it comes to sexual morality?

> Yes. Yeah, yeah. They tell you, I don't know what it tell you, but it say something about sex. I know it say something about fornication, yeah. [*Do you know what it says?*] About fornication? [*Yeah.*] They tell you not to, I think. I'm not sure, but I know it say something in the Ten Commandments. [*Do you think you'd agree with what your church would say, or what your religion would say?*] Oh, I agree. 'Cause that's, I mean 'cause that's what I govern my life by. So I, that's the only thing I know. I don't, I don't agree or disagree. That's what I live by, you know. [*OK, so let's, so if it says that you don't, that you're not supposed to and you're doing it anyway, then how do you deal with that?*] I just, just ask God to forgive me.

## Justin

Justin is a 17-year-old Roman Catholic from an upper-middle-class suburb of Providence, Rhode Island. Although on the survey he reported a fairly high degree of religiosity, in person he too seems only nominally religious. He also appears mildly depressed with his life, though he actively tries to suppress this. His parents split up when he was three, and his mother remarried when Justin was in eighth grade, after living with his stepfather for at least a year. His stepfather is "such a different person than me that I don't think there's any way we could get along well." By Justin's account, his stepfather is to blame; he "puts up a big barricade" to prevent a relationship: "I don't really think he likes me." As with most of the adolescents with whom we spoke, Justin claims to be friends with all sorts of people, that "there's no one I don't get along with." His demeanor, however, is out of step with this claim.

When he was younger, and whenever he wasn't at his father's house, he would attend church with his mother: "[w]e're pretty much every-week people." His father is "Protestant" (no clarification) and his stepfather is Catholic, but neither is active. Unlike Kristin, who takes her religious faith in stride (if not seriously), Justin wishes he could escape his religious responsibilities. His religious sense is indeed shallow: "I'm not really a big fan of pondering the meaning of life here, so." Later he confessed that "very few things interest me.... there's not really much substance to my life right now, and if I think about that stuff [the purpose of life] too much I'm gonna be miserable."

Justin perceives himself as honest; he doesn't deceive, cheat, or lie. He is hardly happy, though. Recently arrested for possession of marijuana, he keenly feels the pressure of expectations on him: "[t]eenagers today are a lot more emotionally fragile." In his assessment, parents couldn't care less about their kids; they simply don't pay attention, and Justin cannot conceive that they might.

The arrest has not diminished Justin's interest in pot or alcohol. A sizable young man, "it takes a lot to get me puking." He has nevertheless recently slowed a drinking-every-other-day habit (he doesn't want a drinking offense on his nascent criminal record), but his marijuana use has increased. When asked how much his parents discipline him when they find out he's done something wrong, he replies tersely: "They're assholes. [*They're assholes?*] Yeah, they suck. [laughs] [*Like, what do you mean?*] They just take my car and stuff.... it's just like, come on, I didn't do anything that bad." Unlike Kristin, who finds her mother's interest in her life annoying yet comforting, Justin evaluates his mother's (and, to an extent, his stepfather's) concern as entirely negative: "[t]hey make doing everything a pain in the ass."

To Justin, religion is "something that hasn't come into play with me yet. I think it probably will sometime ... after I have a better understanding of the way everything works." He *has* belief, but he feels no need to question much of anything: "[y]ou know, I'm Catholic, and I don't really necessarily have to think about it [religion]. I don't have to question it, 'cause, you know, it works." He likes God, he admits, but doesn't think much about religion. He does not disagree with church teachings; they just play very little active role in his life. They probably would later, "when you're about to die." A former priest of Justin's was under fire in the wake of the priest sex scandal, but Justin still feels that the average priest is a good guy. He attended CCD (Confraternity of Christian Doctrine; the standard Catholic religious education course), but it was "just a chance to clown around on Sundays after church." Ironically, at the conclusion of our interview, Justin speculates that he might "be a little bit better than I am now" when he hits age 50 or 60, and he might even be "one of the guys who teaches CCD or, you know, that type of thing."

For now, though, Justin and his friends prefer edgy adolescent fare: music, parties, smoking, drinking, sex, and movies. Parties sometimes entail sex, but "unfortunately I'm not really in that part of, I'm not really, you know, like, into that." Later, he puts it more frankly: "I haven't really recently been too successful with, you know, girls." This depresses him, because dating and sex clearly went together in his experience: "I'd be lying to you if I said, you know, I don't want . . . some, you know, some pussy." Justin has a less romantic view of sexual partnerships than do Ben or Kristin: "[p]eople become assholes when, when they get involved [sexually]," by which he meant that "involved" couples seem to treat each other poorly and cheat on each other. What are his opinions about sexual involvement? Girls who can't "handle it mentally" shouldn't do it. Otherwise, just "don't be an asshole. Don't, I don't like making people feel bad. I mean, I feel bad when people get sad and especially if it's my own doing."

All of this was moot for Justin, since "unfortunately" he has not had sex for about a year. His senior year has been a disappointment in that area, with no imminent prospects. This gap in paired sexual activity should sound familiar to students of human sexuality: necessary resources (e.g., attractiveness, reputation) required to engage in sexual behavior often constrain sexual actors from accomplishing their goals (Laumann, Gagnon, Michael, and Michaels 1994). This is certainly the case for Justin.

Previous sexual partners have cheated on Justin. Though he claims this doesn't affect him, his conversation is raw and revealing: "[n]othing's [no girl is] important to me enough for me to have to, you know, lower my standards. . . . I'm not going to become their bitch, so you know, it's not that big a deal to me." While Justin denies ever participating in any unusual practices like group sex, he asks the interviewer if other adolescents had reported such involvement. While he doesn't surf the Internet for pornography, he thinks there's nothing wrong with it and has even invested in a set of X-rated DVDs. This in turn has brought X-rated junk mail to the house, prompting him to lie to his mother: "I was like, aw shit, mom, I don't know how this happened. [laughs]" Pornography relaxes him, he claims: "[i]t's a nice relaxing way to spend your afternoon."

Christianity has nothing to do with how Justin thinks about sex. Unlike numerous other youths, however, he doesn't report that Christianity teaches that sex outside of marriage is wrong. Instead, he suggests that Christian sexual morality is a social construction meant to curb natural, instinctual behavior in order to limit people's fertility. Left unchecked, people would have too many babies, and at too young an age, and not be able to support them.

### *Carla*

Carla is a 17-year-old evangelical Protestant girl from Florida. An average student and slightly overweight, she nevertheless conveys comfort with her own appearance. She was interviewed in her parents' restaurant, where she works. It's just her and her parents in the "close-knit" household (an older half brother is hooked on drugs and lives elsewhere). Carla was raised in a larger city but has since moved to a smaller town. She and her mother are close. Her father is an ex-Marine with war experience, a recovering alcoholic, and "a very structured, strict, you know, 'we want it done this way, now,' kind of guy." They get along well, and she's "daddy's little girl," but this role comes with some baggage. He prefers to have a schedule of her evening events before she goes out with friends, and she worries about how he will handle her future boyfriends. A recent cancer scare (for her) proved benign but still brought the three of them closer together and closer to God:

> It [cancer] is one of those things that makes me wonder how people can't believe in God. Because, like, my family, that's the only way we got through it was praying together and just thinking, "you know, what's meant to happen will happen." . . . it really pulled us together rather than, you know, like everybody saying "Oh, why did God do this to her?" or "I hate God," you know.

Her parents were not Christians earlier in life. In fact, Carla came to faith before her parents did, after regularly attending church as a five-year-old with a friend. They all started off Baptist but now frequent a nondenominational church. Baptists dominate Carla's local religious scene, and she resents it. She is not given to politicizing religion, as she perceives her fellow Florida Baptists to be doing:

> I mean it's just because we're in the Bible Belt of the South here, but it's, you know, I don't like feeling the influence that the Baptists put on you. You know, like I know that Disney had their Gay Day, but gay families deserve rights, too, you know. I mean like, and I guess that's the difference between me growing up in a big city and this small town here, you couldn't really see their small-town mentality. I know that being gay is wrong in the eyes of God, but at the same time, you're supposed to love everybody. So you know, I just don't like the idea of Baptists telling me what to do.

Carla is an advocate of outcasts and feels hostile toward adolescents who are judgmental about appearances: "I don't want to go somewhere with somebody [if] they're gonna be, 'oh, you can't talk to her' because she doesn't wear the right clothes and all that stuff." Such talk suggests she has been on the receiving end of haughty eyes. In fact, she thinks that personal appearance is one of the two biggest problems facing teenagers these days (the other one is sex):

> There's a lot of pressure on girls, I think more than guys, to look a certain way and to act a certain way. You know, you need to be 5'10", weigh 110 pounds, have long, flowing hair and big boobs and you know all this other stupid stuff. And then when you don't fall into that category, people just kind of look at you like you're second rate. And then if you're not real flirty and flighty and you know "ha-ha" all the time, then you're not a fun girl, I guess, for the guys to be around.

Yet the stress of both fitting in and resisting the pressures to do so are taking a toll on Carla. She takes medication for clinical depression and writes down her feelings in a journal (her doctor's recommendation).

Although Carla is very religious, and she articulates and confesses her belief in the traditional teachings of Christianity, she is not actually very active in her local congregation. She's not in a youth group and only reads the Bible "if something's weighing heavy on my mind." Faith clearly makes a difference in her life. But it does not come easy to Carla; she has to work at it: "[i]t is a struggle because you really understand, like for anybody that says it's not a struggle, then they don't understand Christianity. Because there are so many little things that you don't think about throughout the day that you do that are bad. [laughs]"

Carla occasionally sips alcohol (after all, "Jesus drank. He didn't, you know, drink to get drunk") but swears she will never smoke or touch drugs. Having had a brush with her own mortality, she thinks twice about her legacy before acting: "I would hate for my grandparents and my parents to be at my funeral saying, 'Man, what a loser, you know. She died 'cause she just couldn't resist.'"

She thinks that someday she'll marry her boyfriend of two years, Philip, though for now they maintain clear sexual boundaries: "[t]alking about sex for us was kind of weird because I was like, I don't even know if I should bring it up. But I didn't want him to think that it would be OK, you know. Like no, we have limits and you just have to understand that." He does, and they don't, although they do kiss, which is OK: "[e]ven a little bit farther than that, but you know once you have to start getting in to the, I guess, the truly intimate moments, it's just a little bit too far." Philip "completely understands where I'm coming from and he agrees, so that makes it easy for the both of us."

Carla's parents are open and honest with her about sex, and she appreciates their candor. She is something of a sexual idealist, believing that if two people in love wait, the wedding night will be a grand one: "[t]hat just makes it more special, you know. I mean, your honeymoon will be an experience you'll always remember that way." On the other hand, some adolescents, she thinks, date solely for the sexual benefits: "[t]his sounds horrible, but it's no different than paying a prostitute [laughs], because it's really all you're doing, you're just getting it free." For her, sex is supposed to be the ultimate commitment:

> [It's] being able to say OK, I'm yours for the rest of my life. You have me completely, you know, 100 percent. And then if you're married, and you get pregnant, it's no big deal, you know. You're already married and you're ready for that. You're ready for a family, but you know when you're 16, 17 years old and you get pregnant, what a mess.

Her grandmother got pregnant before her own wedding, and the story has stuck with her: "[s]he said, 'If I had it to do over again, I would've waited, because it was like, you know, bam, we're married, we have no money . . . and we have a kid on the way.'"

Carla is one of the rare adolescents who clearly distinguishes religious from instrumental reasons for abstaining from sex, and sees merit in both: "I mean if you don't do it for religious purposes, then you need to do it just, you know, for street smarts." She applauds recent MTV ads promoting the use of contraception. Although Carla admits feeling pressure to look trim and sexy, ironically she doesn't sense considerable tension over sex, even though she says many of her school peers are sexually active, "more so than their parents might know." She doesn't understand why so many youths are "willing to risk it all for what, like 10, 15 minutes of pleasure, I mean [laughs], it's not like it's all that long when you're young. . . . it just seems like it's overrated to me."

She nevertheless resents the sexual double standard: "[s]ex is sex, and sleeping around is sleeping around. It shouldn't matter who you are [or] what gender you are." Indeed, Carla is something of an evangelical feminist. She's strong-willed, caring, resentful of the small-town, double-standard pecking order based on beauty, and fed up with a Baptist moralizing that she's convinced is only skin deep and at root, unbiblical.

## EMERGING THEMES

There are important questions—especially about distinctly religious influences on sexual decision making—that excerpts from these six interviews with adolescents do not yet begin to address. Nevertheless, several themes are already becoming apparent, and others soon will. While not a summary of the book, these emergent themes are worth noting here.

First, the frenetic adolescent sexuality depicted in documentaries, films, music, and some scholarly books—wherein adolescents widely participate in casual sex, group sex, partner switching, pimping, etc.—is basically fiction. To be sure, one can always read about real-life examples of the bizarre. After all, sex sells. But as *New York Times* columnist David Brooks writes, "You could get the impression that America's young people are leading lives of Caligulan hedonism. . . . You could worry about hookups, friends with benefits, and the rampant spread of casual, transactional sexuality. But it turns out you'd be wrong" (2005: 4–14). Brooks is right. Such accounts are indeed exceptional. Rumors of oral sex parties tend to be just that. Not all adolescents (or parents) think so, though, and many wonder about the "reality" of what they see on the big screen, as shown by Justin's question to the interviewer about what other adolescents are saying. But the findings from most of the interviews suggest that adolescent sexual behavior in America tends to follow traditional patterns, namely, vaginal intercourse with someone of the opposite sex, with some proclivity for oral sex. Nontraditional sexual practices are rare among American youth, though I will present evidence to suggest that this is beginning to change.[4]

Toward this end, it is likewise critical to keep in mind the age-graded nature of sex. The sexuality section of our conversations with most 13- and 14-year-olds was short. Most have not had any type of paired sexual activity, and for many, sex is simply not on their radar screen. As for older adolescents, not all are sexually active or have even had sex yet, nor are they all that interested in sex. Follow-up conversations showed that the sex lives of 17- and 18-year-olds are often light-years different from what they had been just two years before.

Second, sexual activity among youth is often accompanied by feelings of ambivalence, sometimes buried under a mountain of positive peer affirmation. Kristin tells us that she has no regrets about losing her virginity—then losing her boyfriend—but the question of sex arises when we ask her about things she has done that she thinks might be wrong. Justin is clearly unhappy with his life, and not just because he hasn't had sex lately. Valerie has done a good deal of emotional work to "reclaim" her virginity in some sense. Sex simply does not come without emotional strings for the majority of American adolescents, especially girls. As is apparent from Kristin's account, many adolescents do a good deal of mental labor and normative affirmation in order to convince each other that coupled sexual activity during adolescence—a period of relational instability and immaturity—is, in fact, a good idea. Arousal may come naturally during adolescent development, but sexual happiness does not. For some, abstinence guarantees emotional stability. For others, it does not.

Third, religious involvement alone does not equal religious influence on sexual attitudes and behavior. For example, lots of American adolescents attend church regularly or are involved in some sort of religion-oriented youth group (like Kristin's participation in Young Life). Yet such activities do not lead automatically to the attitudes and actions such religious organizations hope to propagate in their youth. Something more is required for religion to make a more apparent difference in the sexual lives of adolescents, and that something is elusive and defies easy description. It certainly involves the internalization of both a belief system and a religious identity. Valerie exhibits it. Kristin does not, despite both young women being involved in organized religion. There is a clear division between Kristin's life of faith and her emerging sexuality. Dating itself implies sexual involvement. Religion doesn't imply anything, except nebulous ideas about giving "order" to her life and teaching her to "respect" others. There is much more I will say about this later in the book.

Fourth, it is hard to live against the grain. Youth with sexually permissive friends or in schools where a high percentage of their classmates have already had sex have a more difficult time avoiding sex, even if they want to steer clear and even if they have the religious resources to do so. In other words, social context matters: what happens *around* teenagers—including the perspectives and behaviors of parents, siblings, peers, and friends—affects their lives, right down to their thoughts, attitudes, intentions, and actions. Very few adolescents admit that they feel pressured by friends. Instead, they tell us they are autonomous decision makers. But the pressure and its influence remains apparent to observers.

There are other themes that will emerge later in the book, including a discussion of the efficacy of abstinence pledging; the frequency, content, and influence of parent-child conversations about sex and contraception; sexual idealism; same-sex experimentation; what happens after virginity is lost; the gap between evangelical attitudes and practices; the phenomenon of "technical virginity," an emerging sexual ethic based less on religion than on social class; and a new way of thinking about how religion influences not only adolescent sexual behavior, but human actions of all sorts. Before we explore these themes, however, we would do well to understand something of how social scientists decide whether religion actually shapes adolescent decision making.

# Chapter 2

## CAN RELIGION CAUSE BEHAVIOR?

It has always been too much to assume that beliefs consistently lead to behavior. All of us are guilty of innumerable hypocrisies. Nevertheless, it is reasonable to conclude that sometimes people do in fact do things for God (Stark 2000). In other words, religion *can* directly influence people's attitudes, perceptions, and behaviors. It *can* alter the conduct of life on Monday as well as on Sunday. What I am interested in is whether it *does*. For the purposes of this book, I wonder how religion might influence adolescent sexual attitudes and behavior. Can social scientists confidently speak of real religious influences, even if the research subjects are not aware of them? Shouldn't we be skeptical of religious influences, especially when teenagers themselves seem religiously disconnected and see no link between religion and their own actions? After all, how could only modest religiosity actually make a difference in adolescents' lives? And if religion does not really influence human behavior, what typically makes it appear to?

## SOURCES OF RELIGIOUS INFLUENCE

For starters, "religion" is hardly a unidimensional concept. It can be a type of *involvement* in pursuits that affirm conventional forms of achievement, so it might be measured as attendance at church services or youth group activities (Elder and Conger 2000). Indeed, the local religious congregation is the most popular voluntary organization in America and often provides adherents with readily available social networks. Religion can also refer to *beliefs* in and *commitments* to the tenets of a particular tradition. Additionally, religion can be about *subcultures* reflecting distinct norms and habits. Because of this complexity, simply stating that "religion affects sexual behavior" would be both unenlightening and unhelpful. What *about* religion affects sex? How so? Is it religious involvement that does so, by taking up some of an adolescent's time that might otherwise be spent hanging out with a boy- or girlfriend? Or is it a teenager's commitment to a set of religious beliefs, some of which address sexuality? Or is it how enmeshed an adolescent is in a particular religious subculture where sexuality is high in religious applicability?

Christian Smith (2003c) identifies nine plausible sources of religious in-fluence on adolescents, which are thought to cluster around three dimensions: moral order, learned competencies, and social and organizational ties. Put dif-ferently, he refers to religious teachings, skills learned in a religious community, and the importance of fellow believers. Together, he argues, these encompass most explanations of the influence of religion in adolescents' lives.

### Moral Order

Smith (2003c: 20) suggests the idea of "substantive cultural traditions grounded upon and promoting particular normative ideas of what is good and bad, right and wrong . . . just and unjust, and so on, which orient human consciousness and motivate human action." Such a moral order is not established by people's own desires and decisions but instead exists apart from and above them, pro-viding standards by which to evaluate those desires and decisions. The three key ways in which moral order is thought to influence youth are particular moral directives, spiritual experiences, and role models. Smith asserts that American religions promote moral directives "of self-control and personal virtue grounded in the authority of long historical traditions and narratives," which youths may internalize and use to guide their own choices and decisions (2003c: 20). Spiritual experiences, such as the "mountaintop" inspirational feelings that may infuse teenagers at a Youth for Christ convention, for example, reinforce moral orders. Such experiences, Smith suggests, can solidify adolescents' moral commitments and positive life practices. Finally, role models offer adolescents practical, real-life examples to emulate.

### Learned Competencies

Religion can influence adolescents by "increasing their competence in skills and knowledge that contribute to enhancing their well being and improving their life chances" (Smith 2003c: 22). The specific ways by which religion is thought to enhance adolescents' learned competencies are leadership skills, coping skills, and cultural capital, the latter of which can be defined as distinctive skills, knowledge, dispositions, and practices objectified in particular cultural/ religious credentials (Holt 1998). For example, being an elder in a Presbyterian church may enhance social trust when one attempts to secure a loan for a business venture, or active youth membership at a particular Catholic parish may resonate with the admissions staff at an elite Catholic university. Such religiously generated cultural capital is often subtle in its manifestations and effects and difficult if not impossible to document with certainty, but it is nonetheless widespread.

### Social and Organizational Ties

The third hypothesized dimension of religious influence on American teenagers concerns the social and organizational ties that religion affords young people (Smith 2003c). Religion builds youths' social and organizational ties through social capital, network closure, and extra-community skills. Network closure— sometimes considered an aspect of social capital—concerns the extent to which people pay attention to the lives of children and youth. These people include not only parents but also those who oversee adolescents and can share information about them with their parents. Family involvement in a religious community often brings neighbors, teachers, parents of children's friends, and the parents' own friends into sustained contact with a family's younger members. Consequently, parents in religious communities tend to enjoy a wider network of people who care about their children. An early figure in identifying and studying social capital, James Coleman (1988) suggested that better youth outcomes are found where there are higher densities of social relationships among youth, parents, and other interested adults, as well as among parents whose children are friends. Finally, participation in religious organizations provides youth access to experiences and events (like mission trips) that expand their horizons, expose them to new knowledge, and encourage their maturation and development (Smith 2003c).

Several of the nine factors that Smith presents concern mechanisms (or means) of influence, wherein something "secular" provides the actual pathway by which religion influences the outcome under consideration. Others refer to unmitigated influences from the religious elements themselves (moral order, spiritual experiences). That is, sometimes religious teenagers do something—or don't do something—because of their faith commitments, not out of a desire to conform, obey parents, or please friends. The nine factors also do not typically operate apart from each other. Such interdependence presents researchers with interpretive difficulties, especially when survey research uses only standard measures of religiosity like church attendance. Even so, it's still helpful to think of these factors as analytically distinct influences. Smith notes that not all religious organizations provide youth with the same quantity or quality of these influences. Some churches "may neutralize whatever it is helpful that they do provide with other detrimental practices and influences—such as abusive leaders, adult hypocrisies, and dysfunctional organization" (Smith 2003c: 27).

Organized religion is, of course, not the only place where these kinds of social influences affect adolescents. Parallel secular contexts abound as voluntary associations, civic organizations, schools, sports clubs, etc. Whether they are as proficient at influencing adolescents is debatable. I would argue that when someone is infused by religion and its moral directives, however uncommon such a scenario may be in reality, there is no immediate equivalent motivator available from secular alternatives. Recent social movement research has underscored this evaluation, documenting the religious sources of the emergence of the modern social movement in America (Young 2002, 2006).[1]

It's evident, then, that religion can affect youth in a number of different ways and means. Unfortunately, social scientists seldom have the luxury of evaluating all nine of Smith's factors. Researchers typically have access to only a handful of religious measures from social surveys originally designed for other purposes. And sometimes even those surveys are poorly constructed (for example, measuring religious affiliation as a selection among Protestantism, Catholicism, or Judaism). What is worse, many social scientific studies focus entirely on the direct (or main) effects of a particular phenomenon and do not even mention possible indirect effects, giving the common and often incorrect impression that religion "doesn't matter" for a particular behavior. This is a problem, since the overall (or total) effect of religion can be quite substantial, just spread across a variety of pathways. Moreover, indirect effects are often the results of earlier causal effects, but it's the most recent and proximate causes that tend to receive more scholarly attention.

## DIRECTIONS OF RELIGIOUS INFLUENCE

Most research on religion and adolescents suggests that religion is largely about forbidding things, and this is certainly true for the literature on adolescent sexual practice. That is, religion functions as a source of social and individual control, in broad keeping with its assessment by Marx, Weber, Freud, and Durkheim. It helps adolescents to avoid actions they might otherwise have taken. And the network closure fostered by religious communities (noted above) is most often considered a redundant social control system, reinforcing parents' own efforts to guide their adolescent children toward desired goals. The social control model also makes sense from within religious perspectives that are skeptical of human nature: youth are bent toward sinning—doing the wrong thing—and being enmeshed in a religious personal network and community helps prevent them from doing so.

There is mounting evidence, however, that the common survey measures of youth and adult religiosity to which social scientists typically have access—especially church attendance (public religiosity) and the self-rated importance of religion in one's life (private religiosity)—often affect different types of actions. While these two ways of being religious do not often counteract each other, private religiosity seems more apt to affect actions like drug use and delinquency, while public religiosity tends to affect outcomes that are more long term in their development, such as future educational success (Muller and Ellison 2001; Regnerus 2000; Regnerus and Elder 2003).

Hypothetically, let's consider Derek, who could represent lots of teenagers with whom we spoke. Derek attends religious services on a regular basis and is plugged into the local church youth group, but for whatever reason, he hasn't internalized the belief system to which he is exposed. In other words, he is just going through the motions. Still, the ritual practice of rising early and going to church commits him to a habit that fosters the discipline also needed for academic and athletic success. But if the religious belief system is never internalized or grounded in his cognitive identity—if he does not understand himself as, for example, chosen by God or if he does not believe his actions to reflect his relationship with God—then regular church attendance alone will fail to motivate him to resist the more transitory opportunities to shoplift, smoke a joint, or have sex. After all, why obey something in which he really doesn't believe?

On the other hand, both church attendance and success in the classroom or on the sports field are longer-term processes, requiring commitment, diligence, discipline, and the routinization of habits. Internalizing or prioritizing religious belief has little to do with these. After all, even the most devoutly religious students can suffer academic difficulties, since schooling success taps talents and tools that may have nothing to do with how religious they consider themselves to be. Religiously grounded beliefs that suggest Derek ought to treat his body as a temple, honor his parents, show kindness toward others, etc., may do little to foster high evaluations in school. But they may be the exact source of influence that will help him to avoid other actions.

When paired together, religious involvement *and* valuing can prove to be one powerful, comprehensive motivator. Adolescents' own valuing of their religious involvement and beliefs and their embeddedness in religious communities that care about them enhance the power of the religious messages they receive and may well shape their sexual choices in several ways, including limiting their sexual options and opportunities by their participation in alternate, desexualized social networks and by offering a less permissive sexual "script" (set of norms) and expectations for devoutly religious adolescents, as we saw in chapter 1 (Ellingson, Van Haitsma, et al. 2004).

## RELIGIOSITY AND ROLE SALIENCE

Embedding oneself in religious networks does not guarantee a particular outcome, of course, especially since people occupy multiple roles (student, friend, girlfriend, daughter). Social psychologist Dale Wimberley (1989) suggests that sometimes the behaviors called for by one's multiple roles are compatible, and sometimes they are not. For example, a devout Christian adolescent may feel pressure from his friends to prove his masculinity by losing his virginity. At that moment, being a compliant friend and being a good Christian will be incompatible. When role identities are incompatible, the "hierarchy of salience" is thought to influence the choice of behavior. That is, which identity is more important to this adolescent?

Any given behavior may vary in the level of conflict that it generates between religious and other role identities. For persons for whom religious identity is near the top of the salience hierarchy, violation of religious norms can result in considerable cognitive dissonance and guilt. Much less discomfort would tend to be generated in persons whose religious identities are lower on the salience hierarchy.

Public and private forms of religiosity also differ in how directly they influence behavior. Public religiosity, like church attendance, is generally considered to be *indirect* in its influence. That is, it suggests the presence of underlying religiosity but is not the thing itself. (After all, how can going to church *cause* anything?) On the other hand, Wimberley (1989) argues that how important religion is in someone's life (private religiosity) can *directly* shape one's religious norm adherence. That is, it acts as a stimulant to religious beliefs or cognitive structures, a light switch of sorts that turns on the force of religious belief. In spheres like sex, where religious applicability is high, sexual behavior outcomes may well hinge on how important and how internalized religion is in an adolescent's life.

In sum, paired adolescent sexual behavior often follows, in the end, from (a) quick decisions made in transient moments, and (b) planned but unstructured time spent together.[2] Private religiosity is thought to affect (a), and public religiosity is known to affect (b). Thus, researchers often find that multiple sources of religiosity affect adolescent sexual behavior and decision making in multiple ways (Ku et al. 1998; Sheeran et al. 1993).

## DISPUTING RELIGIOUS INFLUENCES

Not all social scientists, however, believe that religion actually influences human sexual behavior—or other behaviors, for that matter. After all, if adolescents or adults are not consciously aware of and cannot articulate religious reasons for their actions, pessimism about religious influence may be well founded. There are three common reasons offered for such skepticism:

1. Selection effects
2. Reverse causation
3. Social desirability bias

First, apparent religious influence may actually be the result of selection effects (or selectivity). Selection effects are used to explain an association between a predictor and a particular outcome that really has nothing to do with the predictor's causal influence, but instead both the predictor and the outcome actually result from some other factor that causes each. In other words, certain young people self-select both toward religion and away from sexual behavior, for whatever reason. Some even appear to use religion as a strategy to steer clear of risky situations and actions. Second, the direction of effects may be reversed; perhaps changes in religion or religiosity are in fact the product of changes in behavior—like sex or delinquency—rather than the other way around. Third, apparent religious influence may be reducible to social desirability bias: religious individuals may want to appear better than they actually are, and so offer deceptive answers to survey questions, especially sensitive ones like those about sexual behavior.

### The Selection Effects Explanation

The religion-as-selection-effect hypothesis would go something like this: some other unknown factor causes adolescents both to be religious *and* to avoid sexual intercourse, etc. As a result, statistical estimates of the effects of religion on sex may be inflated due to the presence of this unknown and unmeasured factor that causes both greater religiosity and more conservative sexual attitudes or behavior. In other words, there exists no real relationship between religiosity and sex, despite appearances. Religion conducts, but does not cause, sexual conservatism.

The primary argument in favor of the selection effects hypothesis here is that being religious is a choice. It is self-selected. And the nature of choosing suggests in turn a variety of questions about why people choose to be more or less religious or why they choose to affiliate with a particular religious group. And what ramifications do these choices have for predicting a particular outcome? Some other factors are obviously *not* self-selected, such as one's gender and race/ethnicity, and thus they are not at risk for selection effects.

Additionally, it is thought that *any* observed associations between religiosity and sexual behavior may be the result of different (or even combinations of different) possible processes, relationships, and directions of causal influences than those that researchers have considered. Thus, many social scientists are uncomfortable with even inferences that religion may cause behavior. Terms or phrases such as "influence" or "have an effect on" often elicit subtle reprimands within the contemporary social science community.

If these critics are correct, then religion does not deserve as much attention as it has been getting, and we would be much wiser to focus on the more basic characteristics that actually account for the direction of a person's life—whatever those are (Batson, Schoenrade, and Ventis 1993).[3] For the sake of argument, I will presume that teenagers always *choose* to be more religious or less religious, and that I should document as completely as possible what might shape that choice. If the same factors that shape teenagers' religiosity also shape their sexual behaviors and attitudes, then I could have a problem with selection effects; in other words, I may have overestimated religious influences on their sexual decision making.

So what might "cause" religiosity? Several factors—including family, friends, gender, and formal religious education—have been consistently linked with greater religiosity in adolescents (Erickson 1992; King, Furrow, and Roth 2002; Regnerus, Smith, and Smith 2004). Parents' religiosity easily constitutes the strongest and most reliable influence across studies of adolescents, and religious socialization is more apt to occur in families characterized by considerable warmth and closeness (Myers 1996; Ozorak 1989). But families cannot be thought to *cause* religiosity in a strong sense, but instead to provide the *context* in which its development is much more likely to occur.

Similarly, studies nearly universally find girls to be more religious than boys (King, Furrow, and Roth 2002; Miller and Hoffmann 1995), but simply being female will not *cause* any particular young woman to be religious. Again, gender is simply a more conducive factor for religiosity to develop and thrive, perhaps in step with girls' more rapid moral maturation (Gilligan 1982). Moreover, most social science researchers are well aware of a variety of demographic differences in religious practices, and they typically account for them in their analyses of adolescent behavior.

Alan Miller and Rodney Stark (2002) provocatively assert that gender differences in religiosity really imply gender differences in proclivity for risk taking. That is, they argue that being religious is essentially about reducing the risk of possible eternal judgment, and women—since they are inherently less oriented toward risk taking than men—are for that reason more drawn to organized religion. This controversial notion has forced social scientists to rethink the nature of religiosity. That is, religiosity may be the result of hard-wired personality differences. We already know that "safe," or risk-aversive, people are more likely both to display greater religiosity and to exhibit positive health practices, lifestyles, and generally prosocial behavior.[4] These are people already inclined toward conformism, "clean living," and, presumably, less sexual risk taking (Ellison 1991). Risk-aversive teenagers may in turn be more comfortable with religious social control or be immersed in nuclear families that further reinforce their risk aversion (Ellison and Levin 1998). Thus researchers might erroneously attribute influence to religiosity when it would more appropriately be accorded to whatever it is that causes *both* religiosity and risk aversion.

My own analyses of the Add Health data on temperament and personality orientations indicate that hot-tempered adolescents report lower attendance at religious services than do youth whose parents say their child has no temper problem (see Table 2.1). Only 27 percent of adolescents who attend weekly were reported as having a temper, compared with 38 percent of youth who never attend. Having a temper decreased the odds that teens would report higher attendance by about 23 percent in multivariate analyses (results not shown). Analyses of NSYR data on adolescents' temperament confirm these associations.[5] Adolescents who like to take risks are similarly less likely to attend religious services. Just under two-thirds of those who never attend reported that they liked to take risks, compared with about 54 percent of teens who attend regularly.[6] Hot-tempered and risk-taking youth also report that religion is *less* important to them, in about equal ratios to that found for lower attendance.

Documenting that personality traits—such as temper and risk aversion—are linked to religiousness is only one part of the selection-effects puzzle, however. The personality effects that predict religiosity must *also* predict the outcome of interest (sexual attitudes and behaviors) and should—if religiosity is effectively "caused" by personality effects—reduce religious influence to insignificance. In previous research on a variety of adolescent outcomes (though not sex), religiosity is both subject to selection effects and yet independently influential (Regnerus and Smith 2005). In other words, while religiosity is associated with certain personality traits and orientations, its influence on

TABLE 2.1  Personality Orientations, by Adolescent's Religiosity
(in Percentages unless Noted)

| | Has a temper | Likes to take risks | Avoids socially desirable answers | Mean score on strategic behavior index |
|---|---|---|---|---|
| *Church Attendance* | | | | |
| Once a week or more | 26.8 | 54.3 | 90.4 | 18.32 |
| Once a month or more, but less than once a week | 28.5 | 57.6 | 91.3 | 18.14 |
| Less than once a month | 32.1 | 60.8 | 91.9 | 18.19 |
| Never | 37.9 | 62.8 | 90.6 | 17.79 |
| *Importance of Religion* | | | | |
| Very important | 27.3 | 54.8 | 89.4 | 18.53 |
| Fairly important | 31.3 | 58.4 | 92.3 | 17.96 |
| Fairly unimportant | 34.1 | 62.3 | 93.4 | 17.64 |
| Not important at all | 37.3 | 63.7 | 90.3 | 17.13 |

*Source*: National Longitudinal Study of Adolescent Health

adolescent behavior *cannot* be explained away by personality. Whether this is true of religious influences on sexual outcomes will be addressed throughout the remainder of this book (and documented in the appendix tables).

## The Religious-Strategy Explanation

Actually a version of the selection-effects hypothesis, religious strategy suggests that religion is an active means (or strategy) employed by adolescents to achieve a desired outcome. For example, teenagers who wish to retain their virginity (or avoid alcohol, etc.) may *choose* to become religiously involved as an instrumental strategy toward achieving such a goal. This hypothesis implies that observed outcomes in adolescents' lives do not directly result from the influence of religion. Rather, they are the result of a larger, preceding life orientation to avoid trouble, to attain personal goals (graduate, be admitted to a good college, etc.), and to be as happy and self-fulfilled as possible. Such youths then choose to implement a variety of strategies at different levels and in different areas of their lives to achieve this kind of generally positive, constructive life. Participating in organized religion is one of those strategies.

The religious-strategy hypothesis differs from the general selection-effects hypothesis in that it recognizes that religion may still wield real influence. Its influence would not spring from the motivating power of a belief system, but instead from a need for social support in avoiding negative behaviors and achieving desired goals. Millions of parents send their children to religious day schools every year for just such strategic reasons. Even if teens utilize religion to help, say, avoid an unplanned pregnancy by pledging sexual abstinence until marriage, this hardly implies *no* religious influence. Indeed, such a strategy might make a considerable difference toward achieving the desired outcome. But religion is the means rather than the motivator. The motivation arises from some other source, perhaps the desire to avoid trouble, to please parents, or simply to be happy.

Unfortunately, evidence for distinctly religious strategizing is difficult to document with confidence. It would certainly vary across religious traditions, some of which consider such "extrinsic" religiosity shameful. Presuming it exists, getting people to admit extrinsic religiosity to themselves—much less to an interviewer/stranger—can be a challenge. However, it is clear from the Add Health study that "strategic" or "planful" adolescents *are* significantly more likely to attend church services and to think that religion is important.[7] And the association strengthens as religious salience increases: adolescents who say that religion is "very important" are more strategic than other youths, even those who say religion is "fairly important." In more rigorous analyses, the association between being strategic and both attending religious services and saying religion is important remains, even after controlling for other effects (results not shown).

### The Reverse Causation (or Religious Exit) Explanation

Another possibility is that researchers have the direction of influence backward. In this explanation, reverse causation is responsible for apparent religious effects. Here's how: it is entirely conceivable that some religious teens, for whatever reasons, become interested in—and engage in—paired sexual activities that are no doubt at odds with their religious belief systems. Many experience cognitive dissonance as a result: they know they shouldn't do what they're doing, but they do it anyway. As a result, they stop participating in religious activities and become less religious, preferring this to the guilt and shame that may accompany their continued religious involvement. This phenomenon then creates observed—but again, not real—associations between religiosity and sexual behavior among those religious adolescents who did *not* decrease their religious involvement. But as you can see, the association would be ephemeral, the result of the sexually active dropping out of organized religion, leaving behind other religious adolescents who have not yet had sex. In this way, religion doesn't influence youths' sexual choices, but rather is avoided by those who have chosen to become sexually involved. The same pattern could hold for lots of different outcomes, such as depression, delinquency, or alcohol use. In other words, religion does not influence positive or negative outcomes in people's lives. Instead, other nonreligious (and perhaps unknown) factors effectively weed out those who display religiously undesirable outcomes.

Solid studies confirm that religiosity can in fact be diminished or strengthened as a result of a person's behaviors (Thornton 1985; Thornton and Camburn 1989). In a pair of studies of cohabitation and marriage using different data sets, the practice of cohabitation reduced religious attendance among young adults, while marriage (without previous cohabitation) tended to increase religious involvement (Thornton, Axinn, and Hill 1992; Uecker, Regnerus, and Vaaler 2006). Other religiously problematic behaviors—such as drug use, excessive drinking, and nonmarital sexual behavior—are also positively associated with diminished religiosity in early adulthood (Uecker, Regnerus, and Vaaler 2006).

In general, then, there is sufficient evidence across a variety of outcomes to suggest that changes in behaviors may also produce changes in visible religious involvement. However, a pair of recent Add Health studies found *no* evidence that adolescents reduced their religiosity after experiencing virginity loss (Hardy and Raffaelli 2003; Meier 2003). My own analyses of the Add Health data reveal evidence to support bidirectional effects in many areas of adolescent behavior (Regnerus and Smith 2005). Virginity loss and self-reported theft predict subsequent declines in both church attendance and self-reported religious salience (Regnerus and Uecker 2006). To summarize, associations between religiosity and a variety of adolescent behaviors are often two-way, suggesting that a cycle of sorts is at work. We will examine this further in chapter 5.


### *Religion and Social Desirability Bias*

Finally, people often try to appear "better" than they believe they really are. In survey research, this tendency can affect how respondents answer researchers' questions. This is known as social desirability bias and manifests itself in at least two forms: self-deception, the tendency to give biased but honestly held descriptions of oneself; and other-deception, the tendency to give overly favorable self-descriptions to a researcher (Paulhus 1984). Related to these, there is also the phenomenon of "retracting" self-reported behaviors, where respondents could say that "yes, that is true" of them at one point in time and "no, it's not true" at a later point in time. This may affect sensitive self-reported behaviors, like sex, in Add Health. While more than 10 percent of respondents later contradicted their initial reports of sex, pregnancy, and taking a pledge of abstinence, less than 1 percent of them contradicted simple demographic details about their lives (Rosenbaum 2006).

However, social desirability is not necessarily problematic to a study, especially if all respondents are equally subject to the tendency. But it can bias estimates of religious influence if there are systematic differences among respondents. For example, *if* evangelical Protestant youths are more likely to underreport their sexual behavior, then bias would be introduced that would mischaracterize the real association between evangelical Protestantism and sexual behavior. So, being an evangelical might appear to be protective against sexual activity but might, in reality, make no difference. Indeed, certain phenomena are considered to be at elevated risk of social desirability effects, including sexual behavior and religious activities (Batson, Naifeh, and Pate 1978; Hadaway, Marler, and Chaves 1993; Leak and Fish 1989; Presser and Stinson 1998; Trimble 1997; Watson et al. 1986). If social scientists fail to account for social desirability effects in studies of religious influence, or in studies of sex, this could introduce bias and skew their results.[8] So, does religion correspond with heightened social desirability in adolescents?

No substantively significant connection appears between social desirability[9] and self-reports of religious service attendance (see Table 2.1). Adolescents who report more socially desirable answers on surveys are only slightly more likely to report that religion is of considerable importance, but the relationship is weak and diminishes entirely when accounting for personality traits (temper, risk aversion, and strategizing or instrumentalism; results not shown). Social desirability *is* related to a variety of adolescent outcomes, but this does not diminish religion's effects on these same outcomes. So while it is wisest to always evaluate the role of social desirability in shaping patterned survey responses among adolescents, I can state with confidence that religious influences on adolescent behaviors *cannot* be explained away by social desirability effects (Regnerus 2004; Rowatt and Kirkpatrick 2002; Rowatt and Schmitt 2003).

## CONCLUSIONS

There has been considerable research lately on how religion influences adolescent and adult behaviors and outcomes. Some researchers disagree with the conclusions, suggesting that apparent religious influences are due instead to selection effects, reverse causation, or social desirability bias. So where does this leave us? Should we be confident or skeptical of suggestions that religion influences the lives of American teenagers? What if the adolescents themselves cannot articulate their own religious beliefs? Could religion still shape their actions?

Yes. It is well documented that religion can affect adolescents either directly by motivating particular actions or indirectly by shaping other influences in their lives, such as friendship choices, time use, etc. But I also acknowledge that a healthy dose of skepticism will always serve researchers well. There is selectivity going on among religious youth: strategic and risk-aversive adolescents tend to be more religious, and temperamental adolescents tend to be less religious. There is little evidence, however, that social desirability bias can either account for or confound apparent religious effects. And *none* of these phenomena altogether mitigate the influence of religion on a variety of adolescent behaviors and outcomes. Demographic, family, and personality characteristics each shape the actions of adolescents, but none systematically explains away religious influences. On occasion, they may conduct an indirect effect of religion. There is more evidence of reverse causation—or, more likely, bidirectional relationships—than of selection effects. Yet, given all this, the suggestion that religious influence is entirely the result of personality effects or social desirability bias, or the claim that religion is more product than producer, are overreaching conclusions.[10]

# Chapter 3

⨭

## LEARNING SEXUALITY

*To hear many religious people talk, one would think
God created the torso, head, legs and arms, but the
devil slapped on the genitals.*

—Don Schrader

It is widely believed that today's adolescents typically know more about sex than their parents did at their age. When researchers probe their knowledge, however, what is often uncovered is a hodgepodge of facts and fictions, myths and truths (Bartle 1998; Hockenberry-Eaton et al. 1996). Their vocabulary of sexual physiology may be astute, but their wisdom often ends there—knowledge of words without an understanding of what sex entails both physically and emotionally (Crosby and Yarber 2001; Padilla and Baird 1991). That teenagers often misunderstand sex while talking a great deal about it may comfort some parents and frighten others. The topic of adolescent sexuality is unsettling for many parents. Should an adolescent only be told "the facts" about reproduction, or should parents explain further and correct misunderstandings? Will talking about sex encourage sexual activity? What if adolescents quiz parents about their own sexual pasts?

What parents choose to tell their children about sex and birth control—and how frequently they have such conversations—is of course linked with their own beliefs and attitudes about sex and its appropriateness for adolescents (Jordan, Price, and Fitzgerald 2000; O'Sullivan, Meyer-Bahlburg, and Watkins 2001). And beliefs about sex often follow directly from religious commitments and sentiments. Additionally, parent-child conversations about sex have a way of mirroring the parents' own experiences with such talks when *they* were younger. But exactly how the transmission of sexual values and information occurs is remarkably unclear.

This chapter examines religious influences on parent-child communication about sex, birth control, and the morality of adolescent sex; the ease with which parents communicate about these topics; the behavioral ramifications of such communication; and how much teenagers actually know about sex and pregnancy risks.[1] What are parents telling their adolescents about sex, and what do adolescents know about sex? What types of parents speak easily on the topic?

57

What types stumble when they try, or avoid it altogether? When parents say they're talking to their kids about sex or birth control, what are they communicating? Are religious parents less likely to talk about birth control? I conclude this chapter on learning sexuality with a brief discussion of the emergence of homosexual and bisexual attractions and identities during adolescence and religious patterns in relation to them.

## THE IRRELEVANT SEX EDUCATION DEBATE

As I documented in chapter 1, most Christian religious traditions tend to assert social influence and control over sexual behavior by promoting some cultural scenarios and sexual standards (the what, when, where, how, and with whom) and resisting others. An actual educational curriculum for a distinctly religious sex education, however, is uncommon and certainly underutilized. What does exist varies widely in quality.[2]

Most of us, however, think of schools when we think of sex education. Although church and state are separate spheres in America, they are increasingly partners in the sexual education of American teenagers, given the recent popularity of abstinence-based education in public schools. In a 2005 cover story from *U.S. News & World Report*, journalist Katy Kelly cites a "commonly accepted" figure of 15 percent to denote the number of American parents who prefer an abstinence-only approach to sex education in schools. As recently as 1988, only 1 in 50 junior and senior high schools employed abstinence-only sex education programs (CBS News, "Taking the Pledge," September 18, 2005). Yet schools that take this particular pedagogical approach—which provides little or no information on a variety of sex-related topics—have been the preferred recipient of federal funds during the George W. Bush administration. Abstinence-only sex education is now the primary approach in 35 percent of American public schools. An additional 50 percent teach "abstinence plus," in which other contraceptive methods are discussed, though not preferred. The remainder of schools—just under 14 percent—choose to forgo the offer of federal dollars and teach a more comprehensive sex education, including discussions of types of sex and topics like contraception, masturbation, homosexuality, and abortion. This situation remains the case despite the will of the vast majority of American parents—including conservative Christians—for a wider dissemination of sexuality information (Kelly 2005; Rose 2005).[3]

I would argue that the issue of sex education is a very urgent one, but *not* because of the political hype about abstinence-based education. Rather, few Americans realize the immense consequences that the digital communications revolution and the shift from typographic to image-based learning has for sex education. As the Internet expands its reach and influence, there is an increasingly open market congested with ideas and information—and not only about sex—that have not been evaluated or judged, a process to which "old-fashioned" publications like books and magazines are typically subjected (Smith and Denton 2005). Simply put, whether or not Jane Q. Teacher is allowed to talk about condoms pales in significance and gravity to the democratized availability of the so-called sexual education that is available in the mass media, especially on the Internet. Filmmakers understand that Internet pornography is certainly the primary—and, for some, the only—sexual education that teenagers now receive (Gehmlich and Collett-White in the *Washington Post*, May 24, 2006). Debates about whether educators will or will not address oral sex or anal sex or condoms or gay or lesbian sex are quickly becoming utterly irrelevant, since a few clicks of a mouse will bring any of us to a demonstration of exactly how each is performed and "experienced." For example, anal sex can be far more easily exhibited—and also presumed to be both normal and mutually pleasurable—in a few minutes' time on the Internet than by reading symbolic, stick-figure, dated "facts" about the practice in a health class textbook. (On the other hand, no one ever sees a porn star pop birth control pills.)

In an article addressing this, British columnist Johann Hari (2005) relays a particularly troubling account that is without doubt becoming more normal all the time. Hari (2005: 33) speaks of a 17-year-old boy as he laments about how far contemporary sex education lags behind electronic media:

> The [school] sex education we got was like something from another age. We were told in class what a vulva was when I was 14, but by that time I had been inspecting them in detail on my computer screen for years, and so had every other lad in the room.

While the young man knew human anatomy inside and out, he didn't know about the "huge emotional gap between porn and reality. That's what they need to teach," he pled (Hari 2005: 33).

Much more than simply "catching up" is needed from today's parents of adolescents. And just because any given adolescent does not log-in and "learn" does not mean they will not be instructed from their friends and peers who have. Parents can only protect their children so far here, and no further. Unless this digital revolution in sexual education and socialization is recognized and contested—and soon—the school sex education instructor will become, as Pink Floyd put it, "just another brick in the wall." Thus, *what parents say* about sex has probably never been more important than it is today.

## TALKING ABOUT SEX

Evidence from studies across cultures and of other species suggests that human sexuality is governed largely by social conditioning, rather than endocrinal stimulation (Bandura 1977). In other words, although sexual arousal may come naturally, we have to *learn* sexual intercourse (as well as other forms of sexual expression). A variety of studies concludes that parents of American adolescents often play a modest role in the transmission of information about sex and birth control (Ansuini, Fiddler-Woite, and Woite 1996; Moran and Corley 1991). Most parents trail adolescents' own reading, their peers, their siblings, and school (and now, the Internet) as a source of information about sex (Ammerman et al. 1992; Andre, Frevert, and Schuchmann 1989). A very common learning pattern among girls does not involve parents at all, but rather a process that begins when a friend or peer engages in intercourse, and information about the experience trickles back to friends in a direct or circuitous path. Parents' own perception of themselves as a key source of sexual information also tends to considerably outpace or contradict children's assessments of parents as sex educators (Newcomer and Udry 1985).[4] The extent of disagreement about who is talking to whom, and how often, can vary widely. In one study, 72 percent of mothers "strongly agreed" that they had talked with their adolescent children about sex, but only 45 percent of the youth concurred (Jaccard, Dittus, and Gordon 1998). Even if parents are accurately reporting their own communication efforts, adolescents' reports of communication will likely reflect only those conversations that were influential or retained in memory (Jaccard, Dittus, and Gordon 2000). A discussion might be memorable for an anxious parent, but unless the messages are clear, an adolescent may either not recall it or have a muted idea of the conversational intent (Whitaker et al. 1999). Despite the anxiety and disputed reports, youth actually tend to prefer a parent to a peer as a source of information (Hutchinson and Cooney 1998; Whitaker and Miller 2000) and typically rate parents *highest* in measures of overall influence (Sanders and Mullis 1988).

Figure 3.1 displays a conceptual model of religious influence on the sexual socialization of adolescents. I assert that devoutly religious parents make communication decisions not only based on their own sexual attitudes and morality, but also as a response to their unique perceptions about their own children (the child's immediate "risk" of virginity loss, parents' awareness of the adolescent's dating patterns and sexual activity, the adolescent's own stated sexual values, gendered expectations of sexual behavior, etc.). Thus the influence of parental religiosity on communication about sex is not only direct—determining in part what they ought to say—but also indirect, influencing their judgment of an adolescent's readiness for information. For example, if a teenager has taken a

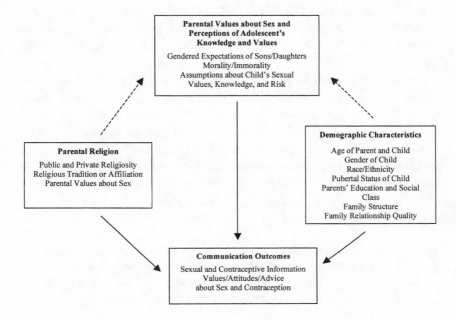

FIGURE 3.1. Conceptual Model of Religious Influence on the Sexual
Socialization of Adolescents

pledge of abstinence, her parents might feel less pressure to discuss sexual issues
with her; after all, the perceived risk of paired sexual activity might appear to
them to be low. On the other hand, if parents perceive an elevated risk of sexual
activity (say, their son is 16 years old and has a steady girlfriend), then the need
for communication might seem more urgent and affect the content and frequency of their conversations.

### The Content of Conversations

What exactly parents tell their adolescents remains less well documented. Some
parents no doubt talk about the physical mechanics of sex, about birth control,
about the emotional aspects of sexual activity, and about sexually transmitted
infections. Probably the most frequent topic of such conversations, however,
is the moral aspects of sexual behavior. As a result, parents are more likely
to shape adolescents' attitudes and beliefs about sex than their knowledge about
sex (Fisher 1986; Sanders and Mullis 1988). Many parents believe that this is
their primary responsibility: to convey normative—rather than informative—
messages about sex (Sanders and Mullis 1988; Thompson 1990). Many parents

presume that adolescents are a bundle of "raging hormones," that they already know plenty about sex, and that sexuality is an overpowering force that parents must help their teenagers to contain, control, and redirect (Schalet 2004).

Other parents tend to divide conversations into different purposes: some are meant to impart information and others are meant to teach values (Hepburn 1983). Many conversations are motivated by parents' perceptions of risk to their adolescent child (Jaccard and Dittus 1991). In one enlightening study, parents more frequently cited immediate risks, such as STDs (93 percent) or pregnancy (86 percent), than the immorality of adolescent intercourse (78 percent) as reasons for avoiding sex. In a fascinating set of in-depth interviews with Canadian youth—most of whom were only marginally religious by their own report—all interviewees

> recalled a lack of free dialogue around the issue of sex . . . and described ex-
> periencing a sense of shame when they attempted to talk with adults about
> [it]. . . . They had learned at an early age to remain silent about, keep secret, or
> never to directly describe their own sexual experiences. (Shoveller et al. 2004:
> 480)

Interviewees related experiences where "adults had closed-off dialogue about sex by using authoritative tactics ['You better not be having sex at your age!'], extremely vague and indirect messaging, and/or highly clinical and instructive approaches," perceived to be ways of avoiding the more complex emotional and pleasurable aspects of sex (Shoveller et al. 2004: 480). Some topics, the youth felt, were simply *intentionally* off limits with their parents.

One NSYR interviewee with whom we spoke, a 13-year-old Hispanic, Catholic girl from Florida, indicates that conversations about sex-related matters are one-sided, contain little about religion, and are short and clinically oriented:[5]

> [*Do you talk to your parents about it?*] No. [*Have they ever talked to you about it?*]
> Yeah. [*What do they say?*] My mom says that no having sex until I'm mar-
> ried, that that's not right for a teenager to do it. Um, that later who knows what
> the consequences might be. That there's AIDS, um, I never know if the guy
> has AIDS or stuff like that.

Conversations about sex can be uncomfortable for both parent and child, but not having them—or handling them poorly—can cause long-term damage. Multiple studies confirm that adolescents who have no communication with their parents about sex tend to evaluate such silence negatively, both in the short run and later as adults (Bartle 1998; Feldman and Rosenthal 2000; Hepburn

1983; Shoveller et al. 2004). In other words, very few adolescents want their parents to say *nothing* to them about sex. And for those whose parents are silent on the topic, the result is usually pain and resentment. Nearly 70 percent of adults in one study indicated that inaccurate sexuality information has had a negative effect on their emotional or physical well-being at some point in their life (Ansuini et al. 1996).[6] Additionally, adolescents who communicate little with their parents are more likely to misunderstand their parents' attitudes about sex (Jaccard et al. 1998; Newcomer and Udry 1985). Consistently negative messages can be just as damaging: parents who rely on negative sexual messages toward their younger children may "find it difficult to switch gears and provide open communicative information sources during their child's adolescence" (Andre et al. 1989: 243).

Overall, the two best predictors of the frequency of parent-child conversations about sexual matters are gender (of both parent and child) and race/ ethnicity.[7] Mothers are the primary go-to parent for sexual information, especially by daughters. Mothers are also more apt to be direct in their conversations with sons. Fathers, on the other hand, are most comfortable with public conversations about general sexual issues, rather than private conversations on more specific sexual topics (Jaccard and Dittus 1991). Adolescent boys are "talked to" much less frequently than are adolescent girls. In one study, only about 50 percent of boys had a parent who agreed that they had talked about sex, compared to 85 percent of the girls (Jaccard and Dittus 1991). Parents are also more likely to discuss the emotional impact of sex, the potential loss of respect, and the virtues of virginity with girls than with boys (Jaccard and Dittus 1991). Indeed, both religious and popular sexual ideologies still unwittingly reinforce different sexual standards for girls and boys.[8] Across multiple studies, only the mother-daughter combination displays something besides a negligible pattern of communication about sexual matters (Fisher 1986).

Communication patterns also vary by race/ethnicity. More frequent communication about contraception and encouragement to postpone sex occurs in African-American families. In fact, the more sensitive the subject matter (like intercourse), the greater the disparity between the proportion of black mothers and of white mothers who have *never* talked with their daughters about it (Fox and Inazu 1980). In one particularly compelling study of how Mexican immigrant women socialize their daughters, Gloria González-López (2004) notes that premarital virginity loss constitutes less of a religious norm violation than the loss of a commodity that could otherwise be traded for marital happiness and financial stability. As one of her interviewees confesses, "I did not follow them [teachings regarding virginity] because of religion. . . . I followed them because of fear of my mother!" (2004: 234).

## Religion and Parent-Child Communication about Sex

So what role does religion play in fostering or curbing sexual conversations between American parents and their teenagers? Table 3.1 displays frequencies of select responses (the top and bottom ends of the ordinal scale) of Add Health parents about their communication about sex-related topics, and Table 3.2 displays NSYR frequencies documenting the ease with which parents talk about sex.[9] Nearly 21 percent of parents who attend church at least once per week report never talking about birth control with their adolescent child, which is higher than parents with more modest attendance habits. (No clear differences appear with respect to talking about sex, just birth control.) Just over 48 percent of weekly churchgoers report talking "a great deal" about the moral issues of sex, compared with as little as 29 percent among those parents who never attend services. Comparable numbers appear for parents who hold their religious faith to be "very important" when compared with those for whom religion's value is less than that. An exception to this is found with talking "a great deal" about sex, where the numbers are reversed when compared with attendance. That is, a higher percentage of parents for whom religion is very important appear (at face value) to talk about sex "a great deal" than do parents who value religion less than this.

Conversations about sexual morality display the most polarized numbers, as might be expected. Since sexual morality is often closely connected with religion, nonreligious parents might naturally report fewer conversations about it. Parents of children who have pledged sexual abstinence until marriage display few notable differences from parents of nonpledgers, except when the conversation is about sexual morality. Parents of pledgers, of course, talk more about sexual morality than do other parents.

The different religious affiliations present a more nuanced portrait. Parents who affiliate with traditionally black Protestant[10] churches clearly talk the most (and with the greatest ease) about all sex-related topics, while Jewish and unaffiliated parents are distinguished by their lower levels of communication about sexual morality. Mormon parents are more likely than most other religious types to shun conversations about birth control. Mainline Protestants (in the NSYR) are the least likely to find talking about sex to be very easy and are the most likely to find such conversations somewhat or very hard. Roman Catholic, Jewish, and Mormon parents report comparably low levels of ease in communication. On the other hand, only about 12 percent of black Protestant parents report feeling great difficulty in talking about sex. Just under half of all religiously unaffiliated parents told us that they found talking about sex to be very easy. The interviews suggest that they may not only be easier to talk to about sex but even may be cooperative in their adolescents' sexual involvement:

TABLE 3.1 Parent-Child Communication Patterns about Sex,
Birth Control, and the Morality of Adolescent Sex

| Parent Characteristics | Percentage of parents who do "not at all" talk to their children about | | | Percentage of parents who talk a "great deal" to their children about | | |
|---|---|---|---|---|---|---|
| | Sex | Birth control | Morality of sex | Sex | Birth control | Morality of sex |
| *Church Attendance* | | | | | | |
| Weekly | 7.9 | 20.6 | 9.4 | 32.3 | 24.0 | 48.2 |
| Once a month but less than weekly | 7.0 | 15.8 | 11.2 | 33.3 | 28.4 | 35.8 |
| Less than once a month | 5.5 | 11.7 | 12.6 | 35.7 | 31.7 | 34.0 |
| Never | 7.9 | 16.2 | 20.0 | 36.3 | 32.3 | 28.6 |
| *Importance of Religion* | | | | | | |
| Very important | 7.2 | 18.0 | 10.2 | 36.6 | 28.7 | 46.3 |
| Fairly important | 6.3 | 14.3 | 13.5 | 31.4 | 28.5 | 28.6 |
| Fairly unimportant | 8.9 | 16.0 | 24.1 | 25.8 | 22.9 | 17.6 |
| Not important at all | 8.8 | 14.4 | 23.4 | 29.5 | 29.7 | 22.5 |
| *Religious Tradition* | | | | | | |
| Evangelical Protestant | 5.4 | 15.2 | 9.0 | 36.8 | 27.6 | 46.2 |
| Mainline Protestant | 5.5 | 15.9 | 10.9 | 28.5 | 24.4 | 31.6 |
| Black Protestant | 5.0 | 12.0 | 10.4 | 55.1 | 46.3 | 54.6 |
| Catholic | 9.9 | 19.9 | 15.2 | 29.7 | 25.2 | 33.8 |
| Mormon (LDS) | 6.7 | 21.4 | 11.7 | 34.3 | 22.5 | 52.3 |
| Jewish | 1.9 | 11.7 | 24.9 | 27.7 | 25.1 | 17.1 |
| Other religion | 8.0 | 18.2 | 12.0 | 33.6 | 28.5 | 41.2 |
| No religion | 9.5 | 15.2 | 24.0 | 28.6 | 29.1 | 22.1 |
| Child has taken pledge of abstinence | 8.0 | 19.2 | 9.1 | 32.7 | 23.8 | 49.9 |
| Child has not taken pledge of abstinence | 7.0 | 16.3 | 13.3 | 34.4 | 29.1 | 36.6 |

*Source*: National Longitudinal Study of Adolescent Health

Jillian, a 15-year-old nonreligious girl from Ohio, was asked: "What about your parents? Do they talk to you much about these things?"

No. They're really laid back about a lot of that kind of stuff. I've, I think they've told me before, like, they don't think I should be, like, having sex, but if I was having sex, they'd rather know so they could get condoms for me. . . .They'd

TABLE 3.2 Patterns of Parent-Child Communication about Sex

| | Percentage of parents who find talking about sex | |
|---|---|---|
| Parent Characteristics | Very easy | Somewhat or very hard |
| *Church Attendance* | | |
| More than once a week | 46.5 | 18.9 |
| Weekly | 40.2 | 25.4 |
| Up to 2–3 times a month | 47.0 | 21.3 |
| Never | 48.3 | 17.9 |
| *Importance of Religion* | | |
| Extremely important | 40.2 | 25.4 |
| Very important | 47.4 | 21.0 |
| Somewhat or fairly important | 49.5 | 22.7 |
| Not very important | 45.4 | 20.7 |
| Not important at all | 48.3 | 17.9 |
| *Religious Tradition* | | |
| Evangelical Protestant | 45.1 | 19.4 |
| Mainline Protestant | 37.9 | 29.5 |
| Black Protestant | 68.4 | 11.7 |
| Catholic | 39.0 | 25.2 |
| Jewish | 42.7 | 20.0 |
| Mormon (LDS) | 40.7 | 29.1 |
| Other religion | 49.4 | 15.2 |
| No religion | 47.9 | 23.8 |
| *Race/Ethnicity* | | |
| White | 40.9 | 22.3 |
| African American | 65.2 | 13.9 |
| Hispanic | 47.2 | 22.8 |
| Asian American | 31.7 | 39.5 |

*Source*: National Survey of Youth and Religion

rather know about it and they'd be OK with it, but I mean they'd probably be mad if I was having sex right now, when I was this young. But they say that they'd rather know than not know. Maybe they just want to find out. [laughs]

James, a 17-year-old boy from Kentucky who is likewise not religious, also has parents (or at least a father) who do not mind his having sex:

My dad, a long time before I did [have sex], he expected me to be doing it like for, for a long time before I actually did. And I was always telling him, you know, I talked to him about it, but I mean, I hadn't done it, so. He kind of expected me to be doing it before I actually did, so we, he kind of made sure that I was [informed, that] I knew as much as he could tell me at my age. So I don't feel like I didn't know anything or anything like that.

The strong influence of both parental religiosity and religious affiliation on sexual morality conversations remains even after accounting for parental disapproval of adolescent sex and whether their own adolescent has taken an abstinence pledge (results in Tables A3.1 through A3.3). When the topic shifts from morality to sex and contraception, however, a number of things change (results in Table A3.2). One that does not, however, is the greater likelihood of black Protestants to discuss sex and birth control with their children consistently more frequently than other types of parents.

Unlike with conversations about sexual morality, parents who attend church regularly clearly have misgivings about the subjects of sex and birth control. Even after controlling for parental attitudes about sex, church attendance is associated with diminished frequency of communication about both sex and birth control. Curiously, this association is much stronger among white parents than among parents of all other races/ethnicities (results in Table A3.4). In other words, while devoutly religious parents in general talk less about sex and birth control, white parents who attend church regularly are even less likely than other types of religiously active parents to talk about them.

While at first it appears that the more important religion is to the parent respondents, the more frequently they report talking to their adolescents about both sex and birth control, an illuminating story emerges when I take into account the frequency with which parents say they talk to their children about the *moral* issues of adolescent sex (Table A3.2, column 3). This not only diminishes the association between parental religious salience and communication about sex and birth control, it in fact becomes significant in the other direction: parents for whom religion is important communicate *less* often about birth control than parents whose religious faith is not important. This suggests that when devoutly religious parents say they are talking regularly with their adolescents about sex and birth control, it means they are talking with them about morality rather than sharing information.

Evangelical Protestants' (and, to a less consistent extent, Mormons' and those of other religions) communication patterns about sex and birth control likewise hinge on sexual morality; once I account for their morality conversations, their likelihood of talking about either sex or birth control diminish. For them, talk about sex *is* talk about values. Less religious parents have a clearer sense of the difference.

Thus, it is clear that many parents think their primary responsibility is to convey normative—rather than informative—messages about sex. But sometimes information is what adolescents need. Parents tend to gauge how much their teenagers know about sex from the language they use (and from assumptions about their mass media exposure to sex). Yet while adolescents may know the vocabulary, they may misunderstand what it all means (Bartle 1998). As a result, many parents—religious or otherwise—overestimate adolescents' knowledge about sex and birth control. They presume, perhaps incorrectly, that accurate information about sex and birth control is widely available and that their child knows all the pertinent facts. What is lacking, such parents may perceive, is clear guidance about what is right and wrong. Other parents recognize (the truth) that they know more about sex than their adolescent does and seek to balance morality with information and instruction, an approach which tends to be appreciated by adolescents. Carla, the 17-year-old evangelical featured in chapter 1, was grateful for her parents' offer of information, moral values, and the freedom to make her own decisions:

> My parents were really, my mom was pretty cool about it, you know. We had the talk when I was like in fourth grade. She made just, you know, a general assumption for me. She didn't get all detailed and gory about it, but it was just kind of like, "This is what happens; this is how you got here. Don't do it until you're married." And then as I got older, they told me it was my personal choice. They were never like, "Don't ever touch a boy. Stay within arm's [length]," you know. It was never anything like that. It was just like, you know, it's, it's up to you. It's a personal choice. We can tell you all day not to, but we're not gonna be there holding your hand.

Carla gave voice to at least one problem with the "just say no" morality-only message:

> It's just like if somebody says "don't go in that room." And they tell you that every day. Before too long, you're gonna go in that room because you want to know what's in there that you can't see. And so I think a lot of parents make a mistake by always saying "don't do it."

Cami, an 18-year-old Roman Catholic from Massachusetts, echoes Carla's concern. Her mother sought to establish conversational honesty with Cami at an early age—not because of perceived risk but out of principle. When asked about the important influences on how she thought about sex, Cami talked about her mother:

> She's never been like, "don't have sex until after you're married," that kind of thing, but she's always been, um, like, honest with me. She's like "Cami, if

you ever [have sex]," she's like "I want [you] to be honest with me," you know. Like when I was little she would, I could just turn around and not look at [her] and "You won't look me in the eye, just be honest with me." She was always talking about, like, um, how um, how you should use condoms and stuff like that. I guess just like hearing that, you know, it just helped me make the decision that I wouldn't have sex. And she actually told me that she didn't have sex until she was married. And I thought that was pretty cool. But she never, like, pushed it on me. Which is also, I think is cool. I think that if she had, then maybe I would have, like, rebelled, I don't know. But the way she did it worked out well because I just, logically, just don't see the point [in having sex now], you know.

## WHY SOME PARENTS AVOID TALKING ABOUT SEX

Not a few parents find such conversations to be uncomfortable and potentially embarrassing to both parties (Schalet 2004). Many consider themselves uninformed and feel they have little information to offer (Sanders and Mullis 1988). Nevertheless, most parents push through their discomfort and talk with their adolescent children, especially girls. Why do some parents struggle with such conversations more than others, and what are the reasons that some altogether fail to communicate? Do religious and moral convictions have anything to do with such reticence?

One study identified more than 20 common reservations that parents give for avoiding conversations with their adolescent children about sex and birth control (Jaccard et al. 2000). Mothers of boys were more apt than mothers of girls to fear that talking wouldn't do any good, that they wouldn't know the answers to his questions, that it would raise parent-child trust concerns, that her son was too busy to talk, and that he would think she might approve of him having sex. Reservations about discussing birth control included the assumption that their children would find such information elsewhere, anticipated difficulties in explaining how contraception works, and the obvious concern that discussing birth control would hasten their children's sexual activity (Jaccard and Dittus 1991).

The Add Health survey queried parents about four particular misgivings about sex-related conversations. They were:

1. You (the parent) really don't know enough about sex and birth control to talk about them with (adolescent child's name).
2. It would be difficult for you to explain things if you talked with (name) about sex and birth control.

3. (Name) will get the information somewhere else, so you don't really need to talk to (him/her) about sex and birth control.
4. Talking about birth control with (name) would only encourage (him/her) to have sex.

While religion plays a key role in the frequency and content of parents' communications about sex, religious factors are largely unimportant in predicting two particular parental misgivings. Parental religiosity is entirely unrelated to the "I don't know enough to talk" answer, and the "my child will learn about sex elsewhere" excuse (results in Table A3.5). There are modest religious effects on the other two reasons. The more important religion is to parents, the more likely they are to say that talking about birth control would only encourage their adolescent to have sex. A more modest attendance effect also appears with this reason. Parents who attend religious services more frequently are also slightly more likely to say that talking about birth control would only encourage sex and that it would be difficult to explain sexual matters.

Race and ethnicity, not religion, best predicts such misgivings (Fox and Inazu 1980; Moran and Corley 1991). Ironically, white parents were the least likely to cite any of the four reasons, despite being considerably more likely than African-American parents to refrain from communication (results not shown). This may indicate that white parents have a stronger sense that they *ought* to be talking to their kids, or that there are no good reasons to give for their relative silence. Hispanics and Asian Americans—each less likely than African Americans to communicate—are more apt to nominate these reasons for their reticence. Older parents were consistently more likely than younger ones both to refrain from communication and to cite the offered reasons as explanations, indicating a generational or cohort difference in norms about sexual socialization.

## CONSEQUENCES OF CONVERSATIONS

Talking to one's adolescent children about sex and contraception equips them with valuable information, but what teenagers *do* with this information is not well established. Opinions vary widely. Some scholars assume that adolescents whose parents communicate with them about sex will avoid the early initiation of sexual behavior and exhibit greater subsequent responsibility in their sexual relationships. A number of studies support this position (Adolph et al. 1995; Newcomer and Udry 1985). Others suggest that communication about sexual and contraceptive matters *enhances* the likelihood that adolescents will subsequently experience intercourse (Bersamin et al. 2005; Taris and Semin 1997). This is what the more religious parents in the Add Health study tend to think (see Table A3.5). Still other research claims that the association between the two hinges on other variables: in one study, peer pressure to have sex was more effective in the absence of parent-child communication about sex (Whitaker and Miller 2000). Finally, some studies disagree with all of these, suggesting that parent-child communication has little effect at all on sexual involvement (Casper 1990; Inazu and Fox 1980; Rodgers 1999).[11]

So which is it? Do religious parents who worry that talking about contraception will encourage sexual activity have reason for concern? The answer is yes, though the effect is not all that large. Table 3.3 displays predicted probability of first sex among a sample of Add Health respondents who were virgins at Wave I of the survey administration.[12] More frequent parent-child communication about sex *slightly* elevates the probability that an adolescent child will subsequently lose his/her virginity before adulthood. Other analyses (shown in Table A3.6) confirm that this relationship is weak; it disappears altogether with additional controls. The association between talking about contraception and having sex, though, is stronger. Among parents who report no communication about birth control, 41 percent of their adolescent children subsequently experienced first sex by the next survey wave. Among parents who talk "a great deal" about birth control, 53 percent of their children did so. Given the number of important control variables for which I accounted—including dating patterns, race/ethnicity, religiosity, and pledging abstinence—I maintain this association is quite resilient. (Nevertheless, talking about birth control is *not* as powerful an influence on subsequent virginity loss as the number of recent dating partners or the age of the child.)

Before concerned parents prematurely conclude that contraceptive conversations should be ceased, we should remind ourselves that—in keeping with the conceptual model in Figure 3.1—many parents decide to talk to their adolescents about sex-related matters *because* they perceive that their adolescents' participation in sexual activity may be imminent. This perception is impossible to control for in such models and is likely at work in the results here. The most likely scenario, then, is that parent-child communication about contraception increases when parents perceive sexual *intentions* in their adolescents (from their dating behavior, age, language, time use, etc.) and that the conversations themselves are not the cause of the subsequent sexual activity. I cannot, however, conclude this with complete confidence.

On the other hand, conversations about the morality of adolescent sex display no evident associations with loss of virginity. They may exhibit indirect effects,

TABLE 3.3 Predicted Probability of Experiencing First Sex, by Differing Levels of Parent-Child Communication about Sex, Contraception, and Sexual Morality

| *Frequency of conversation about* | | *Probability* |
| --- | --- | --- |
| Sex | Not at all | 0.41 |
| | Somewhat | 0.44 |
| | A moderate amount | 0.48 |
| | A great deal | 0.51 |
| Contraception | Not at all | 0.41 |
| | Somewhat | 0.45 |
| | A moderate amount | 0.49 |
| | A great deal | 0.53 |
| Sexual morality | Not at all | 0.48 |
| | Somewhat | 0.47 |
| | A moderate amount | 0.47 |
| | A great deal | 0.47 |

*Source*: National Longitudinal Study of Adolescent Health

*Note*: Generated from probit regression models, controlling for age, parents' education, family structure, conversations about contraception, conversations about sex, conversations about sexual morality, number of adolescent's recent romantic partners, adolescent religious salience, and adolescent religious service attendance, and setting each at its mean level.

such as the influence that such conversations about sexual morality have on adolescents' own attitudes about sex or their likelihood of pledging abstinence.

## WHAT ADOLESCENTS KNOW ABOUT SEX

Up until now, this chapter's focus has been largely on parents and what they tell their teenagers about sex, why some avoid it altogether, and how their conversations about sex are received. I have yet to hint about how effective their communication has been. So, what *do* teenagers know about sex and contraception? Since devoutly religious parents talk more about sexual morality than about sexual mechanics, do their adolescent children display limited knowledge about sex?

In general, most estimates of adolescents' knowledge about sex and related topics are quite low. When quizzed, teenagers often answer correctly no more than 50 percent of the time (Ammerman et al. 1992; Padilla and Baird 1991). Although religion is seldom a key concern of researchers in this area, one study that did explore religious differences in perceived versus actual knowledge about correct condom use notes that religiously affiliated youth are 20 percent more likely to believe misconceptions about condoms than are unaffiliated (or nonreligious) youth (Crosby and Yarber 2001).

In a study of Atlanta area mothers and their adolescent children, researchers asked each to define seven terms related to sexual development: ejaculation, hormones, menstruation, ovulation, puberty, semen, and wet dreams (Hockenberry-Eaton et al. 1996). The adolescents display a marked inability to accurately define most of these terms. Mothers fared *no better* than their adolescent children in identifying sexual development terminology. Less than half of the respondents in a study of adolescent girls correctly identified such body parts as the clitoris, cervix, and urethra, and they could recognize male external anatomy and function better than their own (Ammerman et al. 1992). They also found slang terms easier to identify than medically correct ones.

On the other hand, boys are even less able than girls to correctly define sexual terms—even male-specific ones—or to recognize pregnancy risks and understand contraceptive practices. Surprisingly, the influence of age and sexual experience on accurate knowledge is weaker than expected (Ammerman et al. 1992; Feldman and Rosenthal 2000; Finkel and Finkel 1975; Freeman et al. 1980; Hockenberry-Eaton et al. 1996; Mueller and Powers 1990). The jury is still out on the link between parent-child communication about sex and adolescents' knowledge about sex. Some studies document a clear connection (Miller and Whitaker 2001), and some find nothing (Fisher 1986). If conversations are largely about sexual values, however, such communication may not raise sexual awareness and understanding at all.

Table 3.4 displays the average number of correct answers to a five-question quiz about sex and pregnancy risk administered to adolescents at both waves of the Add Health study.[13] The numbers tend to confirm previous research wisdom: adolescents' scores huddle closely around 50 percent. Unfortunately, scoring 50 percent on a true/false quiz does *not* indicate that teens know the correct answer to half of the questions. Flipping a coin would produce the *same* score, on average. Until a category of adolescents scores reliably better than 50 percent, we cannot have confidence that they know *any* of the correct answers.

Religion matters, in keeping with the results from the parent-child communication patterns noted earlier. Youth who report weekly church attendance and who say that religion is "very important" to them score lower than less religious adolescents at both waves of data collection.[14] The same is true of abstinence pledgers. The difference is not remarkably large, but it is nonetheless robust to the inclusion of a set of control variables (see Table A3.7). Adolescent boys, African Americans, adolescents whose parents are less educated, and sexually inexperienced youths also score lower. The gap between abstinence pledgers and nonpledgers is larger at Wave II than Wave I. Yet, given that so

TABLE 3.4 Average Correct Answers (Out of Five Questions) from a Sex and Pregnancy Risk Quiz, by Adolescent Religious Variables

|  | *Wave I* | *Wave II* |
|---|---|---|
| *Religious Tradition* | | |
| Evangelical Protestant | 2.47 | 2.43 |
| Mainline Protestant | 2.57 | 2.60 |
| Black Protestant | 2.48 | 2.37 |
| Catholic | 2.59 | 2.65 |
| Mormon (LDS) | 2.43 | 2.56 |
| Jewish | 2.79 | 2.92 |
| Other religion | 2.60 | 2.61 |
| No religion | 2.65 | 2.70 |
| *Church Attendance* | | |
| Weekly | 2.44 | 2.48 |
| Once a month but less than weekly | 2.61 | 2.58 |
| Less than once a month | 2.69 | 2.64 |
| Never | 2.59 | 2.67 |
| *Importance of Religion* | | |
| Very important | 2.44 | 2.41 |
| Fairly important | 2.62 | 2.67 |
| Fairly unimportant | 2.67 | 2.71 |
| Not important at all | 2.65 | 2.69 |
| | | |
| Has taken abstinence pledge | 2.34 | 2.31 |
| No abstinence pledge | 2.59 | 2.61 |
| | | |
| "Born again" | 2.46 | 2.41 |
| Not "born again" | 2.60 | 2.63 |

*Source*: National Longitudinal Study of Adolescent Health

many fare so poorly on this quiz, I hesitate to accord too much weight to these findings, except one unmistakable conclusion: most teenagers know very little about sex and about pregnancy risk.

## RELIGIOUS PARENTS AND SEXUAL SOCIALIZATION

From popular authors, we know that devoutly religious parents often see themselves as competing with a sex-saturated popular culture and mass media for the sexual socialization of their children (Dobson 1989; McDowell and Hostetler 2002). Religious parents must choose either to educate their adolescents about sex or to risk abandoning the task to information sources (media, the Internet, friends, school) whose values are perceived as neutral at best and hostile at worst. At the same time, such parents often remain committed to the ideal that their children should not engage in sex until marriage. Clearly, then, what parents tell their children about sex, and when, and whether they discuss birth control or not, can be a struggle for adults who hold traditional religious beliefs about sex. From the results here, we know that regular churchgoers have *less* frequent conversations with their youth about birth control and sex but *more* frequent conversations about sexual morality. The interaction effect between white parents and church attendance (see Table A3.4) suggests that this particular group is even more reticent to broach the subjects of sex and birth control than are other religious parents. Open dialogue about sex is clearly not the norm among devoutly religious families (Thornton and Camburn 1989).

The stronger influence of religion on birth control conversations implies that—while theoretically sex and contraception may go together for some parents—the two are distinctly different topics for religious families. Talking to one's child about sex may seem harmless, even appropriate, but talking about birth control may appear only to equip them to engage in sexual behavior—and in fact, there is something to this. Nevertheless, the probability that an adolescent will lose his/her virginity if his/her parents never talk about birth control is not much lower than if they talk a great deal (0.41 compared with 0.53), and exactly *why* such conversations occur when they do may matter here. Parents judge the urgency and appropriateness of sexual conversations with their children based in part upon their perceptions of immediate risk. Parents whose children have pledged sexual abstinence may feel that a discussion of birth control is simply unnecessary, and adolescents who take such a pledge tend to score slightly lower on the pregnancy-risk quiz, reflecting their disinterest in getting the facts straight at this point in their lives.

In practice, the difference between parents talking about sex and parents not talking about it may be in how spontaneous or planned their adolescents' first experience of intercourse is, as well as their choice to use contraception or not. The old, tired phrase "good girls don't plan" comes to mind here. Planning intentional sexual activity may produce in religious youth (and their parents, if they find out) feelings of guilt or disappointment of a higher order than the feelings experienced with spontaneous sexual activity, in spite of the obvious increased pregnancy risk that accompanies spontaneity (Bartle 1998). What I'm saying is that religious parents may find avoiding sex-and-contraception conversations to be functional: that way, their children would not likely intentionally pursue sex, or if they did, their parents would not blame themselves.

## EMERGING HOMOSEXUALITY AND BISEXUALITY

Up to this point, I have been implying adolescent heterosexuality. Not all adolescents turn out to be heterosexual, however. Although my intention for this book is to better understand how religion shapes contemporary hetero-sexual attitudes and expression among American teenagers, a few pages' inquiry into current data on homosexuality—and any associations with religion that may emerge—is certainly merited. Indeed, little is known about the pair, though much in the way of incompatibility—if not outright hostility—is popularly assumed. Church leaders, youth pastors, and a variety of Christian authors instruct adolescents a great deal about how to avoid premarital het-erosexual behavior. Yet subsumed in their conversation is the notion that while heterosexual desire is normal-but-to-be-channeled-or-resisted, homosexual behavior is always sinful and therefore is to be avoided at all costs. Most of them believe in the malleability of sexual orientation. At the same time, their voices are finding increasing competition from those of universities, school systems, and certainly mass media and pop culture, which continue to give increasing voice to the acceptance and normalization of a variety of sexual orientations.

Nevertheless, most adolescents are presumed heterosexual until proven otherwise. Indeed, most homosexual Americans do not "come out of the closet" and self-identify as such until after their adolescent years. Thus, doc-umenting homosexuality in adolescence is a challenge, one which Add Health and the NSYR did not undertake. The 2002 National Survey of Family Growth did, however, ask a variety of questions to youths aged 15–19 about homo-sexuality, including perceived orientation, same-sex attraction, and homosex-ual behavior—three distinct (though related) phenomena. And the manner in which they asked the questions seems clear.[15]

Table 3.5 displays the frequencies of same-sex attraction, sexual relations, and self-identification as homosexual among NSFG respondents aged 15–19, sorted by categories of religiosity and religious tradition. The first row presents the overall percentages, from which it can be concluded that there are *degrees* of homosexual identification and that actual same-sex behavior is more common than self-identification as homosexual. More than double the number of teenage girls say that they have had same-sex relations (10.7 percent), compared with boys (4.3 percent), but only about half as many girls as boys self-identify as homosexual (1 percent versus 2 percent). On the other hand, more than four times as many girls as boys identify themselves as bisexual, reinforcing the emerging notion that experimenting with bisexual relationships is popular among a minority of teenage girls.

To students of sexual development, these numbers will not surprise, es-pecially since during adolescence sexual orientation for many is still developing,

TABLE 3.5 Same-Sex Characteristics of Unmarried 15- to 19-Year-Olds (in Percentages), by Religiosity Measures

| | Has had same-sex relations | | Is at least sometimes attracted to members of same sex | | Identifies as homosexual | | Identifies as bisexual | |
|---|---|---|---|---|---|---|---|---|
| | Boys | Girls | Boys | Girls | Boys | Girls | Boys | Girls |
| All 15- to 19-year-olds | 4.3 | 10.7 | 5.4 | 15.5 | 1.9 | 1.0 | 1.4 | 6.4 |
| *Church Attendance* | | | | | | | | |
| More than once a week | 2.2 | 8.5 | 2.2 | 7.7 | 0.0 | 0.5 | 0.2 | 3.4 |
| Once a week | 3.4 | 5.1 | 3.2 | 9.0 | 1.2 | 0.7 | 0.6 | 3.9 |
| One–three times a month | 4.1 | 6.2 | 6.1 | 13.0 | 1.6 | 0.7 | 3.2 | 4.8 |
| Less than once a month | 5.2 | 12.6 | 7.1 | 16.9 | 2.5 | 0.7 | 1.8 | 5.9 |
| Never | 5.5 | 18.8 | 7.0 | 27.0 | 2.9 | 2.2 | 1.1 | 12.5 |
| *Importance of Religion* | | | | | | | | |
| Very important | 3.1 | 6.3 | 3.2 | 9.0 | 1.2 | 0.6 | 1.4 | 3.6 |
| Somewhat important | 4.2 | 10.4 | 4.4 | 15.0 | 0.8 | 0.8 | 1.8 | 6.0 |
| Not important | 5.9 | 19.2 | 9.2 | 27.6 | 4.3 | 1.8 | 0.8 | 11.5 |
| *Religious Tradition* | | | | | | | | |
| Evangelical Protestant | 0.8 | 10.6 | 2.6 | 12.6 | 0.2 | 1.0 | 0.7 | 7.0 |
| Mainline Protestant | 0.7 | 6.5 | 1.4 | 12.1 | 1.0 | 0.8 | 0.0 | 5.3 |
| Black Protestant | 4.2 | 12.1 | 5.2 | 10.1 | 0.8 | 1.7 | 0.9 | 3.4 |
| Catholic | 5.0 | 5.0 | 3.8 | 9.7 | 1.3 | 0.7 | 1.4 | 3.0 |
| Other religion | 11.6 | 10.8 | 14.0 | 20.7 | 6.3 | 0.6 | 4.9 | 7.1 |
| No religion | 4.7 | 24.0 | 8.4 | 32.7 | 2.8 | 1.7 | 0.8 | 14.6 |

*Source*: National Survey of Family Growth, Cycle 6

and some youths experiment with same-sex relationships—which may not include actual sexual relations—before coming to understand themselves as one thing or another. The numbers also suggest that female sexuality appears to be more "open" to direction and alteration, even later in the developmental process, than is male sexuality. Indeed, while 6.4 percent of 15- to 19-year-old women identify as bisexual, these numbers decline to 3.5 percent of 20- to 24-year-old women and just 2 percent of women aged 35–44. No such linear pattern exists among men. Despite claims that their share of the general population may approach 10 percent, only 2.3 percent of all men and 1.3 percent of all women ages 18–44 in the NSFG self-identify as homosexual.

Moreover, the LUG ("lesbian until graduation") phenomenon may require some updating: relatively few adolescent girls went so far as to self-identify as homosexual. BUG (bisexual until graduation) would be a more accurate description. One particularly enlightening study of 80 nonheterosexual women between the ages of 18 and 25, conducted over the course of five years, revealed that more than a quarter of the sample relinquished a lesbian or bisexual identity during the study phase (Diamond 2003). Nevertheless, those who did alter their sexual identity were not apt to label what they experienced as a "phase."

While such numbers interest scholars of sexuality, this book is also about religion, and about teenagers. There is more in Table 3.5 that illuminates than just the overall numbers. Several interesting religion stories emerge. First, there are perceptible linear associations between all same-sex measures (except bisexual identity) and the two religiosity measures (church attendance and importance of religion). Fully 27 percent of the least religious girls say they are at least sometimes attracted to other girls, while only 8 percent of the most religious girls say the same thing. Similarly, while as many as 19 percent of the least religious girls report having had same-sex relations, only about 7 percent of the more religious report the same.

Identical patterns appear among more or less religious boys as well, though the overall numbers are well below those of girls. Indeed, the least religious boys still report *fewer* instances of same-sex relations than the most religious girls. Just about the same can be said for same-sex attraction. Nevertheless, a linear association exists between religiosity and all same-sex measures except for bisexual identity (and religious salience on homosexual identity) among adolescent boys. There is simply very little evidence of same-sex *anything* among the most religious boys. Not a single 15- to 19-year-old boy in the NSFG who reported attending church more than once a week self-identified as homosexual.

Since these data are cross-sectional, it is impossible to suggest a unidirectional causal association, and I would err on the side of suggesting self-selection—that is, youth who experience same-sex attraction or wish to identify themselves as something besides heterosexual likely self-select away from extensive religious participation. In other words, same-sex sentiment is far more likely to affect religiosity here than the other way around.

Same-sex patterns among religious traditions are informative as well. The categories "no religion" and "other religion" tend to exhibit the highest percentages in most of the same-sex outcomes. But these too vary by gender. Almost 1 in 4 nonreligious girls say they have had same-sex relations, but only about 1 in 20 nonreligious boys report this. One in 3 nonreligious girls report a same-sex attraction, and 15 percent identify themselves as bisexual.

On the other end of the spectrum, no more than one in a hundred evangelical, mainline, or black Protestant boys self-identify as homosexual, and only slightly more Catholics do so. Similar percentages mark bisexual self-identity among boys, though 7 percent of evangelical girls identify as such. Indeed, the evangelical rate of female bisexuality trails only the nonreligious and is statistically indistinguishable from girls of some "other religion." Again, I would caution that a good deal of selectivity is likely going on: youth who feel homosexual or bisexual attraction (and admit it on a survey) may actively avoid religious groups that they perceive to be unfriendly to either alternative sexual orientations or to indecisiveness about the same (Newman and Muzzonigro 1993).

More rigorous regression models predicting each of these four outcomes, split by gender, reveal a rather weak set of religious effects across the board, especially when predicting homosexual or bisexual identity (see Tables A3.8 through A3.11). While one or the other religiosity measure often predicts a diminished likelihood of reporting a same-sex experience, attraction, or self-identity, only one religious effect remains robust when including multiple controls (including religious tradition variables): boys who say religion is very important are significantly less likely to report a same-sex attraction. Indeed, very few variables are consistent predictors in any of these models, likely reinforcing conclusions about genetic and developmental tendencies toward different sexual orientations and practices.

While the NSFG numbers suggest that youth who struggle to understand or define their sexuality are more likely to avoid extensive religious involvement, this depicts only one part of the story about the association between sexual orientation and religion today. Although we didn't specifically ask NSYR interviewees about homosexuality, the subject did arise with some degree of regularity.[16] Thirty-three interviewees talked about homosexuality, bisexuality, or both. On the one hand, interviewees who brought up the topic of homosexuality almost universally defined themselves as neither homosexual nor unclear about their own orientation, regardless of whether they were religious or not. But neither did many of them actively decry homosexuality. If I could characterize a perspective that recurred across interviews—meaning, a majority of those who spoke about homosexuality would fit this pattern—these would be its hallmarks:

- I myself am not homosexual.
- I believe that homosexuality is not normal and is either against the Bible, nature, or both.
- I don't agree with what homosexuals do, namely, have same-sex relations.
- Nevertheless, I have a homosexual friend, and I don't wish to stop being their friend.
- My parents tend to be more uncomfortable with homosexuality than I am.

- I sense increasing societal openness to homosexuality, especially on TV ("Will & Grace").
- Judging people because they are homosexuals seems wrong and un-Christian to me.

This set of common responses may convey that all interviewees felt that homosexual practice was wrong or abnormal, which is not the case. Several were passionate advocates of gay and lesbian rights, despite being heterosexual themselves. But a clear majority would fit the above description. Moreover, religion did *not* seem to shape most interviewees' responses. When it did, more devoutly religious interviewees felt the push-and-pull of judgment and mercy most keenly: they intellectually object to homosexual behavior as wrong, but they also believe they are to be interpersonally tolerant, perhaps even empathetic. Heather, a 17-year-old Mormon from Utah—who might be expected to voice more evident hostility, given the LDS monopoly there—nevertheless eloquently captured the dual nature of the most common religious perspective we heard. In almost the same breath as she states, "I don't like all this, um, lesbian crap and gay stuff," she empathizes with particular individual homosexual students she knows and respects. After a fellow student let fly a disparaging comment about gays, Heather responded affirmatively, then panicked:

> I realized that my, a particular [gay] guy was right behind me and I just felt, I don't, I don't know what would be the right thing to, to do. Because my values—I don't believe in that and yet he's my friend and he's that way and so I didn't really know how to respond. So I just kinda kept quiet. [*So how did you decide what the right thing was to do in that situation?*] I think I decided that, you know, he has, he has his way and if he thinks that that's the way that he is, and I certainly think that, you know, people have tendencies towards that. I do think they, they can change, and that's what I believe. And, you know, he believes that he can't, you know, and so I, I just chose that I'll let him decide who he is and I'll just keep quiet during this, and it was really awkward 'cause I did blurt out just a kind of a sigh, like, "Oh, that's disgusting," you know. And I think, I don't know if our relationship's quite the same [since].

Very seldom did we hear unsolicited criticism of both homosexuality *and* particular homosexual people. More commonly, we heard the former, but not the latter. There is a growing tolerance of gays and lesbians in the United States, even among those adults and adolescents who would still insist that homosexual practice is morally wrong. The American "live and let live" spirit is triumphing over judgment. Alternately, the importance of personal relationships trumps strong evaluations of sexual orientation.

References to bisexuality or to adolescent girls' "temporary" lesbianism surfaced occasionally, as did "experimenting," but hardly enough to verify the pattern in the 2002 NSFG data. Far more common were references to homosexuality of the above type. We heard no references to personal struggles with sexual orientation, although this is not surprising, given the very private and sensitive nature of the topic.

## CONCLUSIONS

To summarize this chapter, popular commentaries report that adolescents are being exposed to sex—including alternative sexualities—more intensively and at earlier ages than ever before. While sex education debates continue to rage, most parties seem entirely unaware that in adolescents' lives—which is all that really counts—school-based sex education is rapidly being replaced as authoritative by uncensored and unchallenged sexual content on the Internet. Parents, educators, and politicians are truly fiddling while Rome burns.

Second, although many parents claim to be talking to their adolescent children about sex and birth control, how much information these parents are actually communicating is debatable. Devoutly religious parents are somewhat less apt than nonreligious parents to talk to their children about sex and birth control, and they are more likely to report difficulty communicating. When such parents do communicate, they mostly convey sexual values. But religion is much less influential on communication practices than are the demographic characteristics of parent and child, like age, race/ethnicity, and gender. Some parents also distinguish between sex and birth control, and between information and values, when examining their own role.

Third, most parents—religious or otherwise—do attempt to communicate about sex and birth control with their adolescent children, especially their girls. Religious parents are less at ease with these conversations. They suspect that conversations about contraception may lead to sexual practice, and their hunches are somewhat supported by the evidence. Nearly all categories of adolescents consistently display marked misinformation about reproduction and score low on tests of knowledge about sex and pregnancy risk. More religious youth are even less informed.

Fourth and finally, while all humans must learn sexuality, not all humans will be heterosexual. The 2002 wave of the National Survey of Family Growth suggests that self-identifying as homosexual is very uncommon in adolescence, though same-sex attractions and actual relations are slightly more common. Bisexual attractions, relations, and identities are far more common, primarily among girls. Religiosity and religious affiliation are associated with almost all of these, though in more rigorous analyses, they seldom stand out. When homosexuality came up spontaneously in interviews, most adolescents indicated they were not gay or lesbian and, despite their own sentiments on the topic, knew someone who was and felt empathy for them. Most American adolescents—even religious ones—tend toward tolerance of alternative sexualities, short of approval. Labeling them homophobic would miss the mark.

# Chapter 4

## Motivating Sexual Decisions

*Life in Lubbock, Texas, taught me . . . that sex is*
*the most awful, filthy thing on earth and you should*
*save it for someone you love.*

—Butch Hancock

Sexual ideologies and standards vary across the globe (DeLamater 1989), and every society has means by which it attempts to control youthful sexuality (Brooks-Gunn and Paikoff 1997). Yet adolescent sexuality is not simply a raw force that would rage unchecked were it not for institutional social control. Far from being purely about physiology and testosterone, sex is cued by cultural scripts that shape what is "sexual" and who is sexually desirable (Ellingson 2004; Laumann et al. 1994).

In this chapter, I examine heterosexual attitudes and motivations, which are the precursors to actual heterosexual activity. The strongest associations between religion and anything related to sex appear here (Miller and Olson 1988; O'Donnell et al. 2003; Sieving, McNeely, and Blum 2000; Thornton and Camburn 1989). First, I explore the associations between religious youth and the idea of—and actually taking—a pledge to abstain from sex, the anticipation of guilt from sexual activity, and the belief that parents are hostile toward adolescent sexual activity. Second, I take an extended look at the abstinence pledge, its idealism, and whether or not it works. Third, I look beyond the right-or-wrong attitudes about sex to the host of other motivations to pursue or avoid sexual activity. Some motivations display strong associations with religiosity, while other motivations display more social class–based links. Finally, I conclude with an extended discussion of a key contemporary barometer of sexual preparedness: emotional readiness. What does it mean, who refers to it, and who thinks they are emotionally ready?

## The Place of Attitudes and Motivations in Predicting Action

The theory of reasoned action proposes that decisions to engage in sexual activity are the function of sexual intentions, which are in turn the product of two things: personal attitudes about sex and perceived social norms about sex (Forehand et al. 2005; Gillmore et al. 2002). While not rocket science, the theory—when applied to the study of sex—provides a helpful clarification of a proper time order to the causal processes about religious effects on sex, which sometimes get lost in the variable and statistical models talk of social science. In other words, once we know something about what adolescents think about sex, their reasons for having or avoiding sex, and their intentions to act or refrain, we will better understand who acts sexually and why.

Many adolescents who want and intend to have sex nevertheless do not—or at least not as soon as they might prefer—and many who wish to long delay having sex nevertheless become sexually active. A recent longitudinal study of adolescents found that 37 percent of virgins who subsequently did have sex had planned *not to* when asked about their intentions a year earlier (Gillmore et al. 2002). Intentions to act are more proximate to actual decision making than are attitudes, motives, and perceived norms and thus tend to have a stronger effect on adolescents' sexual decisions (Gillmore et al. 2002). Unfortunately, I do not have measures of sexual intention in either the Add Health or NSYR data sets, so I am left to focus on its building blocks—sexual attitudes and motivations.

## Pre-Premarital Sex

For a long time in America, the term "premarital sex" popularly referred to acts of sexual intercourse between a *couple* that occurred prior to the issuance of a legal marriage certificate binding them. The focus remained squarely on a pair of people who would eventually marry, either in front of the people of God, the eyes of God, the state, or some combination thereof. Indeed, pregnancies would often hasten weddings and could serve as the occasion for public confession in many congregations. No doubt many sexually-active-but-unmarried couples were not caught in the "act" of pregnancy and so evaded this painfully embarrassing experience. (This practice of confessing premarital sex is now rare, having gone the way of Sabbath blue laws and bans on playing cards.)

Today, however, premarital sex tends to refer to any act of sexual intercourse that occurs prior to a *person* getting married. Whether the sexual acts occur with an eventual marriage partner, an old boy- or girlfriend, or a one-night stand is less important. John Gagnon and William Simon (1987) label this more accurately as "pre-premarital sex," since most contemporary adolescent sexual partnerships are not composed of eventual spouses. Premarital sex no longer means what it used to mean. And we should change how we speak about it, if in fact we don't mean it. What most people are actually referring to by the phrase is *nonmarital* sex—a sexual relationship that occurs outside of marriage and typically without marital intent. This would profitably distinguish it from both true premarital sex (sex between eventual spouses) and extramarital sex.

Regardless of terminology, there is no doubt that the expanding maturity gap is a primary contributor to the growing toleration of pre-premarital sex. By "maturity gap," I mean the increasing decoupling of marriage from physical sexual maturity in advanced industrial societies like the United States. Better nutrition during the twentieth century has contributed to a trend toward earlier menarche—girls' first experience of menstruation and the beginning of reproductive maturity. Boys' average age at spermarche—when sperm production begins—is about 14, while their average age at marriage is just over 26 (Brooks-Gunn and Paikoff 1997). Girls' average age at menarche is now under 13, and at marriage, just over 24. Together with cultural and economic emphases on acquiring more extensive (and expensive) education, and a trend toward career building and later marriage, these diverse forces combine to produce a significant lag between reproductive maturity and marriage in twenty-first-century America (Brooks-Gunn and Paikoff 1997). The maturity gap for both men and women now averages about 12 years and shows no signs of diminishing. Twelve years of sexual maturity is a long time to avoid sex, so most do not.

The trend affects everyone. Fewer and fewer religious individuals marry following high school, choosing instead to seek education and career stability before settling down. Thus, in contrast to previous generations, fewer of them are choosing to marry in order to legitimate their sexual activities. Over time, the actual prevalence of—and tolerant attitudes toward—premarital sex have increased. Yet it would be premature to say that the maturity gap has successfully altered opinions about premarital sex in *all* religious traditions. A comparison of General Social Survey (GSS) data on adults from 1972 through 1993 found evidence for a substantial decline in support for traditional beliefs about premarital sex among the general population, but *no* substantial decline among evangelical Protestants (Petersen and Donnenwerth 1997). Mainline Protestants and Catholics, though—regardless of attendance—exhibited increasingly tolerant attitudes toward premarital sex. During the 1970s, 51 percent of evangelical Protestants and 30 percent of mainline Protestants indicated that a sexual relationship before marriage was "always wrong" (Wilcox 2004). By the 1990s, these two percentages had dipped to 45 and 21 percent, respectively. When we qualify this by examining only religiously active evangelical and mainline Protestants, the numbers rise to 63 and 34 percent, respectively (for the 1990s). One study notes that the gap in disapproval of premarital sex (between evangelicals and mainliners) has actually grown from about 20 to nearly 30 percent between 1972 and 2002 (Wilcox 2004).

Clearly, there has been a redrawing of the acceptable sexual boundaries for unmarried men and women within mainline Protestantism and, to some extent, Roman Catholicism. Active participation in church life tends to mitigate this somewhat, but not much. After all, only one in three mainline Protestants who regularly attend church unilaterally oppose premarital sex.


## Delay Sex until Marriage?

The GSS, however, is a study of adults. What do adolescents, religious or otherwise, think about premarital sex? In the NSYR survey, we asked adolescents the question: "Do you think that people should wait to have sex until they are married, or not necessarily?" and they could respond with "Yes, they should wait," or "No, not necessarily wait." Their answers clearly vary by religious traits (see Table 4.1). More than seven out of ten evangelical Protestant adolescents respond with a "yes, wait" reply, topped only by Mormons, at 77 percent. Catholics, mainline and black Protestants, and adherents of other religious traditions are split nearly down the middle, while just under 30 percent of Jewish youth and unreligious youth support the idea of waiting until marriage.

Both forms of religiosity are powerful predictors, even more than religious tradition. Regardless of affiliation, 83 percent of youths who are in church more than once a week support waiting until marriage to have sex. Even those who attend once a week are considerably less likely to support this idea (by 16 percentage points). And only 35 percent of those who never attend religious services support waiting. The difference is even more striking when we compare the religious salience categories: only 23 percent of teens who say that religion has no importance in their daily life think waiting until marriage to have sex is the best idea, compared with 81 percent of teens for whom religion is extremely important. So both forms of religiosity (attendance and importance) show remarkably linear patterns in predicting support for waiting. Youth who align themselves (more or less) with the label "spiritual but not religious" are more ambivalent about waiting than youth who don't.

TABLE 4.1 Attitudes about Waiting until Marriage to Have Sex and Perceptions of Parental Emotions (in Percentages), by Religious Variables

|  | Supports waiting until marriage to have sex | Parents would be "extremely mad" if they had sex |
|---|---|---|
| *Religious Tradition* | | |
| Evangelical Protestant | 73.7 | 66.7 |
| Mainline Protestant | 51.9 | 56.8 |
| Black Protestant | 54.8 | 46.8 |
| Catholic | 51.2 | 55.4 |
| Jewish | 27.0 | 48.6 |
| Mormon (LDS) | 77.3 | 79.7 |
| Other religion | 50.7 | 53.4 |
| No religion | 29.3 | 41.2 |
| *Church Attendance* | | |
| More than once a week | 82.9 | 74.7 |
| Weekly | 66.2 | 66.5 |
| Up to 2–3 times a month | 48.5 | 50.3 |
| Never | 34.8 | 42.2 |
| *Importance of Religion* | | |
| Extremely important | 80.8 | 74.7 |
| Very important | 67.2 | 60.5 |
| Somewhat important | 44.7 | 50.7 |
| Not very important | 30.8 | 42.0 |
| Not important at all | 22.5 | 37.2 |
| *Spiritual but Not Religious* | | |
| Very true | 52.7 | 48.4 |
| Somewhat true | 48.4 | 51.0 |
| Not true at all | 64.5 | 63.8 |

*Source*: National Survey of Youth and Religion

Tonia is a 17-year-old daughter of a Jewish father and Christian mother. She regularly attends a Christian church and feels keenly alone in her commitment to waiting until marriage to have sex. Her friends, she notes, have a different criterion:

> I think I'm the only one in my circle of friends who believes in waiting. Um, my other friends kind of believe in the length of time you've been dating should decide when you should be ready. Like if you've been dating for a long

time, they believe that you're more ready. But I think that waiting is the better idea.

Evangelical Protestant teens were much more likely to support waiting until marriage in their interviews as well as on the survey:

- "Marriage and sex is [a] great gift that God gave and so, and I think it should only be used then, when you're married."
- "It's the best gift that you could give to that person that you're going to spend the rest of your life with. So I definitely think it's worth waiting for."

Many of them, even including those who had already had sex, continue to convey the idea of sex as a gift and its ideal relationship with marriage (Carpenter 2005b). Cameron, a 15-year-old evangelical girl from Florida, remarks:

> I felt like I could, you know, do anything I wanted, and that led on to sex. But also I feel that I should have waited. . . . I don't regret doing that with that person, but like, I wish that I would have waited. We both say the same thing. [*Why do you wish you would have waited?*] Just, just for good, I guess. You know, like our beliefs. Because Christians think that way, like you should wait until you get married before you have sex.

Some evangelical youths were more sensitive than others to nuances, real-life circumstances, and varying situations. Hannah, a 17-year-old from Alabama, recognizes the ideal yet notes, "Everybody makes mistakes. So it's not always gonna happen that way. But it should come as close to that [waiting until marriage] as possible. At least engagement, I think."

While around 75 percent of evangelical youth support sexual abstinence until marriage as an ideal, only about half of all mainline youth say the same. The interviews reinforced this distinction. Megan, a 15-year-old religiously active mainline Protestant from Mississippi, says that religious teachings about sex were not only *not* forced by her church, they weren't really spoken of at all: "[*Does your religion have any particular teaching when it comes to sex?*] Not that I've been told. They encourage, um, to save sex for marriage and stuff like that. But that's pretty much it; it's not forced."

Megan's flat response is remarkably like that of Jonathan, a 16-year-old mainline Protestant from Texas. He too struggled to come up with cogent religious guidelines about dating and sexuality. When I spoke with him two years later (at age 18), he had recently lost his virginity, an experience which he regretted. Although he wishes he would have waited, he cannot articulate why, even when I press him. Clint, an 18-year-old mainline Protestant from Michigan who is a virgin and attends his church sporadically, takes into account unique social situations in fashioning his sexual ethic: "There's going to be exceptions to the rule where two 17-year-olds are really like, in love, and you know they think they're ready. Like I'm, I'm not gonna say 'oh well, no, that can't happen.'" Later in the same interview, Clint expands upon his ambivalence about waiting until marriage to have sex:

> There's no reason, um, that, you know, you should save yourself for marriage in every single instance, no exceptions. . . . You know it's, it's a situational thing. But um, I didn't find myself in that situation, and I think I'm kind of grateful for that, you know. 'Cause that's, again, one less thing to worry about in trying to figure out, you know, what's important to me and things like that.

It's no news flash that mainline Protestantism has become more tolerant of premarital and nonmarital sex. Most mainline Protestants live fairly traditional sexual lives but accommodate alternatives in reality, especially if those alternatives are practiced in private (Ellingson et al. 2004).

If the gap between mainline and evangelical abstinence ethics is widening, the one between the religious and the nonreligious is already a chasm. Kevin, an 18-year-old religiously unaffiliated adolescent from Maryland, is frank about his disdain for abstinence (although incorrect in his association of abstinence with higher subsequent divorce rates):

> [*Do you think young people should wait to have sex until after they're married or not?*] No. [*How come?*] Uh, I think it's something you need to know about before you get married. [*And you know about it when you, by being involved sexually with somebody* . . . ] Yeah, it's, I guess it's an important part of a relationship. I mean you get married and then realize that it's not gonna work. You didn't have sex and then have to get divorced. Just seems like a waste, I think.

We also asked youths to estimate how upset their parent(s) would be if they found out they were having sex. Curiously, for those who guessed "extremely mad," the gap between evangelical Protestants and mainliners/Catholics is a good deal narrower than the gap in support of waiting until marriage. Regardless of their own views about abstinence, roughly about half of all youths (except evangelicals and Mormons) say their parents would be "extremely mad" if they were discovered to be sexually active. Again, both forms of religiosity reflect a linear pattern—the more religious the adolescents, the more upset they feel their parents would be with their sexual behavior. Nonreligious youth were much less concerned: only 37 percent of those who completely devalued religion and 42 percent of youth who never attend religious services thought their parents would be extremely mad if they had sex, compared to 75 percent among the most religious. These numbers substantiate the claims of James and Jillian (from chapter 3), the nonreligious youths who report that their parents would be OK with their sexual activity.

Catholic and Protestant religious doctrines on sex are not remarkably different. So why the widening discrepancies in their sexual attitudes? It might appear that mainline Protestants and Catholics are *interpreting* the doctrines differently than evangelical Protestants. In reality, the average mainline Protestant or Catholic is simply less concerned than the average evangelical about *adhering* to the doctrines. Their lack of concern grows over time as well. Figure 4.1 graphs the percentage of NSYR virgins who support abstinence (waiting until marriage to have sex), by their age. Notice the almost-flat line for evangelical Protestants and how the other three slopes decline with age. Though evangelicals, mainliners, and Catholics start adolescence within about a dozen percentage points of each other, they hit the peak of adolescence (age 16) quite far apart in their attitudes about delaying sex until marriage. While 80 percent of 13-year-old and 16-year-old evangelical virgins support abstinence, the share of mainline Protestant youth who agree with them declines from 73 to 43 percent in those three years.

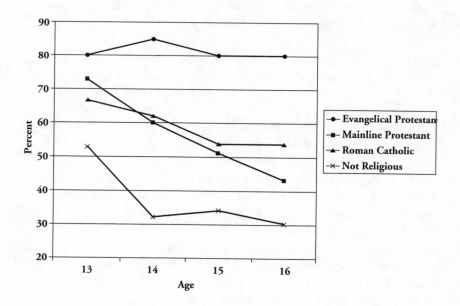

FIGURE 4.1. Adolescents Who Support Abstinence (in Percentages), Virgins Only
*Source*: National Survey of Youth and Religion

For mainline and Catholic youth, "the failure of a belief system to require conformity to orthodox doctrine clears the way for the adoption of views inconsistent with such doctrine.... [and] network participants who express liberal views about premarital sex are unlikely to receive frequent or strong negative sanctions for their views" (Petersen and Donnenwerth 1997: 1084). In other words, there is very little organizationally that prevents mainline and Catholic youth from changing their minds about sex. Many do not give up on idealizing abstinence, of course, but they are in the minority now—or very nearly so. Condoning sex before marriage remains off limits to the faithful evangelical, although as we will see in chapter 5, it is nonetheless practiced by plenty.

## TAKING THE PLEDGE

Nowadays, most evangelical Protestant couples can safely see a movie or even dance without offending their church's sense of behavioral orthodoxy. Premarital sexual intercourse, though, remains a signifier against a well-lived adolescence (Hunter 1987). And some religious youth remain firm in resisting. Toward reducing instances of nonmarital sex, the "abstinence pledge" movement has emerged. This loosely linked group of interdenominational organizations encourages youth to take a public pledge to remain "pure" (sexually abstinent) until marriage, at which time the abstainer does not become impure, but rather sex becomes legitimate. Popular evangelical authors such as Josh McDowell and parachurch organizations such as True Love Waits, the Pure Love Alliance, and the Silver Ring Thing actively reinforce this notion by a variety of means—some religious and some pragmatic—including "promise rings," signed agreements, support groups, and topical Bible studies.[1] Ring ceremonies may involve hundreds of participants and include laser light shows and public pledges made in front of family and friends (Rosenbloom 2005). Event leaders affirm the sacred mystery and power of sexuality (White 2004). Then, employing a variety of methods, they warn adolescents about pregnancy and STDs, and typically claim that condoms will *not* protect them from pregnancy and sexually transmitted diseases. Some leaders attempt to demystify or profane sexual intercourse by noting that "even my dog has sex." Outright scare tactics are not unheard of and sometimes include slide shows of the bodily damage done by (presumably untreated) sexually transmitted diseases (Ali and Scelfo 2002). Make no mistake, though—the abstinence pledge movement is no small undertaking: nearly 13 percent of Add Health Wave I respondents said they had taken such a pledge. Nationwide, the number of pledgers was estimated at one point at more than 2.5 million (Bearman and Brückner 2001).

While its popularity may wax and wane, the idea and the organizations promoting it are here to stay (Rosenbloom 2005).

A helpful way of understanding the abstinence pledge concept is as a "change in script." Organizations like True Love Waits accept the presumption that the norm among adolescents is to be sexually active. They in turn press adolescents to adopt this "new," alternative sexual script—that sex is best within the security of marriage—in the hopes of a verifiable drop in sexual activity among adolescents and an improvement in emotional and physical health among them. The underlying assumption of the abstinence pledge is consonant with social control theory—that adolescents naturally gravitate toward sexual activity like a magnet to a refrigerator door. I find this assumption unwise and unsupported by evidence. Some youth who take the pledge are sexually disinterested to begin with and at low risk for becoming sexually involved in the near future. Indeed, the pledge is most popular among younger adolescents, many of whom are just reaching puberty. The appeal of the pledge diminishes as the sex drive increases with age. Just under 20 percent of 12-year-olds had pledged abstinence at Wave I of the Add Health, while about 9 percent of 18-year-olds had. This is the case with evangelicals as well: 33 percent of evangelical 12-year-olds had taken the abstinence pledge, but only 16 percent of 18-year-olds had. One wonders whether such efforts are in fact equipping these younger adolescents for their upcoming battles with sexual temptation or simply getting them to agree to resist a temptation they don't yet feel.

Despite their popularity, particular virginity-pledge organizations were seldom identified by name in our interviews, even by those who had taken such a pledge. One young man who does identify with a particular movement is Dalton, an 18-year-old evangelical from Texas who has just started college at a Christian university:

> Uh, I don't think it [sex] is appropriate when [a couple] is not married. Um, if you mean physically, like kissing and stuff, of course I've kissed, I mean, a couple of girls. And I've kissed my girlfriend and stuff like that. Um, we never got really physical and stuff, just because that's something that we had pledged not to do. [*Where'd you, how did you come to decide these things?*] Um, she was the one that, and I'm glad she brought it up 'cause I didn't want to bring it up . . . but she was the one that brought it up and said, "How about we pledge to do this?" And I was like, "Wow, that's great with me." So that's how we came to that decision.

When asked about how he could tell if potential romantic interests were virgins (and thus ideal for him), Dalton responds:

> They had their True Love Waits rings. Of course I didn't know for sure, but I mean I could pretty much tell just by the way that they acted and stuff. [*True love what?*] Like some kids will get True Love Waits rings and um, those rings are like, it was a big Southern Baptist push like way, about four years ago, and they still do it now. Like you get a ring when you turn like 15 or something like that and you pledge to save yourself for your marriage and stuff. [*Did you do that?*] Did I do that? Yeah. I did it.

Unfortunately for Dalton, he once accidentally (temporarily) misplaced his ring, making for an interesting interaction with his very conservative parents. When I spoke with him two years later, however, the ring was still on his finger.

Of course not all virgins have maintained their virginity *because* of the pledge, and such pledges were infrequently mentioned in our interviews. Indeed, the average teenager who steers clear of sexual intercourse during the high school years does so without reference to the abstinence pledge movement. Some religious traditions have their own similar concepts, such as the Mormons' emphasis on age "goals" that correspond with common age-at-marriage patterns. Many young people do not take a formal, public pledge but nevertheless privately pledge or promise to themselves that they will wait until they are married before having sex. One study of California adolescents estimated that just under half of its sample of 870 youth made such a private pledge (Bersamin et al. 2005). Less than a quarter of such private pledgers had also made a more formal, public pledge.

Table 4.2 displays the percentage of Add Health respondents who have taken a pledge to remain abstinent from sex until marriage, split by religious categories. These percentages are also divided into three types: pledged at Wave I, pledged at Wave II, and pledged at both waves. The phenomenon is understandably most popular among evangelical Protestants and Mormons, although only a maximum of one in four adolescents reports making such a promise at any one wave, and no more than one in seven are consistent about it. Very few Jewish and nonreligious youths have taken such a pledge, and only 8–12 percent of youths in other Christian traditions have ever done so. Pledging corresponds not only with affiliation but also with religiosity. Although the likelihood of pledging abstinence appears to rise in linear fashion with church attendance and religious salience, the real action remains at the top: the most religious teens are more than twice as likely to have promised abstinence when compared with teens in the next most religious category. And they are four to six times more likely than the least religious adolescents to have pledged. The gap among consistent pledgers is even wider. More rigorous statistical analyses (in Table A4.1) of pledging abstinence suggest that the evangelical Protestant and Mormon effects are not ephemeral. Even

TABLE 4.2 Pledged Abstinence from Sex until Marriage at Waves I and II
and Both (in Percentages), by Religious Variables

|  | Wave I | Wave II | Both waves |
|---|---|---|---|
| *Religious Tradition* | | | |
| Evangelical Protestant | 22.3 | 22.9 | 14.0 |
| Mainline Protestant | 12.4 | 11.9 | 5.9 |
| Black Protestant | 12.4 | 10.5 | 4.2 |
| Catholic | 10.7 | 8.3 | 3.3 |
| Mormon (LDS) | 27.1 | 25.5 | 12.3 |
| Jewish | 2.4 | 1.8 | <1.0 |
| Other religion | 13.9 | 14.1 | 6.6 |
| No religion | 6.1 | 3.4 | 1.2 |
| *Church Attendance* | | | |
| Weekly | 21.6 | 22.5 | 12.6 |
| Once a month but less than weekly | 9.9 | 8.7 | 3.9 |
| Less than once a month | 8.1 | 4.7 | 2.1 |
| Never | 6.3 | 3.7 | 1.3 |
| *Importance of Religion* | | | |
| Very important | 21.5 | 21.4 | 11.8 |
| Fairly important | 8.9 | 7.7 | 3.4 |
| Fairly unimportant | 4.0 | 4.7 | 1.8 |
| Not important at all | 5.9 | 3.7 | <1.0 |
| "Born again" | 24.9 | 24.3 | 14.6 |
| Not "born again" | 9.0 | 7.6 | 3.0 |

*Source*: National Longitudinal Study of Adolescent Health

after numerous controls, adolescents from these two traditions are still more likely to have pledged abstinence than mainline Protestants, black Protestants, Catholics, or Jews. Youth who attend religious services more frequently and who think that religion is important are also each more likely to have pledged at Wave I. These particular findings are even stronger when we consider consistent pledging across waves (not shown). Other notable associations with pledging include greater family satisfaction, less individual autonomy, and a strategic orientation. The pledge is also more popular with girls than boys.

The pledge is not always so memorable, however. Pledge "retraction" is common in the Add Health data: over 50 percent of respondents who said at Wave I that they had taken such a pledge denied it at Wave II (Rosenbaum 2006). Retractors are more likely to be African American, either not a "born again" Christian or no longer one, or newly sexually active. The popularity of the pledge among evangelical youth should not surprise, since they are the target market of most of the movement organizations, and they are also less likely to retract.

Despite its popularity, the pledge movement reaches far fewer teenagers than abstinence-based sex education in schools, which is currently favored by the George W. Bush administration. Unlike pledge organizations, however, abstinence education programs that receive federal funds under Title V of the Social Security Act are *not* legally allowed to discuss religious perspectives. Taking the morality out of sexual abstinence advocacy seems crippling, however, especially since popular American cultural and media institutions are hardly pro-abstinence. One wonders how effective abstinence-based education can possibly be when stripped of all theological and moral motivation and left to compete in the adolescent marketplace of ideas. Somehow, I suspect, MTV, BET, and VH-1 garner a wider and more attentive audience.

## IN LOVE WITH AN IDEAL?

To many abstaining adolescents, marriage is the "golden light at the end of the perilous tunnel of dating" (Ali and Scelfo 2002: 61). Pledgers are encouraged to speak of giving their future spouse the ultimate wedding present—their virginity (Carpenter 2005b; White 2004). The right person, after all, is "worth waiting for." Talk of "ultimate loves" and "soulmates" abounds. This begs the question: are abstinence pledgers and devoutly religious adolescents blowing marital sexuality out of proportion, investing the wedding night with far more significance and anticipation than it can bear? While the evidence for it would be difficult to accurately amass, some of the adolescents with whom we spoke seem to do this. Jana, a 17-year-old evangelical Protestant from North Carolina, articulates such hopes:

> My belief is that you're supposed to wait until you get married, because that just makes it more special, you know. I mean your honeymoon will be an experience you'll always remember that way, and it's just you know, the ultimate commitment to somebody.

Kathleen, a 17-year-old mainline Protestant from California, holds high expectations for both marriage and her eventual husband, and she puts them bluntly:

> Sometimes I've thought maybe if I had sex with someone and I felt loved, then things would change. But then I thought no, you know what, that's kind

of, no, I'd ruin my life, 'cause I'm waiting for my husband. If he's not a virgin, I'm going to be really pissed. Going to be really mad, you know. But it's OK, if I love him, I'm still going to marry him anyway.

While such talk may please some parents and leaders of the abstinence pledge movement, other Christians are not so sure. Lauren Winner (2005: 95), herself an advocate of chastity, complains about such idealism: "we spend years guarding our virginity, but find, upon getting married, that we cannot just flip a switch." When, in marriage, sex is finally OK, even encouraged, many young women "are stuck with years of work (and sometimes therapy) to unlearn" the habits of sexual denial (2005: 95). Young people trained to put up barriers against sex often cannot deconstruct them rapidly upon marrying (Rose 2005). What was very wrong a day before is not easily understood to be very right a day later. Just how common this scenario is remains unknown, though I suspect it is more typical than many think.[2]

Abstinence pledgers are not the only sexual and romantic idealists. Many adolescents—especially girls—are immersed in a culture of romance, regardless of their religiosity or their attitudes toward sex. Karin Martin (2002: 144) refers to stories of "ideal love," which "are not stories of passion and sexuality but are stories of romance and what sociologist Arlie Hochschild calls magnified moments." She argues that first dates, first meetings, first sexual experiences, and even break-ups serve for many adolescent girls as magnified moments of such idealistic love. Such idealism need not end with a girl's first sexual experience, either. Amanda, a 15-year-old mainline Protestant from Tennessee, remarks about the ex-boyfriend to whom she lost her virginity: "It was my first love and i'll love him forever for it." It is perhaps not accidental that all of the more articulate interviewees about the pledge and sexual idealism are girls. Boys, Martin (2002) writes, rarely use the word *love* in discussing their sentiments within romantic relationships. They also tend to anticipate sexual pleasure more than girls and are in turn less likely to value abstinence (Martin 2002).

Other girls criticize abstaining adolescents for just such idealism. Diane, a 17-year-old Jewish girl from Illinois, actually thinks that waiting until marriage is a good idea, but she doesn't think it's practical to expect: "It is a good idea, but it's very idealistic. . . . I think that some of the people that say they're going to wait and have signed pledges are kidding themselves and are trying to make their parents feel better." Leah, a 15-year-old Jewish girl from Maryland, counts a variety of religious types among her wide circle of friends, including two devout Christians. When asked whether she thinks religious faith shapes her friends' relationships with the opposite sex, Leah speaks disparagingly of the abstinence ideal:

Definitely. Like those [Christian] girls I was talking about. They will only date if they think they can marry the person. They . . . believe in abstinence before marriage. . . . I know some of my Catholic friends . . . they don't believe in birth control. Um, some won't date unless they think—like the girl I was talking about who is just so naïve and like, she's like, "everything's so perfect," and, like, can't do anything bad—wants to date somebody who's perfect. She won't kiss. She doesn't want to kiss anyone before she gets married because it has to be perfect, like [laughs] . . . like marriage is . . . the only perfect, holy thing you can share . . . with each other. And it's mostly a religious thing.

Carol, a 17-year-old nonreligious girl from Florida, wonders aloud about why some people make such a big deal out of sex:

I don't see why sex is such a sacred thing to so many people. Um, I guess to some people sex is a way of expressing love. But to me it's not. It's just not. . . . It's just pleasure, it's physical pleasure and that's what it is. Yes, you can express that you love someone through having sex with them, but just because you're having sex doesn't necessarily mean that you love the person.

She guesstimates that she's had 10 or 11 sexual partners.

Criticism of the pledge even comes from within evangelicals' own ranks. Kara, a 17-year-old evangelical Protestant from Texas, knows the lingo and is aware of a key organization promoting the pledge. She's not yet had sexual intercourse but has given oral sex to a previous boyfriend, which she regrets. The experience led her to reevaluate her expectations of romantic relationships, and she's now dating someone who, though previously "promiscuous" (in her own words), is no longer sexually active. Whether her remarks about pledging would have been different had she been dating someone with a less checkered sexual past, we cannot know. But her choice of words is revealing: she describes her religious community in oppositional terms as "they" instead of as "we." When asked about her religion's teachings on sex, she responds:

Um, they practiced something called True Love Waits. I wasn't really involved with it at the time. But that's where you take a vow to God that you will wait 'til marriage and whatnot. They were really based on waiting 'til marriage. [*OK. And, um, how did you feel about it?*] I agreed with it, if that was like the right thing for you, but I didn't think that you'd have to be that strict with it. I mean, yes, it has to be with as few people as possible, but you don't have to wait until you're tied into somebody for the rest of your life. I mean, it's still something that you know, every person's different about it and sometimes it's better to experience different ways and experiences.

Nevertheless, idealism combined with a supportive and watchful moral community can give unusual sticking power to an abstinence commitment. Katie, a 17-year-old evangelical (and self-reported virgin) from Indiana, thinks premarital sex is "wrong, wrong. Save it for marriage. You have your whole life." An attractive young woman, Katie does not lack potential suitors, at least one of whom attempted to take advantage of her. No way:

> [I]n February, I was dating this guy, Matt, um, and it was like Valentine's Day, and he like wanted to take me out. And at first I knew he was like a forceful guy 'cause I'd gone on a date with him before. But he was, like, at church and stuff. He played it out so well in front of my parents and he told them all this stuff. He just seemed like such a great guy. And then, um, took me out and then, like, you know, pretty much just . . . yeah . . . but nothing went too far 'cause I pulled out my cell phone and had the number ready. I was like, "Take me home now," but it was terrible. So, I guess that's why I've just had the whole thing about saving myself and I've been really sketchy, you know, with guys. I want to date them first, 'cause I want to be able to trust them. [*Yeah, so in that last situation, you were able to just call your parents and they came and got you?*] Oh no, he took me home. I had 911 in there. [*Oh wow.*] I was like, "don't even play with me" 'cause if I told my parents, they would, they would kill him. . . . 'Cause he knew being in our church . . . people would find out. And you know, yeah, he came to his senses.

## Is the Abstinence Pledge Movement Effective?

Promising to avoid sexual intercourse until marriage is of no interest to some adolescents, an uphill struggle for some, and seemingly easy for others. Some pledge because it seems like a good strategy to help avoid pregnancy, STDs, guilt, or a bad reputation. Others feel destined to fail their own ideals without it. Still others pledge because it is a popular thing to do in their church or school, or because their parents expect them to. But do such pledges really work? Is promising virginity to one's family and peers enough to withstand the sexual assault on the senses so commonly associated with the adolescent years?

### The Limits of Pledge Effectiveness

The answer to this question depends on how one defines a "successful" movement. If success is defined here as a *drastic* difference in the percentage of pledgers and nonpledgers who remain virgins until marriage, then the answer is no. Hannah Brückner and Peter Bearman's (2005) recent evaluation of Add Health's Wave III data, which by now contain a significant number of married young adults, finds that 99 percent of nonvirgins who had *not* pledged at any wave had lost their virginity before their weddings. Among nonvirgins who *had* pledged to abstain from sex until marriage, 88 percent had broken their pledges.[3] Eighty-eight percent is of course lower than 99 percent, but I suspect that even abstinence-movement proponents are not encouraged by these results. (In other words, sex before marriage is *very* common in American society presently.)[4] Pledge breakers tend not to break their pledge with their future spouse, either. Among those who had ever pledged, were married by Wave III of the survey, and had had premarital sex, 7 in 10 reported having had more than one sex partner.[5] On the other hand, even pledge breakers have *far fewer* sexual partners on average than nonpledgers.

However, we cannot conclude from these numbers (at least not yet) that 88 percent of all pledgers break their pledge. The 88 percent figure does not include respondents who have not had sex yet. About 44 percent of unmarried respondents who claim (at some wave) to have pledged abstinence were still virgins at Wave III. Additionally, the sexual behavior of inconsistent pledgers (or retractors) is distinct from both nonpledgers and consistent pledgers (Brückner and Bearman 2005). Indeed, the outlook improves for abstinence proponents when we examine only those pledgers who have already married, not just those who have had sex. In the sample of *married* young adults, 88 percent of nonpledgers and 68 percent of inconsistent pledgers engaged in vaginal intercourse before marriage, but only 56 percent of consistent pledgers did so. When we consider only *unmarried* respondents, 88 percent of nonpledgers, 77 percent of inconsistent pledgers, and 54 percent of consistent pledgers are sexually experienced. Thus, a significant minority of young adult pledgers have not yet had sex. Since they're not married, however, there is no way to document their complete success in abstinence until marriage, only their present state. These (albeit confusing) numbers may not be enough to thrill pledge advocates, but they do suggest that the pledge indeed reduces the occurrence of sexual relationships prior to marriage.

Ironically, the popularity of abstinence pledging within a school actually diminishes the pledge's effectiveness (Bearman and Brückner 2001). Abstinence pledges are most effective in delaying first sex when a critical mass—neither too few nor too many—of schoolmates has also made such a promise (Bearman and Brückner 2001). They contend that the pledge works by embedding adolescents into a minority, "self-conscious" community that gains strength from identifying itself as "embattled." In schools where the pledge becomes too common, the embattled sentiment is lost, and the pledge is ineffective in stemming first sex. This unique scenario no doubt makes for confusing policy (Winner 2005).

Avoiding vaginal intercourse does not mean, of course, that "successful" pledgers refrain from *all* sexual behavior. One in three adolescents who report being virgins have had genital contact with a partner in the past year (Bearman, Moody, and Stovel 2004). Thirteen percent of consistent pledgers reported oral sex but not intercourse, compared with only 2 percent of nonpledgers and 5 percent of inconsistent pledgers. One particular finding noted by Brückner and Bearman (2005) was a media hit, despite the fact that the authors—for good reason—originally made no particular note of it. In March 2005, CNN, radio talk shows, and a variety of other news media outlets picked up on their ironic finding that abstinence pledgers appear *more* likely to have anal sex than do nonpledgers. However, the statistically significant difference is hardly *substantively* significant. And it only applies to males; too few adolescent girls in the Add Health study reported ever having had anal sex to even generate meaningful estimates about them. Using its survey questions about anal sex (which some adolescents may have difficulty defining), they find that 1.2 percent of virginity pledgers report engaging in anal sex but not vaginal intercourse, compared with 0.7 percent of nonpledgers. Although the media damage is done, I would hesitate to draw any substantive conclusions about pledging and the practice of anal sex as a substitution for intercourse.[6] Anal sex is far from normative as a substitute for intercourse. It is *very* unusual. Finally, young adult pledgers' STD rates are not distinguishable from nonpledgers' rates, suggesting that the former may be more likely to engage in unprotected sex than the latter.

## Successes of the Pledge Movement

On the other hand, if pledging effectiveness were defined more widely as a significant impact on a *variety* of sexual practices and outcomes—such as an increased average age at first sex—then the answer is yes, the movement has been a resounding success. The study authors (Bearman and Brückner 2004; Brückner and Bearman 2005) note this and other conclusions in their summary of the state of knowledge about pledging:

1. Pledgers lose their virginity later than nonpledgers.
2. Pledgers have fewer sexual partners than nonpledgers.
3. Pledgers' partners are less likely to cheat than nonpledgers' partners.
4. Pledgers are more likely to abstain from sex until marriage.

So, while a majority of abstinence pledgers do not wait until marriage to have sex, far more pledgers than nonpledgers do. And despite the fact that many social scientists tend to frown on "early" marriage, pledgers have a penchant for getting married earlier than nonpledgers. This, combined with an average later date of first sex, tends to pay considerable dividends in terms of diminished initial and lifetime risk of acquiring a sexually transmitted disease. Sexual networks are exponential, since a pair of people engaging in sexual relations are essentially "exposing" themselves to every person the partners have ever had sex with. Thus if before marrying an abstinence pledger has had fewer sexual partners than a nonpledger, and his/her spouse also has had fewer partners, then their STD transmission risk is diminished, despite the appearance of no statistical difference in STD status during young adulthood.

Whether the glass is half-empty or half-full depends, of course, on what various interest groups define as "success." Public health officials would be taken aback by pledgers' common failure to consistently use contraception when they do have sex, while the pledge movement no doubt wishes their overall pledging success rates were higher. But both can find reasons to cheer as well as challenges still to be addressed.

### Religion and the Pledge

For all their helpful research, Bearman and Brückner are infrequently concerned about understanding religious influences on pledging behavior and sexual decision making. Still, they (2001) note that religiosity is associated with taking the abstinence pledge and with delayed first sex for white, Hispanic, and Asian adolescents. Table 4.3 displays the percentage of Add Health respondents who were virgins at Wave I but nonvirgins at Wave II, split by both religiosity and Wave I pledging status. Both church attendance and importance of religion predict first sex *regardless of pledging status*. However, each of these is *more* effective in the presence of the pledge than apart from it. The magnitude is small but stable: 13 percent of pledgers who attend church weekly had sex between study waves, compared to 18 percent of nonpledgers who are regular attenders. The difference is comparable for the religious salience measure.

While I can only evaluate the effect of the public abstinence pledge that is associated with the broader movement, there is evidence emerging that suggests that a *private* pledge or promise made to oneself is working at least as well, and perhaps better, than the public pledge. In the study of California adolescents I noted earlier, private pledging reduced the likelihood that teenagers will engage in intercourse and oral sex (Bersamin et al. 2005). A formal public

TABLE 4.3 Adolescents Who Reported First Sex at Wave II (in Percentages), Split by Wave I Pledging Status, Wave I Virgins Only

|  | Experienced first sex | |
|---|---|---|
|  | Pledged at Wave I | Did not pledge at Wave I |
| *Church Attendance* | | |
| Weekly or more | 12.6 | 17.7 |
| Less than weekly | 16.5 | 21.7 |
| Less than once a month | 17.3 | 24.1 |
| Never | 21.2 | 26.1 |
| *Importance of Religion* | | |
| Very important | 12.7 | 18.5 |
| Fairly important | 17.8 | 21.7 |
| Fairly unimportant | 21.9 | 23.3 |
| Not important at all | 22.6 | 28.2 |

*Source*: National Longitudinal Study of Adolescent Health

pledge made little difference by comparison. The authors speculate that while formal pledges may introduce external social control from peers or adults, they may fail if they are simply a response to social pressure to make such a commitment. A private pledge, on the other hand, is thought to capture more intrinsic motivation, resolve that comes from within rather than from outside.

## Secondary Abstinence

The pledge movement is quick to remind both its fans and its critics that it is about *abstinence* and not about virginity per se, since a significant number of youths may have already lost their virginity before deciding that abstaining from sex until marriage is a good idea. Such youths are known as "secondary" abstainers, for whom the pledge is meant to help absolve them of guilt and provide them with a sense of sexual "restoration" in a spiritual and perhaps psychological sense. Just as I noted earlier the phenomenon of pledge retraction, there is also the phenomenon of sex retraction. Youth who said at Wave I that they were not virgins, then reported at Wave II that they are—among other things—are more likely to be recently identified "born again" Christians and those who had newly pledged abstinence (Rosenbaum 2006). Such adolescents may think of themselves as "secondary" virgins. How and why? Janet Rosenbaum (2006) offers a few plausible reasons: first, people have a tendency to want to reconcile their memories with their present beliefs. In other words, many people—adults and adolescents alike—have a tendency to reframe their past in such a way that their present makes more sense. Whether such respondents are intentionally trying to deceive the survey administrator, or whether they are in fact deceiving themselves and reporting what they honestly think is true is not clear. Second, some respondents may view their previous sexual activity as somehow experimental and for that reason think that it doesn't count. In fact, she notes, those who recant their reports of sexual behavior had fewer partners at Wave I. The phenomenon may thus be most popular with youth who have only experienced sexual intercourse once.

Another trend toward secondary abstinence may be in the works, too, one that has less to do with religious motivation and more to do with romanticized ideals. In a 2002 *New York Times* article, Elizabeth Hayt noted the popularity of short periods of sexual abstinence prior to marriage by otherwise sexually active white, southern young women (whose religiosity is unclear). Although she states that this is "increasingly the norm for many brides-to-be across the South," there is presently no social science data to either confirm or reject her interesting claim. Hayt suggests that the practice has gained momentum since the 1990s, fueled by the abstinence movements in sex education and evangelical churches (Aug. 4, 2002, sec. 9). Even the head of the Southern Baptist Theological Seminary recognizes it as largely "a southern thing." It's also a female thing, aimed (apparently) in part at reducing the higher-than-average level of guilt that southern women experience about sex. No doubt it is an attempt to recover sexual idealism and make the wedding night and honeymoon feel fresh and exciting. Hayt quotes one 38-year-old who abstained for a month before her wedding: "the holding out makes you feel like you've been a good girl."

## GETTING MOTIVATED FOR SEX

To be sure, individuals' sexual choices are channeled by social networks and shaped by organizations and cultures, but in the end it is attitudes that shape motivations, and motivations that shape intentions and actions (Ellingson 2004; Gillmore et al. 2002). The Add Health study asked adolescents a series of questions about possible motivations to engage in or to avoid sex (see Table 4.4). Since adolescents who have already had sexual intercourse would very likely display different attitudes or motivations about sex, I restrict my analyses here to youth who reported being virgins at Wave I. What is immediately striking is the consistent difference between black Protestant adolescents and

TABLE 4.4 Motivations to Have or Avoid Sex (in Percentages), by Religious Variables, Wave I Virgins Only

| | Friends would respect you more | Partner would lose respect for you | After sex, you would feel guilty | If you had sex, it would upset your mother | Sex would give you much pleasure | Having sex would make you attractive | Pregnancy would embarrass you |
|---|---|---|---|---|---|---|---|
| *Religious Tradition* | | | | | | | |
| Evangelical Protestant | 8.3 | 33.4 | 65.8 | 88.8 | 33.1 | 8.9 | 77.2 |
| Mainline Protestant | 9.6 | 20.3 | 51.6 | 83.3 | 36.1 | 6.6 | 79.9 |
| Black Protestant | 14.7 | 22.5 | 50.5 | 71.9 | 33.1 | 11.8 | 62.4 |
| Catholic | 11.2 | 21.0 | 46.9 | 81.0 | 40.6 | 8.5 | 74.1 |
| Mormon (LDS) | 2.2 | 31.6 | 77.1 | 96.4 | 42.8 | 6.1 | 82.0 |
| Jewish | 5.5 | 9.0 | 44.6 | 79.0 | 56.4 | 6.3 | 93.7 |
| Other religion | 8.5 | 29.9 | 57.3 | 84.5 | 39.3 | 6.3 | 80.2 |
| No religion | 10.5 | 15.2 | 32.8 | 67.9 | 45.5 | 8.5 | 66.0 |
| *Church Attendance* | | | | | | | |
| Weekly | 8.9 | 31.6 | 65.9 | 89.9 | 35.9 | 6.5 | 80.7 |
| Once a month but less than weekly | 11.8 | 20.7 | 48.1 | 80.2 | 37.9 | 10.5 | 74.9 |
| Less than once a month | 10.1 | 16.0 | 40.5 | 75.8 | 43.3 | 7.7 | 72.7 |
| Never | 10.2 | 15.8 | 35.4 | 70.3 | 39.6 | 9.5 | 67.7 |

*Importance of Religion*

| | | | | | | | |
|---|---|---|---|---|---|---|---|
| Very important | 9.4 | 32.5 | 64.7 | 87.3 | 35.9 | 8.6 | 78.5 |
| Fairly important | 10.8 | 17.6 | 46.2 | 80.6 | 37.1 | 7.8 | 74.3 |
| Fairly unimportant | 8.8 | 15.5 | 34.0 | 79.6 | 45.1 | 6.5 | 77.6 |
| Not important at all | 9.9 | 14.3 | 34.3 | 67.1 | 46.5 | 7.8 | 68.0 |
| "Born again" | 9.9 | 34.6 | 67.8 | 88.5 | 32.5 | 7.8 | 79.2 |
| Not "born again" | 9.9 | 19.3 | 45.4 | 78.8 | 40.5 | 8.3 | 73.6 |

*Source:* National Longitudinal Study of Adolescent Health

*Note:* Calculated as the percentage that "agrees" or "strongly agrees" with the statements.

most other religious groups in at least four types of sexual motivation. Black Protestant adolescent virgins are the most likely to say that their friends would respect them more if they had sex, least likely to say that their having sex would upset their mother (were she to find out), most likely to say that having sex would make them more attractive, and least likely to say that a premarital pregnancy would embarrass them.

Not all sexual motivations differ between races. Both evangelical and black Protestant youth are less likely to say that having sex would give them much pleasure. Evangelicals are most likely to say that having sex would lead to losing the respect of their partner and very likely to anticipate considerable sexual guilt *and* their mother's wrath (second only in each category to Mormons). Jewish adolescents stand out as well. They are least likely to say that having sex would lead the partner to lose respect for them, more likely than nonreligious youth to anticipate sexual guilt, most likely to say that sex would be pleasurable, and most likely to say that pregnancy would be an embarrassment. Religious tradition, perhaps together with race, clearly has something to do with sexual motivations.

Yet, as with other outcomes, the results suggest that religiosity matters more for sexual motivations than does religious tradition. Notice the linear relationship between anticipated sexual pleasure and declining religious salience. Simply put, the more devout an adolescent virgin, the less likely he/she is to anticipate sex as pleasurable. This seems to me a remarkable cultural variation in the emotional and psychological expectations about the physical experience of sex. But if one motivation could be characterized as *most* related to religiosity, it is anticipated guilt. There is a *30 percentage point gap* in anticipated guilt between youths exhibiting the highest and lowest levels of either form of religiosity. However, some may see the glass as half-empty: fully one-third of devoutly religious American adolescents (who are presently virgins) don't think that having sex would make them feel guilty.[7]

While there are linear associations between religiosity and a number of the motivations, no linear logic is apparent between it and friends' respect and sex making one more attractive. Note also the bipolar results about the lost respect of a sexual partner: nearly one in three of the most devout youth anticipate that their sexual partner would definitely lose respect for them were they to have sex. Youth of all other levels of religiosity cluster around 15–20 percent on that question.

Most of the associations between religiosity and sexual motivations hold up even after accounting for demographic controls, family satisfaction, personal autonomy, strategic orientation, previous sexual experience, and dating habits (see Table A4.2). Church attendance and/or religious salience remain *independently* associated with anticipated guilt, lost respect of a sexual partner, upsetting one's mother, and pregnancy embarrassment. Identifying oneself as a "born again" Christian is also—net of religiosity and other controls—associated with greater guilt, loss of respect from one's sexual partner and friends, and a more emotionally upset mother. It is safe to say, then, that most of the sexual motivations evaluated here have stable statistical associations with religiosity.

While the NSYR interviews did not directly inquire about sexual motivations, the topic of guilt emerged with some regularity, largely reinforcing the regression results. For Justin, the 17-year-old Roman Catholic from Rhode Island featured in chapter 1, guilt is not a factor that motivates him to avoid sex:

> I mean, ah, I don't know [what motivates teenagers to have sex]. Guys kind of like, you know, a feeling of . . . achievement. And then the girls, I don't know what motivates girls to have sex. [*So for guys it's achievement?*] Yeah, kind of. I mean . . . it's all positives for guys if you're gonna have sex. There's nothing negative.

Guilt is strongly associated with gender. In the regression models (Table A4.2), adolescent girls' odds of feeling sex-related guilt are 92 percent higher than boys. Melissa, a 15-year-old Roman Catholic from Florida, experienced palpable guilt after performing oral sex. Yet in order to minimize the guilt, she confided about the experience only to "supportive" friends:

> [*OK, how do you feel about it?*] Um, to myself, like guilty. Because, but like, like some of my friends I told, like, that's nothing to them, so. Um, I feel bad, but if I told some friends I know I'd feel worse. But like, I told certain friends that won't, that just think it's OK, I guess to make myself feel better because they've done a lot more, so.

## THE FINAL BARRIER: EMOTIONAL READINESS

As one scholar of adolescent sexuality wisely points out, "Teens do not add up their demographic variables to see if they should have sex. They have sex in the context of their lives and relationships" (Martin 2002: 149). So during our interviews, the research team spent considerable time talking about the context and circumstances in which sex could be considered acceptable or unacceptable. A majority of adolescents revealed their criteria to us, while a minority held that it was never appropriate for teenagers to be having sex. Neither gender nor race nor socioeconomic status distinguishes these two groups, but religion does. Less religious youth are far more likely to offer scenarios in which sex between consenting adolescents is fine. Many adolescents almost entirely lack an articulated, discernible sexual ethic, save for widespread disapproval of casual (or transactional) sex and one-night stands, especially among girls (Risman and Schwartz 2002). Nonreligious youth, together with a significant majority of black Protestant, mainline Protestant, and Roman Catholic youth (and a minority of evangelicals), largely draw upon a language devoid of "traditional" sexual morality as they evaluate the appropriateness of sexual behavior. In their own words:

- "If they want to do it, then it's all right. Just be protected. Don't make stupid choices like not using a condom" (black Protestant, regular attender, age 15).
- "You just should feel that you're mature enough, I guess. . . . I don't know" (Jewish, nonattender, age 17).
- "I guess if they're mentally prepared and aware and they understand what can happen, that's really the main thing. I mean if you want to do it, go for it. Just make sure you're safe about it and you understand" (nonreligious, age 17).
- "Whenever they feel like they're ready" (evangelical Protestant, regular attender, age 16).
- "I guess you should probably know the person's name, you should probably know the person, maybe, spend some time with them before you ever get to that point" (black Protestant, somewhat religious, age 17).
- "I think it's important that they know each other at least" (nonreligious, age 18).

Obviously, we should expect adolescents who have already experienced sexual intercourse to articulate a more tolerant sexual ethic. However, such opinions are not only held by adolescents who have already had sex. They are also the opinions of many who are still virgins:

- "If you want to and you really feel like that for a person, you want to take it to that next level. Then, like, go ahead and do it" (Roman Catholic, regular attender, age 15).
- "If they really like each other, they should" (Roman Catholic, nonattender, age 14).
- "I think it's OK just as long as you're safe about it" (Roman Catholic, regular attender, age 16).

- "I think that it's really who you are and what you're ready for. I think if you're not ready and you say no, it shouldn't happen to you. But other than that, I think it's basically all about the individual" (Jewish, sporadic attender, age 14).
- "I think it's OK if you both want to do it and nobody's feeling pressured [into] doing anything that inside they don't want to do" (mainline Protestant, nonattender, age 14).

Even age does not distinguish their answers. For most adolescents, age is not an important criterion for sexual preparedness. To be sure, most of the 13- and 14-year-olds with whom we spoke are not sexually active and did not anticipate becoming so anytime soon. Yet many of them hesitate to pass judgment on peers who are having sex. The judge-not norm tends to trump any misgivings. Age only contributes to their level of shock, not to disappointment or anger. Beth, a 14-year-old agnostic who says that sex is "not even on my radar screen," puts it this way:

> I mean if one of my friends came up to me and said, "Hey guess what, I had sex last night," I'd be like, "What?" You know, it's not that I wouldn't accept it. I think that I would just be a little surprised.

Christy, an 18-year-old Catholic from upstate New York who attends mass sporadically and has never had sex, told us that one of her friends recently shared with her that she had had sex. Clearly shocked, Christy tries hard *not* to be disappointed in her friend:

> I don't know [if] it scared me, but I just felt like I couldn't believe that she would do that. When I talked to her, I didn't say that. I was just like, "oh, OK." I was just [saying to myself] "hold it in" and things like that. But it just seems like, like protection isn't 100 percent effective, you know. And it just seems so dangerous to do that. I just don't see the point about doing it before marriage. It's just like you're totally one with the person, you know, and I just don't see that I would want to be, like, stressed out and not sure I would want to make that kind of choice. I would rather be just, like, sure. Like, confident in my choice. But, um, she made that decision, so. And she's OK. She's made that decision.

In a nutshell, the norm appears to be "emotional readiness," a catchphrase or action script with which many adolescents identify. A lot of respondents think that waiting until marriage is probably a good idea, but it's not necessary and probably not realistic. So far as I can tell, emotional readiness means that it's fine for you to have sex if (a) you're ready, (b) that's what you want to do, (c) you're not being pressured, and to a lesser extent, (d) as long as you're being "safe" (practicing contraception and protection from STDs). Others add that "it's more than a feeling," that in order to be emotionally ready, "you should realize what you're getting into" and be "old enough to handle the complex emotions of sex." Furthermore, you shouldn't have intercourse with just anyone; it should be a special thing. For many girls in particular, love—however they define it—increasingly justifies the pursuit of a sexual relationship (Risman and Schwartz 2002).

### What Does "Emotional Readiness" Mean?

Ironically, "being emotionally ready" is a familiar and comfortable phrase to many adolescents, but as a norm it largely lacks standardized content and it risks being a platitude. Many definitions of it are hopelessly confusing. Dawn, an 18-year-old practicing Catholic from New York, offers an admirable effort but a convoluted account of the new standard:

> I think that, I mean, I think it's OK. But I mean, I think for me, at least
> I don't think that sex, I just, I can't, because that's just my own personal
> opinion. But I mean, I think it's OK just as long as you're safe about it. If
> you're safe about, I mean, then, you know, just don't be, like, totally reckless
> with it. 'Cause some, you know, you can get hurt. You can, you know,
> get yourself in trouble and get into all kinds of problems. Um, so I think it's,
> you know, I think it's OK, though. You know people, I mean, I could think
> of so many people that do it, but just, you know, it's totally natural. Um,
> I think it's, but you know if it, you have to do it according to how you feel.
> I mean, too, if you really want to, I mean that's fine, you know?

Dawn was far from alone in her inarticulateness. Terrence, a 16-year-old Catholic from Connecticut (who does not actively attend mass), suggests that emotional readiness is unfortunately defined *in hindsight*. If this is true, being emotionally ready would be very difficult for adolescents to use as a yardstick to gauge their own sexual preparedness:

> [I]f you're not ready, and you do it, you know, you might, you might feel
> disgusted with yourself or you might regret it. Or you might just look at it,
> you might, like, just, just be focused on it. Like, "why did I do this, why?"
> They might take it negatively. I, I don't know. [*Is there, like, when is that, or,
> how would someone know that they were ready?*] There's not really a definite
> way of knowing. Just have to, when you, when you think that you're ready
> and you try it, then you know. For sure afterwards.

Cindy is 16 years old, from Indiana, and practices Wicca. She echoes the after-the-fact documentation of emotional readiness:

> If you, like, after you do it, you call up your friend and be, like, "Oh no, I just had sex," then you're not ready for it, you know. But if you're, like, if you did it and you're like, "Wow, that was nice," and you just, like, accept that you did, then it's different. Because then you're not doing it because you want other people to know that you did. You're doing it because you wanted to and you thought it was appropriate for you and your boyfriend to take the next step in that relationship.

Other adolescents disparage talk about emotional readiness. Most (but not all) are very religious or belong to conservative religious traditions. In their own words:

- "I don't think you can ever be emotionally ready as a teenager for anything" (Jehovah's Witness, regular attender, age 16).
- "Whoever came up with that 'ready' stuff was dumb" (evangelical Protestant, regular attender, age 16).
- "I don't think that anybody my age is ready to have sex" (Jewish nonattender, age 17).
- "Most of us have no idea what we're ready for. So it's kind of like, why press your luck?" (evangelical Protestant, regular attender, age 15).
- "If you look at sex as something that's just [only] supposed to be fun and pleasurable, then you're not ready for it, because it's supposed to be so much more than that" (evangelical Protestant, regular attender, age 17).

The ample duration of a romantic relationship is another factor in gauging sexual preparedness. Those respondents who do *not* advocate simple sexual abstinence vary in the length of time that they suggest is sufficient before an exclusive romantic relationship can add a sexual dimension. Most answers range from three to eight months. Very few suggest longer than a year. Theresa, a 16-year-old, unaffiliated, nonreligious girl from Nebraska, thinks seven months is admirable:

> My one friend Terra, her boyfriend, Philip, he's a really shy guy and he didn't even want to have sex until she was ready. And he said that if she didn't want to do it all they didn't have to. And they've been going out for, like, eight months now and they didn't have sex until, like, a month ago. And I just think that if a guy is willing to wait that long without any pressure, then I think he really cares about you.

A year is clearly longer than necessary to the majority of adolescents for whom sexual activity is a live option.

Remarkably, comparatively few adolescents cite a readiness to (a) raise children or (b) make a long-term relationship commitment as key criteria of the emotional readiness for sex. Arguably, if we had fielded this questionnaire to a random sample of adolescents in 1980, these two responses would have been more popular. Today, they are uncommon, mostly limited to the very religious, like Cheryl (a 16-year-old Mormon from Utah): "Being intimate with someone, I think it's very, um, like, sacred, you know. It should be shared with someone that you love and you're willing to spend, like, the rest of your life with."

## The New Rules of Sexual Engagement

In an age when effective contraception can all but mitigate the threat of pregnancy or STDs, what rationale for abstinence is left among those who carry no sense of the sacredness, or even the seriousness, of sex? Sexual ethics appear to be largely self-focused in their present constitution, and they offer little sense of what might be right or good for a *pair* of people, or for the other partner. Sexual morality is seldom categorical. It is fluid in its boundaries and subject to considerable gray areas and alteration on-the-fly. "I think it's basically all about the individual," summarized one adolescent with whom we spoke. If only it were.

One student of adolescence concludes that "there are no longer any rules regarding sexuality in mainstream society, especially for adolescents" (Clark 2004: 127). This, however, is far from true. The rules might look different or sound strange, but they are there. No doubt, contemporary sexual morality is less concerned with the right or wrong of sex or its timing. There are, however, numerous norms of appropriate sexual engagement during adolescence: you should not have sex with your friend's boy- or girlfriend, you should not have sex with "a lot" of people (it may harm your reputation), both partners should be willing, you shouldn't be too young, and—at least from most girls' perspective—you should be in love. Protection is a good idea. There is thus still plenty of sexual morality among contemporary adolescents. It's just not the type with which many adolescents' parents were once familiar and which they might still prefer.

No compelling language will make most American adults feel good about adolescent sexual behavior. The public health community emphasizes terms like protection, safety, respect, responsibility, trust, and consent. The social service community presses youth to avoid risky behaviors that can place them in situations of heightened dependence. But ideas such as patience, commitment, and lifelong love seem out of date, hopelessly romantic, idealistic, and impractical for most. A minority, however, still claims such dying ideals. Christy is one of those minorities. Her internal conflict about the sexual choices of friends reveals a deep-seated link between sex and conceptions of the good life. While she voices her concern about the practical risks of sex, her choice of terms—using words like "scared" and "hold it in"—suggests something deeper than mere interest in a friend's future life chances. Try as she might to not judge her friends, Christy nevertheless finds it impossible to completely bury the moral aspects of sexuality and sexual practice.

## THE SEXUAL BOUNDARIES OF DEVOUTLY RELIGIOUS YOUTH

If sex is out of bounds for some teenagers, just how far is it OK to go? Kissing? Sexual touching?[8] Many religious adolescents inquire of their church youth group leaders about this very thing. Lauren Winner, who has emerged as one of the more popular, contemporary spokespersons among the younger generation of religious conservatives, advocates for not doing anything in private that you would be embarrassed to do in public (Winner 2005). For her, sexual decision making concerns more than just a pair of people but also their religious community and friends, who have (theoretically) invested time, energy, and hope in the bond. While purposefully avoiding categorical claims about this or that action, Winner has hit upon what a majority of religiously conservative adolescents would articulate as acceptable boundaries: everything beyond holding hands and kissing is off limits. Likened to "cheat codes" in video games, sexual touching is simply too far, akin to keeping the letter of the law, but not the spirit of it (Rosenbloom 2005).

"Probably just kissing and making out" was the line of demarcation for Rick, a 14-year-old mixed-race (white and Asian) evangelical from Maryland. Like Rick, Jeanie—a 16-year-old evangelical from California—senses the power and pull of sex. Boundaries are necessary to protect her from doing things she believes she would come to regret: "I think it's unsafe to do anything, like, past kissing, because then you want to do more." The key concern for Rick, Jeanie, and many other religiously conservative adolescents is not that kissing is wrong. To them, it's a morally neutral action. But they believe it could easily lead to other more serious and immoral actions. Although

Brandi, a 15-year-old Hispanic evangelical from Louisiana, is no longer a virgin, she told us that she feels forgiven by God and articulates a new and stricter set of criteria:

> Everything that's not kissing is sex. Like if it's, like, touching and stuff, I think that all has to, like, ends up leading to sex anyway, so I consider that part of sex. That's still something you should wait 'til marriage, 'cause, I don't know, you need to be pure for your husband and everything.

A minority of very religious youth advocate for even stricter boundaries, such as nothing beyond holding hands and "side hugs" instead of chest-to-chest hugs. This is especially the case among younger adolescents, whose rules are understandably more conservative. Darla, a 15-year-old evangelical from California who attends a very conservative church and school, is adamant:

> I don't think a boy and a girl should be touching each other at all. [*Uh-huh, not even holding hands?*] Yeah. [*OK, so there would be no physical contact at all.*] Yeah. [*Between boys and girls until marriage?*] Yeah. [*OK.*] I guess I could see people, like, holding your fiancée's hand or something . . . [or] . . . if she broke her ankle and you had to, like, carry her down the stairs or something.

Since there are essentially no official religious rules on appropriate dating behavior, such rule making is often less about religion and more about adolescents' developmental stage. Tricia, a 14-year-old evangelical from Montana, developed a set of rules based upon how she feels at her age. She acknowledges little religious clarity on the matter: "It's my opinion, that's all. I don't know anything about what the Bible says about [them]." The very religious are not the only ones who advocate conservative boundaries. Kent, a 17-year-old nominally Catholic boy from Ohio who rarely attends mass and identifies himself as fairly unreligious, nevertheless sees little value in sex at his age. A fairly strategic young man, Kent does not profess marriage as his marker of readiness, but he claims he will not likely be ready for sex until he is at least 20 years old and then only with the "right person."

### Masturbation

Many religious adolescent boys—and some girls—struggle with another sexual boundary: masturbation, the most common intercourse substitute, bar none. Popular evangelical author Joshua Harris (2003) humorously notes that devout young men often thumb through Christian books on sex solely to see what they say about this issue. Many evangelical psychologists, including James Dobson (1989) of Focus on the Family, suggest that tolerating adolescent masturbation is less harmful than its condemnation and may serve to provide an outlet for "normal" sexual energy that might otherwise be channeled toward more clearly immoral paired sexual activity.[9] Compulsive masturbation, however, should be avoided. Wheaton College psychologist and sexologist Stanton Jones reinforces Dobson's conclusion, while admitting he has long struggled with what advice to offer in this area (Jones and Jones 1993). In masturbation's place, some focus on the "redirection" of sexual energies into more "positive" outlets, like athletics.

More recently, however, a number of evangelical pastors and authors have addressed masturbation and largely conclude that it should be avoided. In this way, the absence of all conscious, "orgasmic" sexual activity becomes the unwritten norm among them. Joshua Harris and others attempt to redirect attention away from evaluating the morality of the *act* of masturbation and toward the condition of the heart, the motives that underlie the action (Arterburn, Stoeker, and Yorkey 2002; Ethridge and Arterburn 2004; Harris 2003). Here, Harris argues, is where lust, self-centeredness, and a pleasure orientation reside, which do not seek to serve God. Some hold that masturbation is no different than other types of sexual substitution. After all, it is entirely conceivable that adolescents may rationally choose to avoid paired sexual behavior but experience frequent sexual pleasure via masturbation. If I were to summarize contemporary evangelical thinking about masturbation, then, it would be:

- Orgasm is not a sin in itself.
- Masturbation to orgasm may not be sinful in itself, but lust is.
- Since lust almost always accompanies masturbation, almost all masturbation is sin.
- Repressing masturbation may be worse than tolerating it, according to some.
- Masturbation can become compulsive, which is always problematic.
- Ultimately, solo sex is not God's intention for human sexual expression.

Contemporary Catholic and conservative mainline Protestant thought about masturbation tends to avoid the evangelical sense of gravity about it, while not outright advocating for its practice (Sonnenberg 1998). In other words, they are less quick to isolate masturbation as a concern and more apt to echo Dobson's approach.

Regrettably, the NSYR did not intentionally ask our interviewees about masturbation or its morality. (It seems that we too have trouble saying the word.) It is clearly time to collect more reliable data on this subject, especially from adolescents and young adults. The famed Chicago study of human sexuality, published in 1994, notes that 29 percent of men aged 18–24 masturbate at least once a week, compared with 9 percent of 18- to 24-year-old women (Laumann et al. 1994). They also feel the most guilt: 59 percent of 18- to 24-year-old men (and 56 percent of women of the same age) feel guilty after masturbation, the highest level among all age categories. Slightly less than 20 percent of "evangelically oriented" adult men (regardless of age) masturbate weekly, down from 28 percent of mainline Protestant men, 25 percent of Catholics, and 38 percent of nonreligious men. Interestingly, there is race and ethnic variation as well: 17 percent of African-American men masturbate at least weekly, well below the 28 percent figure for whites, 31 percent for Asian men, and 24 percent for Hispanic men.

Despite having little data to go on here, the topic of masturbation nevertheless occasionally surfaced in interviews. David, a 16-year-old evangelical from Oklahoma, told me—after much reassurance of anonymity—that he struggled with masturbation. Two years earlier, he had admitted a "brief" battle with a pornography addiction. So I presumed that the penchant for pornography was back. However, he claimed that it wasn't; the "problem" was strictly about masturbation. A youth group leader from his congregation was calling him regularly to encourage him to read his Bible daily and to see how he was doing with the problem. Indeed, an emerging theme among religious youth is one of accountability groups—pairs or groups of same-sex adolescents who seek via peer pressure to hold each other accountable, which for boys often (symbolically) means saying no to pornography and masturbation. As I noted above, talk of masturbation tends to concern adolescent *male* sexuality. Much, much less has been written about masturbation among adolescent girls.[10]

## Conclusions

Before I switch gears and examine real sex—not just talk of it—a summary of the key findings in this chapter would be good to have fresh in memory.

First, adolescents who say that sex should wait until marriage are usually young (ages 13–15, and prepubescent in terms of their interests and likes) or very religious (mostly evangelical, Mormon, or conservative Catholics or mainline Protestants). Most Jewish, mainline, and Catholic adolescents are unlikely to say that they think waiting for marriage is necessary. And they will often say that if you want to do that, you should (no pressure, though). Thus, religious conservatives and the most devout adolescents tend to hold the least permissive attitudes about sex.

Second, in terms of doing what it is explicitly intended to do, the abstinence pledge doesn't work all that well. Most marrying young people who took the pledge at some point during their adolescence broke it before they wed. Those who are unwavering about the pledge fare better than those who are inconsistent in their reports of pledging. Some suggest that pledgers are more likely to acquire an STD, or put their fellow adolescents at risk by underestimating their own. Perhaps, but real pledges *kept* are clearly effective. They're just uncommon. The pledge *is* effective, though, in delaying first sex and diminishing adolescents' number of sexual partners (and thus lifetime exposure to STDs).

Third, abstinence pledgers—especially girls—are idealists. They expect a lot from marriage and married sex, perhaps too much. On the other hand, numerous sexually active adolescents call sex "no big deal." Sex *is* a big deal, however. Married adults who cheat on their spouses are rarely greeted with apathy. There will always remain a link between sex and conceptions about what a good life looks like.

Fourth, motivations to have or to avoid sex are one step closer in time to actual decisions to engage or refrain. The magnitude of religious effects on sexual motivations (especially guilt) is notable. Church or mass attendance and/or religious salience are associated with more extensive anticipation of guilt from sex, the loss of respect from one's sexual partner, upsetting one's mother, and being embarrassed if pregnancy were to result.

Fifth, emotional readiness is a popular (if obscure) guide for many teenagers to gauge sexual preparedness. Defining emotional readiness, however, is difficult. Some explain it as "when they are ready," "when they're comfortable with it," or "when they won't freak out afterward." Other norms governing adolescents' prospective sexual relationships include the duration of the relationship (at least three months), emotional sentiment (sex should be a special thing), and the use of contraception. In sum, adolescents are emotionally ready when they say they are, even if they're really not, because there is no good barometer they can use to learn the truth, if it can be known. Religious youth are far more apt to disagree with the emotional readiness barometer.

Sixth and finally, most religiously conservative youth tend to articulate a set of boundaries about romantic relationships that could be summarized as "nothing beyond holding hands and kissing." They tend to advocate avoiding in private what would embarrass them in public. While evangelical psychologists have gone on record as suggesting that stifling masturbation may be worse than tolerating it, most evangelical pastors and authors of guides on adolescent sexuality tend to frown on the practice. Whether most American adolescents do or do not masturbate—and, if so, how often—unfortunately cannot be documented using the Add Health or NSYR data.

# Chapter 5

## SEXUAL EXPERIENCE

*The tragedy of sexual intercourse is the*
*perpetual virginity of the soul.*

—William B. Yeats

While the sexual scripts—the attitudes, norms, desires, and motivations—that are available to American teenagers are no doubt interesting, they don't tell us what adolescents actually *do*. To be sure, sexual attitudes and motivations are good predictors of actual activity. But if you were to assume that the *religious* patterns for the former will be the same as for the latter, you would be wrong. This chapter explores religious influences on actual sexual experience. Some teenagers talk a lot about sex, tell us they aren't averse to becoming sexually active, and yet they wait. Others talk about waiting, but don't.

In this chapter, I look at the frequency with which adolescents are having sex, the timing and context of their first sexual experience, the likelihood of experimenting or having sex only once (and then shunning it until much later), attitudes about and use of contraception, sexual regrets and negative sexual experiences (and what those refer to), and how the religious patterns in attitudes (discussed in chapter 4) fare when evaluating actual sexual behavior.

### VIRGINITY LOSS

Virginity has long implied innocence, purity, and freedom from sexual desire, especially among young, unmarried women, and at different historical times it was expected at the time of marriage. In her research on the subjective experience of virginity loss, Laura Carpenter (2001: 128) describes when things began to change: "[a]t the beginning of the [twentieth] century, young men typically saw their own virginity as a neutral or negative attribute, whereas young women perceived theirs as a thing of value."[1] She claims that after about 1920, young people became increasingly likely to lose their virginity prior to marriage, typically to their future spouses. This expanded during the 1960s, when more and more youth began to engage in sexual intercourse with people they did not intend to marry (Carpenter 2001). During and following this period, she writes, women's virginity came to take on a new frame: that of the neutral or negative attribute. In turn, gender differences in sexual experience and age at first sex began to diminish, something most data sets confirm. It has become unusual for adolescent boys or girls to retain and respect virginity. Does religion provide space for subcultures that still value it? If so, for how long, and for what reasons? What happens when religious youth become sexually active?

Most studies of first sex, across a wide variety of data sets, confirm that more frequent attendance at religious services and greater religious salience tends to delay first sex among American adolescents (Beck, Cole, and Hammond 1991; Brewster et al. 1998; Hardy and Raffaelli 2003; Jones, Darroch, and Singh 2005; Ku, Sonenstein, and Pleck 1993; Meier 2003; Sheeran et al. 1993; Thornton and Camburn 1989).[2] Some studies examine denominational differences in first sex, with a variety of results. Several investigators conclude that adolescents from evangelical, fundamentalist, or sectarian (Mormon, Jehovah's Witness) backgrounds are less likely to initiate sex than other youth, especially compared to those from mainline Protestant or nonreligious backgrounds (Beck et al. 1991; Miller and Olson 1988). Other studies report that Catholics are more likely to remain virgins (Brewster et al. 1998; Casper 1990). Using data on Detroit area adolescents, Arland Thornton and Donald Camburn (1989) found that Jewish adolescents are more likely to be virgins than are others. A common problem in several of these studies, however, is that effects of religious affiliation are often estimated and reported without controlling for other religious variables, which can change the results considerably.

Table 5.1 displays the percentage of nonvirgins at Wave I of Add Health, grouped by age and religiosity. At age 13, the range of difference (in the percentage of nonvirgins) between weekly church attenders and those who never attend—and between those for whom religion is very important and those for whom it is not important at all—is only about 7 percentage points. Religiosity is not really a factor at this point. But fast forward *just two years*, and the association materializes quickly. By age 15, the range in sexual experience between the most and least religious youth grows to 16 percentage points for attendance and 19 points for religious salience. By age 17, the attendance range has grown to 22 points: whereas 43 percent of 17-year-old weekly church attenders have already experienced sexual intercourse, fully 65 percent of those who never attend services have. One year later, the range is approximately the same. For religious salience at age 18, we only see two clusters: there is no statistical difference in virginity status among youth who

TABLE 5.1 Nonvirgins (in Percentages), by Age and Religiosity, Wave I

| | Age 13 | Age 15 | Age 17 | Age 18 |
|---|---|---|---|---|
| *Church Attendance* | | | | |
| Weekly | 6.3 | 24.8 | 42.9 | 52.8 |
| Once a month but less than weekly | 9.3 | 34.2 | 62.3 | 67.7 |
| Less than once a month | 16.5 | 36.7 | 65.8 | 70.1 |
| Never | 13.5 | 41.4 | 64.8 | 75.6 |
| *Importance of Religion* | | | | |
| Very important | 7.5 | 26.2 | 48.2 | 55.7 |
| Fairly important | 10.9 | 33.3 | 62.2 | 72.9 |
| Fairly unimportant | 12.5 | 37.6 | 68.9 | 68.3 |
| Not important at all | 14.2 | 45.7 | 61.3 | 71.5 |
| Overall | 9.8 | 32.6 | 57.4 | 65.8 |

*Source*: National Longitudinal Study of Adolescent Health

say religion is fairly important, fairly unimportant, or not important at all. Only those who say it's *very* important stand out, at 56 percent (nonvirgins).

Unlike Table 5.1, which concerns developmental patterns in first sex, Table 5.2 displays the percentage of nonvirgins split by race and religiosity. A linear association between religiosity and sexual experience is present among white, Hispanic, and Asian-American youth, but not among African-American youth. Over 50 percent of African-American youth who attend church weekly have already had sex. On the other hand, Asian-American youth who attend church weekly are the most likely to be virgins (84 percent). White regular attenders follow, at 80 percent.

I am hardly the first to document the race-religion-sex pattern noted here. More than 20 years of research conclusions suggest that the association between religiosity and sexual behavior is considerably weaker among African-American youth than among whites (Benson, Donahue, and Erickson 1989). Is there *any* association between religiosity and sex among African-American youth? The answer, based on previous studies and my own ancillary analyses, is "maybe" for African-American girls, but "not likely" for boys (Bearman and Brückner 2001; Billy, Brewster, and Grady 1994; Durant and Sanders 1989; Ku et al. 1993; McCree et al. 2003; Steinman and Zimmerman 2004; Zelnik, Kantner, and Ford 1981). At least two studies found that, after controlling for conservative sexual attitudes, more religious African-American boys were actually *more likely* to have had sex than their less religious counterparts (Ku et al. 1998; Rostosky, Regnerus, and Wright 2003). Much

TABLE 5.2 Nonvirgins (in Percentages), by Race and Religiosity, Wave I

|  | White | African American | Hispanic | Asian American |
|---|---|---|---|---|
| *Church Attendance* | | | | |
| Weekly | 20.3 | 50.6 | 24.1 | 15.7 |
| Once a month but less than weekly | 35.3 | 60.3 | 30.6 | 25.6 |
| Less than once a month | 42.7 | 64.0 | 40.9 | 22.3 |
| Never | 42.7 | 59.5 | 52.5 | 23.4 |
| *Importance of Religion* | | | | |
| Very important | 23.5 | 51.7 | 26.4 | 16.3 |
| Fairly important | 36.0 | 66.0 | 34.3 | 20.5 |
| Fairly unimportant | 43.5 | 57.0 | 55.7 | 20.4 |
| Not important at all | 44.0 | 57.7 | 54.2 | 31.3 |
| "Born again" | 26.8 | 53.4 | 27.4 | 15.0 |
| Not "born again" | 35.7 | 57.1 | 36.3 | 20.7 |
| Overall | 33.4 | 56.2 | 34.9 | 19.9 |

*Source*: National Longitudinal Study of Adolescent Health

less is known about religiosity and sexual activity among Asian and Hispanic teens.

Table 5.3 displays statistics on vaginal intercourse in the Add Health and NSYR, sorted by religious affiliation and spirituality measures. In general, the NSYR reports lower overall estimates of sexual experience than do the Add Health data. The difference is due primarily to the initial screening questions in the NSYR (which modestly elevate measurement error), its younger average age, and the fact that it was administered seven years later than the Add Health.[3] Indeed, the NSYR and the NSFG are the newest among the surveys from which I report. By different methods and question wording, these two data sources suggest that the age at which youth begin to engage in partnered sexual behavior has increased, though not by much.

Despite the differences between data sets, the patterns among religious affiliations remain stable. Mormon and Jewish adolescents report relatively low percentages of vaginal sexual experience in each data set. Black Protestants are the most likely to have had sexual intercourse, followed by nonreligious youth. Evangelicals and youth of other religions report numbers comparable to each other. The rest of the pack—mainline Protestants, Catholics, Jews, and Mormons—fill out the lower half, roughly in that order in Add Health, though the order is slightly different in the NSYR.

TABLE 5.3 Nonvirgins (in Percentages), by Religious
Affiliation and Spirituality

| | Add Health | NSYR |
|---|---|---|
| *Religious Tradition* | | |
| Evangelical Protestant | 36.2 | 18.5 |
| Mainline Protestant | 30.7 | 15.0 |
| Black Protestant | 57.7 | 28.1 |
| Catholic | 30.3 | 18.0 |
| Jewish | 17.6 | 18.6 |
| Mormon (LDS) | 21.7 | 12.6 |
| No religion | 48.2 | 25.6 |
| Other religion | 32.9 | 19.7 |
| *Spiritual but Not Religious* | | |
| Very true | | 27.6 |
| Somewhat true | | 21.7 |
| Not true at all | | 18.8 |

*Sources*: National Longitudinal Study of Adolescent Health, National Survey of Youth and Religion

Despite all the hubbub about evangelical youth pledging sexual absti-nence, they do not stand out in either of these data sets. Of the eight religious traditions listed, they are third highest (Add Health) and fourth highest (NSYR) in terms of rates of nonvirginity. An accumulating body of evidence has begun to support these underwhelming results (Adamczyk and Felson 2006), and I return to this topic later in the chapter. The most compelling stories to be told here, however, are less about particular religious traditions and more about religiosity and embeddedness.

We shouldn't blind ourselves to the considerable selectivity (noted in chapter 2) that is going on here. That is, what types of youth place themselves in situations that foster sexual activity? The answer is: those who date frequently or spend considerable time with members of the opposite sex and/or have a good deal of leisure time. Do these selection effects alter how well religiosity predicts virginity loss? No. Even *after* controlling for demographic effects, family satisfaction, social desirability, a strategic orientation, the percentage of non-virgins in the respondent's school (which measures peer sexual norms), reli-gious affiliation, the number of recent romantic partners, how much personal freedom they have, and whether or not they've taken the abstinence pledge, *religiosity still matters* in delaying first sex (results in Table A5.1). Only after I introduce three sexual attitudes/motivations (anticipated guilt, friends' respect, and upsetting family) do religiosity effects finally disappear. This by no means suggests that one can eventually "explain away" religious influence. It means instead that religiosity is a robust influence that distinguishes teens who have not yet had sexual intercourse, and it does so via many indirect pathways but certainly through its strong influence on sexual attitudes and motivations, which are themselves powerful predictors of sexual behavior.

No doubt to the disappointment of many youth pastors, evangelical Protestantism (as a variable) continues to fare poorly as a predictor of virginity status. In fact, most other religious traditions are significantly *less likely* than they are to report first intercourse by Wave I. The middle-of-the-road numbers on evangelicals only get higher when we control for other significant effects, including religiosity (in Table A5.1). If I shift to evaluating the NSYR data in this way, the results are comparable (not shown). Keep in mind that this pertains to affiliation only and simply indicates that being an evangelical—apart from personal religiosity—is flatly ineffective for predicting virginity status. Evangelical youth, if their affiliation is not combined with active religious involvement and practice, are not simply identical to the rest of the world when it comes to sexual experience during adolescence; they're actually more active.

### A Time-Order Problem?

It may be premature to give too much credit to the effects of religiosity on adolescents' virginity, since virginity and religiosity are measured at the same time (at Wave I). First sex, however, might have occurred several years *before* the survey's administration (especially among older adolescents), while religiosity is measured at the time of the survey. In order to rectify this time-order problem, I experimented with using parent religiosity variables as proxies for teenagers' religiosity, because it is conceivable that sex has subsequently altered adolescents' own religiosity and left us with the "religious exit" selection-effects problem described in chapter 2. This potential time-order problem should not affect parents' religiosity, however. It simply doesn't make sense that parents would alter their own religiosity because of their children's sexual activity. When I substitute parental religiosity—which is by far the strongest predictor of adolescent religiosity—in the models, parental church attendance has a strong and robust effect on their adolescents' virginity status at Wave II, even after controlling for teens' own sexual attitudes and motivations (results in Table A5.2). The same cannot be said for parental religious salience. This makes sense, since this is a measure of *private* religiosity, and youth might not even know how religious their parents consider themselves to be, much less dwell upon or emulate it.

Table A5.3 enhances the statistical rigor further by limiting analyses to only those teenagers who claimed virginity at Wave I and then predicting their virginity status at Wave II. There should be *no* time-order problem here at all. While the protective influence of both adolescent church attendance and religious salience remains evident, the effects are slightly weaker than in the full sample and not as robust to the addition of important control variables. Yet still religiosity distinguishes the sexually experienced from those who have not yet had sex. This is remarkable in light of the number and types of control variables in the models, including sexual attitudes, abstinence pledging, percentage of nonvirgin schoolmates, proclivity for risk taking, and dating habits.

## Religious Change and Transformation

Another way of detecting real religious influence is by evaluating how change in religiosity *over time* affects virginity status. When I evaluate virginity status at Wave II as a function of religious change, controlling for other variables, adolescent virgins whose frequency of attendance *increased* between study waves were considerably less likely to experience first sex than those virgins who stayed the same (results in Table A5.4). When the change is drastic—or perhaps transformational[4]—the results are even more striking. Adolescent virgins who exhibited rapid declines in attendance or religious salience were much more likely to report having had sex between study waves (the odds increase by 35–50 percent).

## Does Virginity Loss Diminish Religiosity?

So far, I have concluded that religion influences virginity status, without considering that the causal direction may be backward. The problem of reverse causation (or religious exit) may still plague us. Might the experience of sexual intercourse—and any guilt that may accompany it—predict a religious decline or a complete exit among adolescents? Not really. Losing one's virginity has little effect on subsequent church attendance patterns, which barely vary at all between virgins and recent nonvirgins, regardless of gender (Table A5.5). The story changes slightly when we consider the importance of religion in teenagers' lives. Girls outpace boys overall in how important they think religion is, but the religiosity only of girls is affected by recent sexual experience. That is, girls who recently experienced first sex are likely to have subsequently told us that religion is *not as important* in their lives as it was the first time we spoke with them.

However, the numbers are not as large as I might hope if I were convinced that sexual behavior shapes religiosity, more than the other way around. Adolescents' church attendance patterns are altogether unaffected by virginity loss, and their assessment of their own personal religiosity is only modestly diminished by sexual experience (and that only among girls). Several other studies have also suggested that the association between religiosity and sex is not two-directional (Hardy and Raffaelli 2003; Meier 2003).

### Other Notable Effects on Virginity Status

The effects of religion on virginity status, while compelling, are not the only findings worth noting. Analyses of both data sets show a variety of other variables besides religion that influence first sex:

- *Strategic orientation*: Strategic adolescents hold more conservative sexual attitudes and are more apt to pledge abstinence, regardless of religiosity. They also significantly delay first intercourse (even after controlling for sexual attitudes).
- *Parents' average education*: Adolescents from homes where both parents are college educated are more likely to delay intercourse. This is true in multiple models and in both data sets.
- *Risk orientation*: Youth who are *not* averse to risks are more likely to report having had sex.
- *Family satisfaction*: Adolescents who say their families understand them, have fun with them, and pay attention to them are more likely to hold conservative sexual attitudes and motivations, and they are more likely to delay first sex, regardless of religiosity.
- *Biologically intact family*: Youth who live with both their biological mother and father are less motivated to have sex and more likely to delay first sex.
- *Dating behavior*: Adolescents who date several different people in a short period of time are more motivated to pursue sex, have greater opportunity to do so, and thus are more likely to report having had sex. In the NSYR, teenagers who were currently dating were also more likely to have had sex, regardless of age and religiosity.
- *Schoolmates' sexual behavior*: In Add Health, youth attending schools in which higher percentages of fellow students have had sex—which creates a more permissive atmosphere—were more likely to themselves report having had intercourse. School sexual norms definitely matter for sexual decision making.

## AGE AT FIRST SEX

Up until this point, I have limited my discussion to virginity status and have not addressed the adolescents' age at first sex. I give it less attention in part because of a pattern of understandable inconsistencies in Add Health adolescents' self-reports of age at first sex: at both waves, they were not asked how old they were when they first had sex, but were instead asked the month and year of their first experience of intercourse. This can be challenging to recall, especially some years after the fact. At Wave III, however, respondents were simply asked how old they were when they first had intercourse. This is a much easier question to answer, and while the likelihood of recall error may increase over time, any social desirability bias should diminish. Table 5.4 displays the average age at first intercourse for all Wave III nonvirgins, sorted by religious affiliation and two measures of religiosity (from Wave I). The numbers make sense in light of what we have already learned. Black Protestant and nonreligious adolescents report the youngest average age at first sex: just under age 16.

TABLE 5.4 Mean Age at Sexual Debut (Retrospective),
by Religiosity Measures, Wave III

| | |
|---|---|
| *Religious Tradition* | |
| Evangelical Protestant | 16.3 |
| Mainline Protestant | 16.7 |
| Black Protestant | 15.9 |
| Catholic | 16.7 |
| Jewish | 17.5 |
| Mormon (LDS) | 18.0 |
| Other religion | 16.6 |
| No religion | 15.9 |
| *Church Attendance* | |
| Weekly | 16.9 |
| Once a month but less than Weekly | 16.3 |
| Less than once a month | 16.3 |
| Never | 16.0 |
| *Importance of Religion* | |
| Very important | 16.7 |
| Fairly important | 16.4 |
| Fairly unimportant | 16.2 |
| Not important at all | 16.0 |

*Source*: National Longitudinal Study of Adolescent Health

Evangelical adolescents are slightly older than this, just over 16. Mormon adolescents report the highest age, 18. All other groups fall in between them.

In keeping with what we have seen with virginity status, the average age at first sex follows a linear pattern with both religious service attendance and the importance of religion in respondents' lives. Among young adult nonvirgins—and remember, there are some young adults who have not yet had sex—those who attended church once a week as teenagers told us they lost their virginity just prior to age 17, on average, while those who never attended as teenagers reported an average age at first sex right at 16. The linear association is nearly identical with importance of religion as it is with attendance  Thus, the difference in timing of first sex between the most and least religious is just under one year, keeping in mind that some respondents were still virgins.


## THE CONTEXT OF FIRST SEX

We asked our interviewees who had experienced sexual intercourse about the context, setting, and nature of their first sexual relationship, and we heard a fair amount of spontaneity in adolescents' accounts: "We were just hanging out at my house" or "It just sort of happened." If I could identify the single most common context for having sex, it is no longer while on a date and in the back seat of a car (if it ever was), but at home, late at night, when parents are asleep. For some, this spontaneity was accompanied by a distinct lack of preplanning, not to mention a diminished likelihood of using contraception. Karin Martin (2002) and Sharon Thompson (1990) discovered a similar level of spontaneity in their studies and also noted a distinct lack of agency in many girls' discourse. Phrases like "I don't know, it just happened" and "It seemed kind of natural" suggest to Martin that girls in particular experience first sex not so much by choice but as a consequence of growing up in a society wherein girls are subject to great sexual pressure, even coercion. "It just sort of happened" is their way of saying that the decision to have sex was made passively, often in order to maintain a valued relationship.

Others with whom we spoke, however, had planned their first time in considerable detail, and it involved ample agency and volition. While such accounts are less common than the passive stories, Thompson's (1990: 351) study compared the two approaches. Those who told the passive story didn't plan ahead for sex:

> They didn't prepare. They didn't explore. Often they didn't even agree to sex. They gave in, they gave up, they gave out. At most they waited. At least,

that's how they told it. [Other girls] describe taking sexual initiative; satisfying their own sexual curiosity, instigating [sexual activity].

In general, accounts of subjective planning appear to be a "girl thing," and planning tends to involve a measure of romantic idealism that spontaneity lacks. Adolescent boys are less apt to report about planning in general and more apt to indicate that they were waiting on their girlfriends to decide they were ready. Courtney, a 17-year-old nonreligious girl from Tennessee, had been deliberate, "looking into every single possible contraceptive and, like, ridiculous caution and all that stuff." She was glad she planned ahead:

> I had a much more positive experience than most teenagers do, because I know most people I know have felt all guilty and all that stuff afterwards. And, like, I think that we were, like, ready in our relationship and secure enough with each other. And we were cautious enough that we didn't, like, we weren't, like, freaking out or anything. So, I think it was an overall good experience.

On the other hand, Renee—a 16-year-old nonreligious girl from Oklahoma—acted upon her feelings of emotional readiness:

> I really, really cared about John. And we've been together for a long time, and just, I don't know, it just kind of happened. [*And um, was John the first person you've had sex with?*] Yep. [*And would you say that was a positive experience or . . . ?*] I think so. It kind of brought us a little bit closer together, 'cause we knew each other intimately.

Amanda, a 15-year-old mainline Protestant from Tennessee, was meticulous in planning and similarly "romantic" in her portrayal of the experience. Despite the fact that she had broken up with her boyfriend (a college-bound high school senior), she says, "We knew we loved each other. And we, we had talked about the consequences and we knew what could happen . . . and we both felt like our relationship was ready for it." So how did she feel about it once the moment arrived?

> I was scared. I was really scared. I had heard a lot about it, and I knew this would be something that was taken away from me for the rest of my life and I would never be a virgin again. So, I was scared and I was nervous, but at the same time I was kind of excited. I was kind of, like, this is a big step in my life, but I think I'm ready for it and, and I, and I never regret who I did it with.

Parties are not a primary venue for first-time intercourse, especially if the encounter is planned. Accounts of experiencing first sex at parties were slightly more common earlier in adolescence. This makes sense, since early adolescents are the least likely—under normal circumstances and with full volition—to willingly choose sexual intercourse. Parties typically mean alcohol and, in turn, impaired decision making and reduced volition.

Drinking is a much more common piece of the puzzle for adolescent boys. Adam, a 17-year-old nonreligious boy from Michigan, had been drinking before losing his virginity with his first girlfriend:

> Yeah, we were [drunk]. It was, it was to a degree, it was, I don't want to say it was like planned out, but it was like we both thought we were ready. And we had been, we had been going out for, I think it was like a month or a couple months or something like that. So I mean it was definitely, it wasn't just like a random thing. It was, it was a, it was kind of an important step.

Some adolescent boys, most notably African Americans, report that intercourse turned out not to be as big a deal as they had thought it would be. One says, "I don't mean to underplay [it], but it's, it's not really that much that people claim it was." Another concurred:

> Telling you the truth, the whole sex thing is just really overrated. 'Cause [laughs] you can't, after a while it just, and you could get it, you could just be getting it, it just get kind of boring, like you look for something more.

Another, an 18-year-old black Protestant (nonattender) from New York, states:

> When it really happens, it's not all that important. 'Cause you're like, man, like, it's, like, it's, I'm not saying it's bad or nothing. I'm just saying that it's, like, let me see. It's like . . . the NBA finals. Like, oh yeah, it's gonna be a real important thing. And then the Lakers come through and sweep everybody and it's not really that important. That's basically how it is.

## AFTER FIRST SEX: POST-VIRGINITY SEXUAL PRACTICE

So did they or didn't they? The dichotomy between virgins and nonvirgins is only one chapter in the story of adolescent sexual development. But it's a symbolic marker, and societal concerns about sexuality often find their locus in the first act of intercourse (Carpenter 2001). Some suggest that virginity status is not all that helpful a marker and that we should instead distinguish among five different types:

- *Delayers*: have not had sex and are in no hurry to
- *Anticipators*: have not had sex but want to
- *One-timers*: have had sex only once, and either regret it or do not have an opportunity to have intercourse again
- *Steadies*: have had sex multiple times within a monogamous sexual relationship
- *Multiples*: have had sex with several people in various relationships

This classification scheme (from Miller et al. 1997) is a smart approach, since virginity loss can occur in a moment of passion or, sadly, without complete volition. Some devoutly religious "one-timers" think of themselves as renewed virgins or "secondary abstinents" (Ali and Scelfo 2002). Indeed, religiosity may have less to do with simple virginity status and more with current sexual activity (Whitaker, Miller, and Clark 2000). Is religion associated with reduced risk across a range of sexual activity patterns, or does it only function as a gatekeeper, delaying first intercourse and that is all (Jones et al. 2005)?

Surprisingly little is known about the frequency with which adolescents (religious or otherwise) are having sexual intercourse or any other sexual activities. Several studies have investigated this, but emerge with mixed results (Benda and Corwyn 1997; Neumark-Sztainer et al. 1997; Sheeran et al. 1993). For instance, one particular study of unmarried, sexually active young women found a modest inverse association between church attendance and frequency of sex, but only for white women, not African-American women (Durant and Sanders 1989). Less frequent attenders had been sexually active for a longer period, regardless of race. Another study reveals intriguing effects of *community religiosity*: evangelical homogeneity within the respondent's county of residence corresponded with a lower frequency of sexual activity among white and Hispanic young women (Billy et al. 1994).

In a fascinating biosocial study of religious influence, Carolyn Halpern and her colleagues (1994) found that adolescent boys with a combination of high testosterone levels *and* high rates of religious attendance were actually less sexually active than boys with low testosterone levels *and* low attendance patterns. Their study is unique in documenting the mitigating, social control effect of religiosity on a hormonal condition (high testosterone) that elevates boys' proclivity for frequent sexual activity.

*Classifying Adolescents' Sexual Activity*

Following the classification scheme outlined above, Figure 5.1 displays the percentage of 16- and 17-year-olds who could be labeled as a delayer, antici-pator, one-timer, steady, or multiple (Miller et al. 1997). Note how few one-timers there are: 3.7 percent, or about 10 percent of all nonvirgins. Clearly, virginity loss tends to signify the commencement of paired sexual practice. While some adolescents may regret their first sexual experience, few stop there. I am not alone in documenting this, either. A recent longitudinal study of adolescents found that 81 percent of nonvirgins had additional experiences of intercourse within the following year (Gillmore et al. 2002). For the most part, teenagers either *are* having sex or they have not yet had it. By logical inference, then, any adoption of a "secondary virgin" self-identity does not typically fol-low *one* regretted instance of intercourse but rather a pattern of sexual activity.

Table 5.5 displays the percentage of all NSYR youth—regardless of age—who fit into each of these categories, split by religiosity and religious affilia-tion. As is evident from previous tables, most NSYR respondents have not had sex and thus are either delayers or anticipators. No single cell in this table should be compared with another cell; rather, the cells and columns should be understood as a whole. For example, I would draw unmerited conclusions about Mormons by focusing on their percentage of one-timers. Since there are more Mormon one-timers than any other religious group, one could erro-neously conclude that Mormons are the most likely to have one-night stands. The truth, though, is that Mormon youths are unlikely to have sex before age

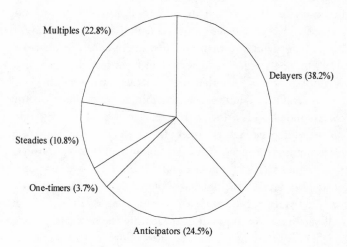

FIGURE 5.1. Sexual Classification of 16- and 17-Year-Olds
*Source*: National Survey of Youth and Religion

TABLE 5.5 Sexual Classifications (in Percentages), by Religiosity Measures

|  | *Delayer* | *Anticipator* | *One-timer* | *Steady* | *Multiple* |
|---|---|---|---|---|---|
| *Religious Tradition* | | | | | |
| Evangelical Protestant | 66.2 | 14.3 | 2.4 | 5.0 | 11.1 |
| Mainline Protestant | 49.2 | 33.8 | 0.7 | 6.6 | 7.8 |
| Black Protestant | 45.7 | 24.2 | 3.6 | 7.3 | 17.2 |
| Catholic | 46.7 | 34.3 | 3.1 | 4.6 | 10.2 |
| Jewish | 38.5 | 42.9 | 0 | 6.2 | 12.4 |
| Mormon (LDS) | 72.5 | 14.9 | 7.0 | 0 | 5.6 |
| Other religion | 48.6 | 31.1 | 0.8 | 3.2 | 15.7 |
| No religion | 26.6 | 47.2 | 1.9 | 7.5 | 16.2 |
| *Church Attendance* | | | | | |
| More than once a week | 78.0 | 11.2 | 2.4 | 2.4 | 5.7 |
| Once a week | 61.8 | 21.5 | 2.5 | 5.7 | 7.0 |
| 2–3 times a month | 46.3 | 29.2 | 2.1 | 7.0 | 14.7 |
| Once a month | 39.0 | 25.1 | 2.8 | 7.2 | 14.7 |
| Many times a year | 49.4 | 22.8 | 4.7 | 6.2 | 14.6 |
| Few times a year | 34.7 | 41.4 | 2.6 | 3.5 | 16.5 |
| Never | 33.3 | 40.9 | 2.1 | 7.3 | 15.4 |
| *Importance of Religion* | | | | | |
| Extremely important | 75.4 | 10.2 | 3.0 | 2.7 | 7.9 |
| Very important | 60.7 | 20.0 | 2.5 | 5.8 | 10.0 |
| Somewhat important | 40.9 | 34.8 | 2.3 | 5.9 | 14.7 |
| Not very important | 28.8 | 49.4 | 1.8 | 5.7 | 13.4 |
| Not important at all | 19.8 | 51.9 | 4.6 | 8.8 | 14.8 |

*Source*: National Survey of Youth and Religion

*Note*: Not all cells sum to 100%, due to missing values.

18 in the first place, but if they *do* have sex, they're more likely to try it once and then refrain from further sexual activity. In the NSYR, *no* Mormons report a steady sexual relationship with one partner, and just under 6 percent of them could be classified as multiples, the fewest of all religious groups.

Among nonreligious adolescents, just under 24 percent have had sex more than once, and among these, there are twice as many multiples as steadies. They are unlikely to be sexual one-timers. So are Jewish and mainline and evangelical Protestant youth. Though mainline Protestant youths are the most likely (at a ratio of just under one-to-one) to be steadies rather than multiples, every other religious group displays a steady-to-multiple ratio of at least one-to-two. This suggests that *any image of long-term adolescent sexual partnerships is a fiction.* Teens are likely to either not have sex at all until late adolescence—the most common pattern—or to have it more often and with more than one partner. One-timers and steadies are not the norm. Once sexual activity has commenced, it usually continues, and with age the sexual network branches out.[5]

Religiosity effects are much easier to interpret than religious affiliation effects. Aside from the presumed associations between either type of religiosity and being a delayer or anticipator, more devoutly religious youth are also less likely to be steadies or multiples: only 2–3 percent of the most devout adolescents could be considered steadies, and 6–8 percent of them are multiples. Results for less religious adolescents are nearly double: 6–7 percent are steadies, and 14–16 percent are multiples. There is little association between religiosity and being a one-timer.

Even after controlling for the influence of friends, personal autonomy, current dating status, popularity, and rebelliousness, church attendance still predicts less frequent sex (results in Table A5.6). It does so until I control for adolescents' patterns of Bible reading and sources of moral authority: teens who say that they do what makes them happy or what helps them to get ahead are significantly likely to report more frequent sex than teens who say that they try to do what the Bible says. And those who read the Bible more frequently report fewer instances of sex.[6]

## Number of Sexual Partners

In chapter 4, I talked about the association between one's number of sexual partners and one's lifetime risk of acquiring a sexually transmitted disease. If an adolescent has one less lifetime sexual partner, and his/her partner also has had one less partner, the decrease in lifetime STD transmission risk rapidly becomes notable. Despite this important link with STDs, only a handful of studies have considered possible links between religiosity and adolescents' (or adults') lifetime number of sexual partners. On average, religious youths are thought to have fewer sexual partners than less devout adolescents (Miller and Gur 2002; Seidman et al. 1992; Thornton and Camburn 1989). In a nationwide sample of adolescent boys, evangelicals or "born again" youth claimed fewer sexual partners over the course of one year (Ku et al. 1993). Nevertheless, the cultural scripts for adolescent sexuality change over time, and most of these studies are now out of date. Are the results different today?

Table 5.6 displays the number of sexual partners among sexually active NSYR youth aged 16–17, grouped by several religion measures. Some of the same patterns from Table 5.5 show up here as well. Mainline Protestants are

TABLE 5.6 Number of Sexual Partners among 16- to 17-year-olds (in Percentages), by Religiosity Measures

| | One | Two | Three or more |
|---|---|---|---|
| *Religious Tradition* | | | |
| Evangelical Protestant | 10.9 | 8.4 | 13.4 |
| Mainline Protestant | 12.6 | 6.1 | 8.9 |
| Black Protestant | 14.3 | 13.0 | 22.6 |
| Catholic | 9.0 | 6.7 | 12.8 |
| Other Religion | 6.3 | 8.3 | 18.1 |
| No Religion | 12.3 | 6.9 | 21.3 |
| *Church Attendance* | | | |
| More than once a week | 6.6 | 6.1 | 4.3 |
| Weekly | 13.6 | 4.8 | 8.0 |
| Up to 2–3 times a month | 9.7 | 11.9 | 17.4 |
| Never up to many times a year | 12.5 | 5.5 | 23.7 |
| *Importance of Religion* | | | |
| Extremely important | 5.0 | 6.2 | 9.7 |
| Very important | 10.7 | 7.1 | 13.7 |
| Somewhat important | 11.9 | 10.8 | 17.5 |
| Not very important | 12.3 | 10.9 | 13.6 |
| Not important at all | 16.1 | 2.9 | 17.8 |
| *Spiritual but Not Religious* | | | |
| Not true at all | 9.5 | 6.1 | 12.2 |
| Somewhat true | 11.5 | 9.5 | 16.2 |
| Very true | 10.8 | 9.9 | 17.4 |
| *Moral Authority* | | | |
| Do what makes me happy | 13.9 | 7.9 | 17.8 |
| Do what gets me ahead | 8.8 | 14.0 | 25.7 |
| Do what an adult or parent says | 10.8 | 8.1 | 12.0 |
| Do what God or Scripture says | 6.3 | 4.0 | 6.3 |
| Some other authority | 0.0 | 9.9 | 15.3 |

*Source*: National Survey of Youth and Religion

*Note*: Jewish and Mormon youth were dropped due to small sample sizes.

the least likely to report three or more sexual partners, while black Protestants report the most among all categories. Teens who attend church sparingly or not at all are *six times* more likely than the most devout youth (24 versus 4 percent) to have three or more sexual partners. Although the comparison is not as striking, the same pattern holds for the measure of religious salience. A modest association also exists between number of sexual partners and teens who think of themselves as spiritual but not religious.

Finally, sources of moral authority are clearly associated with number of sexual partnerships: 26 percent of older adolescents who said (if faced with a dilemma) they would do what gets them ahead report having at least three sexual partners, and 14 percent report two partners. These numbers are even higher than among those who say that they would do what makes them happy. Nonvirgin adolescents who say they would consult Scripture have the fewest sexual partners. Such predictors of respondents' number of sex partners are strong, withstanding controls for age, gender, dating patterns, popularity, family structure, and parental education (results not shown, but they are nearly identical to those in Table A5.6).

## CONTRACEPTION

Perhaps nothing has so powerfully and rapidly altered how adolescents make sexual decisions as their widespread access to contraception. The perceived benefits of sexual intercourse have not changed, but the costs certainly have diminished. The costs for many are no longer primarily physical, but instead psychological and social. Indeed, the most immediate physical risks of sex—pregnancy and STDs—appear increasingly benign to many adolescents, especially the ones actively pursuing sexual relationships. The "scared sexless" mentality that characterized media reports about adolescent sex in the mid-1980s seems outdated now in the wake of recognition that HIV remains confined in America to high-risk populations. In fact, relatively few adolescents we interviewed mentioned STDs or AIDS during our conversation. By far the most references to them were made by African Americans, who tend to bear the brunt of HIV and STD infections in the United States (Centers for Disease Control 2002).[7]

Despite low-cost, accessible contraception, the United States retains one of the highest rates of adolescent pregnancy and childbearing among advanced industrial societies (Singh and Darroch 2000). The most recent national estimates (from 2000) suggest that the annual U.S. teen pregnancy rate is 84 per 1,000 girls aged 15–19, down 28 percent since 1990. The abortion rate among the same is about 24 per 1,000, down from 41 in 1990 (Henshaw 2004). In step with these declines, from 1991 to 2002, the teenage birth rate has dropped some 30 percent, to 43 births per 1,000 girls aged 15–19.

Adolescents are either having less sex or are using contraception more frequently. The former may be true, but not by much. The latter is certainly accurate (Risman and Schwartz 2002). NSFG data from 2002 indicate that 79 percent of young people use contraception during their first act of intercourse, up from 61 percent in the 1980s (Centers for Disease Control 2004). Over 80 percent of these reported using a condom as their primary means of contraception. They were also more likely to have used contraception at their most recent experience of intercourse (83 percent in 2002, compared with 71 percent in 1995). American youth get little contraceptive encouragement from their exposure to mass media: only 3 percent of sex scenes on television involved apparent contraceptive use (Brody 2006).

## Abstinence Pledging and Contraception

One of the more interesting pieces of news on the subject of contraception is that abstinence pledgers are considerably less likely than nonpledgers to use birth control at first sex (Bearman and Brückner 2001). This makes sense, since we can presume that teens who take the abstinence pledge, and then break it, more often than not will have experienced first sex without planning to do so, and lack of planning usually means lack of contraception.[8] For such youth to introduce contraception into their own sexual activity would require a drastic change of script, an alteration of the sexual instructions that their parents, friends, and religious communities have provided them (Laumann et al. 1994). To change scripts is no simple task for pledge breakers. Thus, making use of contraception will not likely occur until *after* such adolescents have come to grips with their status as sexually active and probably not until after the second or third experience of intercourse.

Bearman and Brückner (2004) also note that STD rates are higher in communities where more adolescents take the abstinence pledge. Why this is the case is not immediately clear. Perhaps youth in high-risk (for STDs) communities simply recognize the dangers around them and view pledging as helpful to avoid them. On the other hand, it may be that pledgers underestimate the local STD risk—this is the authors' conclusion—and since pledge failure is fairly common and seldom accompanied by contraception, their relative risk of unprotected sex and STD acquisition is elevated. In turn, their own infections contribute to the pool of infectious persons, increasing others' risk. But given that pledgers tend to break their pledges with adolescents who have had few sexual partners, this conclusion may not be merited. Pinpointing exactly why STD risk is higher where pledging is more popular will likely remain elusive and speculative.

### Religion and Contraceptive Attitudes

Just as I was concluding writing this book, I noticed a remarkable story involving the "religious right" and an American drug maker (Smith 2006). No, it was not about waging war against RU486 (Mifepristone) or the morning-after pill (high-dose oral contraceptives). This story had a peaceful settlement. The pharmaceutical giant Merck was awaiting FDA approval for a vaccine that would be used to inoculate young girls against contracting human papillomavirus, an STD which causes 70 percent of cervical cancer cases in women. Merck's good news was not that FDA approval had been won but that the company had successfully negotiated the support of Focus on the Family and the Family Research Council, two politically powerful conservative religious organizations concerned that use of the vaccine may send a tolerant message about sexual permissiveness. Nevertheless, Merck may face an uphill marketing battle with religious parents, many of whom may not relish the idea of inoculating their preteen children against a disease that is sexually transmitted. To combat this perception, Merck's marketing campaign focuses on health—the prevention of cervical cancer—instead of HPV's sexual origin.

Artificially protecting oneself against STDs and/or pregnancy, whether by use of hormonal contraceptive injections, pills, or condoms, is common today. Most adolescents and young adults—religious or not, sexually active or not—are comfortable with the idea of contraception. This despite the Roman Catholic church's stated doctrine favoring only natural family planning as a means of controlling fertility. Even some evangelical Protestants are beginning to rethink birth control (Torode and Torode 2002). But are these advocates reaching the masses of adolescents—America's newest (or next) cohort of contraceptive users?

Hardly. Table 5.7 displays the percentages of adolescents who agree or strongly agree that using birth control is morally wrong (Add Health, Wave I virgins only), grouped by religion variables. Only two groups even hit double digits—Catholics at 11.4 percent and black Protestants at 12.5 percent. These two groups also exhibit higher-than-average fertility during adulthood as well. (Mormons' fertility is also well known, but they do not stand out here.) Considering that most forms of artificial contraception are comparatively recent, and that up until the early twentieth century many denominations officially condemned contraception, these numbers are remarkably low. A

TABLE 5.7 Adolescents Who Agree or Strongly Agree
That Using Birth Control Is Morally Wrong
(in Percentages), Wave I Virgins Only

| | |
|---|---|
| *Religious Tradition* | |
| Evangelical Protestant | 6.2 |
| Mainline Protestant | 4.8 |
| Black Protestant | 12.5 |
| Catholic | 11.4 |
| Jewish | 6.3 |
| Mormon (LDS) | 7.0 |
| Other religion | 5.2 |
| No religion | 6.8 |
| *Church Attendance* | |
| Weekly | 10.9 |
| Once a month but less than weekly | 6.1 |
| Less than once a month | 3.9 |
| Never | 6.2 |
| *Importance of Religion* | |
| Very important | 11.4 |
| Fairly important | 5.2 |
| Fairly unimportant | 2.2 |
| Not important at all | 5.8 |
| *Abstinence Pledge* | |
| Took the pledge | 12.2 |
| Did not take the pledge | 7.2 |
| Overall | 7.8 |

*Source*: National Longitudinal Study of Adolescent Health

dramatic change has occurred in how young Americans think about controlling their own fertility—and in a relatively short period of time. Yet religious adolescents are still the most likely to protest contraception. Teens high in religiosity are almost twice as likely as other youth to say that birth control is morally wrong. Still, this answer characterizes only about 11 percent of the most religious youth. Even among abstinence pledgers, only 12 percent find contraception to be morally suspect. While the abstinence pledge is more about sex than about contraception, these numbers are nevertheless lower than I expected.

Despite the revolution in attitudes about contraception, few scholars pause to consider any more whether adolescents who forgo contraception actually *intend* to avoid it, not because it interferes with their pleasure (though it may), but because they have moral or other preferential objections to it or believe that it does not work. It is entirely possible that not all sexually active adolescents who avoid birth control do so only because they are foolish or wish to appear as if they are not planning sex. Little attention is paid to religious world views in which contraceptive decision making concerns people's perceptions of "nature" or God's will (Woodsong, Shedlin, and Koo 2004). Indeed, what is "normal" about contraceptive acceptance and usage is defined by shared *culture*, not by innovations in *science*. While contraception enjoys remarkably wide approval, even among the most religious, it is by no means complete approval.

Other youth may associate contraception with premarital sex, and so object to both of them. Table 5.8 displays the percentages, sorted by religion measures, of girls who say their friends would think they were looking for sex if they used birth control. Among religious affiliations, evangelical, Catholic, and black Protestant girls are more likely to think this. A linear association is evident with both forms of religiosity: the more religious they are, the more likely they will think that considering birth control is tantamount to looking for sex. (Still, it's no more than 3 in 10; so this is certainly not how *most* religious adolescent girls think.) Abstinence pledgers likewise associate contraception with sex: 31 percent of adolescent girls who have pledged abstinence agree or strongly agree that using birth control will make their friends think they're looking to have sex, up from 20 percent of nonpledgers.

After controlling for other possible predictors, the associations between religious affiliations and both contraceptive attitudes are considerably weaker than they are with sexual attitudes (results in Table A5.7). At the same time, religiosity (especially church attendance) and abstinence pledging continue to shape contraceptive attitudes even after controls are introduced. Besides religion, white youths, girls, adolescents with educated parents, and those exhibiting a strategic orientation are all less likely than their counterparts to have moral misgivings about birth control.

## Contraceptive Use at First and Last Sex

Most young people—religious or not—favor using contraception. But do they actually use it? In several previous studies, higher religiosity was either unrelated to contraceptive use at first sex (Bearman and Brückner 2001; Zelnik et al. 1981) or predicted *avoiding* its use (Thomson 1982). Two studies, however, note positive effects of religiosity on contraceptive use; one found that more religious youth were more likely to visit a clinic to procure birth control and

Table 5.8 Adolescent Girls Who Agree or Strongly Agree That Their Friends Would Think They Were Looking for Sex If They Used Birth Control (in Percentages), Wave I Virgins Only

| | |
|---|---|
| *Religious Tradition* | |
| Evangelical Protestant | 26.9 |
| Mainline Protestant | 20.4 |
| Black Protestant | 31.7 |
| Catholic | 22.8 |
| Jewish | 9.2 |
| Mormon (LDS) | 8.6 |
| Other religion | 24.4 |
| No religion | 14.3 |
| *Church Attendance* | |
| Weekly | 27.2 |
| Once a month but less than weekly | 23.6 |
| Less than once a month | 18.3 |
| Never | 14.3 |
| *Importance of Religion* | |
| Very important | 28.5 |
| Fairly important | 18.8 |
| Fairly unimportant | 14.9 |
| Not important at all | 13.8 |
| *Abstinence Pledge* | |
| Took the pledge | 30.5 |
| Did not take the pledge | 20.2 |
| Overall | 22.6 |

*Source*: National Longitudinal Study of Adolescent Health

more likely to pause sexual activity in order to use contraception (Miller and Gur 2002). Nevertheless, confusion abounds about the contraceptive strategies of sexually active *religious* adolescents (Brewster et al. 1998; Studer and Thornton 1987; Thomson 1982). In a study of sexually active adolescent girls, white "fundamentalists" were least likely to use condoms during first intercourse (Kahn, Rindfuss, and Guilkey 1990). Adolescent boys who reported no religious affiliation had lower rates of condom use than those who claimed any religious affiliation (Ku et al. 1992). Another study found mainline Protestant women aged 15–24 among the most likely to use contraception at first sex (Jones et al. 2005). Religiosity also predicts skepticism about the efficacy of condoms and oral contraceptives (Wayment et al. 2003).

Indeed, skepticism about contraception's effectiveness was a very common theme among many of our interviewees, religious or not. Some spoke of using multiple methods of birth control since the failure rate for any one of them was thought to be higher than the manufacturers' claims. This cynicism resonates with the abstinence pledge movement's attempt to point out the "failure rates" of most forms of contraception (and by contrast to note the effectiveness of abstinence). Much of their attention is directed at condom failure rates, perhaps since they are the contraceptive of choice among most adolescents and tend to prevent both STDs and pregnancy. What is lost in failure rate debates, however, is the fact that such rates often assume an unclear frequency of sexual activity that nevertheless far outpaces that of most sexually active adolescents, the majority of whom do not have sex multiple times each week. In sum, contraceptives tend to work as advertised for the overwhelming majority who use them.[9]

But in order to work as advertised, oral contraceptives must be taken daily, or condoms used at each instance of intercourse. This is the "failure rate" that is most pertinent. I conversed at length on this matter with a pair of interviewees during the summer 2005 follow-up, and both said that they typically used contraception but could identify multiple instances in which they did not. Sure, it was risky, they admitted. Yet when decision-making time came around, they either chose not to use contraception or had none available. One had sweated through two pregnancy scares—and is hardly alone. Some adolescents refuse intercourse without contraception, or select a different sexual activity, but others forge ahead despite the risks.

Table 5.9 reports the percentage of adolescents who used some form of birth control at their first and last experience of intercourse (and the difference between those two). Do the same religious associations hold for contraceptive use as with contraceptive attitudes? Not really. Among adolescents who were no longer virgins at Wave I of the Add Health study, Mormon youth were the "safest" during first sex, at 92 percent. However, since relatively few Mormons (22 percent of a small subsample) reported being nonvirgins at Wave I, this number may be a statistical anomaly, especially since it does not intuitively follow other stable patterns we have seen.[10] Most religious affiliations crowded somewhere around 65 percent. Jewish nonvirgins—also a small group—reported just over 55 percent contraceptive use at first sex.[11]

The second column displays the use of birth control at the most recent experience of intercourse.[12] Among sexually active adolescents, Mormons and mainline Protestant youth were the safest during their most recent experience of intercourse, at 84 and 71 percent, respectively. Most other religious groups crowded around 70 percent, except for evangelical Protestants, the lowest at 62 percent. Religiosity does not predict actual contraceptive use nearly as well

TABLE 5.9 Adolescents Using Any Method of Birth Control at
First Sex and Most Recent Sex (in Percentages), Wave I

| | *First sex* | *Most recent sex* | *Difference* |
|---|---|---|---|
| *Religious Tradition* | | | |
| Evangelical Protestant | 63.1 | 61.8 | −1.3 |
| Mainline Protestant | 68.2 | 71.4 | 3.2 |
| Black Protestant | 63.4 | 69.7 | 6.3 |
| Catholic | 67.7 | 69.5 | 1.8 |
| Jewish | 56.1 | 69.7 | 13.6 |
| Mormon (LDS) | 91.8 | 84.0 | −7.8 |
| Other religion | 64.6 | 72.7 | 8.1 |
| No religion | 59.5 | 63.9 | 4.4 |
| *Church Attendance* | | | |
| Weekly | 65.2 | 67.4 | 2.2 |
| Once a month but less than weekly | 66.9 | 70.2 | 3.3 |
| Less than once a month | 67.1 | 69.9 | 2.8 |
| Never | 61.0 | 65.1 | 4.1 |
| *Importance of Religion* | | | |
| Very important | 66.1 | 66.4 | 0.3 |
| Fairly important | 66.1 | 71.3 | 5.2 |
| Fairly unimportant | 64.0 | 66.8 | 2.8 |
| Not important at all | 60.1 | 63.7 | 3.6 |
| Overall | 64.7 | 67.8 | 3.1 |

*Source*: National Longitudinal Study of Adolescent Health

as it does attitudes about the morality of contraception. Indeed, no clear pattern is evident. In statistical analyses of actual contraceptive use at first sex and at the most recent experience of intercourse (among the newly sexually active), religion plays a much smaller role in actual birth control decisions than in shaping attitudes about contraception (results in Table A5.8). This was true of sex as well: religion predicts attitudes a good deal better than it predicts behavior. No religious affiliation differences were noted in the models, and they were dropped. Nevertheless, youth for whom religion is more important are still less likely to use contraception at first sex, even after controls are included.

The third column in Table 5.9 displays the percentage point difference between the rates of contraceptive use at first and last sex. Given that the first experience of sexual intercourse is far more likely to be unplanned than the most recent experience, we should expect the difference between the two to be positive. It is *not*, however, for evangelicals and Mormons. And among Roman Catholics, contraceptive use over time only increases by 1.8 percentage points. While I have already noted the small number of sexually active Mormons and do not wish to speculate too much about so few, there are plenty of sexually active evangelicals in the data set. Simply put, about one in three of them—whose overall contraceptive rates are lower than most—are either (1) denying their sexual activity and as a result failing to procure contraception regularly, (2) too embarrassed to obtain contraception regularly, or (3) actively resisting the use of contraception. I cannot easily distinguish among the three, but given their low rates of moral misgivings about birth control, the first answer is more likely.

## Contraceptive Consistency

Up until this point, I have explored contraceptive use at first sex and at most recent sex. What about the times in between? The NSYR asked about consistency in contraceptive use among adolescents who reported having sex more than once, and statistics from that survey appear in Table 5.10, sorted by religion measures.[13] Among sexually active youth, mainline Protestants are clearly the most likely to be consistent. Just under 80 percent say they use contraception every time.[14] Only about 2 percent of them say they never do. By comparison, only 62 percent of sexually active evangelical youths use contraception every time, and 6 percent say they never have. Roman Catholic adolescents display the lowest percentage of every-time users (52 percent), and 5 percent say they never do.

Although church attendance and personal religious salience often predict the same outcomes in the same directions, this is not the case with predicting contraceptive use. Among sexually active adolescents, youth who attend church more than once a week—only about 8 percent of sexually active adolescents—are much less likely to use contraception every time they have sex: 47 percent, compared to 60–64 percent of less religious youth. On the other hand, youth who say that religion is extremely important to them—12 percent of the sexually active population—are the most likely to report using contraception every time: 69 percent.

What might account for this? The most likely explanation has to do with race: African-American youth account for a disproportionate share of the sexually active youths who say that religion is extremely important to them. Additionally, among sexually active adolescents, the correlation between religious salience and educational expectations is highest among African Americans.

TABLE 5.10 Consistency of Contraception Use among Adolescents Reporting Having Had Sex More than Once (in Percentages), by Religiosity Measures

|  | Every time | Almost every time | Some of the time | Never |
|---|---|---|---|---|
| *Religious Tradition* | | | | |
| Evangelical Protestant | 61.6 | 20.3 | 11.8 | 6.3 |
| Mainline Protestant | 78.2 | 11.8 | 8.3 | 1.8 |
| Black Protestant | 57.3 | 27.9 | 11.7 | 3.1 |
| Catholic | 52.4 | 25.2 | 17.4 | 5.0 |
| No religion | 66.9 | 17.4 | 12.1 | 3.6 |
| *Church Attendance* | | | | |
| More than once a week | 47.0 | 23.4 | 21.5 | 8.1 |
| Weekly | 63.7 | 19.7 | 8.2 | 8.4 |
| Up to 2–3 times a month | 63.7 | 21.3 | 12.7 | 2.4 |
| Never | 59.8 | 22.2 | 14.5 | 3.5 |
| *Importance of Religion* | | | | |
| Extremely important | 69.1 | 14.1 | 15.1 | 1.7 |
| Very important | 56.5 | 23.6 | 12.8 | 7.1 |
| Somewhat important | 62.9 | 22.1 | 11.1 | 3.9 |
| Not very important | 62.9 | 22.0 | 14.2 | 1.0 |
| Not important at all | 59.1 | 20.4 | 16.9 | 3.6 |
| *Moral Authority* | | | | |
| Do what makes me happy | 62.4 | 21.0 | 11.4 | 5.3 |
| Do what gets me ahead | 55.4 | 25.5 | 15.2 | 3.9 |
| Do what an adult or parent says | 68.5 | 18.9 | 10.9 | 1.7 |
| Do what God or Scripture says | 50.2 | 20.5 | 19.5 | 9.8 |

*Source*: National Survey of Youth and Religion

*Notes*: Numbers may not sum to 100% due to rounding. Mormon and Jewish youth, in addition to youth from other religions, were dropped due to small sample sizes.

Thus, devout African-American youth—for whom religiosity did not prevent sexual activity to begin with—are more likely than their less devout counterparts to understand pregnancy as limiting their educational life chances and thus pursue contraception.

Back to the results: sexually active adolescents who are frequent church attenders are two to three times as likely as less religious youths to say they have never used contraception (about 8 percent versus 2–3 percent). This corresponds with the Add Health results about both the consistency of and the morality of contraceptive use. As I noted above, devoutly religious youths are clearly more conflicted about the act of sex and about obtaining birth control, but even after first sex, some remain concerned about the morality of using contraception, weighing this against the potential consequences of non-use.

Finally, sources of morality in decision making display clear associations with contraceptive use. Only 50 percent of sexually active youth who try to do what they think God or Scripture tells them is right report contraceptive use every time they have sex, down from 69 percent of youth who say they would do what a parent, teacher, or other (respected) adult tells them. Nearly 10 percent of the God-or-Scripture group say they *never* use contraception, compared with only 2 percent of the parent–respected adult group. The effect of avoiding contraceptive use in the God-or-Scripture group is in fact limited to girls (results not shown).

Again, I don't wish to overstate the strength of these associations. Statistical analyses of both Add Health and NSYR actual contraceptive use outcomes suggest that most of the bivariate associations with religion and religiosity are weak. A pair of findings nevertheless stands out:

- Sexually active mainline Protestant teens are still more likely than evangelical Protestant teens to report using contraception on a regular basis, even after controlling for age, gender, religiosity, parents' education, etc.
- Sexually active teens who say that, when in a moral quandary, they would do what a parent, teacher, or other respected adult advises are more likely to report regular contraceptive use than those who say they would do what God or Scriptures teach.

Although we did not explicitly ask about contraceptive decisions in our in-person interviews, the topic of "safe sex" came up with some degree of regularity. I am struck by how many adolescents—many of them religious but some not—tell us that contraception is not as effective as public health officials suggest. While the vast majority of adolescents approve of contraception, actual usage is sporadic. Why? One recent conclusion favors cultural explanations over emotional or rational ones in explaining high user-failure and discontinuation rates, especially among more religious youth (Woodsong et al. 2004: 72):

[D]istrust of the health care system that provides them, belief in God's will as the paramount authority on childbearing, and a cosmology of natural order are...all intertwined in one of the deepest emotional processes that commonly confronts [us]—the development and maintenance of familial and sexual relationships.

On the other hand, when less religious youth bring up unprotected sex, the conversation ironically can take on a moral tone: people *ought* to use contraception. In a social world in which religious reasons for avoiding sex no longer make sense, religious sexual morality is being replaced by a more individualistic, future-focused morality that guards adolescents' chances at happiness, education, and a prosperous future. Many, many parents reinforce this, which makes sense in light of the findings above about "doing what my parents tell me."

Unprotected sex has thus become—for some—a moral issue like smoking or driving a car without a seatbelt. It's not just unwise any more; it's wrong. We quickly notice how out of place—maybe even immoral—smoking is when we observe it in a hospital room or around small children. Like failing to buckle a child in a car seat, unprotected sex is frowned upon in the new moral order of adolescent sexuality. No one wants to be known for doing it, even if they prefer it. It is becoming socially unacceptable, having been consistently derided by public health officials and sex educators. Also, insisting that they're being safe helps adolescents to convince themselves that they are responsible, and thus ready for sex. Not a few adolescents with whom we spoke—including Kristin in chapter 1—talk about their parents being *more* disappointed in their having unsafe sex than with their loss of virginity. Lots of parents are primarily concerned that their kids not get themselves or someone else pregnant. For adolescents not steeped in a religious tradition, unprotected sex is becoming a new taboo, replacing premarital sex in its ability to provoke shock and concern.

## Regrets and Negative Experiences

First intercourse is no cake walk for many, and plenty regret some aspect of the experience—typically the "when" or the "with whom." In a study comparable to Add Health, fully 55 percent of sexually experienced 15- to 19-year-olds wish they had waited longer to have sex (Albert, Brown, and Flanigan 2003). That number rises to 81 percent of 12- to 14-year-olds. In the National Health and Social Life Survey, fewer women in the youngest cohorts report having wanted their first experience of vaginal intercourse to happen when it did (Laumann et al. 1994). Early adolescents are more likely to regret sexual experience, yet also more likely to subsequently acquire additional sex partners.

The NSYR research team asked interviewees if they had any negative sexual experiences and often inquired about any regrets or things about sex that respondents wish they had known earlier. Most (though not all) of the boys who had already had sex do not regret anything about their decisions. When they do, they tended to regret the *person* with whom they first had intercourse. Brian, a 17-year-old practicing Catholic from Minnesota, complained: "Yeah. I, yeah, I kind of, I do regret losing my virginity, but . . . only because it was with that person. I mean, I'm sure I would have eventually."

Negative experiences are far more common among adolescent girls, although surprisingly the physical pain of first intercourse is not often listed. Pregnancy scares (and actual pregnancies) are rarer than I had anticipated. Girls are also less likely to complain about their first sexual partner than are boys. Christiana, an 18-year-old Hispanic Catholic from California, had numerous grievances, but her particular sexual partner was not one of them. She fits the portrait of the (rare) one-timer perfectly:

> It was just, I don't know, I just felt like it was, I thought I was ready, but you know, obviously I wasn't. [*What do you mean obviously you weren't?*] Because I was young. And then, I was 16, and I was, I was just dumb. And I thought, "Oh, you know," 'cause I was all excited, 'cause he was like, um, probably like the longest boyfriend I've ever had. And I just thought, "Oh, you know. Why not? Whatever; it's no big deal. Everyone else is doing it. Why not?" So I just gave in and it happened. [*How do you feel about that now?*] I regret it. I mean, I don't regret that it was him, but it was just kind of like we were so young, you know, and I wasn't really ready, so, you know. . . . I realized I didn't even like him, you know.

Talli, a 16-year-old inactive mainline Protestant from South Dakota, has several regrets, including the age (14) at which she first had sex and with whom. She manages a competing set of emotions—that sexual choices ultimately don't matter and that they do:

> Yeah, I would, I would regret losing my virginity to who I lost it to. . . . I, uh, I had, you know, 'cause everybody made fun of me 'cause I was a virgin. And I thought it was like a bad thing to be a virgin, so I went out and lost it to this guy I didn't even know, so I regret that. . . . I'd regret just a bunch of things, yeah. [*How do you feel, I mean, you lost your virginity to someone you didn't want to, and based on what you said [earlier] it sounds like you and Lance [current boyfriend] have sex. Um, how do you feel about that? Is it good? Is it bad? Do you have regrets about it?*] Um, it doesn't really matter. It doesn't matter that, I don't think it matters. [*What do you mean it doesn't matter?*] Like sex. It doesn't matter, I don't think.

Tyne, a 17-year-old inactive Catholic from Arizona, had decided at one point to stay a virgin "forever," in her words. But she changed her mind. Why?

I don't know. I just don't want to be a virgin no more I guess. [*OK, and why do you think you didn't want to?*] I don't know. [*And how many people have you had sex with?*] Five. [*OK, and, like, how do you feel about it? Like, how do you feel about it now?*] Um . . . I regret it. I wish I would have waited until I got married, but. [*Why do you wish you would have waited?*] Um, because then you, like, know that that's the right one and stuff like that and just don't, like, give something up and then have them leave or something like that. [*OK, like, how do you feel about that, not having waited?*] Um . . . I'm, like, disappointed in myself. [*And how do you deal with it?*] Um, I deal with it. I don't know, I just . . . don't think about it all that much.

Kimberly, an 18-year-old, religiously inactive Mormon from Utah, states that having sex

messed me up emotionally and physically. . . . I mean I was depressed for a while but my friends helped me through it so. [*And do you think that had an effect on your dating relationships?*] Oh yeah. [*In what way?*] It just, I wouldn't, I wouldn't get close to anybody. . . . I think people don't realize how emotionally involved you get.

Valerie, the 15-year-old active Pentecostal featured in chapter 1, had underestimated the responsibilities that come with sexual activity:

I wasn't thinking about the responsibilities with just doing anything, like, sexual, and you know, there's a lot of responsibilities that come along with it. Like, it's just not, it's not, like, sex and pleasure, but there's, like, things you have to know and, like, protect yourself and stuff.

Laura Carpenter (2005b) notes that many women report feeling disappointed that the loss of virginity failed to feel as "romantic" as they were led to believe. For not a few, it is physically painful (Martin 2002; Thompson 1990). Only about 3 percent of the women in the National Health and Social Life Survey listed physical pleasure as the main reason they engaged in their first experience of sex (Laumann et al. 1994). In her work on mass media, Carpenter (2005a) notes that popular movies that concern virginity loss tend to resolve "non-ideal" experiences in more pleasant or happier ways than is the case in real life. This probably comes as no surprise to many adults, for whom movie sex has long seemed unrealistic, if ideal. Adolescents, however, would not likely understand this unless informed of such. Sharon Thompson (1990) similarly notes that "the letdown so many girls describe is not wholly physical. It is romantic as well. Girls often expect that having sex will transform an uneven relationship into a blissful fusion," only to be disappointed. This is not the case for all teenage girls, she cautions, but perhaps a majority.

Carpenter finds that girls feel the discrepancies between their ideal and real experiences of first sex more poignantly than do boys. Karin Martin (2002) agrees, and notes the narrative work that girls do in order to help themselves feel "better about confusing and disappointing sexual experiences" (2002: 161). She suggests that there are multiple scripts about sex that girls must negotiate, including the cultural script that says sex is wonderful and romantic. Between themselves, on the other hand, they share stories about the physical painfulness of virginity loss, the sexual misbehavior of "sluts," and the necessity of sexual attractiveness to retain boyfriends. Finally, there is the experience itself, which may not fit *any* of these scripts (and may even occur without their full volition). Such narrative work, evident in many NSYR interviewee accounts, "is an attempt to reconcile these contradictory feelings and scripts...a method of balancing what happened, how things are 'supposed' to happen...and how one wants them to be" (2002: 161). She concludes that adolescent girls have to do a good deal of such narrative work in order to come to grips with their sexual experiences. Given the back-and-forth tone of acceptance and denial in many of the girls' accounts featured in this chapter, I think Martin is on to something.

On the other hand, many adolescent boys' accounts (in the NSYR) of negative sexual experiences turn out to be not about emotional pain but rather sexual encounters gone awry, sex that was "less than satisfying," not getting enough sex, being too undiscriminating in their choice of sexual partners, etc. We occasionally encountered one who wished he had waited a while longer, or who feels unprepared and not grown up enough to handle sexual responsibilities, but these are not common, and very few speak of wishing they had waited until marriage. It is as if marriage is a more distant and unattractive ideal for today's adolescent boys than it is for girls. The latter can look ahead and envision it; many of the former cannot see it. Gary, a 17-year-old nonreligious adolescent from Michigan, complained about "bad" sex, but was also one of very few interviewees who expressed concern about how his sexual *partner* felt:

It wasn't until after we had been having sex for a while that she told me that she was having some regrets about not waiting until she was married, and that kind of made me feel bad 'cause I felt like I was, like, harming her. But then that was, but then she never, she never really, that was just something that I think she felt guilty about because that's how she was raised. But then she, I mean, obviously she had her own decision in the matter and she chose to do it. But I think she just felt bad that she went against the way she was brought up.... I think that happened on several different occasions where she brought that up.

Most adolescent boys' accounts of sexual experience fail entirely to mention the emotions of their sexual partners; perhaps most girls don't mention them because they assume their partners had no regrets (and most did not). The fact that so few teenagers we interviewed mention anything beyond a cursory description of their first sexual partner reinforces a point I made earlier in this chapter: sexual relationships have been decoupled. We don't speak of young Americans as having premarital sexual *relationships*; instead, we say they have premarital *sex*.

## Rape and Molestation

The prevalence of negative sexual experiences among adolescent girls we interviewed was higher than anticipated. Eight girls from our sample reported having been raped (or told us their first experience of intercourse was without full volition and choice), and another eight spoke of having been molested. Together, these comprise about 15 percent of the girls we interviewed.[15] Estimates from Add Health suggest that 7 percent of its total Wave I female sample, and 16 percent of all 18-year-old girls, report having ever been forced into sexual intercourse (Raghavan et al. 2004). Additionally, 4 in 10 new reports of forced sex between Waves I and II were from girls who were virgins at Wave I. Since Add Health is a school-based sample, were we able to include school dropouts, the rate would no doubt be higher still. While the NSYR interview sample is not completely random, it is close enough to other national statistics to elicit concern that perhaps one in seven American girls have a forced introduction to sexual activity. Too much has come to light about sexual violence in America to presume this to be a statistical quirk or sampling error. While I have seen no evident religious patterns in either the perpetration of adolescent sexual violence or in its victimization, the issue itself deserves mention here.

Nonconsensual sex seldom includes contraception, almost always involves older adolescent boys or adult men, and certainly does not leave its victims in a position to quickly regain emotional stability and relational trust. Additionally, many victims of nonconsensual sex have trouble confidently defining it as such. There also appears to be a tangible difference for many between unwanted sex and forced sex. In fact, 25 percent of adult women in one nationally representative study call their first experience of intercourse not wanted yet not forced (Laumann et al. 1994). In such confusing situations, adolescent girls seldom seek to prosecute the perpetrator. Rarer still are successful prosecutions. Kendra, a 14-year-old African-American evangelical from Washington, DC, describes such a scenario:

I didn't know him; he didn't know me. We just had a spur-of-the-moment thing. [*Uh-huh, uh-huh, OK.*] It was something that really wasn't, I wasn't raped, but it was something that was taken more than given. It was about 20 percent given and 80 percent taken. [*Why do you say 80 percent taken?*] Because it wasn't something I was prepared to do. [*Yeah.*] It was something that he wanted, and he got it, so. [*Yeah, OK. How did you deal with it?*] I didn't. I tried to rub it off, you know, get it out of my system, get it out of me, get it [out]. But I didn't, I didn't deal with that. I don't think about it.

Several of Karin Martin's (2002: 161) interviewees reported similar experiences. Some of the girls did not know "if sex is something she willed and made happen [or not]," and they feel unclear about their role in its occurrence. She notes that several girls "seemed to have felt they had lost some part of their selves" (2002: 161). Sex for them was not an interaction but rather boys taking something from them.

## RACE MATTERS

Being involved in religion, taking it seriously, and making it a priority helps most adolescents to delay their first experience of intercourse. This is much less true for African Americans, according to Table 5.2, where the association between religion and sex is much weaker overall and is mildly protective only among the most devout.

Most of the African-American adolescents with whom we spoke articulated their churches' position on sexual behavior, and many even agreed with it, but few either practiced it or believed they would continue to live up to it. The standard of waiting until marriage seems hopelessly idealistic and perhaps even inapplicable to their situations. It is *not* a high priority, in no small part because marriage feels distant or unlikely or—as a *Washington Post* column recently speculated—a "white thing" (Jones 2006).[16]

The pervasiveness of sex seems to have spawned a passive, inevitable, "it just happens" perspective for many African-American youth, which was evident in the interviews. When we asked the religiously active Cassandra, a 17-year-old Methodist, about adolescent sexual involvement, she claimed that 99 percent of her friends are sexually active and that she herself has recently become so. Yet she claims, in spite of this, "I haven't really thought about it." Her description stands in stark contrast to many white girls we interviewed, who commonly display a vocabulary of control and sexual strategy or else a constructed helplessness—some said they were romantically overcome "by the moment"—all of which comprise a popular sexual script. But it is different from the more genuinely passive, resigned sexual script evident among African-American girls.

As a result, African-American Christian adolescents appear more likely to understand sex as biological, stimulus and response rather than a battle to be waged (which is more of a white Christian model). Jarrod's words from chapter 1 echo here: "I do think it's [sex is] bad, but I think it's something that most of us can't help, you know. It's chemical, you know, hormones." The locus of control is externalized upon arousal: hormones "take over," and sex happens. If a person can't help it, then all the good intentions, protective attitudes, and religious support in the world may seem powerless.

On the other hand, perhaps white Christian adolescents are far too hung up on sex and that *this* is the unusual phenomenon to be explained, rather than the other way around. However, the black church, white evangelical Protestants, and conservative Catholics do not formally disagree on most sexual issues (contraception notwithstanding). African-American Christians have historically been even more reluctant to tolerate homosexuality within the Church than white Protestants and Catholics. Yet African-American youth are less likely to see themselves as embattled about sex, fighting to resist its lures. The words of one young man quoted in another study capture this well: "[it's] time to be a man and learn the ways of the world. Leave the church to the women" (Lincoln and Mamiya 1990: 305).[17]

## EVANGELICALS' SYMBOLIC SEXUAL TRADITIONALISM

It is popularly held that evangelical Protestants are the most conservative American religious tradition with respect to sexual attitudes and behaviors (Hunter 1987; Penning and Smidt 2002). Perhaps the most stunning finding in this chapter is that the data only offer support for the first of these. Evangelicals do in fact maintain more conservative attitudes about sex than do mainline Protestants, black Protestants, and Jewish youth. They are the second most likely (after Mormons) to think that having sex will make them feel guilty, least likely to think that sex is pleasurable, and most likely to think that having sex will cause their partner to disrespect them (see Table 4.4). But evangelical Protestant youth are *not* the religious group least likely to have sex. Indeed, in both data sets, they are largely indistinguishable from the rest of American adolescents.[18] Mormons, Jews, and mainline Protestant youths are *less* likely to report having had sex, controlling for religiosity. And while evangelicals are the most likely to be sexual delayers, they are far from the least likely to have had multiple sexual partners. For a group that often prides itself on its embattledness with the popular culture around it, such numbers are certainly unnerving (Smith et al. 1998). Why might evangelical youth say one thing about sex but do another?

## Evangelicalism ≠ Religiosity

One key reason that evangelicals often don't stand out is because the measure itself—affiliating with an evangelical Protestant congregation—is not a measure of dynamic religiosity but simply one of affiliation. To sum up several years of my own research on religious influences on adolescent behavior, the real story is almost always about religiosity—how devout people are. This is where the action (the influence) tends to occur, not with something so easy as mere affiliation. However, scholars and practitioners alike tend to equate evangelicalism with religiosity. This is a mistake. Affiliating with an evangelical congregation doesn't make someone devout. There is no shortage of religiously apathetic evangelical adolescents and adults in America. Yet most research conclusions about evangelicals are from studies of affiliation or self-identity alone, not combined with religiosity. Thus, my results may be picking up, in part, on the sexual practices of evangelical youth whose religiosity is average or below average. This certainly cannot explain all of the discrepancy, however. There are several parts to a fulfilling explanation.

## Evangelical and Social Class Distinctions in Sexual Behavior

Another piece of the puzzle has to do with social class distinctions both in sexual behavior and within evangelicalism. In her study of adolescent sexual decision making, Karin Martin (2002) pays little explicit attention to religion but a good deal to social class distinctions. She notes that middle-class girls are more able to say no to sex than are their working-class counterparts. While mine is not a study about social class any more than Martin's is about religion, her findings may help us here. In the NSYR, youth from less-educated families are more likely to have had sex, and the parents of both evangelical and black Protestant youth are, on average, significantly less educated than Mormon, mainline Protestant, and Jewish parents.

Further, Martin notes that girls from middle-class (and upper-class) backgrounds—characteristic of mainline Protestant and Jewish families—have

TABLE 5.11 Evangelical Adolescents Who Experienced First Sex
between Study Waves, Split by Family Advantage
(in Percentages), Wave I Virgins Only

|  | Family advantage | No family advantage |
| --- | --- | --- |
| Overall | 10.2 | 18.5 |
| Attends church weekly | 6.8 | 13.9 |
| Religion is very important | 8.0 | 14.4 |

*Source*: National Longitudinal Study of Adolescent Health

*Note*: Family advantage = one or more parents has/have a college degree, and adolescent lives in a biologically intact, two-parent family.

more subjective knowledge and information about sex, tend to be slightly older when they experience first sex, and are less idealistic about their romantic interests. All of these factors ring true with the data I have presented so far. Table 5.11 displays the share of evangelical adolescents who were virgins at Wave I of Add Health and who reported having had sex by Wave II. I split them into two class-based groups, labeled here as "family advantage." If the respondent lived in a biologically intact, two-parent family and at least one of those parents had a college degree, I identified them as being advantaged; if one or both of those qualifications did not hold, I identified them as not having a family advantage.

What do we learn from this? First, family advantage matters for evangelicals, regardless of religiosity. While about 19 percent of evangelical youth who are not advantaged in this way lost their virginity over the course of a year, just over 10 percent of evangelicals who have such an advantage reported this. Religiosity also helps, but not above and beyond the advantage of family structure and social class. While about 7–8 percent of the most religious evangelicals from advantaged families reported losing their virginity, and around 14 percent of the most religious from less-advantaged families did so, the independent effect of religiosity didn't help either group more than the other. In other words, while religiosity helps evangelical youth, it pales in its influence compared to family and education factors. I should note, too, that high religiosity is more of a trademark of advantaged evangelical families: 75 percent attend church weekly, compared with 51 percent of less-advantaged evangelical families. I conclude from all this that there are social class and family factors that help to account, in part, for sexual behavior distinctions among evangelicals. But these results also tell us that religiosity is not uniquely protective of advantaged evangelical youth; it helps both groups about equally (but does not equalize their outcomes).

## *Evangelicals and Cultural Collision*

A third, more compelling piece of the story has nothing at all to do with measurement or social class. It transcends them. It has to do with the collision of cultures and is grounded in larger historical changes that have altered how Americans understand families. Scholars and observers agree that evangelicals esteem the *idea* of marriage and marital commitment. Evangelicals were much more likely to have gotten married by Wave III of Add Health (29 percent) than mainline Protestants, Catholics, and Jews. Few evangelical youths are looking for sex (see Table 5.5 about sexual anticipators). They are more ambivalent about birth control either in principle or in use. They give voice to conservative sexual mores amid a clearly promiscuous popular culture. So we know that evangelical youths are family traditionalists, at least in their ideals if not always in their actions.

All of this, however, is occurring at a time when adolescent reproductive rights and options appear to remain firmly in place, together with new and popular sources of sexual socialization (the Internet, pornography). The ubiquity of permissive sexual norms from Hollywood and the mass media are not lost on them, either. Evangelical teens are no less likely to appreciate popular films and music than other types of youth. While once parents might have been able to monitor and control evangelical youth media selections, the rapidly increasing number of media sources is making this difficult. Cell phones, MP3 players, iTunes, and the Internet have expanded media access to all youth, evangelicals included. If in the past the battle was keeping kids out of movie theaters and dances—something few evangelical parents even try to do any more—the battle against sexually permissive media content must now be waged on dozens of fronts, most of them well outside parental control.

All of this points to a cultural collision for evangelical adolescents and young adults, who find themselves professing traditional sexual norms yet increasingly tempted by new ones. In such an atmosphere, attitudes about sex may *formally* remain unchanged (and restrictive) while sexual activity becomes increasingly common. This clash of cultures and norms is felt most poignantly in the so-called Bible Belt, the swath of the Midwest and South curving down from Kansas and Oklahoma south to the Gulf Coast and then angling upward into the Carolinas. Indeed, it parallels the high divorce rate problem we see there. While some might suggest that evangelicals are failing to live up to their stated beliefs about divorce and sexuality, I would turn attention instead to the clash of cultures, which is felt most poignantly there.

I don't believe that there are more hypocrites in the Bible Belt than elsewhere. I suspect hypocrisy is more evenly distributed (although some of my colleagues would disagree). Rather, two powerful cultures meet most evidently there: the culture of traditionalist, evangelical religion, with its family-centered ideals and norms, and the culture of postmodern, consumption-oriented, media-saturated, self-focused, individualist capitalism. This is *not* a value judgment—it is simply an observation. As they engage with the surrounding consumer culture, evangelicals are clearly drinking deeply from some of the river's tributaries. And like when a warm and a cold front meet, producing a thunderstorm, so too does the confluence of these two potent cultural forces result in dissonance and conflict. Thus, we see both high marriage rates *and* high divorce rates, together with elevated teenage pregnancy rates, etc. Young evangelicals feel that they "should" get married, but they also feel—courtesy of changing marital norms—that they are entitled to happy marriages, satisfaction from spouses, freedom, sexual happiness, etc. (May 1980). Additionally, the Bible Belt still displays a marrying and childbearing culture (unlike other regions of the country where cohabitation has become normative and childlessness common). But here again, evangelicals feel no less than other Americans the pressures of marriage and childrearing, and many no longer experience the same kind of social support from extended family members they once might have, due to geographic mobility, smaller families, etc. In turn, not a few seek divorce, only to try again at marriage. They *believe* in the institution of marriage, even if a particular marital experience falls short of their ideals.

So it goes for evangelical adolescents with regard to sex; they are at the confluence of cold and warm fronts. They remain in an abstaining religious sexual culture, one that is trying multiple strategies to prevent premarital sex—including both demystifying sex as something that even dogs do and honoring human sexuality by reminding adolescents that God created sex and intended it to be pleasurable. Yet, they are more exposed than ever to the sexualized culture around them. The award-winning documentary *The Education of Shelby Knox* (2005) powerfully documents an example of such a "storm" in Lubbock, Texas, where teen pregnancies and STD rates remained high, even as Shelby—a young woman who took a pledge of abstinence—and others struggled in vain to gain access to a more comprehensive sexual education. Christian teenagers in Lubbock, however, are not very different from youth in other parts of the country. They too like popular music and television shows like "The OC"; they too like to hang out with friends; they too like to surf the Web; they too feel pressure to be in the "in" crowd and have a boyfriend or girlfriend. And in their sexually conservative West Texas culture, the fronts collide.

What results from this cultural collision? Evangelical adolescents know they're not supposed to have sex before marriage, but marriage feels like a long way off (and it often is). Few of them are sexual anticipators, so contraception, while it's probably OK for married people, isn't for them since they're not supposed to be thinking about having sex (remember, good girls don't plan). Virginity is a big deal.

As a result, sex eventually "happens" to most evangelical youths, despite their best intentions (and pledges to abstain), and it tends to be within a committed, romantic relationship. Some feel guilty about it.[19] There are few evangelical one-timers, so sex tends to recur. For a significant minority both at first sex and perhaps at subsequent instances, sex doesn't involve contraception. Sharon Thompson (1990: 350) notes that many girls "are stunned by sex several times before they realize that they are very likely to have sex again, and prepare for that eventuality by obtaining contraception." Additionally, for evangelical teenagers within the confines of a committed romantic relationship, the perceived risk of STDs, the thought of pregnancy, and the responsibilities of marriage may not be as intimidating. Remember, evangelicals are sexual traditionalists in a variety of ways: intercourse makes more sense to them than substituting oral sex (Uecker, Angotti, and Regnerus 2006). They are more likely to follow a traditional script in which women follow men's romantic lead. They tend to marry earlier and have earlier first births (Jones et al. 2005; Xu, Hudspeth, and Bartkowski 2005). A team of psychologists of religion and the family has even noted that conceiving of sex as *sacred* can contribute to unmarried intercourse (Mahoney et al. 2003). Certainly, evangelicals are more apt to think of sex as sacred. However, for others in less optimal situations, abortion—something they have always been taught to abhor—comes to be seen as a rational, if regrettable, solution to their situation. In such cases, telling their parents about a pregnancy sounds unthinkable.

### Sex as a Symbolic Boundary

Sex is a symbolic boundary for evangelical Protestants, demarcating the good from the deviant. Some forms of sexual practice, like homosexuality, remain universally wrong among them. Pre-premarital sex is still considered wrong, but premarital sex between engaged adults certainly decreasingly so. Symbolic boundaries are collectively important to voice, but actual enforcement is arbitrary and rapidly disappearing (Smith et al. 1998). This is likewise the case with divorce among evangelicals: it is no more than a symbolic boundary whose transgression is all but universally tolerated. Instead, battles rage over the *definition* of marriage—a symbol. The abstinence pledge movement is the symbolic resistance of evangelical Protestant youth. It is the small but determined force to which a significant minority of these youth claims allegiance, even while they are increasingly sneaking across enemy lines.

Mainline Protestant parents and adolescents, on the other hand, sense no conflict over "new" sexual norms. Sex is no longer a symbolic boundary for them. Instead, they are much more concerned with guarding adolescents' sexual safety and not obstructing their educational and economic futures. Remarkably, this is how mainline Protestant adolescents come to lose their virginity *later* than evangelicals, in spite of their more permissive attitudes. In chapter 6, we will better understand why this is so. Once they decide to have sex, it tends to be with contraception, sometimes even using multiple forms. So it is that mainline Protestants simply experience less of a cultural conflict about religion and contemporary life. There is no battle, nor even a collision.

## PLAUSIBILITY STRUCTURES

In the end, protective religious effects against extensive sexual activity come down to plausibility structures, to use the term coined by the eminent sociologist of religion Peter Berger (1967). *Plausibility structures* are the networks by which beliefs held by individuals or groups are sustained. Since we live in a diverse age when it comes to human sexuality, and since so much about contemporary sexual norms *could* be different—for example, we could just as well be living with Victorian-style norms about sex—the norms that do exist need to be sustained by plausibility structures in order to persist. That is, norms are kept alive by networks of people, organizations, and communities who tell each other that some ideas, actions, and arrangements are good and optimal, and some are bad and ought to be resisted. Teenagers who are embedded in religious plausibility structures—usually by way of more active religious involvement and stronger religious commitments—are more likely to make sense of their developing sexuality in religious terms, using distinctly religious motivation to ride out the storm of the adolescent religion-sex culture collision. Forms of religiosity and religious sources of moral decision making, not particular religious affiliations, are the key religious predictors of sexual outcomes. Evangelical youth are not *uniquely* immersed in such plausibility structures any more than are mainline Protestants, Catholics, and Jews. Some are; some are not. Consider Kristin, the Methodist/Baptist from chapter 1. While she sporadically attends religious services and is active in Young Life, she does not personalize or internalize their belief system or religious identity. She is going through the motions. She doesn't think of her body as "the temple of the Holy Spirit." God is a distant figure to her and is more interested in her personal growth and keeping her life in order than in making demands of her. Pro-sex arguments from her peers, her pursuit of popularity, her sense of being "ready," and her disinterest in virginity make a lot more sense to her than any religious advice she has heard on sex (and considering that she's participated in Young Life, she has probably heard plenty). Her sporadic religious involvement is not enough to affect her, lacking as it is in personal commitment and motivation on her part. Alternative plausibility structures (her friends and peers) that advance permissive norms about sex are much closer and dearer to her and more relevant than any religious messages she receives.

Frederica Mathewes-Green (2005b), a popular Christian writer and cultural critic, picks up on the competition among plausibility structures in her discussion of Christian approaches to discouraging adolescent sexual practice. She notes two common strategies that Christians use to promote abstinence, and she doesn't think either of them works. The first is *practical*: "we tell students to abstain because immorality leads to misery. But the libertines [the critics of abstinence] in the audience don't see evidence that this is so; they're having fun, for the most part, and it doesn't look like anyone is harmed" (2005b: 48). The second strategy she notes is *romantic*:

> We tell students that marriage is glorious. Once again, they don't see a lot of evidence of that, not in the lives of married people they know, perhaps especially in the lives of their parents. What they saw at the breakfast table for the last 18 years doesn't look that great, and what they did last night didn't feel that bad. (2005b: 48)

In the end, she concludes that such reasoning will typically fail: "All the warnings about the dangers of promiscuity, all the [talk of the] vaunted bliss of marriage, can be irrefutably countered by somebody's experience" (2005b: 48). Instead, what is called for is facing the stark reality of the challenge and growing deeper biblical roots: "Doing the right thing is not guaranteed to make you happy . . . but because the love of God constrains us, because our bodies are not our own but bought with a price, we persevere in a difficult path," motivated instead by the "self-abandoning love of God."

Lauren Winner (2005) concurs that sexual decision making may be most effectively shaped by the type and depth of the religious world view one occupies and immersion into a network of like-minded friends and family, rather than a particular religious behavior, a pledge ring, or membership in the local evangelical church or Catholic parish. A youth's training to remember proof texts or Bible verses that pertain to sex, such as Paul's advice to "flee sexual immorality" (1 Cor. 6:18) may fall flat in the heat of the moment, when neither partner feels much like fleeing.

Cultural critics like these, however, generally play to adults, who have had much more time and experience to reflect on sexuality than have adolescents.

Whether such complex and nuanced messages as theirs are making inroads among adolescents and young adults is difficult to document.

## CONCLUSIONS

Besides the biggest story of the chapter—that evangelical Protestant youth don't always practice what they preach about premarital sexual behavior—there are a few other themes worth reiterating.

First, American adolescents are not as oversexed as some observers have feared. There is a clear difference between perceptions of adolescence as a hypersexual life course period and the reality of what teenagers tell us in person. In fact, many of them do *not* want to have sex yet and plainly told us so. While this response is much more likely from girls, a number of boys—including some 17- and 18-year-olds—are either in no particular hurry to lose their virginity or else recognize the emotional and physical risks of sexual activity and have simply decided that they can afford to wait. The Internet and pornography, however, would have us believe that alternative sexual practices and group sex are increasingly common, even among adolescents. So far as I can tell, this is not true of teenagers. What is true, however, is the decoupling of how we talk about sexuality. Instead of youths having premarital sexual *relationships*, we say they have premarital *sex*. Even that is a misnomer, especially since marriage is a distant or optional notion, and for roughly half of the population is a temporary arrangement.

Second, solitary instances of sexual intercourse are unusual. Instead, virginity loss tends to commence a pattern of paired sexual activity, most commonly with more than one partner. By and large, teenagers either *are* having sex or they have not yet had it. Long-term, monogamous adolescent sexual partnerships are less common than a series of short-term sexual relationships.

Third, the idea of birth control and contraceptive protection against STDs enjoys very wide approval among contemporary teenagers. Yet actual contraceptive use is remarkably difficult to predict by religious, demographic, or any other variables.

The fourth and final story, and perhaps the most untold one, is that nearly across the board, religious influence on sexual decision making is most consistently the result of high religiosity rather than certain religious affiliations. This fact may be less exciting for scholars, religious leaders, and media pundits who enjoy pitting religious groups against each other, but the fact remains: if you really want to know what distinguishes youth who delay sex, who are less sexually active, and who have fewer lifetime sexual partners, you must look beyond the particular doctrines they espouse, their denominational figure-heads, and even any particular oath or attitude they might hold, to how immersed they are in religious plausibility structures and how connected they feel to family and friends who are—for lots of reasons—committed to helping them effectively navigate adolescence and its sexual pressures.

# *Chapter 6*

## IMITATION SEX AND THE NEW MIDDLE-CLASS MORALITY

*There's not really anything in the Bible that talks*
*about that kind of stuff.*

—Alison, 14-year-old evangelical Protestant

As most teenagers figure out, there's more than one form of sexual activity. Since virginity is clearly valued—and, to a lesser extent, practiced—among more devoutly religious youth, one might wonder whether the same value applies to abstinence from other forms of sexual activity. The NSYR asked questions about oral sex and the use of pornography. What emerges when I evaluate these two—in conjunction with the last chapter's focus on sexual intercourse—is evidence of a religious and social class patterning of sexual activity preference and a nascent middle-class sexual morality that is neither about religion nor about abstinence, but about risk reduction, safeguarding one's future, and sexual substitution.

### ORAL SEX

Much is made in the news media and in films, high school locker rooms, and parental conversations about the perceived rise in prevalence of oral sex. Media outlets have taken note of the "friends with benefits" phenomenon, which refers to casual oral sex (and occasionally intercourse) between friends who are not romantically involved with each other. Curiously, none of our interviewees volunteered the phrase "friends with benefits." Some no doubt experienced what the term captures, but the phenomenon is certainly less common than concerned parents may have been led to believe. Most adolescent sexual activity occurs within exclusive relationships, albeit comparatively short-term ones, not mere associations.

While oral sex can be given or received by either gender, when most adolescents talk about oral sex in the interviews, they are typically referring to the action that adolescent girls perform upon adolescent boys. Jeannette, an

18-year-old Catholic girl from New York state (who attends mass sporadically), intends to avoid sexual contact altogether until marriage, and she hasn't given much thought to distinguishing between oral and vaginal sex: "I don't even know what I think about oral sex. I don't know why anyone would want to do that." Among adolescent girls who have not had sex and are not dating anyone, this is the most common answer. Dating or being in a relationship with someone of the opposite sex, however, tends to color girls' perspectives on the topic.

There has also been a lot of talk about oral sex as a means by which youth maintain a technical virginity, as "third base," as "starter sex," and as a way to avoid pregnancy risks and some types of STDs (Lewin 1997; Remez 2000; Schuster et al. 1996).[1] Third base or not, oral sex is a more common introduction to sexual activity than is intercourse. Indeed, oral sex is about 50 percent more common than vaginal intercourse up until age 15 (results not shown). Somewhere between ages 15 and 17, intercourse catches up and surpasses oral sex in popularity. Whether its practitioners are trying to maintain a technical virginity is another matter, one to which I return shortly.

Table 6.1 displays statistics on oral sexual experience among 13- to 17-year-olds in the NSYR, sorted by religion and spirituality measures.[2] Teenagers of different religious affiliations range in oral sexual experience from a low of about 9 percent to a high of 30 percent. The difference in preference for *type* of sexual activity (in the NSYR) by religious affiliation is striking

TABLE 6.1 Respondents Who Have Experienced Oral Sex (in Percentages), by Religious Affiliation and Spirituality

| | |
|---|---|
| *Religious Tradition* | |
| Evangelical Protestant | 20.7 |
| Mainline Protestant | 24.5 |
| Black Protestant | 11.9 |
| Catholic | 18.7 |
| Jewish | 29.7 |
| Mormon (LDS) | 9.0 |
| Other religion | 21.5 |
| No religion | 28.0 |
| *Spiritual but Not Religious* | |
| Very true | 28.3 |
| Somewhat true | 21.6 |
| Not true at all | 18.8 |

*Source*: National Survey of Youth and Religion

when contrasted to the intercourse numbers in chapter 5 (see Table 5.3). Whereas black Protestant youths are the most likely to have had sexual intercourse, they display one of the lowest rates of oral sex. On the flip side, Jewish and mainline Protestant youths display a much clearer preference for oral sex rather than intercourse. Youths who claim to be spiritual but not religious report slightly higher prevalences of both types of sex. Of the seven religious traditions listed, evangelicals are the fourth lowest in terms of oral sex—right in the middle of the pack, just like with intercourse.

Are these apparent religious influences more than just ephemeral? Yes. Black Protestants are statistically less likely than evangelicals to report having had oral sex (results in Table A6.1). So are Catholic and Mormon youth. Prior to controls, youths who consider themselves spiritual but not religious are more likely than those who do not to report having experienced oral sex. And while personal religiosity curbs the likelihood of reporting oral sex (by 23 percent for each incremental change in religiosity), this association disappears after I account for strong influences from dating, attitudes about abstinence, and parents' sexual values. This should not surprise; youth for whom religion is an important part of their lives tend to hold less permissive attitudes about sex (and to have less permissive parents), and these attitudes reduce their likelihood of having had oral sex.

The 2002 NSFG helpfully distinguishes between giving and receiving oral sex, although its religious affiliation categories unfortunately do not allow me to distinguish Mormon and Jewish youth.[3] Table 6.2 displays the percentage of adolescent boys and girls aged 15–17 in the NSFG who have given or received oral sex, sorted by religion categories. Overall, 40 percent of adolescent boys aged 15–17 have received oral sex, and 28 percent have given it. Among 15- to 17-year-old girls, 38 percent have received and 30 percent have given oral sex. Such disjointed numbers suggest some level of misperception about what actually constitutes giving and receiving oral sex, since both males and females were more apt to report receiving oral sex than giving it.

Several numbers stand out. The nonreligious, the never-attenders, and the religion-isn't-important crowd distinguish themselves in all categories and in both genders. They are more than twice as likely as more religious youth to give or receive oral sex. Mainline Protestant girls exhibit comparably high rates of both giving and receiving oral sex, second only to nonreligious girls. Evangelical youths in the NSFG are the least likely to say they have *received* oral sex, which distinguishes them from their average rate in the NSYR, but they report middle-of-the-road numbers on *giving* oral sex.

Black Protestant adolescents display the most evidently disjointed answers— both girls and boys are more than twice as likely to report receiving oral sex as

TABLE 6.2  15- to 17-Year-Old Adolescents Who Have Given or
Received Oral Sex (in Percentages), by Religiosity Measures

|  | Boys | | Girls | |
|---|---|---|---|---|
|  | Given oral sex | Received oral sex | Given oral sex | Received oral sex |
| *Religious Tradition* | | | | |
| Evangelical Protestant | 28.8 | 25.9 | 25.2 | 28.9 |
| Mainline Protestant | 24.1 | 31.2 | 42.0 | 47.6 |
| Black Protestant | 14.2 | 40.5 | 16.9 | 41.6 |
| Catholic | 21.3 | 43.2 | 26.0 | 31.4 |
| Other religion | 28.0 | 27.6 | 25.2 | 30.3 |
| No religion | 49.5 | 61.5 | 52.4 | 61.8 |
| *Church Attendance* | | | | |
| More than once a week | 13.5 | 18.4 | 13.3 | 20.5 |
| Once a week | 15.4 | 26.7 | 21.8 | 30.7 |
| 1–3 times a month | 27.0 | 44.8 | 37.8 | 44.3 |
| Less than once a month | 34.4 | 49.1 | 32.1 | 43.7 |
| Never | 43.8 | 53.5 | 47.0 | 49.7 |
| *Importance of Religion* | | | | |
| Very important | 13.2 | 24.5 | 18.6 | 27.4 |
| Somewhat important | 32.4 | 43.5 | 33.6 | 38.7 |
| Not important at all | 40.4 | 54.4 | 51.6 | 59.6 |
| All 15- to 17-year-olds | 28.0 | 39.8 | 30.4 | 37.9 |

*Source*: National Survey of Family Growth, Cycle 6

giving it. Why *both* genders state this is unclear, though it may have to do with distinctive interpretations of the survey questions themselves. Catholic boys are also twice as likely to have received it as to have given it. Religiosity again clearly distinguishes answers here: it is both very influential and linear in its association with oral sex. Between 13 and 27 percent of the most religious youth say yes to any one of the questions, far below the 40–60 percent among the least religious teenagers.

This remains true even when controlling for family structure, demographics, and parents' education (results in Table A6.2). Both church attendance *and* the importance of religion are independently associated with a lower likelihood of either giving or receiving oral sex (in the NSFG). When controlling for these two forms of religiosity, no clear distinctions remain among the various religious affiliations.

*The Technical Virginity Debate: Is Oral Sex Really Sex?*

Do teenagers think oral sex is really sex, or something distinct and less serious than intercourse? We asked our interviewees this question, especially since we were interested in gauging whether oral sex is a popular means by which teenagers maintain their virginity technically, while still participating in nonvaginal forms of paired sexual activity. There is no clear consensus, however. For some, "sex" runs the gamut of all coupled sexual activity, especially when it results in the exchange of bodily fluids. For others, there are shades of gray. Religion often distinguishes opinions on the question. Evangelical Protestant and other religiously conservative teens tend to consider oral and vaginal sex in the same light, at least in theory. Jennifer, a 17-year-old evangelical from Georgia, takes a simple approach to the definition: "I think oral sex is sex, too. You know, I mean, it's all the same to me. If it has the word sex in it, then it's sex." This definition was repeated with regularity, unlike in Chap Clark's (2004) sample of southern California youth for whom sex refers only to intercourse.[4] Others we interviewed note that the two may be different yet equally wrong. For some religiously conservative adolescents, our even asking them about the definition of what constitutes sex is confusing. When we asked Kelli, a 16-year-old conservative Lutheran from Minnesota, to comment on or distinguish between the morality or acceptability of vaginal versus oral sex, she responds, "Can you explain that?" In general, most of the adolescent virgins we interviewed feel that they are just not ready for intercourse or oral sex yet.

Thus, I find it difficult to believe that very many religiously conservative adolescents would be using oral sex as a primary means for maintaining technical virginity. To be sure, some certainly do take this approach. Ben, featured in chapter 1, does this, although he doesn't explicitly state this as his intention (and he is not an evangelical). However, his account is unusual. There is not a lot of technical virginity language articulated by adolescents, least of all by religious conservatives, in contrast to others' impressions (e.g., Clark 2004; CBS News, "Taking the Pledge," September 18, 2005; DiMarco 2006).

Is there survey evidence for the technical virginity strategy? One study concluded that virgins in serious relationships are just as likely to have had oral sex as nonvirgins (Werner-Wilson 1998). Brückner and Bearman (2005) reported that about 13 percent of consistent abstinence pledgers reported having had oral sex but not intercourse, compared with just 2 percent of nonpledgers and 5 percent of inconsistent pledgers. Table 6.3 displays the percentage of 15- to 17-year-olds in the 2002 NSFG who have already had oral and/or anal sex, but not intercourse. This is the popular definition of technical virginity, which characterizes about 16 percent of all American

TABLE 6.3  Technical Virginity Patterns among 15- to 17-Year-Olds
(in Percentages), by Religious Tradition

| | Technical virgins |
|---|---|
| Religious Tradition | |
| Evangelical Protestant | 13.3 |
| Mainline Protestant | 12.3 |
| Black Protestant | 8.4 |
| Catholic | 19.8 |
| Other religion | 15.6 |
| No religion | 22.5 |
| | |
| All 15- to 17-year-olds | 16.4 |

*Source*: National Survey of Family Growth, Cycle 6

*Note*: Technical virginity = has had oral and/or anal sex only, not vaginal intercourse.

teenagers. As you can see, it is not adolescents from any religious tradition, but the nonreligious, who are most likely to fit this profile. Over 22 percent of nonreligious teenagers have had oral or anal sex, but not intercourse. They are followed in prevalence by Catholics, the mix of those from other religions, evangelicals, mainliners, and—at bottom—black Protestants, who are far more likely to have already experienced vaginal intercourse.

Among NSYR 16-year-olds, about 19 percent of mainline Protestants and 23 percent of Jews opt for an oral-sex-only approach, compared with only 8 percent of evangelicals, 7 percent of Catholics, and a mere 3 percent of black Protestants (results not shown). When I turn the tables and evaluate youth who have *only had vaginal intercourse*, this characterizes about 30 percent of 16- to 17-year-old black Protestant teenagers, but *zero* percent of 16-year-old mainline Protestant and Jewish youths, and only 3 out of 93 17-year-olds. Let me state this plainly: out of 113 Jewish adolescents in the NSYR, *not one* reported having had vaginal intercourse but not oral sex. Only 4 out of 341 mainline Protestant youths reported the same. There is certainly something to this pattern.

The interviews hint at this pattern as well. Naomi, an 18-year-old Jewish girl from Massachusetts, says about oral sex, "I don't think it's as serious, because you don't have to be as careful depending on who you're with. . . . But I think it's still intimate. I don't think you could just do that [have oral sex] for everybody." Rob, a 17-year-old mainline Protestant from New Jersey, doesn't have reservations about teenagers who want to have sex, provided they're in a relationship and are "serious about each other." However, when asked about his friends' sexual behavior, he says: "A lot is oral sex, or just like, you know, like fooling around and stuff. And I doubt, I don't think a lot of people are really getting into it, just like actual sex, for awhile." A virgin himself, he sees sex as dangerous—what with the ever-present threat of pregnancy and STDs—but largely lacking a moral component.

### Is Oral Sex in the Script?

There are good reasons to think that religiously conservative youth might uniquely *avoid* oral sex in a way that they might not avoid vaginal intercourse. After all, the Bible seldom explicitly addresses alternative sexual practices, but when it does, it tends to be disparaging. In other words, many religious youths may prefer to avoid oral sex because it is considered deviant, gross, or simply without precedent—in other words, it's not in their sexual script. Two of the most theologically conservative traditions—black Protestants and Mormons—each display *higher* percentages of vaginal intercourse than oral sex, and black Protestants are the least likely to be technical virgins. A mere 1.5 percent of African-American youth in the NSYR have *only* had oral sex. The same perspective characterizes the most devoutly religious youths, regardless of particular denomination: they are much more likely at age 17 to have experienced vaginal intercourse than to have experienced oral sex (results not shown).

The interviews bear these claims out. Jamaal, an 18-year-old African American, disdains oral sex and wonders why anyone—male or female—would put their mouth on organs that also function to excrete waste products (to paraphrase his words). He prefers "just the regular" method of sex. Another African-American adolescent who has had oral sex complains, "I don't think it's really that rewarding. It's just really kind of boring, when you look at it." Janeena, an African American, thinks—in contrast to how many white youth tend to see it—that "regular" sex is acceptable "first," before marriage, and only then might other forms of sex become legitimate. Lisa, a 16-year-old white Mormon from Nevada, concurs:

> There's a big difference [between the two types of sex], but it's kind of opposite of what most people would believe. I feel that like oral sex is much more beyond than sex. [*So, beyond, you mean*...] Like, more intimate even. Or like, like it would take a lot, like a long relationship or a really good relationship or something.

These are not the words of adolescents looking for alternative sexual pleasures yet keen on remaining virgins. Rather, oral sex is not in their sexual script, and for many it never will be.

Perhaps this preference among religious conservatives reflects their higher fertility rates and even a pronatalist and profamily orientation rather than an anti-sex approach. After all, evangelical Protestants were the most likely (29 percent) to report being married by Wave III of Add Health. This is nearly *twice* as high as mainline Protestants (15 percent) and almost *five times* as likely as Jews (6 percent). By contrast, Randall, a 14-year-old religiously unaffiliated youth from Montana, offered his primary reason for preferring oral sex: you can't get someone pregnant that way. Premarital pregnancy may still be scandalous among religious conservatives, but early family formation is not; it's still in their script. Family formation is no longer a central goal of many other young Americans. It's optional, and considered best delayed. Thus, technical virginity makes far more sense to less religious adolescents than to the most devout.

### Practicing Oral Sex or Just Dabbling?

Is oral sex a short-term, transitional replacement for more satisfying but riskier vaginal intercourse, or does it become a habit in its own right? While we did not ask pointed questions in our interviews about the frequency of oral sex, we did ask this on the NSYR survey. Table 6.4 displays the frequency of oral sex (among NSYR adolescents who have experienced it), sorted by religiosity.[5] The best way to read such a table is by paying attention to the fringes—the adolescents who tried oral sex only once and those for whom it is a common practice. For example, youth who attend religious services more than once a week are the least likely to have had oral sex just once. Still, these religious adolescents are hardly exhibiting patterns of frequent oral sexual behavior. Only 12 percent of them report having oral sex "many times," which is about half the rate reported by youth of more modest attendance levels. The highest frequency of oral sex is among teenagers who attend sporadically (25 percent) and those who say religion is unimportant (30 percent).

Personal religious salience remains a steady predictor of the frequency of oral sex, even in more advanced statistical models (results in Table A6.3). Youth for whom religion is important either avoid oral sex altogether or limit the number of times they experience it. This robust association holds up while controlling for powerful age, gender (male), and race (white) effects, among other influences. Even when accounting for several phenomena that predict more frequent oral sex (popularity, rebelliousness, currently dating, level of autonomy from parents, having "bad" friends, etc.), teenagers who think that religion is an important part of their daily lives are less likely to

TABLE 6.4 Frequency of Oral Sex (among Those Who Ever Have) (in Percentages), by Religiosity

|  | Once | A few times | Several times | Many times |
|---|---|---|---|---|
| *Church Attendance* | | | | |
| More than once a week | 6.2 | 66.2 | 15.2 | 12.4 |
| Weekly | 16.7 | 38.6 | 22.5 | 22.3 |
| Up to 2–3 times a month | 12.1 | 43.2 | 20.2 | 24.5 |
| Never | 10.7 | 41.8 | 23.9 | 23.7 |
| *Importance of Religion* | | | | |
| Extremely important | 9.5 | 47.8 | 18.1 | 24.6 |
| Very important | 11.8 | 48.5 | 22.6 | 17.1 |
| Somewhat important | 13.4 | 41.6 | 21.8 | 23.3 |
| Not very important | 12.6 | 38.8 | 24.1 | 24.6 |
| Not important at all | 10.9 | 45.7 | 13.2 | 30.3 |

*Source*: National Survey of Youth and Religion

have frequent oral sex. Sources of moral authority eventually crowd out most of the *direct* religious influences, suggesting that adolescent religiosity is indirectly effective via its association with avoiding self-centered morality (making decisions based on what makes them happy or what gets them ahead), which in turn displays strong positive (and direct) effects on the frequency of oral sex.

Nevertheless, the NSYR and NSFG cannot yet answer the question of whether oral sex is a transitional experience for adolescents moving toward vaginal intercourse. But the evidence noted about youth who practice one or the other type of sex, but not both, hints at this conclusion: there's no one clear pattern. Some use oral sex as a transitional action, others combine it with intercourse, while the majority avoids them altogether until later in adolescence or adulthood.

## ANAL SEX

Reports of anal sex were very unusual among adolescents in the Add Health study, so much so that I originally gave little thought to addressing the issue in this book. After the 2002 NSFG data were released, however, I could no longer avoid it. The NSFG—several years newer than the Add Health—reported that 8.1 percent and 5.6 percent of 15- to 17-year-old

TABLE 6.5  15- to 17-Year-Old Adolescents Who Have Had
Anal Sex (in Percentages), by Religiosity Measures

|  | Boys | Girls |
|---|---|---|
| *Religious Tradition* | | |
| Evangelical Protestant | 3.6 | 3.6 |
| Mainline Protestant | 2.8 | 9.8 |
| Black Protestant | 11.8 | 6.3 |
| Catholic | 7.5 | 3.2 |
| Other religion | 2.5 | 1.5 |
| No religion | 19.7 | 13.7 |
| *Church Attendance* | | |
| More than once a week | 1.2 | 1.5 |
| Once a week | 3.3 | 2.9 |
| 1–3 times a month | 4.5 | 3.8 |
| Less than once a month | 10.7 | 4.4 |
| Never | 16.8 | 15.0 |
| *Importance of Religion* | | |
| Very important | 2.3 | 3.7 |
| Somewhat important | 9.1 | 4.0 |
| Not important at all | 14.9 | 11.3 |
| All 15- to 17-year-olds | 8.1 | 5.6 |

*Source*: National Survey of Family Growth, Cycle 6

males and females, respectively, say they have experienced heterosexual anal sex.[6] These numbers well exceeded Add Health's, possibly indicating its increasing popularity. Table 6.5 displays the percentage of 15- to 17-year-olds who report having ever experienced anal sex with a member of the opposite sex. Again, the least religious stand out: nearly one in five nonreligious teenage boys have had anal sex, followed at a distance by black Protestants (12 percent), Catholics (8 percent), evangelicals (4 percent), and mainline Protestants (3 percent). Among girls, the nonreligious are also tops—at 14 percent—followed by mainline Protestants (10 percent), black Protestants (6 percent), evangelicals (4 percent), and Catholics (3 percent). Religiosity follows the same linear pattern we have seen throughout this book. While about 15–17 percent of teens who never attend church report having anal sex, less than 2 percent of the most active religious youth say this. As with intercourse, the distinction between these most religious of all youth and teenagers who attend church weekly (still considered to be regular attendance) is notable:

their prevalence rates of anal sex are twice as high as among those who attend church services more than once a week. The religious distinctions are strong: even after controlling for family structure, demographics, and parents' education, church attendance significantly curbs reports of anal sex (results in Table A6.2).

## PORNOGRAPHY

Sexual practices like anal sex no doubt receive a boost from their online visibility. The pornography industry is huge, thrives in the United States, and certainly affects adolescents (Fisher and Barak 2000; Stack, Wasserman, and Kern 2004; Thio 2001). Assisted by technology, people are increasingly able to remove sexual expression from the context of interpersonal relationships. Pornography is no longer the exclusive domain of "adult" shops and the cordoned-off section of select bookstores. Pornography is, as we all know by now, widely available over the Internet and often delivered to us unsolicited in e-mail. As I stated in chapter 3 and repeat here again: for millions of young Americans, Internet pornography is their introduction to sexual information *and* expression. E-mail subject lines invite us to take a look at "sex-starved bitches" or "gorgeous gangbangers." Online, Americans are now never more than a click or two away from it. The popularity of online pictorial diaries at places like MySpace.com enable even amateurs (and teenagers) to participate in the porn industry. Unlike in the past, those who wish to avoid pornography have to go out of their way to do so. In a study released in 2003, one in four adolescents report unwanted exposure to sexually explicit pictures on the Internet in the past year (Mitchell, Finkelhor, and Wolak 2003). By now, that number is certainly much higher. Surprisingly, the level of parental supervision is not associated with such exposure. And filtering software is only modestly protective. Of that original 25 percent, one-quarter report being very or extremely upset by what they saw. One wonders if the same would be true today, considering the numbness that tends to accompany heightened exposure.

Since the 1990s, the pornography industry is thought to have outgrossed the box office receipts of all of Hollywood's films put together (Fisher and Barak 2000; Thio 2001). Many "normal" corporations and their stockholders directly or indirectly profit from the porn industry's success, since numerous multinational corporations often either own "entertainment" subsidiaries or profit from pornographic rentals. It is thought that roughly 40 percent of American hotels (more than 1.5 million rooms) offer pay-per-view pornography, accounting for several hundred million dollars in revenue per year, and up to 80 percent of total in-room entertainment charges (CNN, August 22, 2006). Despite such popularity, reliable data on and analyses of pornography use are exceptionally rare. Academics are in no hurry to collect such data (Slade 2001). And if studies of adult pornography use are unusual, research on adolescent usage is even more unique.

Perhaps because of this lack of data, speculation abounds about the prevalence of pornography among (mostly male) adolescents and adults. We *do* know that the personality predictors for "old style," offline pornography use are not very relevant to the study of online pornography use (Fisher and Barak 2000). Online porn is much more accessible, and the selection effects for it are different. Pamela Paul (2005) interviewed more than 100 people and noted that pornography tends to distract men from their real sexual partners and as a result harms their social relationships. The debate over these and other harmful effects of pornography continues, but the debate is hardly an informed one, since so few solid social scientists have waded into it.

Data on religion's influence on pornography use are limited as well. Darren Sherkat and Christopher Ellison (1997) note a strong connection between strength of religiosity and condemnation of pornography. Religious organizations, sometimes in unusual alliances with feminist organizations, have been and remain the most common sources of antiporn crusades. A descriptive study of Internet sex chat room participation finds that half of all users report no religious affiliation and that religion holds no influence in their lives (Wysocki 2001). More recently, a rare glimpse into the social science of adult pornography use revealed that the strongest predictors of Internet pornography use are weak ties to religion and the absence of a happy marriage (Stack, Wasserman, and Kern 2004). Religion, the authors conclude, functions as a social-control mechanism that may prevent adult men from doing what might otherwise come naturally to them (looking at pornography).

In the telephone survey component of the NSYR, adolescent respondents were queried in this way about Internet pornography use: "[i]n the last year, how often, if at all, have you used the Internet to view X-rated, pornographic Web sites?" Respondents could reply with: about once a day, a few times a week, about once a week, a few times a month, about once a month, less than once a month, or never. Pornography use is largely a gender-specific practice. The consumers of pornography among America's adolescents are almost exclusively male. Fully 97 percent of surveyed girls in the NSYR state that they never use the Internet for pornography, compared with 70 percent of all adolescent boys (60 percent of 16- and 17-year-old boys). I suspect there also is considerable social desirability bias at work in this question, prompting youths to underreport their involvement in pornography. From our in-person interviews, a majority of adolescent boys do not think there is a problem with viewing pornography, and they admit to doing this very thing ("infrequently," of course). Comparing the interview admissions with the survey data, then, suggests that the latter are undercounting.

Table 6.6 displays statistics on monthly or even more frequent Internet pornography use among the adolescent boys in the NSYR sample (about 80 percent of the overall sample had access to the Internet). Pornography use varies according to religiosity: whereas 18 percent of adolescent boys who never attend services report monthly use, only about 8 percent who attend more than once a week report comparably. So Table 6.6 offers evidence for a nearly linear association between religiosity and pornography use among adolescents. Religion's importance in daily life sorts these youth even more extensively: 26 percent who say religion is not important at all report regular porn use, compared to only 5 percent who say religion is extremely important. Religious affiliation is also associated with this outcome: Jewish and nonreligious youths report the highest rates of pornography use—about 30 and 22 percent, respectively. Evangelicals, Mormons, and youths who identify with another (non-Christian) religion display the lowest stated rates of pornography use here, though these numbers may be artificially low due to stronger than average social desirability bias. The moral source variables (how youth decide between right and wrong) likewise show clear distinctions in their associations with Internet pornography.

The odds of Internet pornography use by spiritual-but-not-religious youth are elevated, even when controlling for their primary religious affiliation (results in Table A6.4). With the addition of controls, the only two affiliations that remain distinctly different from evangelicals are Catholics and Jews, both of whom display significantly higher frequency. Thus, evangelical Protestants are among the least likely to report pornography use. They are statistically comparable to black Protestants, mainliners, Mormons, and nonreligious youth. Interestingly, religious attendance, the key indicator of public religiosity, exhibits little bearing on pornography usage, while religion's importance for daily life matters considerably.

## Gendered and Religious Perspectives on Pornography

Very few adolescent girls with whom we spoke approve of pornography. Religion does not appear to augment their displeasure, either. Cassie, a 15-year-old evangelical from Georgia, is transparent in her repulsion, and her

TABLE 6.6 Male Respondents Who Report
"at Least" Monthly Internet Pornography Use
(in Percentages), by Religion Measures

| | |
|---|---|
| *Church Attendance* | |
| More than once a week | 7.7 |
| Once a week | 8.6 |
| 2–3 times a month | 12.9 |
| Once a month | 15.6 |
| Many times a year | 13.4 |
| Few times a year | 22.5 |
| Never | 18.1 |
| *Importance of Religion* | |
| Extremely important | 5.0 |
| Very important | 9.3 |
| Somewhat important | 16.0 |
| Not very important | 20.0 |
| Not important at all | 25.8 |
| *Moral Authority* | |
| Do what makes me happy | 22.2 |
| Do what helps me get ahead | 20.3 |
| Follow adult or parent's advice | 9.4 |
| Do what God or Scripture says | 6.3 |
| *Religious Tradition* | |
| Evangelical Protestant | 7.5 |
| Mainline Protestant | 13.4 |
| Black Protestant | 13.4 |
| Catholic | 17.4 |
| Jewish | 29.5 |
| Mormon (LDS) | 6.2 |
| Other religion | 6.5 |
| No religion | 22.2 |

*Source*: National Survey of Youth and Religion

sentiment captures the opinion of the majority of the adolescent girls: "I feel betrayed by it really. Because a lot of it is watched by guys really, and I feel like I'm being stripped bare even if it's not my body. And it bothers me."

Samantha, a 15-year-old mainline Protestant from Virginia, speaks disparagingly of pornography, not so much for its immorality but rather because it indicates some pathetic ineptness on the part of users: "I think [pornography] is the dumbest thing [laughs]. . . . Oh gosh. Seriously, though, you're a low life if, like, you can't go out and do your own thing. You have to watch someone else. I think that's disgusting. I think it's retarded. Uh, I think it's so low."

Other adolescent girls tolerate pornography, thinking it might be a safe outlet for adolescent boys' unstable libidos. Patti, a 14-year-old mainline Protestant girl from Pennsylvania, has mixed emotions about the subject:

> I think that a lot of it is really, um, demeaning and degrading towards women. And it objectifies women; and I don't like to see that. [*Uh-huh.*] I, it's not that I have a problem with the female or male body, because I think the body is a beautiful thing. And I think that art and pornography kind of get, sort of, done into one, because I mean there's a lot of really beautiful pieces of art that are of the naked body. [*Right.*] And obviously that's not pornography. [*Right.*] But I think that there's a fine line between art and pornography. And I think that pornography is disgusting and that there's no reason for it, so. But I think that people just have to realize there's a fine line between pornography and art form.

Patti's ambivalence concerns the portrait of the human female form, sans evident sexuality. However, most contemporary pornography is less concerned with conveying the *beauty* of a woman's body and more with its *sexuality*, either alone or with a partner(s) in a sexual act. That, Patti would agree, is objectionable.

Then, there is the other half of all adolescents—boys. I asked Jeff, a 17-year-old Catholic from Illinois, how he felt about pornography. He hemmed and hawed:

> Um, I think it's, I don't know. I don't think it's, oh man. Well you see, it depends on what you use it for, because I think it's good sometimes for teens because they're not having sex. They're taking all of that energy out on whatever, instead of going out and whatever, you know? But. I guess it's a way of, oh [sighs], I don't know, it's a way for teens to get out whatever they have to get out without making a baby or getting an STD.

Luke, a 16-year-old Catholic from New York, relays a common story about pornography use:

> Uh, it's, I don't know how to say it. I mean I'm not going to say I've never watched porn. I mean, what can you do? It's part of life. If you're going to look at it and you're going to watch it, that's your decision, I guess. [*OK. So you mentioned you've seen it. Do you watch it at all on a regular basis?*]

Not on a regular basis. Every now and then of course, but... [*How do you think viewing pornography affects us, do you think it changes us at all?*] I guess it does some people. It really doesn't affect me.

I note above that what little research does exist on this topic suggests that evangelical Protestant adults tend to hold antipornography attitudes (Sherkat and Ellison 1997). From the NSYR survey and interviews, evangelical youth also tend to think uniquely about pornography, feeling distinctly hostile toward it, at least in concept. However, it is not at all clear that their usage patterns differ from other adolescents. We asked Tim, a 14-year-old evangelical from Georgia, about pornography: "It's wrong. [*Have you ever viewed pornographic Web sites or movies?*] [long pause] Say that again? [*Have you ever viewed pornographic Web sites or movies?*] [pause] Can we skip this question?" Dale, a 15-year-old evangelical from Illinois, also takes his time when asked about pornography: "[pause] It's, I don't know. Skip it. [*OK. Ah, have you ever viewed any pornographic Web sites or movies or anything?*] Kind of inadvertently, like, but not really."

Despite their elevated proclivity for either avoiding the question or distorting the answer, evangelical adolescent boys are much more likely to identify the false "reality" of pornographic portrayals, less likely to take the matter lightly, and more likely to recognize its tempting allure. One 15-year-old notes that "you never know the person [in the picture], you're never going to meet them, and even if you did, would you have a chance with them? I don't view it as, as reasonable." Another calls it "not that satisfying.... there's a lot of fakeness to it.... it portrays a false sort of lifestyle." David, the evangelical from Texas mentioned in a previous chapter, not only told me that he struggled for a time with a pornography "addiction" that "desensitized" him, but also that he feels "sorry for the people who watch that. And I feel sorry for the people who make it and star in them. It's sad." He quit looking at it when "it made me start feeling sick inside and empty."

Together, these accounts denote several conclusions about the majority of teenage boys and pornography:

- They look at it.
- They don't like to think that they look at it very often (although they may).
- Many believe it to be helpful (when combined with masturbation) for relieving pent-up sexual tension.
- Some feel guilty about it. Most feel embarrassed to admit it.

- They don't talk about it with their friends.
- Most believe that it doesn't affect them.

## How to Make Love Like a Porn Star?

Not a few adolescent boys, however, express a perspective that most girls would certainly loathe—that of pornography as education about proper sexual technique.[7] That is, some clearly think that what they see online or in videos is not only real sex (which it might be) but *normal* sex. Emilio, a 14-year-old Catholic from Arizona, thinks pornography is completely natural, " 'cause everybody does it. I mean, I'm not saying just 'cause everybody does it I do it, but I do it to learn. To learn or to, just to watch it. Most of the time to learn. [*To learn what?*] Like if I get in that situation, I'll know what to do." One of the more salient criticisms of pornography concerns this very thing—that it provides a false picture of what sexually intimate relations are like.

Although there is clearly variation, much contemporary pornography portrays women in submissive positions and men as sexual aggressors. In an enlightening look at the pornography industry and its delusional subtexts, Gail Dines and Robert Jensen (2004: 374) identify the main themes of heterosexual pornography: "(1) All women always want sex from men; (2) women like all the sexual acts that men perform or demand; and (3) any woman who does not at first realize this can be persuaded with a little force." Male-on-female violence—real, implied, or symbolic—pervades pornographic video. As a result, some adolescent boys approach girls "expecting them to be into anything and everything" (Hari 2005: 33).

Laura Carpenter (2002: 357) relays a similar experience from one of her interviewees who, in the process of losing his virginity, "tried to do what [he] saw the people do in the porno movies." His efforts did not lead to a mutually satisfying experience, to say the least. While it is unclear how common Emilio's distorted perspective on pornography is, it is certainly disconcerting. An equally difficult question to answer is just how much adolescent girls have actually internalized the unrealistic (and emotionally harmful) norms of pornography. Do adolescent girls respond to the perceived "demand" for unusual sexual activities that their boyfriends are learning about online? Do they themselves log on to learn, or is any link between pornography and new sexual trends indirect, via its influence on popular teen magazines and their advice columns? While definitively answering these questions is not yet possible, the increase I note in the prevalence of anal sex among adolescents, however, hints at one answer.

## Middle-Class (Sexual) Morality

A key claim I want to make, and one which I believe the data support, is that a distinctly middle-class sexual morality is visible in the American religious scene, especially (but not exclusively) among mainline Protestant and Jewish youth—traditionally among the wealthiest of religious Americans. This sexual ethic trades the "higher" pleasures of vaginal intercourse for a set of low-risk substitutes: coupled oral sex, mutual masturbation, and solitary pornography use (and masturbation). By "low risk," I mean that the chance of pregnancy is nil, and the threat of transmitting STDs is diminished. Those who hold to this middle-class morality are more apt to think of sexual intercourse as "dangerous"—that is, conducive to pregnancy and diminished life chances.

White, strategically oriented youth with educated parents are among the least likely adolescents to object to contraception in theory and the most likely to say that having sex would upset their mother (for whatever reason) and that pregnancy would embarrass them. What are mainline Protestant and Jewish teenagers like? On average, they are white, not overly religious, very strategic, and from educated homes. Black Protestant, evangelical, Mormon, and some Catholic adolescents are more likely to say that premarital sex is wrong, but they also are quicker to engage in—and to tolerate the potential responsibilities that come with—sexual intercourse. While I don't have enough historical data to suggest that a widespread *change* has occurred in adolescents' sexual scripts, there is sufficient evidence that the behavior of white, middle-class, strategic mainline Protestant and Jewish teenagers reveals a script that is certainly distinct.

Adolescents espousing this new script are generally not interested in remaining technical virgins, though they may nevertheless exhibit that status for a time. They are sexually tolerant. They are interested in remaining free from the burden of teenage pregnancy and the sorrows and embarrassments of STDs. They perceive a bright future for themselves, one with college, advanced degrees, a career, and a family. Simply put, too much seems at stake. Sexual intercourse is not worth the risks. The pleasures of sex could be a foolish transaction, leading to pregnancy, which would in turn require hard thinking about abortion (to which they are generally not opposed, but don't take lightly, either). Thus, vaginal intercourse is replaced *for a time* by alternatives like oral sex and pornography.

Ironically, it is at its root a profamily sexual ethic, since such youths tend to come from what many scholars would label "good homes," and they want this for themselves in the future. Their eventual spouse simply need not be their first and only sexual partner. More important is emerging from pre-premarital sexual relationships free of children and disease. Sandra, a 13-year-old mainline Protestant girl from Washington, articulates the familial aspect of this sexual script. When asked under what conditions it would be OK to have sex, she responds: "(a) you're married. [Or] (b) you are having protected sex. . . . You know, just really safe, you know. I think marriage is a big, big deal." To Elisa, an articulate 14-year-old mainline Protestant girl from northern Virginia, unprotected sex is even a *moral* mistake: "unprotected sex should wait until, not only marriage, but until you're really ready to have a child."

Elisa captures this middle-class morality script concisely: "I don't think that it's imperative that you wait until marriage, but I think it's a good, it's a wise decision." This ethic is not about religion. It's about being shrewd. Solidly middle- or upper-middle-class adolescents have considerable socioeconomic and educational expectations, courtesy of their parents and their communities' lifestyles. They are happy with their direction, generally not rebellious, tend to get along well with their parents, and have few moral qualms about expressing their nascent sexuality. In fact, nowhere in my NSYR analyses does the "parents, teachers, or respected adults" source of moral authority distinguish itself *except for contraceptive use.* Some parents are pushing sexual safety rather than abstinence, and their adolescent children are listening and obeying. Parental expectations are what shape their sexual values and scripts. If religion can help them live up to these values and avoid sexual pain, all the better. But it is not really expected to, since religion is a side item on their menu and not the main course (Smith and Denton 2005).

## CONCLUSIONS

Oral sex, considered to be the primary substitute for vaginal intercourse (perhaps besides masturbation), is a more common *first* sexual activity until about age 16, at which point its preferred status begins to give way to intercourse. It is also more popular among nonreligious, mainline Protestant, and Jewish teenagers than it is among other religious groups.

Although some observers suggest that there is an emerging penchant among evangelicals and abstinence pledgers for technical virginity—the practice of oral or anal sex without vaginal intercourse—there is not much evidence of it when talking with them. Strictly by the numbers, it characterizes about 16 percent of youth. Technical virginity, however, is clearly less about religious rules and more about a strategic approach to steering clear of pregnancy and STDs. Indeed, most technical virgins have no moral objections to intercourse. They simply think it's a risk not worth taking.

Internet pornography is fast becoming a central source of adolescents' information about the sexual practices of others. It's a poor source, no doubt, fraught with unreal accounts of hypersexuality, group sex, fetishes, and women who live only to sexually satisfy men. It does not reflect sexual reality. Just how many American adolescents believe it does is, of course, impossible to gauge. Some interviewees suggested this to us, however. While religious patterns for pornography use are clear, the topic is subject to an elevated level of social desirability bias. Hems, haws, sighs, and long pauses accompanied lots of adolescent boys' answers to our questions about pornography, regardless of religiosity or religious affiliation. I suspect its use is more underreported than other sex-related practices. Its long-term influence on patterned sexual attitudes and behavior remains unknown.

The key story of the chapter, though, is about an evident sexual ethic among strategic, education-minded, moderately religious youth. I call it an emerging middle-class sexual morality, but in truth it is more characteristic of the upper middle class than those—like evangelical Protestants—who are newer to the middle class. It is future-oriented, self-focused (but not anti-family), risk aversive, parent-driven (and subtly class-oriented), yet largely sexually tolerant. It is most apparent among less religious and more affluent mainline Protestant and Jewish adolescents, though others subscribe to it as well. Oral sex is substituted for vaginal intercourse, and in so doing adolescents retain their technical virginity. But this is seldom *intentional*, in contrast to recent research claims to the contrary. Such youth see no need to abstain from intercourse until marriage. They're just abstaining for the present to safeguard their future schooling plans, career trajectories, and life chances.

# Chapter 7

## A TYPOLOGY OF
## RELIGIOUS INFLUENCE

It should be clear by now that the sexual morality of adolescents—even religious ones—is hardly simple and may not always make a great deal of sense to adults. For many adolescents, religious faith plays a confused role in coloring their sexual attitudes and actions. For a small minority, religion is an obvious and vital part of the many decisions they make every day. For still others, religious claims upon their behavior are ignored or unknown. Some adolescents feel unable to live up to religious standards and overwhelmed by outside influences—like peer norms about sex—that are quite powerful yet entirely outside the individual's control. And their intentions to either pursue or avoid sex may be weakened when they are not shared by friends. Thus social scientists know better than to presume that religious claims upon adolescents' sexuality are at the top of their salience hierarchy for all but the most devout among them. Instead, religious claims battle with other compelling scripts. Teenagers' resulting sexual choices—to refrain, to engage, to dabble, or to dwell on the vague boundaries of what is "too far"—nevertheless tend to make sense to them when they give an account of their actions. Some express regrets, but even most of these come—with some effort—to be satisfactorily integrated into their own autobiographies.

A deeper understanding of all this would be impossible if I were content to simply document religious influence on sexual decision making and perhaps hypothesize about its pathways. Such a focus on simple influence, however, is only of modest value in clarifying the role of religion in people's lives. We learn much more when we delve deeper, ask questions of real people, find out what they know and believe, and think historically and contextually about our research questions and subjects. Partly in response to this dissatisfaction, I want to introduce a typology of religious influence and highlight evidence for different types of religious effects. Simply documenting the effects is only so interesting. I want to know *how* religion shapes the behaviors and actions of some and not others, and why. The typology moves us in that direction. It also begs a set of theoretical questions about how social scientists can know that religion shapes adolescent sexual decision making and what we ought to do with the reasons that adolescents themselves articulate. Adolescents' personal accounts matter a great deal, but no less important are those reasons that remain unspoken. Reasons for sexual choices are indeed complex, and sometimes those choices are seemingly against an individual's better judgment. Since things are not always as they seem, as the sociological adage goes, I've enlisted survey research and statistical analyses to help document the unstated influences on sexual decision making and patterns of which adolescents may themselves be unaware.

Applying this typology of religious influence to the study of adolescent sexuality suggests that while religion certainly *influences* the sexual decision making of many adolescents, it infrequently *motivates* the actions of religious youth. In other words, religious teens do not often make sexual decisions for religious reasons. The ones who articulate religious reasons and act in step with their stated beliefs are the exception, not the rule. Most religious adolescents remain influenced by their faith tradition and practices, but not motivated by them.

## Six Types of Religious Influence

The conversations to which we have been privy—about adolescents' religious ideals, their motivations, and their actual sexual behavior—provide tangible examples of six types of consequential relationships between religion and adolescent sexual behavior.[1] Although my concern here is with adolescents, the typology should work for adults as well and for a variety of other actions that are subject to religious teachings and normative expectations. The typology implies that religion gives direction, speaks authoritatively, and can motivate action. Whether or not the adolescent is aware of religion's direction and motivation is addressed in the columns of the typology of religious influence. The rows address the other half of the equation: whether the actions taken are in keeping with the choices suggested by religious authorities or teachings. Two cells are further subdivided to reflect whether the "obedience" seems purposeful or accidental, and whether the "disobedience" reflects awareness or disregard. The six types of relationships are:

1. *Intentional religion*: Religion influences the actor's behavior, and the actor is aware of it, acknowledging its effect by using religious language.

2. *Instrumental religion*: Religion may influence the actor's behavior, but the influence is essentially pragmatic, that is, the actor employs largely secular reasoning for avoiding undesirable consequences of behaviors.
3. *Invisible religion*:[2] Religion influences the actor's behavior, but the actor is not aware of it and may even deny religion's relevance.
4. *Inconsistent religion*: Religion does not influence the actor's behavior, but the actor acknowledges its relevance and feels that it ought to influence his/her actions.
5. *Irrelevant religion*: Religion does not influence the actor's behavior, and although the actor is aware of religious claims, he/she does not care about them or denies their relevance.
6. *Irreligion*: Religion does not influence the actor's behavior, because the actor is not religious, has little knowledge or interest in religious claims, and/or does not apply them to him- or herself.

Many American teenagers would be placed in the irrelevant or invisible religion categories outright, since a majority of them, while belonging to a

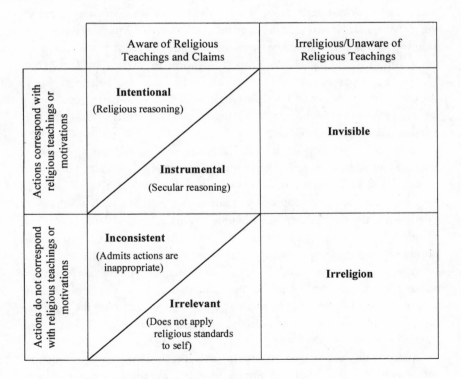

FIGURE 7.1. Typology of Religious Influence

religious tradition, are not actively religious and exhibit little reflection about religious claims upon their sexual attitudes and activities. The most interesting work involves distinguishing among the intentionally, instrumentally, and inconsistently religious adolescents—those youth who tend toward religion and can articulate some awareness of religious claims upon their sexual attitudes and actions.

This typology is not rigid; adolescents, like all of us, may feel regret and alter their behavior. For pornography addiction, the force of habit can effectively mitigate the best intentions to avoid it. Additionally, some well-meaning youths (mirroring adults, no doubt) are much clearer on religious teachings about some aspects of their lives than about others. For instance, I would expect evangelical Protestant teenagers to be fairly fluent in the language of biblically based sexual abstinence but less so in biblically based environmental stewardship or race relations, since sexuality is invested with considerable religious relevance, and their congregations and youth leaders tend to think more individually than collectively about human obligations (Emerson and Smith 2000; Smith et al. 1998).

What if researchers cannot document whether or not their study participants or survey respondents know what their religion teaches about sex? Or what if the participants' accounts of their religion's teachings about sex are simply way off the mark? The typology is still helpful for those situations, being optimally designed for mixed-methods research.[3] In fact, complementing in-person interviews with survey data analyses is the best way to document the presence of invisible religious influence—when youth are not aware of religious influence but survey analyses document significant effects of religion on a given behavior.

These six types also suggest that the story of the relationship between religion and adolescent sexual behavior is not entirely dependent upon what teenagers think this relationship is. Good sociology, while it values people's own perspectives, is not content to assume that people always think about their own actions and describe their motivations *accurately*. We must take a broader view, examining contemporary and historical contexts, cultures, and norms of the social worlds we inhabit. None of us invents the sexual scripts upon which we draw. Instead, under the influence of others, we unconsciously adopt (and, to a lesser extent, adapt) ours from the pool of those available around us. Most of us *think* we know why we act as we do, but there are boundaries to our self-knowledge, and social scientists (like marketing experts) know better than to always take people at their word.

Additionally, sociology is an interpretive undertaking, which entails further potential pitfalls. Subjective meanings and intentions are not directly observable; motives are slippery, complex, multivalent, mixed, and not easily sorted. But this does not make the study of them a hopeless cause. Yes, meanings are observable only indirectly and imperfectly, but to press forward without them is to severely limit our understanding of human behavior, lapsing instead into a purely positivist model of social science, whose deterministic theories are altogether out of touch with the ways we actually live. Good sociology must always be interpretive, because humans are mental, not only organic, beings (Smith 2003b).

## INTENTIONAL RELIGION

It is clearly too much to presume that religion *infuses* the lives of most contemporary American Christians, whether adults or adolescents. Religion can directly influence attitudes, perceptions, and behaviors, but it often does not. It can have consequences for how people act on Monday as well as on Sunday, but it often fails to.[4] Intentional religious action isn't the most common type of religious influence. But it's perhaps the easiest to spot. In this type of association, religion is thought to provide adolescents with sets of moral teachings and directives of self-control and personal virtue about how they ought to live (Smith 2003c).[5] Such teachings and directives are typically augmented by relational and material resources and by incentives for adherence, such as congregational support or sanction. In turn, intentionally religious individuals are aware of the religious teachings and directives and articulate them when explaining the reasons for the actions they take. Cami, an 18-year-old Roman Catholic from Massachusetts, exemplifies the intentionally religious adolescent. She is clear about a link between religion and sexuality, and when asked whether her religion has any particular teaching on sex, she articulates the Church's position, including its "openness" to conception:

> My religion, yeah. It teaches that you should wait just because of the value of life and just, like, the sacred bond you have between, like, a man and a woman. It's like, so much more, like, a good environment to have sex in a positive [way], and to bring a baby into the world. And, like, if you have sex before you have marriage, you don't want to have a baby. And, like, our religion teacher was explaining that if you do that, and say, then you're kind of, like, shutting that out of the picture. Because God, like, created sex so that you could welcome him into the picture and, like, possibly bring a baby into the world. And that's like the point of it. I guess that's cheesy, but I guess I kind of believe that too.

Cami is a virgin, and in her words, "I'm not planning on having sex with anybody [soon]." She knows that church teachings frown on nonmarital sexual behavior and bless marital relations. So far, she's had little difficulty living this out.

Sunny, a 16-year-old evangelical girl from Oregon, notes several aspects and nuances of religious teachings about sex. To begin with, sexual attraction is not wrong: "When guys like girls it's [not] like a sin or anything because that's how God made us, you know. You're gonna have those emotions. It's what you choose to do with them [that could be right or wrong]." In fact, she suggests that "marriage and sex is a great gift that God gave, and so I think it should only be used then, when you're married." She finds the emotional-readiness language insufficiently directive, unlike her religious teachings.

When religious messages diverge distinctly from social norms or institutional expectations, social scientists should expect to find significant religious effects on behavior. But if most individuals and institutions oppose a particular behavior—like criminal activity—then religious voices in opposition to it are not unique and will simply join the chorus of opposition (Burkett and White 1974). Since much of adolescent sexual behavior is perfectly legal, and even normative in some social circles, religious messages about sex are often distinctive and uniquely "noisy." Yet intentional religious influence is probably the rarest of the six types of association between religion and adolescent sexual behavior. Many times, we asked teens for a religious message about sex, and they came up with little or nothing.[6] Having been well socialized into competing sexual scripts, *most* Christian teenagers in America do not think or articulate their responses in religious or moral terms: "Religious teachings may be more like ad hoc scripts that guide people momentarily rather than fundamentally shape their values, and these scripts may be narratives that provide after-the-fact accounts of behavior rather than channeling behavior through deeply held inner dispositions," suggests sociologist Robert Wuthnow (2004: 211). Deeply held religious commitments about sex are simply uncommon among youth, even religious ones.[7]

Some may argue that adolescents are generally not as religiously astute or aware as adults, but there is little evidence to suggest that NSYR adults far outpace adolescents here. Religious "maturity" is hardly a trait that is exclusive to adults, or even widespread among them. As Smith and Denton (2005) conclude in their extensive analysis of adolescent and adult religiosity, parents should expect adolescents to mirror their own depth of religiousness, suggesting a strong patterned socialization of beliefs and behaviors.

## How Cognitive Is Sexual Decision Making?

Discussing intentional religious motivation invites the question: just how cognitive is adolescents' sexual decision making? Since the sexual decision-making process is largely mental and thus cannot be observed, aspects of it may well elude the decision makers. As noted earlier in the text, the theory of reasoned action (and its successor, the theory of planned behavior) points out that behavior is almost always preceded by the *intention* to perform that behavior (Ajzen 1991; Ajzen and Fishbein 1980; Cook, Moore, and Steel 2005; Gillmore et al. 2002). This is rather commonsensical, of course, but the theory raises some pertinent issues. Even when we can pin down motives, we have only made modest progress, documenting what pushes a person *toward* a decision to act but not why they acted as they did. With respect to adolescent sexual motivations and intentions, I have no doubt that the average teenage sexual anticipator will become sexually active before the average delayer. But not always. As the results about evangelicals' sexual attitudes and practices suggest (chapter 5), intentions are clearly not enough. Many teenagers do not live up to the sexual norms—whether permissive or restrictive—that they profess.

Alternatively, religious motivation may simply belong to the practical consciousness of adolescent actors. Social theorist Anthony Giddens (1979: 5) distinguishes between *practical* consciousness, those "tacit stocks of knowledge" upon which a person draws when acting, and *discursive* consciousness, the self-knowledge to which a person is able to give words. When we take action, suggests Giddens, we do not have access to all the reasons that we choose a particular course. Some reasons are literally unspeakable yet remain influential. We might say that we just can't quite put our finger on it. Or, together with Woody Allen, we conclude that "the heart wants what it wants, and the heart has its reasons that reason does not know."[8] Yet these reasons of the heart tend to be more powerful than the ones we can recall and express, Giddens suggests. People like to rationalize their actions, finding reasons for why they did what they did. But these reasons are only the *accessible* ones, those residing in our discursive consciousness. A search into the complex motives of adolescent sex may well conclude that self-interest, trust, mistrust, guilt, delight, jealousy, loneliness, status expectations, longing, pride, insecurity, ambition, and self-loathing all emerge in adolescents' sexual motives (and human motives in general) with greater or lesser regularity. The sources of these feelings are manifold, and some (like pride and self-loathing) are unlikely to appear in teens' own accounts of the reasons for their sexual action or inaction.

Thus, perhaps the reason that intentionally religious motivation appears rare is because religious reasons may more commonly be located in the practical consciousness. There they remain deep-seated accounts difficult to express yet nonetheless influential in shaping intentions and actions. When looking, then, for religious motivation for sexual decision making, we may be hard pressed to discover it as an account that adolescents are able to verbally express to a researcher.[9]

Alternately, maybe there is little hidden religious motivation after all. Perhaps, instead, there are just very few intentionally religious adolescents, end of story. After all, the most compelling sexual scripts—the ones that get the most face time with all but the most sheltered youth—are not religious ones, but secular and permissive ones. If we consider how often during the average day any of us receive what we might call a restrictive sexual cue, and compare that with how often we are treated to more permissive sexual scripts or suggestions, I suspect the scales would quickly tip toward the permissive (unless we actively avoid televisions, radios, billboards, and people). Add to this eight hours a day in high school—a sexual marketplace itself—and it becomes remarkable that the primary language that *any* adolescent would use to talk about sexuality would be religious. No wonder the intentionally religious adolescent sexual decision maker is so unusual. The competition between religious scripts and mass media scripts about sex is almost no contest.

Finally, might we be witnessing a loss of religious motivation about adolescent sex that was once operative in previous generations of Americans? I'd answer no. Although adolescent sexual habits have no doubt changed, and first sex is experienced earlier on average than, say, 60 or 70 years ago, I would hesitate to conclude that adolescents growing up in the 1930s or 1940s were more explicitly motivated by religious discourse about sex. The average sexual script was simply more consonant with a religious script than it is today. If anything, religious discourse about sex is *more* public today, if for no other reason than as a response to the sexualized nature of nearly ubiquitous mass media messages. Permissive scripts are the new norm. Restrictive scripts are uncommon. Distinctly religious motivation no longer gets lost in the crowd of restrictive scripts. As a result, distinctly religious motivation to avoid sex is arguably at an all-time high.

## INSTRUMENTAL RELIGION

As an alternative to intentional religion, a more rationalized, instrumental religion shapes in adherents particular preferences and interests which redefine what they understand to be in their self-interest (for example, treat others kindly and you may expect it in return). Instrumentally religious actors pursue actions that maximize their interests, which are not at bottom distinctly religious ones involving transcendence and divinely ordained purpose (as for the intentionally religious actor). Instead, multiple roles—like religious believer, athlete, popular classmate, college-bound 18-year-old, and girl- or boyfriend— can be simultaneously relevant for sexual decision making, a condition dubbed "structural overlap" (Wimberley 1989). The awareness of religious claims may be present, yet the language employed when describing why one or another path was chosen is largely devoid of religious content. This is a much more common scenario than intentional religion.

Many religious adolescents make what may appear at first to be religiously inspired decisions about sex (to avoid it or to intend to wait until marriage), but when pressed, the reasons they offer have little or nothing to do with religion:

- They don't think that teenagers can be emotionally ready.
- They think they're just not mature enough to handle having sex.
- They don't want to complicate their lives with the emotional ties that accompany sex.
- They fear that pregnancy could limit their options for the future.
- They perceive that high school is just not the time for it (but college may be).

Solomon, a 16-year-old black Protestant from Louisiana, responds this way when asked if his religion has any particular teaching or morality when it comes to sex: "You shouldn't have sex until you're married." Does he agree with that?

> Yeah, I agree, because if you don't, you will most likely just bring pain or suffering to, like, if you plan on going to college or something. And then you end up, get a girl pregnant in high school and that just totally changed your whole future. Like, what could've happened [if you had avoided sex].

While Solomon acknowledges and articulates that religious reasons for avoiding sexual behavior exist, his motivation for steering clear of sexual involvement is largely pragmatic: it would bring emotional pain and possible pregnancy, which would constrain his future. Religious teachings on sex are "back row" reasons that may occasionally come in handy but are not nearly as compelling as "front row" concerns like pregnancy. Pragmatism is at the heart of this approach. Religion *helps*, and that is what it is for. It does not really motivate, but instead serves in a supporting cast role.

Some adolescents are aware of the instrumental nature of their approach, but most are not. Carla, the 17-year-old evangelical from chapter 1, is exceptional for her ability to distinguish between intentional and instrumental types of influence, suggesting, "if you don't [abstain] for religious purposes, then you need to do it just, you know, for street smarts, I guess." "Street smarts" are by far the most popular reasons offered by adolescents for delaying sex.

Researchers distinguish instrumental religion from intentional religion by the *language* respondents use to explain the reasons for the attitudes they hold and the actions they take. But sometimes this language is hard to detect. Not only do restrictive sexual scripts tend to get drowned out by more permissive ones, there is also competition between religious and nonreligious restrictive sexual scripts. The public health community presses health-related motivations for delaying sex and for using contraception. Educators encourage youth to keep their futures in mind. Religious messages, while they don't usually contradict these other scripts, are kept by law from wider distribution. Federal abstinence-based educational grants disallow explicitly religious content, meaning that public health messages based on select scientific studies are the scripts that are most commonly heard by adolescents in public schools.

Thus, evidence for religious instrumentalism can be subtle. It is not as if the actors have well-established goals in mind and consciously choose to participate in organized religion to help meet those goals. Most teenagers do not actively adopt religious beliefs and teachings that they didn't already hold in order to help meet certain ends.[10] I would argue that many adolescents are not even aware that religion tends to have emotional, social, and familial benefits. Most simply want to be happy and secure, do well in school, have fun with their friends, and anticipate college. Being somewhat religious and participating in religious activities seem generally to cohere with meeting those goals.

Where does religious instrumentalism come from? Most adolescents inherit it from their parents, who very much want to protect their teenagers from unwanted pregnancy and STDs (as noted in the middle-class morality phenomenon discussed in chapter 6). Reflecting on his interviews with fathers, family sociologist Nicholas Townsend (2002: 66–67) noted that most of the men "equated 'high morals' with not using drugs and with wearing a seatbelt rather than with thirsting after righteousness, sacrificing for the common good, or speaking truth to power." Religion is seen as a form of protection or insurance that is wisely adopted in the pursuit of certain ideal goals. Townsend noted that parents, especially fathers, "enlist religion as a source of values to inoculate their children against danger." When we asked Valerie, the 15-year-old Pentecostal featured in chapter 1, what her religious practices do for her, she responded with an answer that resonates with Townsend's argument:

They [my religious practices] make me just a nicer person, just respectful, just to older people and stuff. Like things that you have, like, learned since you were little, like respect your elders and stuff, like, those things come easier for me now. Like before, I, like, hated adults, you know, but now it's a lot easier just to be lovable and caring to people.

## INSTRUMENTALISM ≠ INSINCERITY

Religious instrumentalism does not equal religious insincerity. Many of the instrumental adolescents with whom we spoke are pleasant, admirable, and religiously involved. The label is simply an observation and a classification: avoiding pregnancy, strategizing about your future, and recognizing your own emotional immaturity are all admirable actions, but they are common norms and not religious per se. Most people live their lives "negotiating the demands of multiple religious and nonreligious moral orders—compromising here, synthesizing there, compartmentalizing elsewhere" (Smith 2003b: 106). In this common scenario, religion plays a role but is hardly a totalizing influence. It has to get in line with the other competing demands (and helpful resources).

The instrumental approach is common among very religious adolescents, evangelical Protestants included. Perry, a 14-year-old evangelical from South Carolina, offers only instrumental reasons for avoiding sex: "Because you have a better chance of not getting diseases or something, if they wait until they're married and you got better chances of having a healthier child . . . and better chances of not getting divorced after you've done it." Nicole, a 16-year-old evangelical from California, advocates for sexual abstinence until marriage not primarily for religious reasons, but because it will make for a better marriage:

Just because I think you're definitely going to have so much better of a relationship if you can wait until you're married. But it's a really hard thing to do. But it's pretty, um, um, honorable, you know, and it's the best gift that you could give to that person that you're going to spend the rest of your life with. So I definitely think it's worth waiting for.

An alternative interpretation of instrumental religious influence, one that gives the benefit of the doubt to the inarticulateness of many religiously conservative teenagers, might go like this: God's laws exist for the good and protection of his people. In other words, because God loves people, he gave them commands to which they ought to adhere (like keeping sex within the boundary of marriage). By obeying God's commands, people avoid the destructive consequences of sin (STDs, pregnancy out of wedlock). Breaking God's rules is thought to bring disorder and pain. While such logic tends to be unreflective about the nature and purpose of the command itself—why God might want to restrict intercourse to marriage—this may be due primarily to the pragmatic, ends-oriented nature of American evangelical Christianity.

In other words, it may *not* be the case that adolescents are ignoring the point of religious teachings on sex, but that those religious teachings are never relayed to them in the first place.[11] The evangelical youth pastor featured in the documentary *The Education of Shelby Knox* fit this model: his technique focused on doing whatever it takes—including denigrating sex as a simple act that even dogs do—to deliver youths to their wedding night with their virginity still intact. The message becomes less about understanding and articulating *why* God made the rule than remaining clear *that* God made the rule. Since God said it, it's good enough for them. But is it enough to direct their actions?

## INVISIBLE RELIGION

Invisible religion is likewise common, but it is also the most difficult to detect. It occurs when youth who do not consider themselves very religious *inadvertently obey* religious norms. For obvious reasons, it's less easily distinguished in conversations with individual adolescents. Yet just because many youth do not exude religiousness, we should not presume that religion bears no relationship to their actions. After all, how adept are we adults at really understanding and articulating the forces that shape our own decisions and priorities? We think we know why we act as we do, but we are easily deceived and often only account for socially acceptable aspects of our motivations.

The trained observer can often note the presence of invisible religion by asking questions about parents' and adolescents' religious practices and affiliations, how valuable religion is in their lives, and their religious commitments, together with a close examination of how these are associated with the personal resources and protective factors available to them: perhaps a two-parent family, ample parental monitoring, a healthy self-image, good relations with family members, family with adequate interest in their education and future, etc. This is not to say that these phenomena cannot occur apart from religious families, but rather that, when they do occur within religious families, it is unlikely that religion has nothing to do with them.

Consider Jonathan, the young man quoted in chapter 4. Although he attends religious services with some regularity, he does not articulate any religious teachings about sex or even awareness that his faith *has* rules and resources addressing human sexual expression. But Jonathan lives in an intact, two-parent family, with a mother who cares about and watches out for him and a father who provides responsibly for his family. The family's religious involvement may indeed have something to do with those phenomena and, in turn, with Jonathan's behavioral choices.[12] When I spoke with Jonathan in 2005, he wasn't actively going to church any more and had lost his virginity, but for reasons he could not explain (despite my efforts to explore them), he very much regretted the incident and was content to avoid further sexual contact for the time being. While some social scientists may disagree with me here, the events and traits of his life and home suggest to me that religion retains an invisible influence upon Jonathan. Religion constitutes a "horizon of significance" for him and for many—an inescapable, meaningful identity that can continue to shape the course of lives long after people stop actively recognizing it (Taylor 1991). Like the "Catholic guilt" felt on occasion by many people who no longer practice the faith, religion can remain influential, even while invisible.

So how do social scientists document something that is invisible? Evidence from survey-based research is the easiest way to detect the presence of invisible religious influence on a particular behavior, although survey research makes it impossible to document its presence for any particular person. Church attendance is an example of a form of religiosity whose influence is almost always indirect and frequently invisible to the adherent. Simply attending church, with its greetings, readings, songs, sacraments, and sermons, is not going to *cause* adolescents to delay first sex or engage with fewer sexual partners. While there could be a zero-sum time-in-church-equals-time-not-spent-with-one's-boyfriend-or-girlfriend scenario at work here, the more likely explanation is that church attendance is related to delayed first sex and fewer sexual partners via certain (potentially unmeasured) pathways. We know that church attendance can be a socially integrative force, creating social support networks (Ellison and George 1994), and that regular religious involvement reinforces traditional authority structures, especially the family unit (Brody et al. 1994; Pearce and Axinn 1998; Wilcox 2002). In turn, social support, heightened monitoring, and strong families each contribute to diminished sexual activity among adolescents (Jacobson and Crockett 2000; Upchurch et al. 1999). Having sex is difficult in the absence of opportunities to do so, and there is no doubt that more extensive involvement in organized religion curbs available free time and makes it less likely that some adolescents will get into circumstances where they might have to come up with superhuman efforts to resist sex in the heat of the moment. All of these influences may occur without the religious individual making any use of religious language about avoiding a particular behavior. The effect is invisible but clearly real.

## MORAL COMMUNITIES

Another way in which religion wields invisible influence is in the broader social context or community where people live. That is, religion is not only the property of individuals but of groups. This is referred to as the "moral communities" thesis, prompted by Emile Durkheim and more recently popularized by Rodney Stark. Durkheim found that collective religiosity and common ritual practice provides individuals with both an obligation and a desire to conform to community norms. Stark (1996) argues that individual religiosity is related to conformity (obedience to norms) only in distinctly *religious* contexts, communities where the mean level of religiosity is high (Stark and Bainbridge 1996). Without the support of fellow believers, he suggests, the influence of religion on personal behavior is weakened. I refer to this as the "light switch" part of the moral communities thesis. For example, the influence of religion on a particular adolescent's sexual choices is different for one who is surrounded by like-minded friends than for one in a distinct religious minority (be it a *true* minority, such as the only Muslim in a Catholic high school, or a *perceived* minority, such as the only Christian who thinks teen sexual relationships are wrong.) Such youths face a tougher battle than others do to act according to their particular religious principles. Research on first sex suggests that sexual decision making is "strongly bound to social context," with school peers playing a critical role in "creating a sense of normative behavior" (Kinsman et al. 1998: 1185; also see Bearman and Brückner 2001; Teitler and Weiss 2000).

Thus, some knowledge of the religious and normative settings in which adolescents live is important—but seldom considered—for adequately understanding how religion affects their sexual decisions. Additionally, just how embedded any given adolescent is in a social and friendship network may matter as well. Stephen Ellingson and his colleagues (2004: 19) note in their study of the Chicago sex market that "the more firmly embedded individuals are in a network, the more likely other network members are to influence their sex-market choices." Thus, not only the sexual behavior of our friends and neighbors affects our own sexual decisions, but also how enmeshed we are in those networks. Isolates are less affected than those more deeply embedded.

Unfortunately, most social science data only have measures of religion and religiosity at the level of the individual, not a collective. Add Health data, however, *do* include measures of social context (for example, see Tables A5.1 and A5.3, where I control for the percentage of schoolmates who are non-virgins). Drawing upon these data, Amy Adamczyk and Jacob Felson (2006) explore whether the religiosity of adolescents' friends and characteristics of the friendship network influence adolescents' own sexual decision making, something I did not explicitly consider in chapter 5. They focus on three aspects of the structure of adolescents' friendship groups: sociability, popularity, and density. They define "sociability" as an adolescent's level of participation in activities with friends. Low sociability could reduce attachment to the group, lowering the likelihood of adhering to group norms. "Popularity" is fairly self-evident, and network "density" refers to how much members of a friendship network know and interact with other members of the group. When friendship networks are denser, the researchers hypothesize, friends will know and interact with each other more frequently, and more monitoring should result, as well as limited opportunities to meet outsiders. Obviously, these friendship-group traits do not inherently lend themselves toward pursuing or avoiding sex. However, in the presence of high religiosity among one's friends, these network traits may enhance adherence to religious sexual norms. The opposite may also be true: if Joe is the only devoutly religious believer among his friends, his restrictive attitudes about sex will not likely alter the group's more permissive sexual norms. It is much more likely that Joe will alter his sexual attitudes and practices in consonance with group norms, or else struggle to adhere to them while under normative assault.

What Adamczyk and Felson have discovered is striking: when a youth's friends display elevated personal religiosity, her/his own odds of having had sex diminish considerably. Moreover, devoutly religious friends have a leavening effect—influencing the sexual decision making of both religious and irreligious adolescents alike. The authors also noted that as youths spend more time with their friends, their friends' religiosity becomes a more important predictor of whether or not they have had sex.

Particular aspects of the friendship group's structure also make a difference. First, the protective effect of friends' religiosity increases as the friendship group's network density increases. In other words, when adolescents are embedded in a tight set of friendships, the effect of their friends' religiosity is more likely to delay their virginity loss than would the religiosity of a friend in a sparse friendship network. Network density in religious friendship groups enhances monitoring and thereby limits opportunities for sexual intercourse (while perhaps elevating the opportunity to meet like-minded members of the opposite sex). So the researchers concluded that adolescents embedded in cohesive friendships with religious teens are more likely to conform to religious norms against premarital sex.

What does this have to do with invisible religious influence? Simply put, the influence of friendship group traits are largely invisible to the individuals. While parents may have conceptions in their minds of how "good" or "bad" friends may affect their adolescent children, the actual influence on the individual is difficult to document. Network density, sociability, and shared religiosity all exist and can—with considerable effort—be measured. But they are not visible or audible. I myself am not aware of how dense my own friendship networks are, or how sociable I actually am. By evaluating a group of individuals from the outside, however, researchers can uncover such invisible religious influences by employing statistical methods of analysis.

## INCONSISTENT RELIGION

Adolescents often act out of step with their religious ideals, in ways they themselves would call inconsistent. This is hardly unusual and certainly does not end with the arrival of adulthood. Why do religious ideals often fail to translate into action?

There are three best assumptions that scholars examining potential religious influences should hold with respect to social behavior. First, people may not do what they want to do. This continues to surprise social scientists, especially those who believe that humans are rational actors. Paul of Tarsus—the biblical missionary and author—characterizes this phenomenon in his letter to the Christian church in Rome: "For what I do is not the good I want to do; no, the evil I do not want to do, this I keep on doing" (Rom. 7:19). Many Christians—young and old—are familiar with this text and join Paul in bemoaning their own failures.

Second, people may not put into practice what they say they believe. This is a variant of the first assumption and no less obvious to astute observers of human actions. It too may be largely unconscious. Michael Emerson and Christian Smith (2000) document the reality of this in the lives of American evangelical adults who voice a commitment to end racism and to promote racial reconciliation. Sometimes, they simply do not understand the nature of the problem; other times, they have trouble carrying out what they believe to be right. Religious traditions, texts, and leaders themselves acknowledge that adherents often fail to live up to the expectations of their faith traditions and communities. Thus, social scientists ought to expect to see weaknesses, shortcomings, and failures in the lives of religious believers.

Third, religious expectations for actions often compete with other preferences and normative expectations. Adolescents regularly experience moral dilemmas about what course of action to take. And American society has experienced considerable secularization at the macrosocial level: many of the public institutions under and within which adolescents live their lives (the state, mass education, the media) have undergone a historical process of excluding religious interests and discourse as irrelevant or illegitimate (Smith 2003a). As the moral orders of contemporary institutions continue to diverge from historic religious moral orders (for example, self-interest versus the religious ethic of self-sacrifice), pressure is placed on people to act in ways contrary to their religious traditions. In other words, religious teens may act irreligiously at times as they carry out the expected behaviors of competing scripts. This incongruity of action may be most clearly visible during adolescence, as religious teachings against property destruction, drunkenness, and fornication clash with teenage social norms prescribing "trashing" and theft, parties, and losing your virginity.

For Rosita, a 17-year-old Hispanic girl from Arizona who attends mass only sporadically, church teachings are clear on sexual matters. But her behavior, she acknowledges, is not in line with them. She admits that the church is probably right:

> Yeah, because you're supposed to wait until you're married. [laughs] You're supposed to wear a white dress, but... [*Do you agree with it?*] Well, I was taught to believe, to agree with it, so, I think I, I don't know. Even though it's, like, I don't really practice it, I think I do agree with it.

The Church is right and she is wrong, she says, but little evidence suggests that Rosita is prepared to bring her behavior in line with her church's teachings anytime soon.

Tony, a 14-year-old Hispanic Catholic from California, could be classified as a sexual anticipator from our conversation about sexual attitudes and motivations. But he's also somewhat aware of where his church stands on adolescent sex:

> My religion says that you should just have it when you're married, or at least I think that. I don't really know. Yeah, I really don't know. [*Do you agree with that?*] Ah, yes. [*Why?*] Because it's my religion; I was taught to believe in it. [*OK, but um, earlier you said if you had the opportunity, you might do it anyway.*] Yeah. [*So would you follow with your religion, or would you follow with the moment?*] The moment.

Although Tony has not yet disobeyed church teachings on sex, he still fits the inconsistent class of the typology rather well. In fact, a disproportionate number of Latino Catholics express such a sense of "I know I'm not living up to my church's teachings about sex." Whether linked to the Catholic guilt phenomenon I noted above or not, inconsistent religion is not as common as invisible or irrelevant religion.


## IRRELEVANT RELIGION

In contrast to those displaying inconsistent religion, a person may know what her/his belief system says, but may not care or may actively disagree and act in opposition to it. Such people exhibit irrelevant religion. Such adolescents are not irreligious, since they report a religious affiliation, are often involved in organized religious activities, and may be aware of the religious teachings and claims upon their behavior. But they just don't care, because such claims are irrelevant and need not be obeyed. Amanda, a 15-year-old mainline Protestant from Tennessee quoted briefly in chapter 4, fits this category:

> I was confused before I had sex, 'cause here I am going to church and people
> are telling me wait 'til you're married, and here I am having friends that
> have already done it millions of times. And so you're kind of stuck with, you
> don't know, I mean, excuse me, you *know* when you're ready.

A regular churchgoer, Amanda nevertheless has no regrets about losing her virginity to her ex-boyfriend, despite her perceptions of church teachings: "I just, I don't think you should have to wait 'til you're married." It's as simple as that—she doesn't believe the rule applies to her. By both her actions (extensive sexual activity) and her words (disregard for the church's teachings on sex), she distinguishes herself from other adolescents for whom religion may have an invisible influence on their behavior. She carries forward with her the experience of religious socialization that is either ignored or perhaps actively rebelled against. Jeremy, a 17-year-old Catholic from Connecticut, puts such an approach in frank terms when he speaks about his own faith and that of his friends: "[Religion] really doesn't come into play with any of us, not at all in terms of our interactions. Religion may influence [my friends]. I have no idea."

For some adolescents, their motivations and decisions for such actions stem in part from a desire to violate the religious traditions or teachings with which they grew up and which they have grown to resent. This too, strangely enough, signifies an enduring effect of religion (see my discussion of Taylor's horizon of significance earlier in this chapter). Bart, a 15-year-old evangelical Protestant from Alabama who doesn't attend church much, nevertheless discerns with considerable acumen a pattern of "age-appropriate" religious irrelevance in his town that repeats itself with each generation. It leaves him skeptical of claims about religious motivation, even in conservative Alabama:

> I've noticed that most adults, particularly in our church . . . most of them don't realize or change or repent of their ways. Or they don't realize it until they're like 20 or 30. And so, like, also at school, particularly at school, most of the kids there, they don't have, they don't think a single idea or thought about anything [concerning] religion or dating or anything.

God, Bart told us bluntly, would pretty much have to lay his hand directly on a teenager if her/his dating and sexual behavior were going to be affected by religion. Instead, Bart thinks religion is simply scripted as irrelevant during this phase of the life course. Adults, even religious ones, are complicit in this, and each generation is "allowed" to ignore religious moral directives about sex until it's time to get serious, settle down, and have a family.

## IRRELIGION

Finally, some youths are not religiously observant (so far as surveys and interviews can tell), know very little about any religious claims upon their behavior, and act without regard for any particular religious teachings. I label this irreligion, or the absence of religion and its influence. It is found among youth who are either entirely devoid of religion or who are religiously inactive and neither know nor care about any religious claims on their behavior. Despite how morally charged adults may think adolescent sexual practice is, for these adolescents sex seems largely (but perhaps not entirely) devoid of moral implications. Little needs to be said about irreligion, since it should be straightforward in documentation and interpretation.

Kelly, a 17-year-old girl from Nevada, provides an example of irreligion. When asked whether she thinks young people should wait until marriage to have sex, she opines: "I think people should make up their own decision and not worry about pleasing God and say, 'Oh, I'm sinning.' Because God didn't write that book. Someone else did." Kelly has had five sexual partners, the first at age 15. Unlike Amanda, who attends church regularly, this irreligious young woman nevertheless indicates regret about her sexual activity. When asked how she feels about her decisions, Kelly responds, "Um . . . I'm, like, disappointed in myself." How does she deal with that? "I don't know, I just . . . don't think about it all that much." Recall the words of Carol, a 17-year-old nonreligious girl I quoted in chapter 4: "I don't see why sex is such a sacred thing to so many people. Um, I guess to some people sex is a way of expressing love. But to me, it's not. It's just not." How does she feel about having had 10 or 11 sexual partners already?

> I'm fine with [it]. It doesn't bother me at all. I really don't like the stereotype that if a girl sleeps with more than one guy she's a whore [and] if a guy does it he's a pimp. I think that a girl can be as sexually active as she wants to be. Just, she needs to be safe about it.

Survey research from both Add Health and the NSYR, and likely from other sources, reinforces the conclusion here that irreligious youth exhibit far fewer boundaries around sexual behavior. Tables in chapters 4 and 5 suggest that they exhibit less anticipated guilt from sex, tend to have first sex earlier, and have more numerous sexual partners, but do not distinguish themselves in terms of contraceptive use.

In sum, the question of religious influence does not yield a yes-or-no answer. The real challenge lies in documenting the *type* of influence that religion has on adolescent and adult behavior. Six variations characterize my typology of religious influence: intentional, instrumental, invisible, inconsistent, irrelevant, and irreligion. In terms of religious influence on adolescent sexual decision making, the most common types are instrumental and invisible religion, with irrelevant religion marking a significant minority as well. Irreligion and inconsistent religion follow, and intentional religion appears from all accounts to be the rarest form of religious influence. The case may be altogether different for other outcomes besides sex, or if applied to the study of adult religious influence. The typology is a flexible one.

# CONCLUSIONS

By now, it is no surprise that mixed messages are being issued in the realm of adolescent sexuality, from both adolescents themselves and the adults and social institutions around them. In this book, I have focused my attention on organized religion, its identities and practices, and I've concerned myself with how they shape adolescents' sexual perspectives and actions. Some of the stories have been predictable ones, like the sexually conservative attitudes of evangelical Protestant teenagers and the more permissive practices of nonreligious youth. Other stories are surprises: the anomalies of evangelical conservative sexual attitudes versus their permissive practices, and mainline Protestants' tolerant attitudes and penchant for delaying first sex. Out of these results, both the expected and the astonishing, twelve key themes have emerged.

First, religiosity almost always makes a difference. The key story of religious influence on adolescent sexual decision making is typically best captured by religiosity, not differences between religious groups such as evangelical Protestants, Catholics, Mormons, and Jews (interesting as those are). But just because it makes a difference does not mean that religion *motivates* adolescents' sexual decision making. For not a few youths we interviewed, religious involvement alone does not equal religious influence on their sexual attitudes and behavior. Something more is required for religion to make a more apparent difference in the sexual lives of adolescents, and that something is a plausibility structure—a network of like-minded friends, family, and authorities who (a) teach and enable comprehensive religious perspectives about sexuality to compete more effectively against ubiquitous sexually permissive scripts, and (b) offer desexualized time and space and provide reinforcement of parental values (including the importance of education and a future orientation). While relatively rare, such plausibility structures enable youth to actively choose to hold sexual attitudes or to shun certain sexual practices for *religious* reasons.

Such religious intentionality is the hallmark of a small segment of American adolescents, excluding even most religious adolescents.

Second, more devoutly religious parents tend to talk less often to their adolescent children about sex and birth control, and most often about sexual morality. They fear that conversations about contraception may lead to sexual practice, and their hunch about this is not entirely without evidence. Parents' religion is considerably less influential on their communication habits than several demographic characteristics of parent and child (including the age of both, race/ethnicity, and the teen's gender). Yet most parents, religious or otherwise, do attempt to communicate about sex and contraception with their adolescent children, especially girls. African-American parents talk more, and with greater ease, likely in response to their perceptions of urgency, since their adolescent children tend to experience first sex at earlier ages. When religious parents do talk, some of them struggle with such conversations, in no small part because their own religious traditions have not done a good job of helping them to understand sexuality through theological lenses. Despite all of the sexual communication that is allegedly occurring, most adolescents do not know very much about sex and pregnancy. Adolescents higher in personal religiosity tend to know slightly less about both. In the end, balancing information about sexuality with expectations about boundaries is a rare but optimal approach to a well-rounded, morally sensitive sexual socialization and is appreciated by most teenagers.

Third, religion affects adolescents' sexual attitudes and motivations more than their actions. More devoutly religious youth anticipate considerable guilt from sexual activity, are least likely to think that sex is physically pleasurable, and told us that their parents were opposed to adolescent sex. Other sexual motivations displayed more class-based associations that reflected a fear of harm to adolescents' future educational and earning power. Adolescents from "higher-class" religious affiliations like mainline Protestantism and Judaism were among the most likely to fear pregnancy. There is also religious and social class patterning of sexual activity preferences. Mainline Protestant and Jewish adolescents are more likely to delay vaginal intercourse, given its threat to their life chances, and are instead among the most likely to experience oral sex and (among boys) to use pornography.

Fourth, emotional readiness, a key barometer of contemporary sexual preparedness, is a slippery term. It displays few connections to religion, apart from a predictable disdain among adolescents who think it wise to wait until marriage. While it resonates with many adolescents, some note that it can only be understood in hindsight. If they end up regretting their first sexual experience, then they weren't ready. If they don't, then they were. Most adolescents, including many religious ones, hint at an emerging set of sexual norms that has little to do with religion, including (a) don't be pressured or pressure someone else into sex, (b) don't sleep around, for the sake of your own reputation, (c) the only person who can decide whether a sexual relationship is OK is you, and (d) sex should optimally only occur within the framework of a "long-term" relationship: at least three months, by their accounts.

Fifth, the success of abstinence pledging is mixed. Evangelicals, Mormons, and generally more religious adolescents are the most apt to like the idea of—and take—a pledge to abstain from sex until marriage. Pledgers, especially girls, are idealists. They expect a lot from marriage and from married sex. (For all its naïveté, this view is a refreshing break from the description of numerous sexually active teens that sex is "no big deal.") Documenting pledging success is a challenge, however. The majority of pledgers do indeed break their promise somewhere on the way to the altar (and in up to 7 of 10 cases, it is *not* with their future spouse). Yet there is good news for the pledge movement as well: most pledgers significantly delay their experience of first intercourse, which reduces their lifetime exposure to STDs. They have fewer sexual partners than do nonpledgers, and more faithful sexual partners. They are, however, more likely to avoid contraception at first sex. In the end, real pledges successfully kept are inarguably effective. They're just unusual. And we haven't heard the final word on the 45 percent of pledgers (in Add Health) who are both still unmarried and still virgins.

Sixth, American teenagers are far from oversexed. There is a difference between popular, mass media perceptions of adolescence as a hypersexual time of life and the reality of what teens tell us in person. Most have not yet had sex, though most will before the conclusion of their teenage years. Experimenting with bisexuality is considerably more common among adolescent girls than boys, though this diminishes in early adulthood. Less religious youth are more likely than devoutly religious teenagers to report—and probably feel more comfortable reporting—same-sex attraction, same-sex sexual experience, and a bisexual self-identity. When adolescents do experience first (heterosexual) sex, few try it just once. That is, most heterosexual teenagers are either sexually active or have never had sex. A significant minority nevertheless expresses sexual regrets and describes negative sexual experiences. Gender is the key distinction: girls' accounts of regrets are much more frequent than boys', for whom a bad sexual experience tends to amount to a disappointing choice of sexual partner or an unfulfilling encounter.

Seventh, evangelical Protestant youth may hold less sexually permissive attitudes than most other religious youth, but they are *not* the last to lose their virginity, on average. Not even close. This is one of the most interesting and ironic stories emerging from these analyses. Apart from being enmeshed in plausibility structures that redefine and rechannel their priorities, evangelical teenagers don't display just average sexual activity patterns, but rather above-average ones. There are several plausible explanations for this anomaly, but I give most weight to the clash of cultures that evangelical adolescents are experiencing: they are urged to drink deeply from the waters of American individualism and its self-focused pleasure ethic, yet they are asked to value time-honored religious traditions like family and chastity. They attempt to do both (while other religious groups don't attempt this), and serving two masters is difficult. What results is a unique dialectic of sexual-conservatism-with-sexual-activity, a combination that breeds instability and the persistent suffering of consequences like elevated teen pregnancy rates. African-American Christians display the earliest average age at first sex among religious adolescents. While religiosity may modestly delay virginity loss among African Americans, even the most religious among them tend to exhibit first sex about as early as the least religious white adolescents.

Eighth, contraceptive use enjoys wide approval but inconsistent use among sexually active American teenagers. While less than 8 percent of all teenagers—primarily Catholics, Mormons, and black Protestants—question the morality of contraception, fully 30–40 percent of them fail to use contraception during their first experience of intercourse. Religiosity is associated with thinking that birth control is immoral and that it makes you look like you want sex, but there is little evidence to suggest that any particular religious traditions, even Catholicism, actually shape contraceptive use.

Ninth, anecdotes and media reports aside, there is little evidence of adolescents practicing oral sex without vaginal intercourse for the purpose of maintaining a sense of purity. Nevertheless, the technical virginity description still fits around 16 percent of American youth. Since those religious adolescents most likely to engage exclusively in oral sex—mainline Protestant and Jewish youth—also tend to be more sexually tolerant in general, it is more precise to dub this practice "substitution." Such teens are simply abstaining from vaginal intercourse for the present, in order to safeguard their educational futures. This middle-class sexual script is parent-driven and is not sexually conservative in a religious sense. Thus, the practice is about risk reduction, not morality.

Tenth, there is evidence that the practice of anal sex is beginning to increase among heterosexual American teenagers. I say this because its prevalence is considerably higher in the 2002 NSFG than in the Add Health, administered in the mid-1990s. Here again, this is not due to a religiously motivated pursuit of technical virginity. Rather, greater religiosity decidedly diminishes this practice. It is far more common among adolescents who say they are not religious, who never attend religious services, and who think that religion is unimportant. So while American teenagers largely appear to be traditional in their sexual practices, there are hints that this may be starting to change. If true, the ubiquity of pornography is likely playing a role in such evolution.

Eleventh, the typology of religious influence is a useful tool as social scientists investigate the variety of ways in which religion shapes human behavior, whether studying adolescents or adults. The most popular types of religious influence on the sexual decisions of teenagers are invisible, instrumental, and irrelevant religion, followed by inconsistent religion and irreligion. Intentional religiosity is rare among teenagers.

Twelfth and finally, few adolescents, no matter how religious, articulate a deep, nuanced sexual ethic. Although many religious traditions and texts suggest that sex is part of the good created order, that its connection to the formation of human life is not accidental, that sex outside the context of a committed relationship harms both participants, etc., the only sexual message most religious youth are getting is, "Don't do it until you're married." And this message doesn't go far at all toward shaping sexual decision making.

# Unscientific Postscript

My purpose in writing this book has been to convey what is, not what ought to be.[1] I want to close now with several reflections about investigating the social science of adolescent sexuality in a manner that attempts to value solid research, and yet pays adequate deference to the interests of adolescents, their parents, and the organizations that serve them. A Weberian approach seeks to understand the expressed ends of the research participants and their communities, to evaluate their likelihood of attaining them, and to suggest alternative ways of reaching those goals. In this tradition, I offer my thoughts.

## SUBOPTIMAL SEX

Adolescents are not alone in articulating confusing and nebulous sexual norms. Researchers and experts often fare no better, and they increasingly struggle to identify what is wrong, if anything, with adolescent sexual behavior. Until recently, studies of adolescent sex have often been grouped together with studies of juvenile delinquency or deviance. But sex has become more evidently normative during adolescence, so it is by definition no longer deviant or forbidden. In light of this, some scholars have wished to altogether deproblematize adolescent sexual behavior, emphasizing instead values such as mutual consent, positive body image, sexual self-esteem, the development of a sexual activity "skill set,"[2] and the use of contraception as linchpins of a "healthier" adolescent sexuality (Brooks-Gunn and Paikoff 1997; Risman and Schwartz 2002; Schalet 2004; Thompson 1990). From within this approach, the language of religious morality sounds senseless beside the languages of law, public health, and the social service sector (Ellingson 2004). The only wrongs, then, are underage sex (statutory rape), molestation,[3] nonconsensual sex, and unequal sexual power. Deviant sexual practices become those that pose a threat to an adolescent's physical health or long-term economic life chances.

I want to assert several important reasons why we may still wish to consider sex as suboptimal for adolescents. First, adolescents lack secure and stable romantic relationships, and while security may not be requisite for good sex, it does make for emotional health and deeper sexual contentment, goods most of us would agree are valuable (Giordano 2003; Waite and Joyner 2001). As adults, we often refer to sex within a stable relationship as "making love," and a fleeting sexual partnership as "hooking up" or as an "affair." Then there's also the crudest form of faceless, transactional sex between entirely self-focused individuals, commonly referred to with an expletive. But none of these terms seem to fit for teenagers. Most of them, especially girls, do not respect the brevity of short-term hooking-up relationships and are certainly averse to crude, faceless sex. But neither do we think of their sexual activity as making love, because love entails relational stability and commitment (Risman and Schwartz 2002). It's as if we don't believe adolescents can make love because we don't believe they can make relationship promises they can keep. Instead we say, as I have throughout this book, that adolescents "have sex." Would we want to accept for our adolescents, then, something we adults tend to *not* wish for ourselves: sexual relationships largely divorced from real intimacy, security, love, and commitment? Presently, we are threatening to not only accept such half-baked relationships, but even encourage them.

Second, while sexual development may be complete by mid-adolescence, teenagers are in a state of constant emotional maturation and development over the entire course of this life stage (Weinberger, Elvevåg, and Giedd 2005). Moreover, the moral development of boys in the West tends to lag behind that of girls (Gilligan 1982). Duty-based and other-oriented norms are simply slower to form in boys, and they tend to develop more rapidly in early adulthood, alongside significant life course transitions such as marriage and child-rearing. As a result, boys are more likely to compartmentalize moral claims upon their sexual behavior and less likely to understand sex as optimally involving relational commitment. Fathers do not get anxious about their daughters' boyfriends without reason. Adolescent boys are simply more likely than girls to see sex as an unmitigated good (Martin 2002).

Perhaps, instead, we ought to give adolescent girls, who are more apt to both anticipate and exhibit regret, the benefit of the doubt, rather than a push toward "liberation" from how they think about sexual relationships.[4] It seems wiser to trust their moral senses on this count. Teenage girls may actually like the idea that they could "take charge of their romantic relationships and may not have to barter their bodies to get boys' attention" (Smith and Denton

2005: 194). In a society bursting with sexuality and increasingly relying on the Internet for sexual socialization, why would we want to suggest to adolescent girls that their sexual reticence is a problem?

Third, sex for adolescents is often (although certainly not always) expressed within relationships that display clear power differences between girls and boys (Martin 2002). Sometimes this is reflected in age differences, and on rare occasions we penalize this with the force of law. To be sure, some things have certainly improved, including a declining sexual double standard and a decreased likelihood of adolescent girls understanding sex as more transactional than relational. Yet the prevalence of rape and molestation reported in our interviews and the significant age differentials in sexual pairing are worth our concern. By definition, such acts entail less power among adolescent girls to make their own sexual decisions and to feel good about them. I suspect that even the most libertine of advocates for a freer adolescent sexuality would not like the idea of their own 13-year-old son or daughter becoming sexually active. Nor would most parents feel comfortable with their 17-year-old "making love" to a 30-year-old, legal though it is in most states.

Viscerally, we react to such scenarios because morally something is amiss. Sex is a moral act, and it is impossible to think about adolescent sexual attitudes and behavior in morally neutral terms. Changing the salient language to emphasize "healthy" or "unhealthy," "wise" or "unwise" cannot bury the reality that some conception of what is "good" will win out and another will be lost by the wide adoption of such linguistic conventions. Official moral neutrality about sex is a fiction: it merely disguises the moral assumptions upon which actors draw and which institutions purvey (Ellingson 2004; Smith 2003b). *There is no value-free perspective on sex.*

Sex is far from a *simple* pleasure. The emotional pain that lingers after poor sexual decision making, at any age, is evidence of the complex morality inherent to human sexuality. The sexual human begs for something better and more lasting than hooking up or satiating a partner's will. Sexual intercourse has connectional qualities that, when experienced within committed, loving relationships, touch our souls. Girls especially sense this, while adolescent male culture tends to suppress and redirect this insight. Disconnection and loneliness can both trigger and result from adolescent sexual activity (Clark 2004; Hallfors et al. 2005).[5] For all of these reasons, sex without security tends to damage people on the inside. Serial monogamy fares only slightly better, while multiplying opportunities for pain and disconnection. Simplifying and disenchanting human sexuality nets few returns, save for irresponsibility, unhappiness, and fractured relationships and families. Personally, I continue to be mystified—and not infrequently frustrated—by my own sexuality and desire. Yet I dread the day when sex is no longer mysterious or occasionally frustrating. Do we really wish it differently for our own children?

## PARENTAL RIGHTS AND RESPONSIBILITIES

Distinctly religious claims on adolescent sexual behavior should not be thought of as illegitimate by researchers and academics. Many of the noisiest religious voices talking about sex today would heartily agree with the importance of positive body image and the emergence of legitimate sexual desire, even while disputing that paired sexual practice is acceptable for youth (McDowell 2002; Winner 2005). I might be more amenable to the health-and-life-chances approach to evaluating adolescent sexuality if I could see that sexually active teenagers actually exhibited better emotional health, happiness, heightened respect between genders, a more mature sense of responsibility, and an improved ability to make lasting, intimate relationships. It's *just not there*—not in the survey data, the interviews, or other published studies.

While most devoutly religious parents may see the world differently than do researchers and public health professionals, parents should never be considered the enemy whose outdated norms need to be overcome. They are the legal guardians and, indeed, the first loves of their children. Girls especially rely on their fathers' attention to tide them over until they transfer allegiance to another (Martin 2002). Parents are more than monitors to be eluded; they are stakeholders in their adolescents' sexual decision making (Ellingson et al. 2004).[6] A thousand anecdotes about overbearing parents can never merit a categorical dismissal of their right and obligation to socialize their children as they see fit.

Parents and religious organizations are not off the hook, however. Far from it. The evidence presented in chapter 3 suggests that many religious parents avoid talking openly with their adolescent children about sex and contraception. This is at best foolish and potentially harmful to the development of a healthy sexuality, and at worst maddeningly irresponsible as we enter an era of the Internet-as-sex-educator. Popular, media, and peer cultures are well positioned as sex educators if parents are not.[7] We owe our children a more comprehensive sex education—moral advocacy *and* information—than most of them are getting. Their pledges of abstinence are not valid reasons to avoid informing them about sexual matters. Mothers and fathers have the power—and, I would argue, the responsibility—to break any legacies of secrecy about sex, to resist sexual double standards, to both instruct their adolescents about the beauty, pleasures, and complexities of sex and human anatomy *as well as* pass on to them their own moral assertions about sexual boundaries. Not only would this approach function to improve the sexual experience of women and men and the marital happiness of many, but it would also likely function to reduce both the teenage pregnancy and abortion rates—something we all agree would be a good thing.

## (ANTI-)FAMILY MATTERS

There remains an almost categorical disregard concerning family health in debates about adolescent sexual behavior. First and most obvious is the anti-marriage sentiment at work within the social science research community. In its eyes, marriage (if ever entered into at all) and childbearing should be put off until one's education is complete and one's career trajectory is secure. Families are mere additions to the unrivaled, unfettered individual. Fertility control has become not only an assumption but a new moral imperative. Few Americans—including most religious ones—disagree.

Religious conservatives deserve little credit here as well, given their narrow vision of marriage and family. They esteem the institution of family, fight over its definition, and war against abortion, yet laws about the definition of marriage will do little to stimulate values like self-sacrifice and fidelity. Although marriage rates remain high among them, many of their families continue to break apart on the shoals of individualism and consumer capitalism and the self-focused desires it creates. (No battle over the redefinition of marriage will ever do as much damage to the institution as this undisputed modern force.) Religious groups would do well to think more creatively about the health of families as they ponder how to advocate for positive sexuality within the bounds of marriage. Little effort is expended on preparing adolescents for marriage and family life (Holman and Li 1997; Martin, Martin, and Martin 2001). Instead, family-focused religious conservatives want to have their cake (no sex before marriage) and eat it too (delayed marriage and family formation—the triumph of free market consumer-oriented individualism).[8] Having to wait until age 25 or 30 to have sex *is* unreasonable. Yet if religious organizations and their adherents are going to continue advocating for Christian chastity, and I have no reason to suggest they won't or shouldn't, they must work more creatively to support younger marriages. This is not the 1950s (for which I am glad), where one could bank on social norms, extended (and larger) families, and clear gender roles to negotiate and sustain early family formation. We have none of those realities.

Instead of old-style finger wagging at premarital sexual behavior, congregations need to find new and practical ways to undergird the family, an institution of which they claim to be strong defenders. Congregations and parents would do well to involve their youth as more central participants rather than relegate them to the youth group, hold their breath, hope for the best, and breathe easy only after the adolescents have made it out of high school alive and without any life-altering episodes. Youth groups are not social control organizations tasked with preventing teenagers from acting like adults.

Religious conservatives have still more to worry about. The majority of religious interviewees with whom we spoke, the ones who might possibly own some sort of religious ethic concerning human sexuality, could articulate nothing more about what their faith has to say about sex than a simple no-sex-before-marriage rule. For most of them, this is the sum total of Christian teaching on sex. For the most part, congregations are doing a terrible job of fashioning distinctively Christian sexual ethics. Abstinence organizations seem primarily interested in pragmatically doing whatever it takes to stop adolescents from having sex. In fact, despite its numeric successes, the movement is hamstrung and self-limited because of American Christians' disinterest in taking a firmer position on marriage and the family. If family formation is best postponed, and any given marriage can be undone without consequence, why should young people wait to enjoy the benefits of sex within an unstable and temporary arrangement (marriage)?

Moreover, such a dualistic focus—the "did they" or "didn't they" question—unwittingly reinforces the sexual double standard. Nonvirgins are prompted to "reclaim" their virginity, but few young men seek such "restoration" (Hayt 2002). This emphasis is almost entirely about women's bodies and sexuality.[9] Adolescent boys and young men, as noted throughout the book, feel less sexual guilt and mention fewer negative sexual experiences. No one expects boys or men to cooperate in the first place. Indeed, the sexual revolution has ironically benefited men no less than women: men increasingly resist marriage, since without the threat of family formation (pregnancy), their sexual relationships are low risk (Ehrenreich 1983).

In sum, if congregations intend to be faithful to their own traditions about the body and sexuality, they should stop winking at this double standard, acknowledge it, and start having more frank conversations about the real sexual issues that real people face. Combined with a recovered understanding of Christian sexual ethics, such a course would be prochastity, profamily, *and* pro-sex.

# Appendix A

## REGRESSION MODELS

Regression analysis is a statistician's way of performing a controlled experiment. In order to isolate the effects of one variable on another, I must account for, or hold constant, other factors that might confound the association. Regression allows me to do this by simultaneously evaluating the independent effect of each variable on the outcome of interest. When coefficients are presented, a number greater than zero means that an increase in that variable has a *positive* association with the dependent variable (outcome) under examination. If the coefficient is less than zero, then an increase in that variable has a *negative* association with the outcome. When odds ratios are presented, a value greater than one indicates an *increase* in the odds of a higher level of the dependent variable, while values less than one are indicative of a reduction in the odds of a higher level of the outcome.

These tables also bring up the question of statistical significance. Because the surveys I use are samples of the American adolescent population, there remains the possibility that findings are a result of chance due to sampling error. That is, results may vary slightly because different samples of the population would yield slightly different results. Because of the large number of respondents in the NSYR, Add Health, and NSFG data sets, however, we can be confident that the results are similar to what would be obtained from analyses of the total population of American adolescents. Furthermore, I have performed tests of statistical significance that determine the actual likelihood that my findings are due to chance, or sampling error. A coefficient or odds ratio with a + next to it suggests that there is less than a 10 percent chance that the difference is due to sampling and is not a "real difference." One star (*) means there is less than a 5 percent chance, two stars (**) indicates less than a 1 percent chance, and three stars (***) signifies that there is less than a one-tenth of 1 percent chance that the finding is due to sampling error. If nothing appears next to a coefficient or odds ratio, it is implied that there is no statistically significant effect of that variable on the outcome.

Performing multivariate analyses like these boosts confidence that the associations between religion and sexual outcomes are actually the result of religion and not some other variable, such as race/ethnicity, gender, or age.

TABLE A3.1 Odds Ratios from Ordered Logit Regression Estimates of the Parent-Reported Frequency of Discussion about Sexual Morality

|  | *Model 1* | *Model 2* |
|---|---|---|
| *Parental Religion Measures* | | |
| Church attendance | | 1.148** |
| Importance of religion | | 1.448*** |
| Evangelical Protestant | 0.811* | 1.139 |
| Mainline Protestant | 0.502*** | 0.819 |
| Catholic | 0.491*** | 0.770+ |
| Jewish | 0.189*** | 0.357*** |
| Mormon (LDS) | 0.993 | 1.364 |
| Other religion | 0.650*** | 0.998 |
| No religion | 0.254*** | 1.157 |
| *Parental Controls* | | |
| Parents' average education | | 0.819** |
| White | | 0.804+ |
| Hispanic | | 0.757+ |
| Asian American | | 0.559** |
| Age | | 0.979*** |
| Female | | 1.306** |
| Bio-intact, two-parent family | | 0.974 |
| Disapproves of sex at child's age | | 1.188*** |
| Thinks their child has already had sex | | 1.244*** |
| *Adolescent Controls* | | |
| Female | | 1.648*** |
| Age | | 1.066** |
| School has sex education | | |
| Curriculum | | 0.928 |
| Has taken abstinence pledge | | 1.330*** |
| Family well-being | | 1.026** |
| Number of recent romantic partners | | 1.076** |
| *Model Fit Statistics* | | |
| −2 log likelihood | 37,706.5 | 36,595.3 |
| Pseudo $R^2$ | 0.016 | 0.045 |
| N | 13,726 | 13,726 |

+ $p < .10$; * $p < .05$; ** $p < .01$; *** $p < .001$.

*Source*: National Longitudinal Study of Adolescent Health

TABLE A3.2 Odds Ratios from Ordered Logit Regression Estimates of the Parent-Reported Frequency of Discussion about Sex and Birth Control with Their Adolescent Child

| | Frequency of talk about sex | | | Frequency of talk about birth control | | |
|---|---|---|---|---|---|---|
| | Model 1 | Model 2 | Model 3 | Model 1 | Model 2 | Model 3 |
| *Parental Religion Measures* | | | | | | |
| Church attendance | | 0.902*** | 0.796*** | | 0.893*** | 0.816*** |
| Importance of religion | | 1.224*** | 0.970 | | 1.101* | 0.887** |
| Evangelical Protestant | 0.516*** | 0.757+ | 0.637** | 0.501*** | 0.671** | 0.582*** |
| Mainline Protestant | 0.428*** | 0.671* | 0.698* | 0.484*** | 0.705** | 0.722** |
| Catholic | 0.369*** | 0.648** | 0.689* | 0.424*** | 0.664** | 0.701** |
| Jewish | 0.394*** | 0.638+ | 1.305 | 0.517*** | 0.814 | 1.531+ |
| Mormon (LDS) | 0.508*** | 0.935 | 0.696 | 0.379*** | 0.634* | 0.497*** |
| Other religion | 0.454*** | 0.708* | 0.635** | 0.481*** | 0.677** | 0.629*** |
| No religion | 0.365*** | 0.679+ | 0.531** | 0.528*** | 0.676* | 0.559** |
| *Parental Controls* | | | | | | |
| Parents' average education | | 1.063 | 1.241*** | | 0.946 | 1.036 |
| White | | 0.755* | 0.802* | | 0.841 | 0.891 |
| Hispanic | | 0.542*** | 0.549*** | | 0.660** | 0.701** |
| Asian American | | 0.295*** | 0.340*** | | 0.407*** | 0.479*** |
| Age | | 0.965*** | 0.972*** | | 0.962*** | 0.968*** |

*(continued)*

217

TABLE A3.2 (continued)

| | Frequency of talk about sex | | | Frequency of talk about birth control | | |
|---|---|---|---|---|---|---|
| | Model 1 | Model 2 | Model 3 | Model 1 | Model 2 | Model 3 |
| Female | | 1.300** | 1.159+ | | 1.231* | 1.102 |
| Bio-intact, two-parent family | | 0.780*** | 0.751*** | | 0.768*** | 0.745*** |
| Disapproves of sex at child's age | | 1.094*** | 0.988 | | 1.011 | 0.921*** |
| Thinks child has already had sex | | 2.359*** | 2.542*** | | 2.949*** | 3.116*** |
| Frequency of talk about morality of sex | | | 3.787*** | | | 2.841*** |
| *Adolescent Controls* | | | | | | |
| Female | | 1.544*** | 1.201*** | | 1.228*** | 0.977 |
| Age | | 1.096*** | 1.070*** | | 1.134*** | 1.120*** |
| School has sex education curriculum | | 1.132 | 1.230 | | 1.143 | 1.205 |
| Has taken abstinence pledge | | 1.092 | 0.920 | | 0.983 | 0.839* |
| Family well-being | | 1.036** | 1.027** | | 1.028** | 1.018* |
| Number of recent romantic partners | | 1.154*** | 1.138*** | | 1.128*** | 1.105*** |
| *Model Fit Statistics* | | | | | | |
| −2 log likelihood | 36,581.1 | 35,159.6 | 30,060.2 | 39,603.6 | 37,806.5 | 34,324.0 |
| Pseudo $R^2$ | 0.012 | 0.051 | 0.188 | 0.008 | 0.053 | 0.140 |
| N | 13,726 | 13,726 | 13,726 | 13,726 | 13,726 | 13,726 |

+ $p < .10$; * $p < .05$; ** $p < .01$; *** $p < .001$.

Source: National Longitudinal Study of Adolescent Health

TABLE A3.3 Odds Ratios from Ordered Logit Regression Estimates of the Parent-Reported Frequency and Ease/Difficulty of Talking about Sex

| | Frequency of talking about sex | | |
|---|---|---|---|
| | Model 1 | Model 2 | Model 3 |
| *Parental Religion Measures* | | | |
| Church attendance | | 0.952* | 0.980 |
| Importance of religion | | 1.107* | 1.091* |
| Evangelical Protestant | 0.700* | 0.708* | 0.587* |
| Mainline Protestant | 0.514*** | 0.525*** | 0.444** |
| Catholic | 0.533*** | 0.544*** | 0.519* |
| Jewish | 0.625* | 0.641* | 0.585[+] |
| Mormon (LDS) | 0.720 | 0.730 | 0.544 |
| Other religion | 0.474* | 0.478* | 0.582 |
| No religion | 0.702[+] | 0.727 | 0.728 |
| *Parental Controls* | | | |
| Parents' average education | | | 1.007 |
| White | | | 1.403 |
| Hispanic | | | 0.937 |
| Asian American | | | 0.323** |
| Age | | | 0.977*** |
| Female | | | 1.982*** |
| Respondent parent is married | | | 0.862 |
| Thinks people should wait to have sex until married | | | 1.037 |
| Knows or thinks child is dating | | | 1.200*** |
| Frequency of talking about sex | | | |
| *Adolescent Controls* | | | |
| Female | | | 1.703*** |
| Age | | | 1.084* |
| Has already had sex | | | 1.313* |
| Thinks people should wait until married to have sex | | | 0.999 |
| Quality of relationship with parents | | | 1.042 |
| *Model Fit Statistics* | | | |
| −2 log likelihood | 6,391.7 | 6,381.1 | 6,157.8 |
| Pseudo $R^2$ | 0.005 | 0.007 | 0.041 |
| N | 3,089 | 3,089 | 3,089 |

(*continued*)

| | Ease of talking with child about sex | | | |
| --- | --- | --- | --- | --- |
| | Model 1 | Model 2 | Model 3 | Model 4 |
| *Parental Religion Measures* | | | | |
| Church attendance | | 0.920*** | 0.936** | 0.938* |
| Importance of religion | | 1.115** | 1.080$^+$ | 1.058 |
| Evangelical Protestant | 0.415*** | 0.414*** | 0.577$^+$ | 0.677 |
| Mainline Protestant | 0.273*** | 0.266*** | 0.414** | 0.485* |
| Catholic | 0.334*** | 0.330*** | 0.484* | 0.574$^+$ |
| Jewish | 0.334*** | 0.322*** | 0.585 | 0.655 |
| Mormon (LDS) | 0.303*** | 0.312*** | 0.466$^+$ | 0.561 |
| Other religion | 0.438** | 0.425** | 0.695 | 0.719 |
| No religion | 0.489*** | 0.438*** | 0.670 | 0.683 |
| *Parental Controls* | | | | |
| Parents' average education | | | 0.940** | 0.938** |
| White | | | 0.757 | 0.646 |
| Hispanic | | | 0.728 | 0.693 |
| Asian American | | | 0.515 | 0.685 |
| Age | | | 0.991 | 0.998 |
| Female | | | 1.494*** | 1.220* |
| Respondent parent is married | | | 0.902 | 0.908 |
| Thinks people should wait to have sex until married | | | 1.132 | 1.136 |
| Knows or thinks child is dating | | | 1.138* | 1.078 |
| Frequency of talking about sex | | | | 2.923*** |
| *Adolescent Controls* | | | | |
| Female | | | 1.546*** | 1.341*** |
| Age | | | 1.029 | 1.005 |
| Has already had sex | | | 1.457*** | 1.407** |
| Thinks people should wait until married to have sex | | | 1.058 | 1.070 |
| Quality of relationship with parents | | | 1.094*** | 1.093*** |
| *Model Fit Statistics* | | | | |
| −2 log likelihood | 6,344.4 | 6,326.8 | 6,191.1 | 5,776.0 |
| Pseudo $R^2$ | 0.017 | 0.020 | 0.041 | 0.105 |
| N | 2,840 | 2,840 | 2,840 | 2,840 |

$^+$ p < .10; * p < .05; ** p < .01; *** p < .001.

*Source*: National Survey of Youth and Religion

TABLE A3.4 Race/Religion Interaction Effects from Ordered Logit Regression Estimates of Frequency of Discussion about Sex and Birth Control with Their Adolescent Child

|  | Frequency of talk about sex | Frequency of talk about birth control |
| --- | --- | --- |
| *Parental Measures* | | |
| Weekly church attendance | −0.303** | −0.412*** |
| Parent is white | −0.484*** | −0.483*** |
| *Interaction Effect* | | |
| Weekly church attendance × white | −0.330** | −0.286* |
| *Model Fit Statistics* | | |
| −2 log likelihood | 27,173.5 | 31,227.1 |
| Pseudo $R^2$ | 0.179 | 0.123 |
| N | 12,233 | 12,233 |

<sup></sup>+ p < .10; * p < .05; ** p < .01; *** p < .001.

*Source*: National Longitudinal Study of Adolescent Health

*Note*: Control variables are included but not shown and are identical to those displayed in Table A3.2.

TABLE A3.5 Odds Ratios from Ordered Logit Regression Estimates of Parental Misgivings about Discussing Sexual Issues with Their Adolescent Child

|  | Respondent doesn't know enough about topic | Difficult to explain things to child | Child will learn about sex elsewhere | Talking about birth control would only encourage sex |
| --- | --- | --- | --- | --- |
| *Parental Religion Measures* | | | | |
| Church attendance | 1.043 | 1.066* | 0.985 | 1.059* |
| Importance of religion | 1.039 | 1.029 | 1.060 | 1.135** |
| *Model Fit Statistics* | | | | |
| −2 log likelihood | 28,527.7 | 29,624.5 | 28,527.4 | 27,813.5 |
| Pseudo $R^2$ | 0.100 | 0.110 | 0.116 | 0.077 |
| N | 13,726 | 13,726 | 13,726 | 13,726 |

+ p < .10; * p < .05; ** p < .01; *** p < .001.

*Source*: National Longitudinal Study of Adolescent Health

*Note*: Model includes (but does not display) controls for parent religious affiliation; parent race, age, and gender; parents' average education; adolescent gender, age, and family satisfaction; intact family; exposure to a school sex education curriculum; whether the parent thinks sex is inappropriate during adolescence; parent's communication about sex and sexual morality; and whether the parent thinks his/her adolescent child has already had sex.

TABLE A3.6 Odds Ratios from Logistic Regression Estimates
of First Sex (Virginity Loss) as a Function of Parent-Child
Communication about Sex, Contraception, Sexual Morality,
and Several Control Variables, Wave I Virgins Only

|  | Model 1 | Model 2 |
|---|---|---|
| Parent talks about sex | 1.147[+] | 1.129 |
| Parent talks about contraception | 1.265*** | 1.228*** |
| Parent talks about sexual morality | 0.903* | 0.961 |
| Parent thinks adolescent has had sex |  | 2.386** |
| Adolescent's church attendance |  | 0.918[+] |
| Adolescent's importance of religion |  | 0.914 |
| Adolescent has taken an abstinence pledge |  | 0.796* |
| *Model Fit Statistics* |  |  |
| −2 log likelihood | 7,664.1 | 7,573.0 |
| Pseudo $R^2$ | 0.132 | 0.142 |
| N | 6,385 | 6,385 |

[+] $p < .10$; * $p < .05$; ** $p < .01$; *** $p < .001$.

*Source*: National Longitudinal Study of Adolescent Health

*Note*: Model includes controls for age, gender, parents' average education level, biologically intact two-parent family, race/ethnicity, and number of adolescent's recent romantic partners.

TABLE A3.7 Odds Ratios from Ordered Logit Regression Estimates of
the Score on Adolescent Pregnancy Awareness Quiz

|  | Wave I | Wave II |
|---|---|---|
| Church attendance | 1.000 | 1.019 |
| Importance of religion | 0.948[+] | 0.925* |
| Identifies as "born again" | 0.909 | 0.875 |
| Female | 1.406*** | 1.476*** |
| Age | 1.096** | 1.058[+] |
| White | 1.145[+] | 1.460*** |
| Asian American | 1.513** | 1.443* |
| Hispanic | 1.081 | 1.292* |
| Parents' average education | 1.444*** | 1.281** |
| Has had sexual intercourse (by Wave I) | 1.595*** | 1.218** |
| Has had sexual intercourse (by Wave II) |  | 1.383*** |
| Frequency of talking to parent about sex | 0.990 | 1.013 |
| Frequency of talking to parent about contraception | 1.021 | 1.004 |
| Frequency of talking to parent about sexual morality | 0.963 | 0.990 |
| Has taken an abstinence pledge | 0.853* | 0.762** |
| *Model Fit Statistics* |  |  |
| −2 log likelihood | 32,972.8 | 20,901.5 |
| Pseudo $R^2$ | 0.011 | 0.010 |
| N | 9,716 | 6,297 |

[+] $p < .10$; * $p < .05$; ** $p < .01$; *** $p < .001$.

*Source*: National Longitudinal Study of Adolescent Health

TABLE A3.8 Odds Ratios from Ordered Logit Regression Estimates of Attraction to Members of the Same Sex, among Unmarried 15- to 19-Year-Olds

| | Boys | | | Girls | | |
|---|---|---|---|---|---|---|
| | Model 1 | Model 2 | Model 3 | Model 1 | Model 2 | Model 3 |
| Church attendance | 0.762* | | 0.960 | 0.743** | | 0.863 |
| Importance of religion | | 0.472** | 0.443* | | 0.549*** | 0.894 |
| Evangelical Protestant | | | 1.502 | | | 1.114 |
| Black Protestant | | | 1.112 | | | 1.060 |
| Catholic | | | 1.408 | | | 0.807 |
| Other religion | | | 7.828** | | | 2.308* |
| No religion | | | 1.550 | | | 2.622* |
| Age | 1.145 | 1.153 | 1.132 | 1.052 | 1.087 | 1.073 |
| African American | 1.821 | 2.213 | 2.718 | 0.787 | 0.850 | 0.813 |
| Hispanic | 2.098+ | 2.460* | 2.963** | 0.483* | 0.513+ | 0.605 |
| Other race | 1.965 | 2.190 | 1.313 | 0.783 | 0.789 | 0.664 |
| Lives in the suburbs | 2.089+ | 2.199* | 1.944+ | 0.756 | 0.723 | 0.679+ |
| Lives in rural area | 2.711* | 2.869* | 3.039* | 0.602 | 0.589 | 0.623 |
| *Model Fit Statistics* | | | | | | |
| −2 log likelihood | 540.5 | 531.6 | 508.5 | 1,096.0 | 1,088.3 | 1,066.7 |
| Pseudo $R^2$ | 0.047 | 0.063 | 0.103 | 0.058 | 0.065 | 0.084 |
| N | 1,068 | 1,068 | 1,068 | 1,083 | 1,083 | 1,083 |

+ p < .10; * p < .05; ** p < .01; *** p < .001.

*Source:* National Survey of Family Growth, Cycle 6

*Note:* Models include controls for parents' average education level, biologically intact two-parent family, whether the respondent still lives with his/her parent(s), educational status, and whether the respondent has ever had heterosexual sex.

TABLE A3.9 Odds Ratios from Logistic Regression Estimates of Ever Having Had Same-Sex Relations among Unmarried 15- to 19-Year-Olds

| | Boys | | | Girls | | |
|---|---|---|---|---|---|---|
| | Model 1 | Model 2 | Model 3 | Model 1 | Model 2 | Model 3 |
| Church attendance | 0.842 | | 0.984 | 0.805$^+$ | | 0.953 |
| Importance of religion | | 0.653 | 0.636 | | 0.581** | 0.706 |
| Evangelical Protestant | | | 0.917 | | | 1.579 |
| Black Protestant | | | 0.561 | | | 3.345$^+$ |
| Catholic | | | 2.848$^+$ | | | 0.782 |
| Other religion | | | 8.704*** | | | 1.681 |
| No religion | | | 1.556 | | | 2.076 |
| Age | 1.506* | 1.528* | 1.547* | 0.943 | 0.960 | 0.950 |
| African American | 1.769 | 1.960 | 3.071* | 0.832 | 0.921 | 0.420 |
| Hispanic | 1.718 | 1.904 | 1.554 | 0.403* | 0.425* | 0.499$^+$ |
| Other race | 1.143 | 1.216 | 0.663 | 0.321$^+$ | 0.318$^+$ | 0.315$^+$ |
| Lives in the suburbs | 1.945 | 2.002$^+$ | 2.096$^+$ | 0.819 | 0.797 | 0.773 |
| Lives in rural area | 2.789* | 2.899** | 3.367** | 0.682 | 0.703 | 0.696 |
| Has had heterosexual sex | 2.759* | 2.675* | 2.926* | 3.151*** | 2.977** | 2.957** |
| *Model Fit Statistics* | | | | | | |
| −2 log likelihood | 339.3 | 337.2 | 312.7 | 643.2 | 623.6 | 634.9 |
| Pseudo $R^2$ | 0.136 | 0.142 | 0.204 | 0.114 | 0.141 | 0.125 |
| N | 1,079 | 1,079 | 1,079 | 1,100 | 1,100 | 1,100 |

$^+$ p < .10; * p < .05; ** p < .01; *** p < .001.

*Source:* National Survey of Family Growth, Cycle 6

*Note:* Models include controls for parents' average education level, biologically intact two-parent family, whether the respondent still lives with his/her parent(s), and educational status.

TABLE A3.10 Odds Ratios from Ordered Logit Regression Estimates of Homosexual Sexual Orientation, among Unmarried 15- to 19-Year-Olds

| | Boys | | | Girls | | |
|---|---|---|---|---|---|---|
| | Model 1 | Model 2 | Model 3 | Model 1 | Model 2 | Model 3 |
| Church attendance | 0.694** | | 0.914 | 0.777 | | 0.933 |
| Importance of religion | | 0.416 | 0.399 | | 0.560 | 0.575 |
| Evangelical Protestant | | | 0.184 | | | 1.010 |
| Black Protestant | | | 0.143 | | | 1.105 |
| Catholic | | | 0.653 | | | 0.776 |
| Other religion | | | 5.514 | | | 0.632 |
| No religion | | | 0.436 | | | 0.829 |
| Age | 1.355 | 1.378 | 1.295 | 1.409 | 1.443 | 1.427 |
| Intact family | 0.723 | 0.786 | 0.642 | 3.124 | 3.412 | 3.278 |
| Lives with parents | 1.767 | 1.662 | 1.659 | 0.156* | 0.133* | 0.142* |
| Model Fit Statistics | | | | | | |
| −2 log likelihood | 167.5 | 164.3 | 144.7 | 103.1 | 102.2 | 101.9 |
| Pseudo $R^2$ | 0.110 | 0.127 | 0.231 | 0.078 | 0.086 | 0.088 |
| N | 1,047 | 1,047 | 1,047 | 1,070 | 1,070 | 1,070 |

+ p < .10; * p < .05; ** p < .01; *** p < .001.

Source: National Survey of Family Growth, Cycle 6

Note: Race and parents' education predict statistical failure perfectly among girls. They are dropped from the analyses. All models include controls for race, suburban/rural residence, parents' average education level, educational status, and whether the respondent has ever had heterosexual sex.

TABLE A3.11  Odds Ratios from Ordered Logit Regression Estimates of Bisexual Sexual Orientation, among Unmarried 15- to 19-Year-Olds

| | Boys | | | Girls | | |
|---|---|---|---|---|---|---|
| | Model 1 | Model 2 | Model 3 | Model 1 | Model 2 | Model 3 |
| Church attendance | 0.914 | | 0.795 | 0.758[+] | | 0.886 |
| Importance of religion | | 1.216 | 1.242 | | 0.555** | 0.727 |
| Evangelical Protestant | | | 2.287 | | | 1.564 |
| Black Protestant | | | 2.895 | | | 2.210 |
| Catholic | | | 3.329 | | | 0.729 |
| Other religion | | | 16.601** | | | 1.948 |
| No religion | | | 2.327 | | | 1.996 |
| Age | 1.419 | 1.401 | 1.351 | 0.961 | 0.881 | 0.861 |
| African American | 1.151 | 0.930 | 0.708 | 0.638 | 0.679 | 0.451 |
| Hispanic | 5.064* | 4.730* | 5.181* | 0.635 | 0.678 | 0.825 |
| Other race | 2.419 | 2.222 | 1.515 | 0.294 | 0.303 | 0.289 |
| In high school | 4.174 | 4.400 | 3.828 | 1.513 | 1.489 | 1.310 |
| High school degree or less | 1.191 | 1.294 | 0.841 | 5.471** | 5.622** | 5.071** |
| Has had heterosexual sex | 0.817 | 0.896 | 0.944 | 1.477 | 1.463 | 1.396 |
| *Model Fit Statistics* | | | | | | |
| −2 log likelihood | 128.6 | 128.6 | 118.4 | 444.8 | 440.1 | 432.3 |
| Pseudo $R^2$ | 0.136 | 0.136 | 0.204 | 0.094 | 0.104 | 0.120 |
| N | 1,047 | 1,047 | 1,047 | 1,065 | 1,065 | 1,065 |

[+] p < .10; * p < .05; ** p < .01; *** p < .001.

*Source:* National Survey of Family Growth, Cycle 6

*Note:* Models include controls for suburban/rural residence, parents' average education level, biologically intact two-parent family, and whether the respondent still lives with his/her parent(s).

TABLE A4.1 Odds Ratios from Logistic Regression
Estimates of Taking a Pledge of Sexual
Abstinence until Marriage

|  | *Model 1* |
|---|---|
| Church attendance | 1.251*** |
| Importance of religion | 1.460*** |
| Mainline Protestant | 0.577*** |
| Black Protestant | 0.512** |
| Catholic | 0.664** |
| Mormon (LDS) | 1.437 |
| Jewish | 0.184* |
| Other religion | 0.788 |
| No religion | 2.048** |
| Identifies as "born again" | 2.169*** |
| Age | 1.011 |
| Female | 1.704*** |
| Family satisfaction | 1.051** |
| Level of autonomy | 0.915** |
| Strategic | 1.066*** |
| *Model Fit Statistics* | |
| −2 log likelihood | 10,123.5 |
| Pseudo $R^2$ | 0.156 |
| N | 14,501 |

$^+$p < .10; $^*$p < .05; $^{**}$p < .01; $^{***}$p < .001.

*Source*: National Longitudinal Study of Adolescent Health

*Note*: Model also includes controls for parents' average education level, southern residence, biologically intact two-parent family, social desirability, race/ethnicity, virginity status, and number of adolescent's recent romantic partners.

TABLE A4.2 Odds Ratios from Ordered Logit Regression Estimates of Motivations to Have or Avoid Sex

| | After sex, you would feel guilty | Friends would respect you more | Partner would lose respect for you | Having sex would make you attractive | Sex would give you much pleasure | Having sex would upset your mother | Pregnancy would embarrass you |
|---|---|---|---|---|---|---|---|
| Church attendance | 1.267*** | 0.950+ | 1.148*** | 0.978 | 0.987 | 1.310*** | 1.171*** |
| Importance of religion | 1.176** | 0.954 | 1.088+ | 0.911+ | 0.956 | 1.157** | 0.972 |
| Mainline Protestant | 0.806* | 1.031 | 0.842+ | 1.123 | 0.887 | 0.789* | 0.995 |
| Black Protestant | 0.657* | 0.977 | 0.763+ | 1.068 | 0.833 | 0.544*** | 0.808 |
| Catholic | 0.735** | 1.100 | 0.854 | 0.979 | 1.044 | 0.852 | 0.974 |
| Mormon (LDS) | 1.475 | 0.683 | 1.102 | 0.772 | 0.928 | 1.711+ | 1.005 |
| Jewish | 0.543** | 1.274 | 0.656+ | 0.776 | 1.510 | 0.420*** | 1.678* |
| Other religion | 0.905 | 0.805+ | 0.816 | 0.879 | 1.008 | 0.949 | 0.997 |
| No religion | 1.230 | 0.817 | 1.134 | 0.756+ | 0.878 | 1.022 | 0.927 |
| Identifies as "born again" | 1.419*** | 0.831* | 1.260* | 0.905 | 0.855+ | 1.332*** | 1.076 |
| Age | 0.947* | 1.004 | 0.932* | 0.934* | 1.167*** | 0.841*** | 0.917*** |
| Female | 1.915*** | 0.278*** | 1.213*** | 0.346*** | 0.283*** | 2.086*** | 1.361*** |
| African American | 0.792* | 1.732*** | 0.837+ | 1.079 | 1.008 | 0.859 | 0.516*** |
| Bio-intact, two-parent family | 1.198*** | 0.861* | 1.101+ | 0.939 | 1.044 | 1.733*** | 1.351*** |
| Strategic | 1.034*** | 0.950*** | 0.994 | 0.950*** | 1.019* | 1.030* | 1.056*** |
| Has already had sex | 0.266*** | 1.557*** | 0.465*** | 1.192* | 1.843*** | 0.456*** | 0.464*** |
| *Model Fit Statistics* | | | | | | | |
| −2 log likelihood | 29379.7 | 27171.0 | 28706.3 | 26891.8 | 27001.9 | 25846.5 | 28820.1 |
| Pseudo $R^2$ | 0.087 | 0.059 | 0.029 | 0.042 | 0.072 | 0.093 | 0.060 |
| N | 9,688 | 9,688 | 9,688 | 9,688 | 9,688 | 9,688 | 9,688 |

+ $p < .10$; * $p < .05$; ** $p < .01$; *** $p < .001$.

*Source:* National Longitudinal Study of Adolescent Health

*Note:* All models include controls for parents' average education level, southern residence, level of autonomy, social desirability, other races/ethnicities, and number of adolescent's recent romantic partners.

TABLE A5.1 Odds Ratios from Logistic Regression Estimates of Having Experienced Sexual Intercourse by Wave I

|  | *Model 1* | *Model 2* | *Model 3* | *Model 4* |
|---|---|---|---|---|
| Church attendance | 0.821*** | 0.828*** | 0.856*** | 0.927 |
| Importance of religion | 0.883*** | 0.929* | 0.876** | 0.969 |
| Mainline Protestant |  |  | 0.671*** | 0.744+ |
| Black Protestant |  |  | 1.246 | 1.213 |
| Catholic |  |  | 0.610*** | 0.600*** |
| Mormon (LDS) |  |  | 0.333* | 0.289* |
| Jewish |  |  | 0.459* | 0.330* |
| Other religion |  |  | 0.691* | 0.702* |
| No religion |  |  | 0.589** | 0.716 |
| Identifies as "born again" | 0.981 | 0.973 |  |  |
| Age | 1.811*** | 1.601*** | 1.567*** | 1.452*** |
| Female | 0.937 | 0.886+ | 0.892 | 1.371*** |
| Parents' average education | 0.501*** | 0.557*** | 0.532*** | 0.522*** |
| Lives in the South | 1.309** | 1.234** | 1.192* | 1.237* |
| African American | 2.718*** | 2.416*** | 2.115*** | 1.594* |
| Hispanic | 1.090 | 1.210 | 1.540*** | 1.028 |
| Asian American | 0.599+ | 0.597+ | 0.732 | 0.818 |
| Bio-intact, two-parent family | 0.557*** | 0.593*** | 0.630*** | 0.671*** |
| Family satisfaction |  | 0.879*** | 0.896*** | 0.895*** |
| Level of autonomy |  |  | 1.085*** | 1.054 |
| Strategic |  | 0.942*** | 0.952*** | 0.962** |
| Social desirability |  | 1.126 | 1.183* | 1.146 |
| Number of recent romantic partners |  |  | 1.609*** | 1.609*** |
| School percentage nonvirgins |  | 9.118*** | 7.709*** | 5.373*** |
| Has taken an abstinence pledge |  |  | 0.246*** | 0.298*** |
| Sex would bring guilt |  |  |  | 0.584*** |
| Sex would upset your mother |  |  |  | 0.817*** |
| Sex would bring friends' respect |  |  |  | 1.230*** |
| *Model Fit Statistics* |  |  |  |  |
| −2 log likelihood | 12081.9 | 11706.2 | 11006.0 | 7386.7 |
| Pseudo $R^2$ | 0.171 | 0.197 | 0.245 | 0.253 |
| N | 10,757 | 10,757 | 10,757 | 6,845 |

+ p < .10; * p < .05; ** p < .01; *** p < .001.

*Source*: National Longitudinal Study of Adolescent Health

TABLE A5.2 Odds Ratios from Logistic Regression Estimates of
Having Had Sexual Intercourse by Wave II, Using Full Sample
and Parent Religiosity Proxies

|  | *Model 1* | *Model 2* | *Model 3* | *Model 4* |
|---|---|---|---|---|
| Parent's church attendance | 0.843*** | 0.855*** | 0.889* | 0.854** |
| Parent's importance of religion | 1.002 | 1.040 | 0.986 | 1.047 |
| *Model Fit Statistics* |  |  |  |  |
| −2 log likelihood | 12930.1 | 12143.2 | 8174.2 | 7706.4 |
| Pseudo $R^2$ | 0.177 | 0.227 | 0.182 | 0.229 |
| N | 11,456 | 11,456 | 7,245 | 7,245 |

$^+$ p < .10; * p < .05; ** p < .01; *** p < .001.

*Source*: National Longitudinal Study of Adolescent Health

*Note*: All models include controls for age, gender, religious affiliation, parents' average education level, southern residence, biologically intact two-parent family, family satisfaction, social desirability, proclivity for risk taking, strategic orientation, school percentage nonvirgins, and race/ethnicity. Model 4 also controls for number of adolescent's recent romantic partners and three attitudes (sex would bring guilt, sex would upset mother, sex would bring respect of friends) about sex.

TABLE A5.3  Odds Ratios from Logistic Regression Estimates of Having
Had Sexual Intercourse by Wave II, Wave I Virgins Only

| | Model 1 | Model 2 | Model 3 | Model 4 |
|---|---|---|---|---|
| Church attendance | 0.880* | 0.890* | 0.888* | 0.914 |
| Importance of religion | 0.851* | 0.864* | 0.814* | 0.803* |
| Mainline Protestant | | | 0.906 | 0.876 |
| Black Protestant | | | 1.511+ | 2.112* |
| Catholic | | | 1.094 | 1.037 |
| Mormon (LDS) | | | 0.798 | 0.981 |
| Jewish | | | 0.509+ | 0.220*** |
| Other religion | | | 1.014 | 1.203 |
| No religion | | | 0.886 | 0.996 |
| Identifies as "born again" | 0.951 | | | |
| Parents' average education | 0.601*** | 0.653*** | 0.595*** | 0.557*** |
| African American | 1.441*** | 1.361*** | 1.190 | 0.875 |
| Hispanic | 1.072 | 1.165 | 1.204 | 0.862 |
| Asian American | 0.854 | 0.869 | 0.969 | 0.930 |
| Bio-intact, two-parent family | 0.562*** | 0.581*** | 0.602*** | 0.723** |
| Strategic | | 0.954** | 0.956** | 0.973 |
| Likes taking risks | | 1.202*** | 1.153*** | 1.036 |
| Number of recent romantic partners | | | 1.625*** | 1.791*** |
| School percentage nonvirgins | | 4.739*** | 4.667*** | 3.254* |
| Has taken an abstinence pledge | | | 0.909 | 0.862 |
| Sex would bring guilt | | | | 0.689*** |
| Sex would upset your mother | | | | 0.974 |
| Sex would bring friends' respect | | | | 1.204*** |
| *Model Fit Statistics* | | | | |
| −2 log likelihood | 7003.2 | 6878.8 | 6550.1 | 3901.9 |
| Pseudo $R^2$ | 0.067 | 0.083 | 0.127 | 0.126 |
| N | 7,117 | 7,117 | 7,117 | 3,833 |

+ p < .10; * p < .05; ** p < .01; *** p < .001.

Source: National Longitudinal Study of Adolescent Health

Note: All models include controls for age, gender, and southern residence. Some models also control for level of autonomy, family satisfaction, and social desirability.

TABLE A5.4 Odds Ratios from Logistic Regression Estimates of Having Had Sexual Intercourse by Wave II, Using Religious Change Measures

|  | Model 1 | Model 2 | Model 3 | Model 4 |
|---|---|---|---|---|
| Change in attendance | 1.016 (0.889**) | | | |
| Change in importance | 0.905 (0.958) | | | |
| Drastic increase in attendance | | 1.097 (0.918) | 1.056 (.892) | |
| Drastic increase in importance | | 1.176 (0.943) | 1.176 (.936) | |
| Drastic decrease in attendance | | 1.082 (1.400*) | | 1.082 (1.398*) |
| Drastic decrease in importance | | 1.514* (1.369*) | | 1.496* (1.380*) |
| *Model Fit Statistics* | | | | |
| −2 log likelihood | 6613.6 (12217.4) | 6603.1 (12212.5) | 6618.1 (12246.8) | 6604.9 (12212.7) |
| Pseudo $R^2$ | 0.112 (0.209) | 0.113 (0.209) | 0.111 (0.207) | 0.113 (0.209) |
| N | 7,430 (11,266) | 7,430 (11,266) | 7,430 (11,266) | 7,430 (11,266) |

+ p < .10; * p < .05; ** p < .01; *** p < .001.

*Source:* National Longitudinal Study of Adolescent Health

*Note:* Coefficients in parentheses are for regression models using the virgin-only sample. Models also control for age, gender, region, race/ethnicity, intact family, planful personality, aversion to risk taking, social desirability, number of adolescent's recent romantic partners, Wave I religious service attendance, and Wave I religious salience.

TABLE A5.5 Reverse Causation–Odds Ratios from Ordered Logit Regression Estimates of Wave II Attendance and Importance of Religion on Having Experienced Sexual Intercourse between Study Waves, Wave I Virgins Only

|  | Attendance | | Importance | |
|  | Male | Female | Male | Female |
| --- | --- | --- | --- | --- |
| Had sex, Wave II | 0.890 | 0.945 | 0.774[+] | 0.749** |
| *Model Fit Statistics* |  |  |  |  |
| −2 log likelihood | 6942.2 | 7670.5 | 6481.5 | 6800.7 |
| Pseudo $R^2$ | 0.246 | 0.227 | 0.238 | 0.235 |
| N | 3,313 | 3,689 | 3,312 | 3,689 |

[+] p < .10; * p < .05; ** p < .01; *** p < .001.

*Source*: National Longitudinal Study of Adolescent Health

*Note*: Models include but do not display estimated coefficients from lagged dependent variable, demographic covariates, social desirability, personality traits, etc.

TABLE A5.6 Negative Binomial Regression Estimates of Reported Number of Times Having Sex on Respondent Characteristics and Behaviors

|  | Model 1 | Model 2 | Model 3 |
| --- | --- | --- | --- |
| Church attendance | −0.080** | −0.073** | −0.043[+] |
| Importance of religion | −0.158** | −0.059 | 0.052 |
| White | −0.223[+] | −0.093 | −0.182 |
| Hispanic | −0.395* | −0.197 | −0.310 |
| Asian American | 0.089 | 0.041 | −0.126 |
| Age | 0.736*** | 0.646*** | 0.642*** |
| Female | −0.080 | −0.100 | −0.107 |
| Parents' average education | −0.099*** | −0.088*** | −0.087*** |
| Parent respondent is married | −0.344** | −0.217* | −0.208* |
| Parent perceives adolescent's friends as positive |  | −0.237*** | −0.220*** |
| Level of autonomy |  | 0.119*** | 0.104*** |
| Is currently in a dating relationship |  | 0.894*** | 0.912*** |
| Parent respondent considers adolescent to be rebellious |  | 0.239*** | 0.225*** |
| Adolescent is considered popular |  | 0.285*** | 0.270*** |
| Spiritual but not religious |  |  | 0.001 |
| Frequency of Bible reading |  |  | −0.120** |
| Do what makes me happy |  |  | 0.697*** |
| Do what gets me ahead |  |  | 0.642** |
| Do what an adult or parent says |  |  | 0.212 |
| *Model Fit Statistics* |  |  |  |
| −2 log likelihood | 4848.4 | 4600.7 | 4556.3 |
| Pseudo $R^2$ | 0.076 | 0.123 | 0.132 |
| N | 2,973 | 2,973 | 2,973 |

[+] p < .10; * p < .05; ** p < .01; *** p < .001.

*Source*: National Survey of Youth and Religion

TABLE A5.7 Odds Ratios from Ordered Logit Regression Estimates of Adolescent Attitudes about Birth Control, Wave I

| | Using birth control is morally wrong (full sample) | | Friends might think respondent is looking for sex if respondent uses birth control (adolescent girls only) | |
|---|---|---|---|---|
| | Model 1 | Model 2 | Model 1 | Model 2 |
| Church attendance | 1.166*** | 1.147*** | 1.168*** | 1.185*** |
| Importance of religion | 1.069+ | 1.144** | 1.004 | 1.078 |
| Mainline Protestant | | 0.883 | | 1.012 |
| Black Protestant | | 0.632*** | | 1.039 |
| Catholic | | 1.190+ | | 0.887 |
| Mormon (LDS) | | 1.142 | | 0.706 |
| Jewish | | 0.440+ | | 0.687 |
| Other religion | | 0.775* | | 0.942 |
| No religion | | 1.281+ | | 1.310 |
| Identifies as "born again" | 0.939 | | 1.225* | |
| Age | 0.968 | 0.966 | 0.869*** | 0.884** |
| Female | 0.593*** | 0.583*** | | |
| Parents' average education | 0.673*** | 0.704*** | 0.786* | 0.819* |
| Lives in the South | 1.054 | 1.032 | 1.096 | 1.051 |
| African American | 1.242* | 1.609*** | 1.149 | 1.050 |
| Hispanic | 1.556*** | 1.407*** | 1.880*** | 1.747*** |
| Asian American | 2.222** | 2.119** | 2.746*** | 2.589*** |
| Bio-intact, two-parent family | 1.019 | 1.012 | 1.105 | 1.095 |
| Family satisfaction | 0.980+ | 0.976* | 0.969* | 0.964* |
| Level of autonomy | | 0.937** | | 0.910** |
| Strategic | 0.937*** | 0.934*** | 0.955** | 0.954** |
| Social desirability | 1.045 | 1.023 | 0.902 | 0.893 |
| Number of adolescent's recent romantic partners | | 0.900*** | | 0.956 |
| Has taken an abstinence pledge | | 1.305** | | 1.447** |
| School percentage nonvirgins | 1.108 | 1.153 | 0.994 | 0.985 |
| Has had sexual intercourse | 0.792*** | 0.852** | 0.512*** | 0.546*** |
| *Model Fit Statistics* | | | | |
| −2 log likelihood | 28684.7 | 28539.6 | 16087.5 | 16027.9 |
| Pseudo $R^2$ | 0.022 | 0.027 | 0.028 | 0.031 |
| N | 10,852 | 10,852 | 5,314 | 5,314 |

$^+$ p < .10; $^*$ p < .05; $^{**}$ p < .01; $^{***}$ p < .001.

*Source*: National Longitudinal Study of Adolescent Health

TABLE A5.8 Odds Ratios from Logistic Regression Estimates of Birth Control Practices among Adolescents Who First Had Sex between Waves I and II

| | Used birth control at first intercourse | Used birth control at most recent intercourse |
|---|---|---|
| Church attendance | 1.154 | 1.169 |
| Importance of religion | 0.793* | 0.967 |
| Identifies as "born again" | 1.371 | 0.888 |
| Age | 1.128 | 1.045 |
| Female | 0.991 | 1.072 |
| *Model Fit Statistics* | | |
| −2 log likelihood | 1086.3 | 1364.2 |
| Pseudo $R^2$ | 0.037 | 0.027 |
| N | 910 | 1,140 |

$^+$ p < .10; $^*$ p < .05; $^{**}$ p < .01; $^{***}$ p < .001.

*Source*: National Longitudinal Study of Adolescent Health

*Note*: Models also include controls for age, gender, parents' average education, southern residence, race/ethnicity, biologically intact two-parent family, family satisfaction, strategic orientation, social desirability, and school percentage nonvirgins.

TABLE A6.1 Odds Ratios from Logistic Regression Estimates of Oral Sexual Experience

| | Model 1 | Model 2 | Model 3 |
|---|---|---|---|
| Spiritual but not religious | 1.293*** | 1.073 | 0.993 |
| Mainline Protestant | 1.184 | 1.051 | 0.786 |
| Black Protestant | 0.445*** | 0.542$^+$ | 0.386* |
| Catholic | 0.736* | 0.562*** | 0.400*** |
| Mormon (LDS) | 0.424$^+$ | 0.375* | 0.392* |
| Jewish | 1.447 | 1.205 | 0.683 |
| Other religion | 0.963 | 0.826 | 0.645 |
| No religion | 1.426* | 0.658$^+$ | 0.533* |
| Church attendance | | 0.938$^+$ | 1.024 |
| Importance of religion | | 0.772*** | 1.024 |
| Female | | 0.740** | 0.765* |
| Quality of parent-child relations | | | 0.850*** |
| Proponent of abstinence until marriage | | | 0.248*** |
| Is currently in a dating relationship | | | 2.212*** |
| Parents would be upset if respondent had sex | | | 0.579*** |
| *Model Fit Statistics* | | | |
| −2 log likelihood | 3157.7 | 2643.8 | 2173.6 |
| Pseudo $R^2$ | 0.024 | 0.183 | 0.328 |
| N | 3,060 | 3,060 | 3,060 |

$^+$ p < .10; $^*$ p < .05; $^{**}$ p < .01; $^{***}$ p < .001.

*Source*: National Survey of Youth and Religion

*Note*: All models also include control variables for different races/ethnicities (coefficients not shown). Models 2 and 3 also include controls for parents' perceptions about respondent's friends, parents' average education, age, parents' marital status, and the perceived rebelliousness of the respondent.

TABLE A6.2 Odds Ratios from Logistic Regression Estimates
of Having Given Oral Sex, Having Received
Oral Sex, and Having Had Anal Sex

|  | Has given oral sex | Has received oral sex | Has had anal sex |
|---|---|---|---|
| Church attendance | 0.778*** | 0.832* | 0.578*** |
| Importance of religion | 0.705* | 0.698* | 1.006 |
| Evangelical Protestant | 1.003 | 0.726 | 0.692 |
| Black Protestant | 1.252 | 1.059 | 1.025 |
| Catholic | 0.720 | 1.022 | 0.621 |
| Other religion | 0.787 | 0.576* | 0.262* |
| No religion | 1.006 | 1.152 | 1.407 |
| *Model Fit Statistics* |  |  |  |
| −2 log likelihood | 12,024.1 | 11,296.4 | 14,478.6 |
| Pseudo $R^2$ | 0.146 | 0.117 | 0.057 |
| *N* | 1,270 | 1,270 | 1,263 |

$^+$p < .10; $^*$p < .05; $^{**}$p < .01; $^{***}$p < .001.

*Source*: National Survey of Family Growth, Cycle 6

*Note*: All models include controls for age, gender, parents' average education level, biologically intact two-parent family, urbanicity of residence, and race/ethnicity. The reference category for religious tradition is mainline Protestant.

TABLE A6.3 Negative Binomial Regression Estimates
of Number of Times Having Oral Sex on Respondent
Characteristics and Behaviors

| | *Model 1* | *Model 2* | *Model 3* |
|---|---|---|---|
| Church attendance | −0.022 | −0.027 | −0.004 |
| Importance of religion | −0.210*** | −0.123* | −0.034 |
| White | 0.674*** | 0.875*** | 0.826*** |
| Hispanic | 0.299 | 0.522* | 0.462$^{+}$ |
| Asian American | −0.102 | 0.175 | −0.172 |
| Age | 0.637*** | 0.543*** | 0.538*** |
| Female | −0.361*** | −0.312** | −0.340*** |
| Parents' average education | −0.068** | −0.046* | −0.046* |
| Parent respondent is married | −0.299** | −0.235* | −0.227* |
| Parent perceives adolescent's friends as positive | | −0.198*** | −0.177*** |
| Level of autonomy | | 0.105*** | 0.088*** |
| Is currently in a dating relationship | | 0.729*** | 0.744*** |
| Parent respondent considers adolescent to be rebellious | | 0.200*** | 0.194*** |
| Respondent is considered popular | | 0.378*** | 0.351*** |
| Spiritual but not religious | | | 0.019 |
| Frequency of Bible reading | | | −0.077* |
| Do what makes me happy | | | 0.545** |
| Do what gets me ahead | | | 0.466* |
| Do what an adult or parent says | | | −0.012 |
| *Model Fit Statistics* | | | |
| −2 log likelihood | 4935.7 | 4723.1 | 4683.2 |
| Pseudo $R^2$ | 0.074 | 0.114 | 0.122 |
| N | 2,972 | 2,972 | 2,972 |

$^{+}$ p < .10; * p < .05; ** p < .01; *** p < .001.

*Source*: National Survey of Youth and Religion

TABLE A6.4 Odds Ratios from Ordered Logit Regression Estimates
of Internet Pornography Use among Adolescent Boys

|  | Model 1 | Model 2 |
|---|---|---|
| Spiritual but not religious | 1.332** | 1.132 |
| Mainline Protestant | 1.925** | 1.437 |
| Black Protestant | 1.533 | 1.400 |
| Catholic | 1.890*** | 1.691* |
| Mormon (LDS) | 1.292 | 0.902 |
| Jewish | 4.655*** | 3.161** |
| Other religion | 1.375 | 1.108 |
| No religion | 1.978** | 1.003 |
| Church attendance |  | 0.996 |
| Importance of religion |  | 0.858* |
| Parents perceive adolescent's friends as positive |  | 0.755*** |
| Parents' average education |  | 1.114** |
| Age |  | 1.322*** |
| Adolescent has autonomy with media |  | 1.182** |
| Quality of parent-child relations |  | 0.866** |
| Proponent of abstinence until marriage |  | 0.587** |
| Is currently in a dating relationship |  | 1.534** |
| *Model Fit Statistics* |  |  |
| −2 log likelihood | 2482.5 | 2328.8 |
| Pseudo $R^2$ | 0.018 | 0.079 |
| $N$ | 1,315 | 1,214 |

+$p < .10$; * $p < .05$; ** $p < .01$; *** $p < .001$.

*Source*: National Survey of Youth and Religion

# *Appendix B*

## RESEARCH METHODS

The data for this book come from the National Study of Youth and Religion (NSYR), the National Longitudinal Study of Adolescent Health (Add Health), and the National Survey of Family Growth (NSFG). In the following pages, I explain how the data for these studies were collected.

### NSYR SURVEY

The National Study of Youth and Religion, funded by the Lilly Endowment Inc. and under the direction of Dr. Christian Smith, professor of sociology, is based at the Odum Institute for Research in Social Science at the University of North Carolina at Chapel Hill. The NSYR survey is a nationally representative telephone survey of 3,290 English- and Spanish-speaking adolescents between the ages of 13 and 17 and of their parents.[1] An oversample of 80 Jewish households (not nationally representative) brings the total number of completed NSYR cases to 3,370. The survey was conducted from July 2002 to April 2003 by researchers at the University of North Carolina at Chapel Hill using a random-digit-dial (RDD) method, employing a sample of randomly generated telephone numbers representative of all household telephones in the 50 United States, including Alaska and Hawaii. The national survey sample was arranged in replicates based on the proportion of working household telephone exchanges nationwide, ensuring equal representation of listed, unlisted, and not-yet-listed household telephone numbers. Eligible households included at least one adolescent between the ages of 13 and 17 living in the household for at least six months of the year. In order to randomize responses within households, and so to help attain representativeness of age and gender, interviewers asked to conduct the survey with the adolescent in the household who had the most recent birthday. Parent interviews were conducted with either a mother or father, as available, although the survey asked to speak with mothers first, believing that they may be better qualified to answer questions about their family and adolescent. Stepparents, resident grandparents, resident partners of parents, and other resident parent-like figures were also eligible to complete the parent portion of the survey.

An RDD telephone survey sampling method was chosen for this study because of the advantages it offers compared to alternative survey sampling methods. Unlike the school-based sampling employed by Add Health, for example, our RDD telephone method was able to sample school dropouts, home-schooled youth, and students frequently absent from school. Using RDD, we were also able to ask numerous religion questions, which school principals and school boards often disallow on surveys administered in schools. Explicit informed consent from parents also proved more feasible using RDD than school-based sampling. And the audible reading of survey questions by trained interviewers facilitated question-and-answer clarifications that increased the validity of answers, compared to paper-and-pencil questionnaires administered en masse in school classrooms. Additionally, the RDD method eliminated potential design effect problems associated with geographic or school clusters. When compared to an in-home survey, the RDD method proved more cost efficient, reduced the possibility of interviewer bias, and increased the validity of answers to sensitive questions. Finally, superior Internet-based methods of sampling and surveying were not sufficiently developed and tested by the time of this survey's fielding to have been useful for the NSYR. Unfortunately, the RDD telephone method was unable to reach the approximately 4 percent of U.S. households without telephones, as well as cell-phone-only households.

Prior to conducting this survey, NSYR researchers (including the author) conducted 35 in-depth pilot interviews, survey-focused interviews, and focus groups to help inform the construction of the survey instrument and to improve question wording and comprehension. There were 175 pretests of the survey instrument, using both nationally representative and convenience samples, which were conducted to help improve question-and-answer categories and survey clarity and validity.

The NSYR survey was conducted with members of both English- and Spanish-speaking households. The English version of the survey was translated into Spanish by a professional translation service and evaluated by translation consultants and Spanish-speaking interviewers. Surveys with Spanish speaking households were conducted by native Spanish-speaking interviewers who are fluent in both English and Spanish and who had extensive experience conducting the survey in English before conducting the Spanish version. The parent and adolescent respondents could each independently choose the language in which to complete the survey.

Prior to conducting all surveys, interviewers obtained respondents' verbal informed consent and provided respondents with information about the confidentiality of their answers and the right to refuse to answer questions. Household eligibility was determined through the use of an initial screening question about resident adolescents. Incentives of $20 to parent respondents and $20 to adolescent respondents were offered to complete the survey, for a total of $40 to completing households. Survey respondents were also able to complete the survey at their convenience by calling a toll-free number which linked to their sample record. Throughout the fielding of the survey, interviewers were monitored using remote technology by project staff to ensure data quality, and the interviewers, monitors, and researchers were routinely debriefed about survey performance. Upon completing the survey, all respondents were given contact information for the researchers, the research firm, and the university's institutional review board to use to verify the survey's authenticity or to ask any questions about the survey or their rights as respondents. This information was also included in written form in thank-you letters accompanying the mailed incentives. To help protect the privacy of survey respondents, the NSYR obtained a federal Certificate of Confidentiality from the National Institutes of Health. With this certificate, researchers with the NSYR cannot be forced to disclose information that might identify respondents, even by a court subpoena, in any federal, state, or local civil, criminal, administrative, legislative, or other proceedings. The certificate was thus useful for resisting any potential demands for information that would identify respondents.

The NSYR survey was conducted over nine months, between the end of July 2002 and the beginning of April 2003. All randomly generated telephone numbers were dialed a minimum of 20 times over a minimum of five months per number, spread out over varying hours during weekdays, weeknights, and weekends. The calling design included at least two telephone-based attempts to convert refusals. Households refusing to cooperate with the survey yet established by initial screening to have children aged 13 to 17 in residence and with telephone numbers able to be matched to mailing addresses were also sent information by mail about the survey, contact information for researchers, and a request from the principal investigator to cooperate and complete the survey; those households were then called back again for possible refusal conversions.

The NSYR survey itself took a mean of 82 minutes to complete—30 minutes for the parent portion and 52 minutes for the adolescent portion. The overall cooperation rate of our national sample was 81 percent. Ninety-six (96) percent of parent-complete households also achieved teenager completes. The final NSYR national sample survey response rate was 57 percent. Multiple diagnostic analyses demonstrate that the NSYR appears to provide a reasonably unbiased representative sample of its target population and so, when weights are applied, can be taken to accurately describe the population of U.S. adolescents aged 13–17 and their parents living in residential households during that time period. The final survey instrument is available by Internet download at the project Web site: http://www.youthandreligion.org/publica tions/docs/survey.pdf. A more extensive demographic and behavioral outcome comparison with other data sets, including Add Health, is available in appendix B ("Survey Methodology," pp. 292–301) of Smith and Denton (2005).

## NSYR In-depth Interviews

The National Study of Youth and Religion conducted in-depth personal interviews with 267 adolescents between March 2003 and January 2004. The purpose of the interviews was to provide extended, follow-up discussions about adolescents' religious, spiritual, family, and social lives. All interview subjects were selected from among the 3,370 adolescents who completed the NSYR telephone survey, and the interviews expanded on the topics included in that survey. All interviews were conducted in person in public settings (public libraries, restaurants, coffee shops, classrooms, etc.) by 17 trained interviewers (including the author) and ranged from about 90 minutes to three hours in length. Each interviewer conducted between 10 and 20 interviews, and interviewers were matched to the adolescent on gender and race in the majority of cases. Interviews were conducted in 45 states, and all interviewees were between the ages of 13 and 18. A cash incentive of $30 was distributed to the adolescent at the conclusion of each interview.

Interviewees were selected from the telephone survey respondents using a stratified quota sample in order to represent a range of demographic and religious characteristics from which substantive conclusions about adolescent experiences in the United States could be drawn. Therefore, the interview sample was drawn taking into account the following demographic characteristics: region, urban/suburban/rural, age, sex, race, household income, religion, and school type. Adolescents attending private school or who were home-schooled were slightly oversampled.

Using a standard call script provided by NSYR, interviewers made contact with potential interviewee households. Interviewers identified themselves as researchers with the "National Youth Study." The full name of the research project was not used in order to avoid any bias introduced by identifying religion as a key focus of the study. If parents or adolescents seemed hesitant about participating, an additional script provided more information about the project and offered the phone number for the principal investigator. In addition, interviewers offered to mail to hesitant respondents written information about the project and then call back in a few days. Interviewers worked hard to obtain consent from the parents. However, when adolescents refused to participate even after being offered additional information, interviewers made no further attempts to convert those who refused.

Interviewers were required to obtain verbal and written informed consent from both parent and adolescent before conducting interviews. In the initial phone contact to set up the interview, interviewers obtained verbal consent from both parent and adolescent. Both were also informed that the adolescent would have the right to skip any question and to terminate the interview at any time for whatever reason. Prior to actually conducting the interviews, interviewers had to collect written consent forms signed by both parents and adolescents; in cases where adolescents were 18 years old, parental written consent was not required. All adolescents were also reminded at the start of the interviews and again in the middle of the interviews that they were free to skip any question they were not comfortable answering. In the event an adolescent revealed personal crises or dangers during the interview, interviewers were instructed about mandatory reporting and how properly to handle cases of abuse, harm to self or others, or other serious issues. In addition, all interviewers had in their possession at all times copies of a teen hotlines resource sheet. Interviewers provided this resource sheet to any adolescent who appeared to be struggling with suicide, mental health problems, eating disorders, family violence, or other serious issues, even in cases that did not technically require mandatory reporting.

Before and after the actual interviews, interviewers followed strict procedures for handling all data and paperwork related to the interviews. The protocol was designed to prevent any of the data files from being linked to the contact information of the adolescent participants. Interviewers were trained to treat all documentation and audio files as confidential and to handle them so as to minimize any risk of adolescents having their interview responses identified by others.

## ANALYSIS OF IN-DEPTH INTERVIEWS

All of the available interview transcripts (N = 267) were read and coded using ATLAS-ti software. Computer-assisted qualitative data analysis programs like ATLAS-ti assist researchers working with large quantities of textual data by facilitating the organizational tasks involved. I created a coding scheme based on the theoretical orientations guiding the research prior to beginning the analysis of the interview data. Throughout the coding process, however, the coding scheme underwent several revisions as new themes and ideas emerged from the data. In this analysis, we applied codes to selections of text, retrieved selected quotations within context, and tabulated the coded quotations, organizing quotations within codes and codes in relation to one another. The in-person interview questions on sexuality are listed in appendix C.

## NATIONAL LONGITUDINAL STUDY OF ADOLESCENT HEALTH

The National Longitudinal Study of Adolescent Health (Add Health) is a nationally representative, school-based study of adolescents in grades 7–12 in the United States and their outcomes in young adulthood. Add Health was designed to help explain the causes of adolescent health and health behavior, paying particular attention to the multiple contexts in which adolescents live. Add Health data collection was mandated to the National Institutes of Child Health and Human Development (NICHD) by action of the U.S. Congress (1993) and is funded by NICHD and 17 other federal agencies.

Fieldwork for the first two waves was conducted by the National Opinion Research Center of the University of Chicago; fieldwork for the third wave was conducted by the Research Triangle Institute in North Carolina. Unlike many contextual studies in which measures are constructed from the respondents' reports, Add Health collected data from the sources that make up some of the most important contexts in an adolescent's life, namely, parents, schools, communities, friends, and romantic partners. Three general theoretical concerns shaped the research design of Add Health, namely, that the health of adolescents is shaped by (1) differential environments, (2) differential behaviors of adolescents exposed to the same environment, and (3) differential health and risk vulnerabilities and strengths of adolescents exposed to the same environment (Udry and Bearman 1998). The Add Health data include a range of topics and variables, including sections on demographic background, religious identity and involvement, sexual behaviors, risk perceptions, and attitudes. Racial and ethnic oversamples of Cubans, Puerto Ricans, Chinese, and high-socioeconomic-status blacks were also gathered. Wave I data collection was undertaken in 1994–1995, Wave II followed approximately one year later in 1996, and Wave III data collection took place in 2001–2002, interviewing respondents during early adulthood.

## Wave I

The first wave of Add Health includes the richest set of respondents and data sources, including parents, school administrators, and several samples of adolescents. The primary sampling frame was a list of all high schools in the United States. To begin the process of data collection, a sample of schools was selected from such a list provided by the Quality Education Database. To ensure diversity, sampling was stratified by region, urbanicity, school type (public versus private), racial composition, and size. Each high school in the sample was matched to one of its feeder schools, with the probability of the feeder school being selected proportional to its contribution to the high school's student body. Over 70 percent of the originally selected schools agreed to participate. Replacement schools for those that refused to participate were selected within each community. This multistage design resulted in a final sample of 134 middle and high schools in 80 communities.

An in-school survey was administered to more than 90,000 students, with a response rate exceeding 90 percent. This survey can be used to construct several school-level variables (e.g., percentage African American, percentage smokers, etc.). A school administrator ($N = 164$) completed a half-hour self-administered questionnaire on characteristics of the school, which can be used to measure aspects of the school environment.

In addition to the in-school and school administrator surveys, a random sample of 16,000 students was selected from school rosters to participate in 1.5-hour, in-home interviews. Approximately 200 students were selected from each school pair, regardless of school size. This subsample of students was stratified within schools by sex and grade. There were 12,105 of these students who completed the in-home interview. Special oversamples were also selected: 1,038 high-education blacks, 450 Cubans, 437 Puerto Ricans, 334 Chinese, 471 physically disabled adolescents, and more than 4,000 adolescents residing in the same household. Additionally, 2 large schools and 14 small schools were completely "saturated," that is, all students ($N = 2{,}553$) enrolled in these schools were selected for in-home interviews. The final number of respondents for the in-home interviews was 20,745. A parent of each respondent was also administered a half-hour interview; approximately 85 percent of parents participated ($N = 17{,}713$).

The in-home interviews were conducted by trained interviewers using laptops to enter the survey responses. The interview included components on a variety of health and health-risk behaviors and mediating influences, including general health and nutrition, physical development, alcohol and drug use, delinquency, sexual behavior, contraceptive usage, AIDS and STD risk perceptions, academics, relationship with parents, self-efficacy, emotional health, family relations, religion, and perceived parental attitudes, among other topics. Sensitive portions of the survey, namely, sections on sexual behavior, were self-administered so that the adolescent respondent was entering responses directly into the computer. Headphones and audio delivery of the questionnaire were provided to assure that the respondents understood such questions. Neither the interviewer nor anyone else in the room could hear any question or response.

For each of the 80 communities represented in Add Health, neighborhoods were specified for each in-home respondent, and 1990 U.S. Census data at the tract, block, and county levels were assembled and merged for possible contextual analysis. Other sources of contextual data—including county-level religious affiliation data from Glenmary Research Center and data from the Uniform Crime Reports—were also merged. School attributes were available from the administrator survey and were also constructed by creating school means on any trait or behavior available from both the in-school and in-home data sets. Similarly, peer or friendship group measures have been constructed from matching friendship nominations, primarily in the saturated school samples.

### Wave II

The second wave of the Add Health in-home survey, collected approximately one year after the first (1996), includes just under 75 percent of the respondents interviewed at the first wave for a total N of 14,738. Of those, sample weights are available for 13,570. Respondents who were seniors in high school during Wave I and thus no longer in school (or had dropped out) were purposely not reinterviewed at Wave II. Thus, Wave II primarily includes only adolescent respondents who were enrolled in high school during both waves of data collection. The interviews were administered in-home, as at Wave I.

### Wave III

The data for Wave III were collected in 2001–2002, approximately five to six years after Wave II was collected. Wave III consists of all Wave I interview respondents (including the Wave I high school seniors who were dropped for Wave II) who were able to be located and interviewed (N = 15,170). Respondents at this wave were between the ages of 18 and 26, and transitions from adolescence to young adulthood can be evaluated. Wave III contains sections related to marriage, childbearing, educational history, relationships, and other areas relevant to young adults in addition to sections similar to those administered at Waves I and II. In addition to the more than 15,000 respondents from Wave I, Add Health brought in 1,507 respondent partners to be interviewed. The interviews were conducted in much the same manner as the other in-home interviews, with an emphasis on relational intimacy and commitment. Approximately 500 were married partners, 500 were cohabiting partners, and 500 were dating partners. Further details regarding the sample and methods of study can be found by visiting the Add Health Study's Web site at http://www.cpc.unc.edu/addhealth.

## National Survey of Family Growth

Cycle 6 of the National Survey of Family Growth (NSFG) is a nationally representative survey of Americans aged 15–44, jointly planned and funded by several agencies of the U.S. Department of Health and Human Services. Interviewing for NSFG Cycle 6 was conducted from January 2002 to March 2003 by the University of Michigan's Institute for Social Research (ISR) under contract with the National Center for Health Statistics (NCHS). In-person interviews were conducted with 7,643 women 15–44 years of age and 4,928 men 15–44 years of age for a total sample size of 12,571. The NSFG employed a four-stage sampling design and included an oversample of 2,271 adolescents (aged 15–19) in order to ensure an adequate sample size for this age group. The NSFG, as its name implies, is designed to provide national estimates of factors affecting family formation and growth, including pregnancy and birth rates, men's and women's health, and parenting. The response rate was 79 percent overall—80 percent for females and 78 percent for males. The questionnaire for males averaged about 60 minutes in length, while the female interview averaged about 80 minutes. Further details about the sample and methods of study can be found by visiting the NSFG's Web site at http://www.cdc.gov/nchs/nsfg.htm.

TABLE B1 Demographic Characteristics Comparing the Survey
and Interview Samples (in percentages)

| | NSYR survey (weighted) | NSYR interviews | Add Health Wave I (weighted) | NSFG (weighted) |
|---|---|---|---|---|
| *Census Region* | | | | |
| Northeast | 17 | 16 | 14 | NC |
| Midwest | 22 | 21 | 31 | NC |
| South | 37 | 30 | 39 | NC |
| West | 24 | 33 | 17 | NC |
| *Gender* | | | | |
| Male | 50 | 53 | 51 | 50 |
| Female | 50 | 47 | 49 | 50 |
| *Age* | | | | |
| 13 | 19 | 6 | 19 | 0 |
| 14 | 20 | 20 | 17 | 0 |
| 15 | 21 | 20 | 17 | 32 |
| 16 | 21 | 20 | 17 | 34 |
| 17 | 20 | 22 | 16 | 34 |
| 18+ | 0 | 12 | 14 | 0 |
| *Teen Race/Ethnicity* | | | | |
| White | 66 | 65 | 70 | 64 |
| African American | 16 | 14 | 15 | 15 |
| Hispanic | 12 | 15 | 11 | 15 |
| Asian | 2 | 3 | 3 | NC |
| Other | 4 | 3 | 1 | 6 |
| *Household Type* | | | | |
| Married-couple household | 70 | NC | 69 | 53 |
| *Income* | | | | |
| Less than $10,000 | 5 | 2 | 11 | 12 |
| $10K–$19,999 | 10 | 6 | 13 | 15 |
| $20K–$29,999 | 10 | 7 | 14 | 14 |
| $30K–$39,999 | 11 | 11 | 14 | 15 |
| $40K–$49,999 | 11 | 16 | 12 | 9 |

*(continued)*

TABLE B1 (*continued*)

| | NSYR survey (weighted) | NSYR interviews | Add Health Wave I (weighted) | NSFG (weighted) |
|---|---|---|---|---|
| $50K–$59,999 | 8 | 10 | 12 | 10 |
| $60K–$69,999 | 9 | 13 | 8 | 9[b] |
| $70K–$79,999 | 8 | 7 | 6 | 17[c] |
| $80K–$89,999 | 6 | 6 | 3 | – |
| $90K–$99,999 | 5 | 5 | 2 | – |
| $100K and up | 19 | 16 | 6 | – |
| N | 3,370 | 267 | 16,865[a] | 1,307 |

*Notes*: [a]Number in sample after listwise deletion of missing values for age, sex, race, and sex of parent respondent
[b]$60K–$74,999
[c]$75K and up
NC = Not calculated

TABLE B2  Religious Breakdown of NSYR
In-depth Interviewees

| | |
|---|---|
| Protestant | 131 |
|    Adventist | 3 |
|    Assemblies of God | 1 |
|    Baptist | 41 |
|    Bible Church | 1 |
|    Brethren | 1 |
|    Christian or Just Christian | 36 |
|    Church of Christ | 2 |
|    Church of the Nazarene | 1 |
|    Congregationalist | 3 |
|    Episcopalian | 1 |
|    Evangelical | 1 |
|    Lutheran | 8 |
|    Methodist | 14 |
|    Nondenominational | 6 |
|    Pentecostal | 3 |
|    Presbyterian | 9 |
| Catholic | 41 |
| Mormon | 21 |
| Jewish | 18 |
| Buddhist | 3 |
| Muslim | 2 |
| Jehovah's Witness | 2 |
| Hindu | 2 |
| Christian Science | 1 |
| Eastern Orthodox | 1 |
| Native American | 1 |
| Pagan or Wiccan | 1 |
| Don't know | 4 |
| Not religious | 39 |

# *Appendix C*

## Interview Questions on Sex

Sexuality Introduction: Now I am going to ask you a few questions about physical involvements or sex with others that may seem a little sensitive.

- All of your answers are totally confidential.
- You are free to not answer any question in this interview you don't want to.
- If you do not understand a question, just tell me that you don't know the answer.
- Please try to be honest in all of the answers that you do give.

* An issue that is a big concern to a lot of teenagers and adults is teenage physical involvements and sexual activity: like what kinds of physical intimacy or sexual activities are good or bad, safe and unsafe, right or wrong for teenagers to do. Different people have different ideas about this. What are your thoughts about teenagers and physical involvements and sex?
* When or under what conditions do you think it is appropriate and not appropriate for teenagers to be physically involved with each other? Why?

- Does this depend on different kinds or levels of physical intimacy? What things do you think are OK and what things, if any, are not? Why?

[Ask all of the following only if respondent seems adequately comfortable discussing:]
* Do you think young people should wait to have sex until they are married or not? Why?

- What do you mean when you refer to sex? What is included and what is not?
- Are there different kids of sex (i.e., oral, intercourse, etc.)? [if yes] Does the type of sex make a difference in whether it is OK for young people, or not?
- [if they should wait] Might it be OK for teenagers to have sex if they are "emotionally ready for it" or not?
- [if they don't need to wait] Under what conditions is it OK for teens to have sex? Do you think it matters how "emotionally ready" someone is?
  - [If "emotionally ready" matters] What do you think it means to be "emotionally ready for sex"? When is that? How would somebody know that they were "ready"?

* How much have you had to deal with questions about physical involvement and sex in your own personal life?
* Are your friends having sex?

- What kind(s) of sex?
- What do you think motivates them (physical pleasure? desire for social acceptance? social status? pressure? feeling grown-up? or what?)?

* Have you yourself ever been physically involved with another person, more than just holding hands or light kissing?

- [if yes] How physically involved have you gotten? In what ways?
- [if R didn't say explicitly] Have you yourself ever had sex?
- [if yes] You mean intercourse, or oral sex, or . . . ? What were/are the circumstances?
  - How do you feel about that?
  - Do your parents know? How would (or do) they feel about that if they knew?
  - Do your friends know? How do/would your friends feel?

* [if physically intimate or sexually active] Are there any things that you wish you would have known earlier about sex, anything you would do differently knowing whatever you know now? What? Why?

- Do you have any regrets?

* Have you ever had a negative or unhappy sexual experience?

  • [if yes] Is that something you would be willing to talk about?
  • [if yes] What were the circumstances? Why was it negative or unhappy for you?
  • How did you deal with it? How do you think it has affected you? [be prepared here to provide help information to respondents in need]

* Do you ever feel pressure now to have sex? By friends, dates, other influences?

  • What do you do with those pressures? Have they influenced you?

* How much is pregnancy or sexually transmitted diseases a concern for teens thinking about sexual activity?

  • Have you personally had to deal with issues of pregnancy or sexually transmitted diseases?

* What do you think have been the most important influences (i.e., people, experiences) on how you think about sex? How have they influenced you? In what ways?

  • [if religious or spiritual] Does your religion have any particular teaching or morality when it comes to sex? If so, what is it?
  • Do you agree with it? Why or why not?
  • How do you think that has worked out in your own life?

# NOTES

1. This number is a conservative estimate based on the Centers for Disease Control (CDC) and National Survey of Family Growth rates of sexual experience in teenagers. Based on an estimate that at least 8.85 percent of teenagers experience first sex in any given year, seven years of adolescence (ages 12–18), and just over 29 million adolescents in the United States, we arrive at a figure of just over 7,000.

2. This phenomenon is also causing considerable consternation in our legal system. Sexually explicit photographs of actual minors—those below the age of 18—are considered child pornography and subject to vigorous prosecution. Nevertheless, only the most obvious sexually explicit photographs of minors—those involving children—are prosecuted with any effectiveness. Additionally, the U.S. Supreme Court ruled in 2002 that "virtual" images of child pornography—while in very poor taste—are nevertheless legal. All of this suggests that in many cases what is legal and what is illegal are difficult to distinguish.

3. Throughout the book, I make reference to the "loss of virginity" and define it as coterminous with the first experience of vaginal intercourse for both boys and girls.

4. Robert Putnam (1995: 66) refers to social capital as "features of social organization, such as networks, norms, and trust, that facilitate coordination and cooperation for mutual benefit." Astute discussions of social capital should not overlook religious institutions as key providers of network ties and social trust (Smidt 2003).

5. Understandably, different surveys tend to produce varying estimates. Four reasons explain most discrepancies. First, different surveys often ask their respective questions in slightly different manners, and the psychology of question wording is sensitive to slight alterations in terms, phrases, and even the placement of questions in a survey (Tourangeau, Rips, and Rasinski 2000). Second, different data sets employ screening questions on different topics. For example, in order for NSYR respondents to even receive a particular question on sexual behavior, they first must pass a screening question that determines whether it is even necessary to ask subsequent questions. Third, Add Health, the NSYR, and the NSFG were administered approximately seven to eight years apart, and things can change in that time. Fourth, survey responses can be biased by systematic errors such as low response rates, response bias, and the survey setting's ability to guarantee anonymity in answering sensitive questions. Unfortunately, it is often impossible to pinpoint the exact source of varying estimates.

6. Seven denominations comprise the overwhelming majority of African Americans' religious affiliations in the United States. They are the African Methodist Episcopal (AME) church; the African Methodist Episcopal Zion church; the Christian Methodist Episcopal (CME) church; the National Baptist Convention, USA, Incorporated (NBC); the National Baptist Convention of America, Unincorporated (NBCA); the Progressive National Baptist Convention (PNBC); and the Church of God in Christ (COGIC). The Steensland et al. (2000) approach used in this book is slightly more encompassing and includes African Americans who report being a part of a Methodist or Southern Baptist congregation as well.

## Chapter 1

1. Elsewhere in the contemporary Christian world, these practices are still observed. In parts of Africa, the biblical concepts of "bride price" and obligations for men to marry deceased brothers' wives remain commonplace, as does the practice of polygamy (which was also practiced during the Old Testament era). American Christians tend to view such practices as either bizarre, or sinful, or both, yet their roots—if not their justification—in biblical themes and texts are evident.

2. Immediately following this command is another one: "Keep your lives free from the love of money and be content with what you have." However, materialism and greed—more common biblical themes than even sexual immorality—are less common signifiers of contemporary sinfulness.

3. Smith and Denton (2005: 162–163) describe the shape and character of "moralistic therapeutic deism" in considerable detail and outline its minimalist creed in five tenets: (1) God exists and created the world and watches over human life; (2) God wants people to be good, nice, and fair to each other—something the Bible as well as other religions' texts tend to teach; (3) the goal of life is to be happy and feel good about yourself; (4) God need not be active in people's lives unless they need resolution of a problem; and (5) good people go to heaven when they die. The authors conclude that this "religion" is very popular, but only loosely Christian (and has in fact supplanted actual historical Christian traditions). It is not so much a secularized version of Christianity, they argue, but an actively colonized, distinct faith that is largely theology-less and Jesus-less (Smith and Denton 2005: 171).

4. Framed in terms of sexual "markets," adolescents largely occupy "relational" sexual marketplaces, not "transactional" ones wherein short-term sexual relationships are more normative (Ellingson et al. 2004).

## Chapter 2

1. I am reminded of the humorous yet grave evaluation offered by an anonymous seventeenth-century English writer: "I had rather see coming toward me a whole regiment with drawn swords, than one lone Calvinist convinced that he is doing the will of God."

2. Certainly there is much more to the story than just quick decisions or opportunities to have sex. Theories about sexual scripts, networks, and choices clarify much about how sexual decisions are made (Laumann el al. 1994). I note this pair here simply because of their apparent associations with religiosity.

3. On the other hand, perhaps the critics have gone too far and are overlooking evident religious influences by using statistical methods that are, in fact, *too* rigorous. After all, if social scientists include enough variables in their statistical models, they can make almost any real and significant effect "disappear."

4. For a more extensive discussion of the relationship between religiosity and risk aversion, see Iannacone (1995), Miller and Hoffmann (1995), and Miller and Stark (2002). The risk-aversion hypothesis about religiosity is certainly complex. Extremely religious persons have consistently filled the ranks of foreign missions and religious relief organizations, often at significant personal risk (Stark 1997). Perhaps the association between religiosity and risk aversion is a curvilinear one.

5. The NSYR survey only asks about temperament: 8–9 percent of adolescents who attend religious services seldom or never are reported to have a "very bad" temper, compared with 3 percent of youths who attend services weekly or more often. Weekly attenders fare best of all—65 percent of them are said to have a "not bad" temper, compared with 49 percent of adolescents who never attend. Ten percent of adolescents who think religion is not important at all are said by their parents to have a very bad temper, compared with only 3 percent of youths who think religion is extremely important.

6. With the addition of a set of demographic measures to the models of adolescent attendance and personal religious salience, these personality effects weaken only slightly. Risk-taking and hot-tempered youth still attend less often, and more strategic respondents still attend more. Even with the use of a lagged dependent variable model, wherein I account for earlier attendance patterns, risk taking still predicts significantly lower attendance.

7. The measure of strategic orientation I use comes from a five-item summed index of how planful or strategic a decision maker the respondent is. All five measures include identical answer categories, ranging (1–5) from strongly agree to strongly disagree, administered to the respondent in the form of statements (that were later reverse coded). The first is: "When making decisions, you usually go with your 'gut feeling' without thinking too much about the consequences of each alternative." The second is: "When you have a problem to solve, one of the first things you do is get as many facts about the problem as possible." The third is: "When you are attempting to find a solution to a problem, you usually try to think of as many different ways to approach the problem as possible." The fourth is: "When making decisions, you generally use a systematic method for judging and comparing alternatives." The fifth and final component is: "After carrying out a solution to a problem, you usually try to analyze what went right and what went wrong." The alpha coefficient of reliability for this set of measures was 0.63.

8. The most popular survey-based means of measuring social desirability are variations of the Marlowe-Crowne Social Desirability Scale (MCSDS; Crowne and Marlowe 1960). The MCSDS items describe desirable but uncommon behaviors, such as "Before voting I thoroughly investigate the qualifications of all the candidates" or denying participation in undesirable but common activities, such as saying "I never gossip." Socially desirable responses are typically measured as strong agreement with statements that are, essentially, humanly impossible. Thus they are intended to pick up on respondents' desire to be thought of in a way that is both ideal and yet highly improbable. Some scholars, however, argue that a number of efforts to account for social desirability bias are actually confounded by "religious relevance" (Watson et al. 1986). That is, some measures of social desirability—such as denying that "I sometimes try to get even rather than forgive and forget"—may actually be measuring religiosity or its effects.

9. The measure of social desirability that I use here is a three-item index of dichotomous variables loosely derived from the MCSDS (Crowne and Marlowe 1960). Higher scores reflect a greater degree of socially desirable responding. In Add Health analyses, respondents who answered "strongly agree" to the statement "you never argue with anyone" were given

one point toward three possible points on the scale. Similarly, one point was given for the same answer to the statement "you never get sad," and likewise for the statement "you never criticize other people." Thus respondents who emphatically agreed with such statements were thought to be characterizing themselves in a more positive light than is possible. While short forms for social desirability scales are often frowned upon (Barger 2002), others find them helpful (Hays, Hayashi, and Stewart 1989). In my case, Add Health did not ask more questions like this, preventing me from adding more measures to the index.

10. In the end, human motivations and actions are no doubt bundled. That is, religious and "secular" influences often work together to reinforce each other and to motivate action in a common direction. Separating them into independent influences will only tell us part of the story, the part about multiple influences. Yet most social scientists would agree, if pressed, that influences on behavior generally do not work in any sort of truly independent fashion.

## CHAPTER 3

1. Some material from this chapter previously appeared in my article in *The Sociological Quarterly* 46 (2005): 81–107, entitled "Talking about Sex: Religion and Patterns of Parent-Child Communication about Sex and Contraception." Blackwell Publishing permitted its reproduction here.

2. I am referring to distinctly *religious* pedagogy here, not to the secular, abstinence-based educational tools presently used in many schools. The most popular religious books about adolescent sexuality are written by and targeted at evangelical Protestants. However, they are much less likely to be educational in their orientation than they are to be uniquely moral in orientation. At least one notable exception to this is the Concordia series on sexual development, published by the Lutheran Church (Missouri Synod). Roman Catholic and mainline Protestant denominations also produce sex education material, but they tend to enjoy a limited readership.

3. Many wonder why abstinence-only pedagogical approaches remain appealing to politicians and policy makers. The answer likely lies in powerful organizations (like Focus on the Family, the Family Research Council, etc.) that are able to reframe political issues like sex education in "culture wars" terminology and threaten to galvanize and sway the popular vote of conservative Christians. Thus, while a majority of conservative Christians may wish for a more comprehensive sex education for their children, the organizations that claim to represent them tend not to echo their interests.

4. In a survey of 374 rural Ohio parents, 87 percent perceive themselves as the leading source of sexual information, while much smaller percentages (41 and 16 percent, respectively) think that the mass media and religious institutions are primary sources of information (Jordan et al. 2000).

5. I quote infrequently from the NSYR interviews on the topic of learning about sex because the question was not on the interview schedule. Instances when the subject came up were sporadic. Thus I hesitate to suggest that the interview quotes on this topic reflect any common patterns among adolescents and their parents.

6. Moreover, it can be difficult for adolescents who've been consistently taught that wrongdoing happens "out there" and who haven't been taught anything about sex to understand the sexual feelings and urges that are inside their own bodies. It may seem to them that something which feels so good can't be wrong, no matter how it is expressed.

7. Other factors also appear to shape the frequency of communication about sexuality. Daughters with *older* mothers report slightly lower frequencies of sexual-risk communication (Hutchinson and Cooney 1998), while overall parent-child relationship satisfaction predicts more extensive conversations (Jaccard et al. 2000).

8. Reiss (1989) maintains that this double standard of sexual socialization and accompanying conflicted and anxious attitudes often works to prevent a more positive approach to sexuality, and ultimately undermines sexual responsibility. While few organizations (like churches, mass media, and the academy) articulate the reality of such a double standard, it remains resilient.

9. The three questions asked of parents in the Add Health study are as follows: (1)"How much have you and (name) talked about his/her having sexual intercourse and the moral issues of not having sexual intercourse?" (2) "How much have you talked with (adolescent child's name) about birth control?" (3) "How much have you talked with (adolescent child's name) about sex?" The questions were asked in the order listed above, and for each one the respondent parent could select one of four possible answers: not at all, somewhat, a moderate amount, or a great deal. In the NSYR, parents were asked a similar question about sex: "How many times, if ever, have you talked with [your teen] about sex? Would you say: never, once or twice, 3–5 times, or 6 times or more?" If parents asked for clarification, interviewers were instructed to state, "That is, how many times has the parent talked to their teen about the teen's own sexuality and sexual practices, not about sex as a topic in general." Few parent respondents indicated "never" (N = 159, or 4.7 percent). To those parents who gave a positive response, interviewers then asked, "How easy or hard is it for you to talk with [your teen] about sex? Is it very hard, somewhat hard, fairly easy, or very easy?" It is this last question that I feature. Since the first question overlapped with the Add Health series, I chose not to feature it here.

10. Race/ethnicity comprises the most powerful predictor of all communication-related variables in both data sets. African-American parents report significantly more communication about both sex and birth control than do parents of any other race or ethnic group. Indeed, African-American parents are almost three times as likely as Asian Americans to talk "a great deal" to their children about sex (in Add Health). The racial/ethnic differences in NSYR appear comparable to those in Add Health. African-American adolescents are also *more* likely than whites, Hispanics, and Asian Americans to say that their church does an "excellent" job in "helping you better understand your own sexuality and sexual morality" (results not shown).

11. While not directly related to the topic at hand, it is generally agreed that more forthright maternal conversations about sexuality and pleasure enhance adolescent girls' likelihood of experiencing pleasure in later sexual experiences (Thompson 1990).

12. It should be acknowledged here that a population of virgins is not "random." Whenever I analyze this population, it is a unique group, subject to considerable selection effects, especially among the oldest adolescents among whom virginity is less common (though by no means rare). I do, however, avoid the time-ordering problem that often plagues studies of sexual behavior. That is, all predictor variables used are measured earlier in time than the outcome of first sex, except for the number of romantic partners (which is a recollection from the past 18 months and was administered at Wave II). What I lose, however, is the ability to assess youths who experienced first sex *before* Wave I data collection, a similarly unique group. Those youths vary systematically on many counts (race/ethnicity, sexual attitudes) from virgins of identical age.

13. The sex and pregnancy-risk quiz was administered at both waves of the Add Health study and comprises five true/false statements. The dependent variable is a count of the number of statements to which correct answers were given. The five questions are:

1. When a woman has sexual intercourse, almost all sperm die inside her body after about six hours (answer = false).
2. Most women's periods are regular, that is, they ovulate (are fertile) fourteen days after their periods begin (answer = false).
3. The most likely time for a woman to get pregnant is right before her period starts (answer = false).
4. Even if a man pulls out before he has ejaculated (even if ejaculation occurs outside the woman's body), it is still possible for the woman to become pregnant (answer = true).
5. In general, a woman is most likely to get pregnant if she has sex during her period, as compared with other times of the month (answer = false).

14. The number of adolescents dips from Wave I to Wave II because high school seniors at Wave I were purposefully not reinterviewed at Wave II.

15. The exact wording for these questions, delivered via the ACASI (Audio Computer-Assisted Self-Interviewing) method in which the respondent reads the questions and answers on a computer screen rather than hears and answers the actual interviewer, was as follows (Mosher, Chandra, and Jones 2005: 9–10):

(For females): The next question asks about sexual experience you may have had with another female. Have you ever had any sexual experience of any kind with another female? [Note that this question is worded in such a way that a variety of experiences could be reported. The wording of this question may elicit more "yes" answers than the more restrictive or behavior-focused wording used for males in the NSFG.]

(For males): The next questions ask about sexual experience you may have had with another male. Have you ever done any of the following with another male? Put his penis in your mouth (oral sex)? Put your penis in his mouth (oral sex)? Put his penis in your rectum or butt (anal sex)? Put your penis in his rectum or butt (anal sex)? A "yes" answer to any of these four questions was classified as "same-sex sexual contact." [Note that these questions are more specific than the single question on female same-sex behavior.]

Respondents were also asked questions on sexual attraction and orientation. For females, the questions were:

People are different in their sexual attraction to other people. Which best describes your feelings? Are you only attracted to males, mostly attracted to males, equally attracted to males and females, mostly attracted to females, only attracted to females, or not sure?

For males, the questions were:

People are different in their sexual attraction to other people. Which best describes your feelings? Are you only attracted to females, mostly attracted to females, equally attracted to females and males, mostly attracted to males, only attracted to males, or not sure?

Finally, both males and females were asked: "Do you think of yourself as heterosexual, homosexual, bisexual, or something else?"

16. I recognize that since we didn't ask about it, those youths who did talk about it are an unusual sample that have self-selected to raise the issue—and therefore they may be systematically different than those who did not talk about it.

## CHAPTER 4

1. Reflecting an international vision, beginning in 2005 the Silver Ring Thing intends to persuade 20 percent of the world's adolescents to put off sex until marriage, according to its founder, Denny Pattyn (Rosenbloom 2005).

2. Among the more common antecedents to the medical condition labeled "vaginismus"—defined as painful or impossible intercourse due to the involuntary contraction of vaginal muscles—are strict religious teachings about sex, stern parenting, and inadequate sexual education.

3. A word on Bearman and Brückner's methodology is in order here. It is impossible to measure whether the respondent actually waited until after the formal wedding date to experience first sex, since Add Health did not ask the respondents whether they waited to have sexual intercourse until after they were married. Instead, the authors calculated whether the report of the timing of first sex corresponded to the year in which the respondent reported getting married. They give the benefit of the doubt to those respondents who reported first sex in the same year that they got married. Thus the measure is a conservative one.

4. Only about 5 percent of the youngest cohort of all adults (and just 2 percent of men) in the National Health and Social Life Survey indicated they were virgins at the time of their marriage (Laumann et al. 1994).

5. The assumption is that such additional sexual partners are premarital sexual partners, but it is conceivable that some of these were extramarital sexual partners. It seems unlikely, however, that that is a typical scenario.

6. However, when interviewed by Ed Bradley on CBS's "60 Minutes" ("Taking the Pledge," September 18, 2005), Bearman contended that "adolescents who take virginity pledges, who remain virgins, that is who don't have vaginal sex, who technically remain virgins, are much more likely to have . . . anal sex." I think the claim about anal sex is an overstatement.

7. Although it is conceivable that some religious respondents answered this and other sexual motivation questions with their future married status in mind—thus making the issue of guilt moot—this should not be the case among most, since the section in which the questions appeared began with these instructions:

> The next questions are about how you would feel about having sexual intercourse at this time in your life. Some people have sexual intercourse before they get married. Others do not. For these questions, it doesn't matter whether you yourself have had intercourse. Just indicate whether you agree or disagree with the statements.

8. A term I do not use in this book is "petting," which has gone out of use. Evangelical books about sex and sexual morality previously paid much attention to the term and the general set of behaviors it represented (fondling another's breasts or genitals, perhaps to orgasm). The actions still concern them, but the terminology has changed.

9. Dobson (1989: 83–84) explicitly argues to adolescents:

> It is my opinion that masturbation is not much of an issue with God. It is a normal part of adolescence which involves no one else. It does not cause disease. It does not produce babies, and Jesus did not mention it in the Bible. I'm not telling you to masturbate, and I hope you won't feel the need for it. But if you do, it is my opinion that you should not struggle with guilt over it. Why do I tell you this? Because I deal with so many Christian young people who are torn apart with guilt over masturbation; they want to stop and just can't. I would like to help you avoid that agony.

10. As one example of this, the popular evangelical book *Every Young Man's Battle* (Arterburn, Stoeker, and Yorkey 2002) devotes more than 40 pages to the topic of masturbation, while *Every Young Woman's Battle* (Ethridge and Arterburn 2004) has only 6 pages on the subject.

CHAPTER 5

1. Gloria González-López notes the same among Latina immigrants and their mothers, many of whom convey to their daughters that their virginity is a valuable commodity (2004).

2. I say "most" because there are always exceptions. Some studies find a protective effect of attendance only among certain subgroups of adolescents, such as white males (Cvetkovich and Grote 1980) or African-American and white females (Billy, Brewster, and Grady 1994). Some find no association at all between religious attendance and sexual experience (Benda and Corwyn 1997; Thomson 1982). But the most common conclusion is that church attendance tends to delay first sex.

3. In order to refrain from introducing potentially sensitive and confusing questions to younger teenagers, NSYR interviewers employed a screening procedure. The exact sequence and text of the NSYR sex question screens are as follows. First, respondents were asked, "How many total different people, if any, have you been physically involved with, more than just holding hands and light kissing, since you turned 13 years old?" If they responded with a number greater than zero, they were eventually asked: "Have you ever willingly touched another person's private areas or willingly been touched by another person in your private areas under your clothes, or not? [not including a physician]" Respondents who said "yes" were then asked the battery of sex questions. If they responded "no," then I have recoded them as having retained their virginity, having no sexual partners, a sexual frequency of zero, no oral sex, etc. Add Health asked about vaginal sexual intercourse of all of its respondents, regardless of age. In general, screening questions— while essential for some aspects of survey research and helpful for others—will tend to produce underestimates of behaviors in question. On the other hand, asking all 13-year-olds (in Add Health) about vaginal intercourse may run the risk of overestimating rates of sexual behavior, if for no other reason than that the question introduces material that not all adolescents yet understand (in turn, boosting the likelihood that they will give erroneous answers). Such different question wording and the use of screens contribute to different survey estimates.

4. I measure "transformational" change as involving a multiple-step increase or decrease in religiosity in a short period of time—the approximate year between Add Health survey waves. For example, if an adolescent reports "never" attending religious services at

Wave I and then reports attending "once a month or more, but less than once a week," I label that as a drastic, or transformational, religious change. The change can be in either direction: an adolescent who says religion is "very important" at Wave I and "fairly unimportant" at Wave II likewise exhibits a (negative) religious transformation.

5. Looking ahead to young adulthood (in Add Health Wave III), this pattern remains stable. Among those young adult respondents who reported having had sex (around 80 percent), about 21 percent reported having had one sexual partner during their life, 14 percent reported two total partners, 12 percent reported having had three, 9 percent each reported four and five sexual partners, and 35 percent reported some number higher than five.

6. I don't wish to make strong distinctions between religious variables like Bible reading and attendance, etc. Suffice it to say that—despite controlling for variables that have strong associations with frequency of sex—religion continues to distinguish adolescents here as well as in analyses of virginity status.

7. Using Add Health's Wave III data, Brückner and Bearman (2005) find that African-American young adults have STD rates roughly eight times that of whites. Asians, Hispanics, and others exhibit rates of trichomoniasis, gonorrhea, and chlamydia that are two to five times that of whites.

8. A variety of studies has concluded that members of groups most likely to delay first intercourse are also less likely to use contraception once they do have sex (Brewster et al. 1998; Cooksey et al. 1996).

9. The Alan Guttmacher Institute reports that between 1.6 and 3.6 percent of condoms break or slip during each coital act (Cates 2001). (While breaking may be a manufacturer's fault, slipping may not be.) The FDA says that 11 women out of 100 will get pregnant while using condoms for one year, yet these numbers range from 1 to 20 percent, depending upon the study in question. In sum, failure rates vary from country to country, by manufacturer, by study, and certainly by method. Indeed, it is probably impossible to calculate one precise rate for any given method.

10. Perhaps the few Mormons who are having sex are trying to hide it, given the high rates of contraception at first sex (92 percent) and at their most recent sexual encounter (84 percent).

11. Since both Jewish and Mormon adolescents are among the most likely to delay first sex, those among them who are sexually active comprise a unique and very nonrandom group. Thus I hesitate to make confident interpretations here about their contraceptive use.

12. Numerous measures about contraception and birth control appear in the Add Health data set, but I have only featured several here. Religiosity does not distinguish between answers to such survey statements as "Birth control is too much of a hassle to use," or "Birth control is too expensive to buy," or "Using birth control interferes (or would interfere) with sexual enjoyment." Perhaps the lack of association is itself interesting, but typically the answers to these questions are more explicable by other key variables like gender, socioeconomic status, and sexual experience.

13. There were not sufficient numbers of Jewish and Mormon youth who had had sex more than once to include them in Table 5.10.

14. What exactly is the difference between "every time" and "almost every time," especially among youths who may not have had sex more than a few times to begin with? The answer could be as simple as one instance. Or, it could be that mainline Protestant youth exhibit comparable contraceptive use, but—in keeping with the popular discourse of public health and sexual education—will not admit to having unprotected sex, suggesting a possible social desirability bias.

15. I don't feature numerous accounts here of negative sexual experiences, since my focus is on how religion shapes sexual decision making, and rape and molestation are certainly not about decision making on the part of the victims.

16. The suggestion that marriage is a "white thing" could also be extended to restrictive norms about sexual behavior. Such an oppositional culture argument suggests that perceived "white" patterns of sexual activity would be seen as an orientation to be challenged, in order to indicate one's true racial membership. However, I detected none of this in the interviews.

17. This quotation, though originally from C. Eric Lincoln and Lawrence Mamiya's (1990) book, was most recently cited in Kenneth Steinman and Marc Zimmerman's (2004: 153) study of religion and risk behavior among African-American adolescents.

18. Considerable angst was raised recently in the evangelical community with the publication of Ron Sider's (2005) book *Scandal of the Evangelical Conscience: Why Are Christians Living Just Like the Rest of the World?* In it, Sider takes American evangelicals to task for saying one thing and doing another. From divorce to racism, domestic violence to sex, Sider concludes that evangelical Christians act very much like their non-Christian neighbors, despite their unique rhetoric and claims of concern.

19. Twelve percent of evangelical youth who experienced first sex between Add Health survey waves "strongly agree" that having sex would/did make them feel guilty. Only one other religious group (those from other, non-Christian religions) broke the 6 percent barrier. In other words, evangelical recent nonvirgins are the most likely to feel bad about sex.

## Chapter 6

1. Oral sex is considered low risk for some sexually transmitted infections (like HIV), but nevertheless can transmit other types of infections, including chlamydia, gonorrhea, and herpes (Edwards and Carne 1998).

2. If respondents made it through the original screening question about sexual activity, the NSYR asked them a general question about oral sex: "Have you ever engaged in oral sex, or not?" This was followed by a frequency question. We also asked about oral sex during the in-person interviews.

3. The NSFG questions were worded as follows, to women: "Has a male ever put his mouth on your vagina (also known as cunnilingus or oral sex)?" "Have you ever put your mouth on a male's penis (also known as fellatio or oral sex)?" To men: "Has a female ever put her mouth on your penis (also known as oral sex or fellatio)?" "Have you ever put your mouth on a female's vagina (also known as oral sex or cunnilingus)?"

4. Clark (2004), however, notes that he did not directly discuss sexuality or sexual behavior with his study participants.

5. A table outlining the frequency of oral sex split by religious affiliation had too few values in several cells to make clear sense of it.

6. The NSFG questions were worded as follows, to women: "Has a male ever put his penis in your rectum or butt (also known as anal sex)?" To men: "Have you ever put your penis in a female's rectum or butt (also known as anal sex)?"

7. This section heading is borrowed from the title of the book by Jenna Jameson and Neil Strauss (2004).

## Chapter 7

1. I am deeply indebted to John Bartkowski for helping me to think through these various categories. He is at least half-responsible (or to blame) for the outlines of the

typology. As a social scientist, I intend to convey no rank order to this typology. It is a classification tool to help us understand the role of religion in motivating behavior.

2. My definition of invisible religion is categorically distinct from that of Thomas Luckmann (1967), whose definition referred to the increasing likelihood of seeing one's religious faith as an entirely private matter. His and my term may not be cut from entirely different cloth, however. It is plausible to suggest that youths for whom religious influence on their actions is invisible are unaware of it precisely because religion has lost public relevance and is compartmentalized.

3. This typology is best used in conjunction with in-person interview data, where we can probe respondents about what they believe and why they take the actions they do. Survey researchers of sexuality, however, could also do a better job of tapping motivations than they currently do. For example, social scientists could ask survey respondents to rank order the "concerns" they have when it comes to making a decision about having sex with a willing partner. Such answer options might include (a) risk of pregnancy, (b) threat of discovery, (c) influence upon reputation, (d) moral or religious guilt, etc. Those respondents who rank order a, b, or c above d would *not* be considered intentionally religious. Perhaps respondents who rank a and b above d could be identified as instrumentally religious, especially if we know (from other survey responses) that they are fairly religious. While such an approach of course introduces new problems, it is nevertheless an innovative way to apply this typology.

4. The "consequential" is one of five aspects of religiosity offered by sociologists Charles Glock and Rodney Stark (1965). In their definition of religiosity, people may or may not:

- Know about their religion (the intellectual aspect)
- Attend or participate in religious services (the ritualistic aspect)
- Attach importance and emotion to religious things (the experiential aspect)
- Internalize their belief systems (the ideological aspect)
- Act on their beliefs (the consequential aspect)

5. Smith's emphasis on moral directives is similar in spirit to Sherkat and Ellison's (1997: 959) discussion of religious cognitive frameworks, which could be defined as religiously derived cultural orientations and "precommitments to particular understandings—often reinforced in social settings—[that] become consequential for motivating actions."

6. For those who were articulate, this ability often spilled over into other facets: if they were intentionally religious about one or two behaviors, they were more likely to be so about others.

7. I should note that not all religions seek to curb sexual permissiveness. Cindy, the 16-year-old Wiccan from Indiana quoted in chapter 4, feels that adolescent sexual *pursuits* could be religiously motivated. Her account blends unusual religious sources with public health concerns that were taught to her both in school and on television (she mentions learning about condoms from the animated television show "South Park"):

> I think that my beliefs in sex are reflected in my religion, because they say that it's not something that should be shunned, it's something, it's fun. It's what two people do when they're in love with each other, you know, or just when you want to have fun. You know, go ahead. As long as you're careful, you know, do something. Like, don't just, like, go out and have sex with everyone and [not] use a condom, you know. As long as you're careful about it then, hey, go ahead, you know.

8. The human heart is unusual territory for a sociologist, but I cannot deny its reality and power, despite its inability to be measured. After all, why is it that so many novelists seem to understand and capture the human condition far better than do social scientists?

9. In his book *Fear and Trembling*, philosopher Soren Kierkegaard (1954 [1843]) goes on a similar quest to locate the "knight of faith," that person who devotes his/her life toward a single-minded love of the divine. I might call this person the intentionally religious actor, but Kierkegaard would suggest that I won't easily find what I'm looking for. Such a person is religious, he suggests, but nothing about him/her indicates any special spiritual qualities. If one did not know otherwise, it would be impossible to distinguish him/her from other religious individuals.

10. Shuman and Meador (2002) dispute such religious instrumentalism in their book *Heal Thyself: Spirituality, Medicine, and the Distortion of Christianity*. They argue that the religion and health "movement," if it can even be called that, distorts and devalues real Christian faith by mixing the self-interested consumer mentality with the sacred in an exchange relationship. I've found, however, that it would be difficult to argue convincingly that very many people are *consciously* instrumental about religion. The interviews detect little of this among teenagers.

11. Alternately, otherwise very religious adolescents may simply be so familiar with the dominant discourses about sex (such as the public health narratives) that they feel the need to frame their answers to secular researchers in terms that would make sense to someone whom they presume would not understand religious reasoning. So rather than seem overly religious, they prefer to show that their religiously inspired actions have pragmatic justification. Exactly how true this account may be is impossible to know.

12. For evidence on religion's influence on marital stability, see Brody et al. (1994) or Mahoney et al.'s (2001) review of research. Greater church attendance appears linked with lower rates of marital physical aggression (Ellison and Anderson 2001; Ellison, Bartkowski, and Anderson 1999). Pearce and Axinn's (1998) study of mothers and their relationships with their children across 26 years reveals that the more important religion is to a mother, the more likely her child is to report a higher quality of relationship with her. Research on fathers in intact families reveals that fathers' time spent attending religious services is beneficial for their children's school outcomes (Yeung, Duncan, and Hill 2000). These are just a few examples of how religion can indirectly affect children through its direct effects on marital and family processes.

## UNSCIENTIFIC POSTSCRIPT

1. This Weberian tradition has a long history within the social sciences, although it is often co-opted by activist scholarship, which can be of considerable value so long as readers keep their eyes wide open.

2. In her conclusion to what otherwise is a very informative article, Sharon Thompson (1990) advocates that we teach young women—among other skills—how to "fuck" and how to pleasure members of both sexes.

3. Even these "wrongs" may be debatable, as some scholars have taken to speaking about criminal sexual conduct with a child in seemingly neutral terms, labeling it "childhood sexual contact."

4. I am *not* suggesting that all adolescent girls are "by nature" sexually conservative. Some express considerable inhibitions about sexual involvement, while others do not. Rather, girls tend to be more likely to exhibit ambivalence and mixed emotions about sex.

5. Frederica Mathewes-Green (2005a: 7) wisely wonders why "we try so hard to dress in ways that will make people stare at our bodies, when what we really want is for them to look at our eyes."

6. Parents are stakeholders, not owners. A phenomenon I find odd, alarming, and out of step with both ancient and modern religious wisdom about sex is the practice of pledging abstinence *to* one's parents, as if parents *owned* a child's sexuality.

7. Risman and Schwartz (2002: 22) correctly point out that, "while concern with teenage sexuality continues, the public does not seem willing to desexualize the greater culture that shapes teen experiences."

8. More liberal religious traditions have elected not to pursue both goals. Instead, they openly discourage young marriage, choosing instead to shrewdly focus on education and career first. Their sexual relationships may or may not be accompanied by marriage, but when it becomes time for marriage and family, they tend to be more stable and less prone to divorce.

9. Despite suggestions that abstinence organizations target boys and girls equally, for every five girls who take an abstinence pledge, only three boys do (from Add Health Waves I and II).

## Appendix B

1. The information about the National Survey of Youth and Religion (NSYR) is taken, with the authors' permission, from *Soul Searching: The Religious and Spiritual Lives of American Teenagers*, by Christian Smith with Melinda Lundquist Denton (Oxford University Press, 2005). Interested readers can find a more detailed description of the data collection process in appendixes B and C of that source.

# REFERENCES

Adamczyk, Amy, and Jacob Felson. 2006. "Friends' Religiosity and First Sex." *Social Science Research* 35: 924–947.

Adolph, Carol, Diana E. Ramos, Kathryn L. P. Linton, and David A. Grimes. 1995. "Pregnancy among Hispanic Teenagers: Is Good Parental Communication a Deterrent?" *Contraception* 51: 303–306.

Ajzen, Icek. 1991. "The Theory of Planned Behavior." *Organizational Behavior and Human Decision Processes* 50: 179–211.

Ajzen, Icek, and Martin Fishbein. 1980. *Understanding Attitudes and Predicting Social Behavior.* Englewood Cliffs, NJ: Prentice-Hall.

Albert, Bill, Sarah Brown, and Christine M. Flanigan (eds.). 2003. *14 and Younger: The Sexual Behavior of Young Adolescents (Summary).* Washington, DC: National Campaign to Prevent Teen Pregnancy.

Ali, Lorraine, and Julie Scelfo. 2002. "Choosing Virginity." *Newsweek*, Dec. 9, 60–64, 66.

Ammerman, Seth D., Elizabeth Perelli, Nancy Adler, and Charles E. Irwin, Jr. 1992. "Do Adolescents Understand What Physicians Say about Sexuality and Health?" *Clinical Pediatrics* 31: 590–595.

Andre, Thomas, Rita Lund Frevert, and Dana Schuchmann. 1989. "From Whom Have College Students Learned What about Sex?" *Youth & Society* 20: 241–268.

Ansuini, Catherine G., Julianna Fiddler-Woite, and Robert S. Woite. 1996. "The Source, Accuracy, and Impact of Initial Sexuality Information on Lifetime Wellness." *Adolescence* 31: 283–289.

Arterburn, Stephen, Fred Stoeker, and Mike Yorkey. 2002. *Every Young Man's Battle: Strategies for Victory in the Real World of Sexual Temptation.* Colorado Springs, CO: WaterBrook.

Bandstra, Barry L. 2004. *Reading the Old Testament: An Introduction to the Hebrew Bible.* 3d ed. Belmont, CA: Wadsworth.

Bandura, Albert. 1977. *Social Learning Theory.* Englewood Cliffs, NJ: Prentice-Hall.

Barger, Steven D. 2002. "The Marlowe-Crowne Affair: Short Forms, Psychometric Structure, and Social Desirability." *Journal of Personality Assessment* 79: 286–305.

Bartkowski, John P., and Christopher G. Ellison. 1995. "Divergent Models of Childrearing in Popular Manuals: Conservative Protestants vs. the Mainstream Experts." *Sociology of Religion* 56: 21–34.

269

Bartle, Nathalie A. 1998. *Venus in Blue Jeans: Why Mothers and Daughters Need to Talk about Sex.* New York: Dell.

Batson, C. Daniel, Stephen J. Naifeh, and Suzanne Pate. 1978. "Social Desirability, Religious Orientation, and Racial Prejudice." *Journal for the Scientific Study of Religion* 17: 31–41.

Batson, C. Daniel, Patricia Schoenrade, and W. Larry Ventis. 1993. *Religion and the Individual: A Social-Psychological Perspective.* New York: Oxford University Press.

Bearman, Peter S., and Hannah Brückner. 2001. "Promising the Future: Virginity Pledges and First Intercourse." *American Journal of Sociology* 106: 859–912.

———. 2004. "The Relationship between Virginity Pledges in Adolescence and STD Acquisition in Young Adulthood." Paper presented at the National STD Conference, Philadelphia, March 8–11.

Bearman, Peter S., James Moody, and Katherine Stovel. 2004. "Chains of Affection: The Structure of Adolescent Romantic and Sexual Networks." *American Journal of Sociology* 110: 44–91.

Beck, Scott H., Bettie S. Cole, and Judith A. Hammond. 1991. "Religious Heritage and Premarital Sex: Evidence from a National Sample of Young Adults." *Journal for the Scientific Study of Religion* 30: 173–180.

Benda, Brent B., and Robert Flynn Corwyn. 1997. "A Test of a Model with Reciprocal Effects between Religiosity and Various Forms of Delinquency Using 2-Stage Least Squares Regression." *Journal of Social Service Research* 22: 27–52.

Benson, Peter L., Michael J. Donahue, and Joseph A. Erickson. 1989. "Adolescence and Religion: A Review of the Literature from 1970 to 1986." Pp. 153–181 in *Research in the Social Scientific Study of Religion*, edited by Monty L. Lynn and David O. Moberg. Greenwich, CT: JAI.

Berger, Peter. 1967. *The Sacred Canopy: Elements of a Sociological Theory of Religion.* New York: Anchor.

Bersamin, Melina M., Samantha Walker, Elizabeth D. Waiters, Deborah A. Fisher, and Joel W. Grube. 2005. "Promising to Wait: Virginity Pledges and Adolescent Sexual Behavior." *Journal of Adolescent Health* 36: 428–436.

Billy, John, O.G., Karin L. Brewster, and William R. Grady. 1994. "Contextual Effects on the Sexual Behavior of Adolescent Women." *Journal of Marriage and the Family* 56: 387–404.

Brewster, Karin L., Elizabeth C. Cooksey, David K. Gulkey, and Ronald R. Rindfuss. 1998. "The Changing Impact of Religion on the Sexual and Contraceptive Behavior of Adolescent Women in the United States." *Journal of Marriage and the Family* 60: 493–504.

Brody, Gene H., Zolinda Stoneman, Douglas Flor, and Chris McCrary. 1994. "Religion's Role in Organizing Family Relationships: Family Process in Rural, Two-Parent African American Families." *Journal of Marriage and the Family* 54: 878–888.

Brody, Jane E. 2006. "Children, Media and Sex: A Big Book of Blank Pages." *New York Times*, January 31, F7.

Brooks, David. 2005. "Public Hedonism and Private Restraint." *New York Times*, April 17, 4–14.

Brooks-Gunn, Jeanne, and Roberta Paikoff. 1997. "Sexuality and Developmental Transitions during Adolescence." Pp. 190–219 in *Health Risks and Developmental Transitions during Adolescence*, edited by John Schulenberg, Jennifer L. Maggs, and Klaus Hurrelmann. New York: Cambridge University Press.

Browning, Christopher R., Tama Leventhal, and Jeanne Brooks-Gunn. 2005. "Sexual Initiation in Early Adolescence: The Nexus of Parental and Community Control." *American Sociological Review* 70: 758–778.

Brückner, Hannah, and Peter S. Bearman. 2005. "After the Promise: The STD Consequences of Adolescent Virginity Pledges." *Journal of Adolescent Health* 36: 271–278.

Burkett, Stephen R., and Mervin White. 1974. "Hellfire and Delinquency: Another Look." *Journal for the Scientific Study of Religion* 13: 455–462.

Carpenter, Laura M. 2001. "The Ambiguity of 'Having Sex': The Subjective Experience of Virginity Loss in the United States." *Journal of Sex Research* 38: 127–139.

———. 2002. "Gender and the Meaning and Experience of Virginity Loss in the Contemporary United States." *Gender & Society* 16: 345–365.

———. 2005a. "Virginity Loss in Reel/Real Life: Using Popular Movies to Navigate Sexual Initiation." Paper presented at the annual meeting of the American Sociological Association, Philadelphia, August 13–16.

———. 2005b. *Virginity Lost: An Intimate Portrait of First Sexual Experiences*. New York: New York University Press.

Casper, Lynne M. 1990. "Does Family Interaction Prevent Adolescent Pregnancy?" *Family Planning Perspectives* 22: 109–114.

Cates, Williard. 2001. "The NIH Condom Report: The Glass Is 90% Full." *Family Planning Perspectives* 33: 231–233.

CBS News. 2005. "Taking the Pledge." *CBS News*, September 18. Retrieved September 21, 2005, from http://www.cbsnews.com/stories/2005/05/20/60minutes/main696975.shtml.

Centers for Disease Control and Prevention. 2002. "Youth Risk Behavior Surveillance— United States, 2001." Retrieved January 26, 2004, from http://www.cdc.gov/mmwr/PDF/SS/SS5104.pdf.

———. 2004. "Teenagers in the United States: Sexual Activity, Contraceptive Use, and Childbearing, 2002." Retrieved August 29, 2005, from http://www.cdc.gov/nchs/data/series/sr_23/sr23_024FactSheet.pdf.

Clark, Chap. 2004. *Hurt: Inside the World of Today's Teenagers*. Grand Rapids, MI: Baker Academic Press.

Coleman, James. 1988. "Social Capital in the Creation of Human Capital." *American Journal of Sociology* 95: S95–S120.

Collins, Rebecca L., Marc N. Elliott, Sandra H. Berry, David E. Kanouse, Dale Kunkel, Sarah B. Hunter, and Angela Miu. 2004. "Watching Sex on Television Predicts Adolescent Initiation of Sexual Behavior." *Pediatrics* 114: 280–289.

Connolly, Ceci. 2005. "Teen Pledges Barely Cut STD Rates, Study Says." *Washington Post*, March 19, A3.

"Conservatives Ask FBI to Investigate Hotel Porn." 2006. Associated Press, August 22. Retrieved August 22, 2006, from http://www.cnn.com/2006/US/08/22/hotel.porn.ap/index.html.

Cook, Andrew J., Kevin Moore, and Gary D. Steel. 2005. "Taking a Position: A Reinterpretation of the Theory of Planned Social Behaviour." *Journal for the Theory of Social Behaviour* 35: 143–154.

Cooksey, Elizabeth C., Ronald R. Rindfuss, and David K. Guilkey. 1996. "The Initiation of Adolescent Sexual and Contraceptive Behavior during Changing Times." *Journal of Health and Social Behavior* 37: 59–74.

Crosby, Richard A., and William L. Yarber. 2001. "Perceived versus Actual Knowledge about Correct Condom Use among U.S. Adolescents: Results from a National Study." *Journal of Adolescent Health* 28: 415–420.

Crowne, Douglas P., and David Marlowe. 1960. "A New Scale of Social Desirability Independent of Psychopathology." *Journal of Consulting Psychology* 4: 349–354.

Curran, Melissa, and Zach Estes. 1998. "In a Protestant City, Different Paths to Enlightenment." *New York Times*, April 29, G4.

Cvetkovich, George, and Barbara Grote. 1980. "Psychosocial Development and the Social Problem of Teenage Illegitimacy." Pp. 15–41 in *Adolescent Pregnancy and Childbearing: Findings from Research*, edited by Catherine S. Chilman. Washington, DC: U.S. Department of Health and Human Services.

DeLamater, John. 1989. "The Social Control of Human Sexuality." Pp. 30–62 in *Human Sexuality: The Societal and Interpersonal Context*, edited by Kathleen McKinney and Susan Sprecher. Norwood, NJ: Ablex.

Diamond, Lisa M. 2003. "Was It a Phase? Young Women's Relinquishment of Lesbian/Bisexual Identities over a 5-Year Period." *Journal of Personality and Social Psychology* 84: 352–364.

DiMarco, Hayley. 2006. *Technical Virgin: How Far Is Too Far?* Grand Rapids, MI: Revell.

Dines, Gail, and Robert Jensen. 2004. "Pornography and Media: Toward a More Critical Analysis." Pp. 369–380 in *Sexualities: Identities, Behaviors, and Society*, edited by Michael S. Kimmel and Rebecca F. Plante. New York: Oxford University Press.

Dobson, James C. 1989. *Preparing for Adolescence: Advice from One of America's Foremost Family Psychologists on How to Survive the Coming Years of Change*. Ventura, CA: Regal.

Durant, Robert H., and Joe M. Sanders, Jr. 1989. "Sexual Behavior and Contraceptive Risk Taking among Sexually Active Adolescent Females." *Journal of Adolescent Health Care* 10: 1–9.

Durkheim, Emile. 1951 [1897]. *Suicide*. New York: Free Press.

Eccles, Jacquelynne S. 1999. "The Development of Children Ages 6 to 14." *Future of Children* 9: 30–44.

*The Education of Shelby Knox*. 2005. Documentary by Marion Lipschutz and Rose Rosenblatt. DVD. Incite Pictures.

Edwards, Sarah, and Chris Carne. 1998. "Oral Sex and the Transmission of Viral Sexually Transmitted Infections." *Sexually Transmitted Infections* 74: 6–10.

Ehrenreich, Barbara. 1983. *The Hearts of Men: American Dreams and the Flight from Commitment*. Garden City, NY: Anchor.

Elder, Glen H., Jr., and Rand Conger. 2000. *Children of the Land: Adversity and Success in Rural America*. Chicago: University of Chicago Press.

Ellingson, Stephen. 2004. "Constructing Causal Stories and Moral Boundaries: Institutional Approaches to Sexual Problems." Pp. 283–308 in *The Sexual Organization of the City*, edited by Edward O. Laumann, Stephen Ellingson, Jenna Mahay, Anthony Paik, and Yoosik Youm. Chicago: University of Chicago Press.

Ellingson, Stephen, Edward O. Laumann, Anthony Paik, and Jenna Mahay. 2004. "The Theory of Sex Markets." Pp. 3–38 in *The Sexual Organization of the City*, edited by Edward O. Laumann, Stephen Ellingson, Jenna Mahay, Anthony Paik, and Yoosik Youm. Chicago: University of Chicago Press.

Ellingson, Stephen, Martha Van Haitsma, Edward O. Laumann, and Nelson Tebbe. 2004. "Religion and the Politics of Sexuality." Pp. 309–348 in *The Sexual Organization of the*

*City*, edited by Edward O. Laumann, Stephen Ellingson, Jenna Mahay, Anthony Paik, and Yoosik Youm. Chicago: University of Chicago Press.

Ellison, Christopher G. 1991. "Religious Involvement and Subjective Well-Being." *Journal of Health and Social Behavior* 32: 80–99.

Ellison, Christopher G., and Kristin L. Anderson. 2001. "Religious Involvement and Domestic Violence among U.S. Couples." *Journal for the Scientific Study of Religion* 40: 269–286.

Ellison, Christopher G., John P. Bartkowski, and Kristin L. Anderson. 1999. "Are There Religious Variations in Domestic Violence?" *Journal of Family Issues* 20: 87–113.

Ellison, Christopher G., and Linda K. George. 1994. "Religious Involvement, Social Ties, and Social Support in a Southeastern Community." *Journal for the Scientific Study of Religion* 33: 46–61.

Ellison, Christopher G., and Jeffrey S. Levin. 1998. "The Religion-Health Connection: Evidence, Theory, and Future Directions." *Health Education and Behavior* 25: 700–720.

Emerson, Michael O., and Christian Smith. 2000. *Divided by Faith: Evangelical Religion and the Problem of Race in America*. New York: Oxford University Press.

Erickson, Joseph A. 1992. "Adolescent Religious Development and Commitment: A Structural Equation Model of the Role of Family, Peer Group, and Educational Influences." *Journal for the Scientific Study of Religion* 31: 131–152.

Ethridge, Shannon, and Stephen Arterburn. 2004. *Every Young Woman's Battle: Guarding Your Mind, Heart, and Body in a Sex-Saturated World*. Colorado Springs, CO: WaterBrook.

Feldman, S. Shirley, and Doreen A. Rosenthal. 2000. "The Effect of Communication Characteristics on Family Members' Perceptions of Parents as Sex Educators." *Journal of Research on Adolescence* 10: 119–150.

Finkel, Madelon L., and David J. Finkel. 1975. "Sexual and Contraceptive Knowledge, Attitudes, and Behavior of Male Adolescents." *Family Planning Perspectives* 7: 256–260.

Fisher, Terri D. 1986. "Parent-Child Communication about Sex and Young Adolescents' Sexual Knowledge and Attitudes." *Adolescence* 21: 517–527.

Fisher, William, and Azy Barak. 2000. "Online Sex Shops: Phenomenological and Ideological Perspectives on Internet Sexuality." *Cyber Psychology & Behavior* 3: 575–589.

Forehand, Rex, Mary Gound, Beth A. Kotchick, Lisa Armistead, Nicholas Long, and Kim S. Miller. 2005. "Sexual Intentions of Black Preadolescents: Associations with Risk and Adaptive Behaviors." *Perspectives on Sexual and Reproductive Health* 37: 13–18.

Forste, Renata, and David W. Haas. 2002. "The Transition of Adolescent Males to First Sexual Intercourse: Anticipated or Delayed?" *Perspectives on Sexual and Reproductive Health* 34: 184–190.

Fox, Greer Litton, and Judith K. Inazu. 1980. "Mother-Daughter Communication about Sex." *Family Relations* 29: 347–352.

Freeman, Ellen W., Karl Rickels, George R. Huggins, Emily H. Mudd, Celso-Ramon Garcia, and Helen O. Dickens. 1980. "Adolescent Contraceptive Use: Comparisons of Male and Female Attitudes and Information." *American Journal of Public Health* 70: 790–797.

Gagnon, John H., and William Simon. 1987. "The Sexual Scripting of Oral Genital Contacts." *Archives of Sexual Behavior* 16: 1–25.

Gehmlich, Kerstin, and Mike Collett-White. 2006. "Cannes Sex Films Question Role of Porn, Internet." *Washington Post*, May 24. Retrieved May 26, 2006, from http://

www.washingtonpost.com/wp-dyn/content/article/2006/05/24/AR2006052401050 .html.

Giddens, Anthony. 1979. *Central Problems in Social Theory: Action, Structure, and Contradiction in Social Analysis.* Berkeley: University of California Press.

Gilligan, Carol. 1982. *In a Different Voice: Psychological Theory and Women's Development.* Cambridge, MA: Harvard University Press.

Gillmore, Mary Rogers, Matthew E. Archibald, Diane M. Morrison, Anthony Wilsdon, Elizabeth A. Wells, Marilyn J. Hoppe, Deborah Nahom, and Elise Murowchick. 2002. "Teen Sexual Behavior: Applicability of the Theory of Reasoned Action." *Journal of Marriage and the Family* 64: 885–897.

Giordano, Peggy C. 2003. "Relationships in Adolescence." *Annual Review of Sociology* 29: 257–281.

Glock, Charles, and Rodney Stark. 1965. *Religion and Society in Tension.* Chicago: Rand McNally.

González-López, Gloria. 2004. "De Madres a Hijas: Gendered Lessons on Virginity across Generations of Mexican Immigrant Women." Pp. 217–240 in *Gender and U.S. Immigration: Contemporary Trends*, edited by Pierrette Hondagneu-Sotelo. Berkeley: University of California Press.

Hadaway, C. Kirk, Penny Long Marler, and Mark Chaves. 1993. "What the Polls Don't Show: A Closer Look at U.S. Church Attendance." *American Sociological Review* 58: 741–752.

Hallfors, Denise D., Martha W. Waller, Daniel Bauer, Carol A. Ford, and Carolyn T. Halpern. 2005. "Which Comes First in Adolescence—Sex and Drugs or Depression?" *American Journal of Preventative Medicine* 29: 163–170.

Halpern, Carolyn T., J. Richard Udry, Benjamin Campbell, Chirayath Suchindran, and George A. Mason. 1994. "Testosterone and Religiosity as Predictors of Sexual Attitudes and Activity among Adolescent Males: A Biosocial Model." *Journal of Biosocial Science* 26: 217–234.

Halpern-Felsher, Bonnie L., Jodi L. Cornell, Rhonda Y. Kropp, and Jeanne M. Tschann. 2005. "Oral versus Vaginal Sex among Adolescents: Perceptions, Attitudes, and Behavior." *Pediatrics* 115: 845–851.

Hardy, Sam A., and Marcela Raffaelli. 2003. "Adolescent Religiosity and Sexuality: An Investigation of Reciprocal Influences." *Journal of Adolescence* 26: 731–739.

Hari, Johann. 2005. "It's Everywhere: Just Don't Talk about It." *New Statesman*, March 7, 32–33.

Harris, Joshua. 2003. *Sex Is Not the Problem (Lust Is).* Sisters, OR: Multnomah.

Hays, Ron D., Toshi Hayashi, and Anita L. Stewart. 1989. "A Five-Item Measure of Socially Desirable Response Set." *Educational and Psychological Measurement* 49: 629–636.

Hayt, Elizabeth. 2002. "It's Never Too Late to Be a Virgin." *New York Times*, August 4, section 9.

Henshaw, Stanley K. 2004. *U.S. Teenage Pregnancy Statistics with Comparative Statistics for Women Aged 20–24.* New York: Alan Guttmacher Institute.

Hepburn, Eileen. 1983. "A Three-Level Model of Parent-Daughter Communication about Sexual Topics." *Adolescence* 71: 523–534.

Hockenberry-Eaton, Marilyn, Mary Jane Richman, Colleen DiIorio, Teresa Rivero, and Edward Maibach. 1996. "Mother and Adolescent Knowledge of Sexual Development: The Effects of Gender, Age, and Sexual Experience." *Adolescence* 31: 35–47.

Holman, Thomas B., and Bing Dao Li. 1997. "Premarital Factors Influencing Perceived Readiness for Marriage." *Journal of Family Issues* 18: 124–144.

Holt, Douglas B. 1998. "Does Cultural Capital Structure American Consumption?" *Journal of Consumer Research* 25: 1–25.

Hunter, James Davison. 1987. *Evangelicalism: The Coming Generation.* Chicago: University of Chicago Press.

———. 2000. *The Death of Character: Moral Education in an Age without Good or Evil.* New York: Basic.

Hutchinson, M. Katherine, and Teresa M. Cooney. 1998. "Patterns of Parent-Teen Sexual Risk Communication: Implications for Intervention." *Family Relations* 47: 185–194.

Iannacone, Laurence R. 1995. "Risk, Rationality, and Religious Portfolios." *Economic Inquiry* 33: 285–295.

Inazu, Judith K., and Greer Litton Fox. 1980. "Maternal Influence on the Sexual Behavior of Teen-Age Daughters: Direct and Indirect Sources." *Journal of Family Issues* 1: 81–102.

Irvine, Martha. 2005. "Bi? Study Says More Women Try It." "CBS News," September 16. Retrieved November 18, 2005, from http://www.cbsnews.com/stories/2005/09/16/health/main851480.shtml.

Jaccard, James, and Patricia J. Dittus. 1991. *Parent-Teen Communication: Toward the Prevention of Unintended Pregnancies.* New York: Springer-Verlag.

Jaccard, James, Patricia J. Dittus, and Vivian V. Gordon. 1998. "Parent-Adolescent Congruency in Reports of Adolescent Sexual Behavior and in Communications about Sexual Behavior." *Child Development* 69: 247–261.

———. 2000. "Parent-Teen Communication about Premarital Sex: Factors Associated with the Extent of Communication." *Journal of Adolescent Research* 15: 187–208.

Jacobson, Kristen C., and Lisa J. Crockett. 2000. "Parental Monitoring and Adolescent Adjustment: An Ecological Perspective." *Journal of Research on Adolescence* 10: 65–97.

Jameson, Jenna, and Neil Strauss. 2004. *How to Make Love Like a Porn Star: A Cautionary Tale.* New York: Regan.

Jones, Joy. 2006. "Marriage Is for White People." *Washington Post*, March 26, B1.

Jones, Rachel K., Jacqueline E. Darroch, and Sucheela Singh. 2005. "Religious Differentials in the Sexual and Reproductive Behaviors of Young Women in the United States." *Journal of Adolescent Health* 36: 279–288.

Jones, Stanton L., and Brenna B. Jones. 1993. *How & When to Tell Your Kids about Sex: A Lifelong Approach to Shaping Your Child's Sexual Character.* Colorado Springs, CO: NavPress.

Jordan, Timothy R., James H. Price, and Shawn Fitzgerald. 2000. "Rural Parents' Communication with Their Teen-Agers about Sexual Issues." *Journal of School Health* 70: 338–344.

Joyner, Kara, and Edward O. Laumann. 2000. "Teenage Sex and the Sexual Revolution." Pp. 41–71 in *Sex, Love, and Health in America: Private Choices and Public Policies,* edited by Edward O. Laumann and Robert T. Michael. Chicago: University of Chicago Press.

Kahn, Joan R., Ronald R. Rindfuss, and David K. Guilkey. 1990. "Adolescent Contraceptive Method Choices." *Demography* 27: 323–335.

Kelly, Katy. 2005. "Just Don't Do It! Are We Teaching Our Kids Way Too Much about Sex? Or Not Nearly Enough?" *U.S. News & World Report*, October 17, 45–51.

Kierkegaard, Soren. 1954 [1843]. *Fear and Trembling and the Sickness unto Death* (Translated by Walter Lowrie). Princeton, NJ: Princeton University Press.

King, Pamela E., James L. Furrow, and Natalie Roth. 2002. "The Influence of Families and Peers on Adolescent Religiousness." *Journal for Psychology and Christianity* 21: 109–120.

Kinsman, Sara B., Daniel Romer, Frank F. Furstenberg, and Donald F. Schwartz. 1998. "Early Sexual Initiation: The Role of Peer Norms." *Pediatrics* 102: 1185–1192.

Ku, Leighton, Freya L. Sonenstein, Laura D. Lindberg, Carolyn H. Bradner, Scott Boggess, and Joseph H. Pleck. 1998. "Understanding Changes in Sexual Activity among Young Metropolitan Men: 1979–1995." *Family Planning Perspectives* 30: 256–262.

Ku, Leighton, Freya L. Sonenstein, and Joseph H. Pleck. 1992. "The Association of AIDS Education and Sex Education with Sexual Behavior and Condom Use among Teenage Men." *Family Planning Perspectives* 24: 100–106.

———. 1993. "Factors Influencing First Intercourse for Teenage Men." *Public Health Reports* 108: 660–684.

Laumann, Edward O., John H. Gagnon, Robert T. Michael, and Stuart Michaels. 1994. *The Social Organization of Sexuality: Sexual Practices in the United States*. Chicago: University of Chicago Press.

Leak, Gary K., and Stanley Fish. 1989. "Religious Orientation, Impression Management, and Self-Deception: Toward a Clarification of the Link between Religiosity and Social Desirability." *Journal for the Scientific Study of Religion* 28: 355–359.

Leland, John, Pat Wingert, Laura Gatland, Julie Weingarden, Jamie Reno, Margaret Nelson, and D. J. Wilson. 2000. "Searching for a Holy Spirit." *Newsweek*, May 8, 60–63.

Leman, Kevin. 1999. *Sex Begins in the Kitchen: Because Love Is an All-Day Affair*. Old Tappan, NJ: Revell.

Lewin, Tamar. 1997. "Teen-Agers Alter Sexual Practices, Thinking Risks Will Be Avoided." *New York Times*, April 5, 8.

Lincoln, C. Eric, and Lawrence H. Mamiya. 1990. *The Black Church in the African American Experience*. Durham, NC: Duke University Press.

Luckmann, Thomas. 1967. *The Invisible Religion: The Problem of Religion in Modern Society*. New York: Macmillan.

Mahoney, Annette, Kenneth I. Pargament, Aaron Murray-Swank, and Nichole Murray-Swank. 2003. "Religion and the Sanctification of Family Relationships." *Review of Religious Research* 44: 220–236.

Mahoney, Annette, Kenneth I. Pargament, Nalini Tarakeshwar, and Aaron B. Swank. 2001. "Religion in the Home in the 1980s and 1990s: A Meta-Analytic Review and Conceptual Analysis of Links between Religion, Marriage and Parenting." *Journal of Family Psychology* 15: 559–596.

Martin, Karin A. 2002. "I Couldn't Ever Picture Myself Having Sex: Gender Differences in Sex and Sexual Subjectivity." Pp. 127–141 in *Sexuality and Gender*, edited by Christine L. Williams and Arlene Stein. Malden, MA: Blackwell.

Martin, Paige D., Don Martin, and Maggie Martin. 2001. "Adolescent Premarital Sexual Activity, Cohabitation, and Attitudes toward Marriage." *Adolescence* 36: 601–609.

Mathewes-Green, Frederica. 2005a. "Bodies of Evidence: The Real Meaning of Sex Is Right in Front of Our Eyes." *Touchstone Magazine*, June. Retrieved March 29, 2006, http://touchstonemag.com/archives/article.php?id=18–05–027-f.

———. 2005b. "What to Say at a Naked Party." *Christianity Today*, February, 48.

May, Elaine Tyler. 1980. *Great Expectations: Marriage and Divorce in Post-Victorian America*. Chicago: University of Chicago Press.

McCree, Donna Hubbard, Gina M. Wingood, Ralph DiClemente, Susan Davies, and Katherine F. Harrington. 2003. "Religiosity and Risky Sexual Behavior in African-American Adolescent Females." *Journal of Adolescent Health* 33: 2–8.

McDowell, Josh. 2002. *Why True Love Waits: The Definitive Book on How to Help Your Kids Resist Sexual Pleasure.* Carol Stream, IL: Tyndale House.

McDowell, Josh, and Bob Hostetler. 2002. *The Love Killer: Answering Why True Love Waits.* Carol Stream, IL: Tyndale House.

Meier, Ann M. 2003. "Adolescents' Transition to First Intercourse, Religiosity, and Attitudes about Sex." *Social Forces* 81: 1031–1052.

Miller, Alan S., and John P. Hoffmann. 1995. "Risk and Religion: An Explanation of Gender Differences in Religiosity." *Journal for the Scientific Study of Religion* 34: 63–75.

Miller, Alan S., and Rodney Stark. 2002. "Gender and Religiousness: Can Socialization Explanations Be Saved?" *American Journal of Sociology* 107: 1399–1423.

Miller, Brent C., and Terrance D. Olson. 1988. "Sexual Attitudes and Behavior of High School Students in Relation to Background and Contextual Factors." *Journal of Sex Research* 24: 194–200.

Miller, Kim S., Leslie F. Clark, and Janet S. Moore. 1997. "Sexual Initiation with Older Male Partners and Subsequent HIV Risk Behavior among Female Adolescents." *Family Planning Perspectives* 29: 212–214.

Miller, Kim S., Leslie F. Clark, Deborah A. Wendell, Martin L. Levin, Phyllis Gray-Ray, Carmen Noemi Velez, and Mayris P. Webber. 1997. "Adolescent Heterosexual Experience: A New Typology." *Journal of Adolescent Health* 20: 179–186.

Miller, Kim S., and Daniel J. Whitaker. 2001. "Predictors of Mother-Adolescent Discussions about Condoms: Implications for Providers Who Serve Youth." *Pediatrics* 108: 28–35.

Miller, Lisa, and Merav Gur. 2002. "Religiousness and Sexual Responsibility in Adolescent Girls." *Journal of Adolescent Health* 31: 401–406.

Mitchell, Kimberly J., David Finkelhor, and Janis Wolak. 2003. "The Exposure of Youth to Unwanted Sexual Material on the Internet: A National Survey of Risk, Impact, and Prevention." *Youth & Society* 34: 330–358.

Moran, James R., and Deborah M. Corley. 1991. "Sources of Sexual Information and Sexual Attitudes and Behaviors of Anglo and Hispanic Adolescent Males." *Adolescence* 26: 857–864.

Mosher, William D., Anjani Chandra, and Jo Jones. 2005. "Sexual Behavior and Selected Health Measures: Men and Women 15–44 Years of Age, United States, 2002." *Advance Data from Vital Health Statistics 362.* Hyattsville, MD: National Center for Health Statistics.

Mueller, Kay E., and William G. Powers. 1990. "Parent-Child Sexual Discussion: Perceived Communicator Style and Subsequent Behavior." *Adolescence* 25: 469–482.

Muller, Chandra, and Christopher G. Ellison. 2001. "Religion Involvement, Social Capital, and Adolescents' Academic Progress: Evidence from the National Longitudinal Study of 1988." *Sociological Focus* 34: 155–183.

Myers, Scott M. 1996. "An Interactive Model of Religiosity Inheritance: The Importance of Family Context." *American Sociological Review* 61: 858–866.

National Center for Education Statistics. 2002. "Digest of Education Statistics." Washington, DC: National Center for Education Statistics, Retrieved August 4, 2005, from http://nces.ed.gov/programs/digest/d02/index.asp.

National Center for Health Statistics. 2005. "Fertility, Family Planning, and Reproductive Health of U.S. Women: Data from the 2002 National Survey of Family Growth." Retrieved March 29, 2006, from http://www.cdc.gov/nchs/data/series/sr_23/sr23_025 .pdf.

Neumark-Sztainer, Dianne, Mary Story, Simone A. French, and Michael D. Resnick. 1997. "Psychosocial Correlates of Health Compromising Behaviors among Adolescents." *Health Education Research* 12: 37–52.

Newcomer, Susan F., and J. Richard Udry. 1985. "Parent-Child Communication and Adolescent Sexual Behavior." *Family Planning Perspectives* 17: 169–174.

Newman, Bernie S., and Peter G. Muzzonigro. 1993. "The Effects of Traditional Family Values on the Coming Out Process of Gay Male Adolescents." *Adolescence* 28: 213–226.

O'Donnell, Lydia, Athi Myint-U, Carl R. O'Donnell, and Ann Stueve. 2003. "Long-Term Influence of Sexual Norms and Attitudes on Timing of Sexual Initiation among Young Urban Minority Youth." *Journal of School Health* 73: 68–75.

O'Sullivan, Lucia F., Heino F. L. Meyer-Bahlburg, and Beverly X. Watkins. 2001. "Mother-Daughter Communication about Sex among Urban African American and Latino Families." *Journal of Adolescent Research* 16: 269–292.

Ozorak, Elizabeth W. 1989. "Social and Cognitive Influences on the Development of Religious Beliefs and Commitment in Adolescence." *Journal for the Scientific Study of Religion* 28: 448–463.

Padilla, Amado M., and Traci L. Baird. 1991. "Mexican-American Adolescent Sexuality and Sexual Knowledge: An Exploratory Study." *Hispanic Journal of Behavioral Sciences* 13: 95–104.

Paul, Pamela. 2005. *Pornified: How Pornography Is Transforming Our Lives, Our Relationships, and Our Families.* New York: Times Books.

Paulhus, Delroy L. 1984. "Two-Component Models of Socially Desirable Responding." *Journal of Personality and Social Psychology* 46: 598–609.

Pearce, Lisa D., and William G. Axinn. 1998. "The Impact of Family Religious Life on the Quality of Mother-Child Relations." *American Sociological Review* 63: 810–828.

Penner, Clifford, and Joyce Penner. 2003. *The Gift of Sex: A Guide to Sexual Fulfillment.* Waco, TX: Word.

Penning, James M., and Corwin E. Smidt. 2002. *Evangelicalism: The Next Generation.* Grand Rapids, MI: Baker Academic.

Petersen, Larry R., and Gregory V. Donnenwerth. 1997. "Secularization and the Influence of Religion on Beliefs about Premarital Sex." *Social Forces* 75: 1071–1089.

Pope John Paul II. 1997. *The Theology of the Body: Human Love in the Divine Plan.* Boston: Pauline Books and Media.

Pope Paul VI. 1968. *Humanae Vitae.* Rome: Vatican.

Presser, Stanley, and Linda Stinson. 1998. "Data Collection Mode and Social Desirability Bias in Self-Reported Religious Attendance." *American Sociological Review* 63: 137–145.

Putnam, Robert D. 1995. "Bowling Alone: America's Declining Social Capital." *Journal of Democracy* 6: 65–78.

Raghavan, Ramesh, Laura M. Bogart, Marc N. Elliott, Katherine D. Vestal, and Mark A. Schuster. 2004. "Sexual Victimization among a National Probability Sample of Adolescent Women." *Perspectives on Sexual and Reproductive Health* 36: 225–232.

Regnerus, Mark D. 2000. "Shaping Schooling Success: A Multi-Level Study of Religious Socialization and Educational Outcomes in Urban Public Schools." *Journal for the Scientific Study of Religion* 39: 363–370.

———. 2004. "Religious Influences on Sensitive Self-Reported Behaviors: The Product of Social Desirability, Deceit, or Embarrassment?" University of Texas at Austin. Unpublished paper.

———. 2005. "Talking about Sex: Religion and Patterns of Parent-Child Communication about Sex and Contraception." *Sociological Quarterly* 46: 81–107.

Regnerus, Mark D., and Glen H. Elder, Jr. 2003. "Staying on Track in School: Religious Influences in High- and Low-Risk Settings." *Journal for the Scientific Study of Religion* 42: 633–649.

Regnerus, Mark D., and Christian Smith. 2005. "Selection Effects in Studies of Religious Influence." *Review of Religious Research* 47: 23–50.

Regnerus, Mark D., Christian Smith, and Brad Smith. 2004. "Social Context in the Development of Adolescent Religiosity." *Applied Developmental Science* 8: 27–38.

Regnerus, Mark D., and Jeremy E. Uecker. 2006. "Finding Faith, Losing Faith: The Prevalence and Context of Religious Transformations during Adolescence." *Review of Religious Research* 47: 217–237.

Reiss, Ira L. 1989. "Society and Sexuality: A Sociological Explanation." Pp. 3–29 in *Human Sexuality: The Societal and Interpersonal Context*, edited by Kathleen McKinney and Susan Sprecher. Norwood, NJ: Ablex.

Remez, Lisa. 2000. "Oral Sex among Adolescents: Is It Sex or Is It Abstinence?" *Family Planning Perspectives* 32: 298–304.

Risman, Barbara, and Pepper Schwartz. 2002. "After the Sexual Revolution: Gender Politics in Teen Dating." *Contexts* 1: 16–24.

Rodgers, Kathleen Boyce. 1999. "Parenting Processes Related to Sexual Risk-Taking Behaviors of Adolescent Males and Females." *Journal of Marriage and the Family* 61: 99–109.

Rose, Susan. 2005. "Going Too Far? Sex, Sin, and Social Policy." *Social Forces* 84: 1207–1232.

Rosenbaum, Janet. 2006. "Reborn a Virgin: Adolescents' Retracting of Virginity Pledges and Sexual Histories." *American Journal of Public Health* 96: 1098–1103.

Rosenbloom, Stephanie. 2005. "A Ring That Says No, Not Yet." *New York Times*, December 8. Retrieved December 12, 2005, from http://www.nytimes.com/2005/12/08/fashion/thursdaystyles/08purity.html.

Rostosky, Sharon Scales, Mark D. Regnerus, and Margaret Laurie Comer Wright. 2003. "Coital Debut: The Role of Religiosity and Sex Attitudes in the Add Health Survey." *Journal of Sex Research* 40: 358–367.

Rowatt, Wade C., and Lee A. Kirkpatrick. 2002. "Two Dimensions of Attachment to God and Their Relation to Affect, Religiosity, and Personality Constructs." *Journal for the Scientific Study of Religion* 41: 637–649.

Rowatt, Wade C., and David P. Schmitt. 2003. "Associations between Religious Orientations and Varieties of Sexual Experience." *Journal for the Scientific Study of Religion* 42: 455–465.

Sanders, Gregory F., and Ronald L. Mullis. 1988. "Family Influences on Sexual Attitudes and Knowledge as Reported by College Students." *Adolescence* 92: 827–846.

Schalet, Amy. 2004. "Must We Fear Adolescent Sexuality?" *Medscape General Medicine* 6: 1–22.

Schuster, Mark A., Robert M. Bell, and David E. Kanouse. 1996. "The Sexual Practices of Adolescent Virgins: Genital Sexual Activities of High School Students Who Have Never Had Vaginal Intercourse." *American Journal of Public Health* 86: 1570–1576.

Seidman, Stuart N., William D. Mosher, and Sevgi O. Aral. 1992. "Women with Multiple Sexual Partners: United States, 1988." *American Journal of Public Health* 82: 1388–1394.

Sheeran, Paschal, Dominic Abrams, Charles Abraham, and Russell Spears. 1993. "Religiosity and Adolescents' Premarital Sexual Attitudes and Behaviour: An Empirical Study of Conceptual Issues." *European Journal of Social Psychology* 23: 39–52.

Sherkat, Darren E., and Christopher G. Ellison. 1997. "The Cognitive Structure of a Moral Crusade: Conservative Protestant Opposition to Pornography." *Social Forces* 75: 957–980.

Shoveller, Jean A., Joy L. Johnson, Donald B. Langille, and Terry Mitchell. 2004. "Sociocultural Influences on Young People's Sexual Development." *Social Science & Medicine* 59: 473–487.

Shuman, Joel James, and Keith G. Meador. 2002. *Heal Thyself: Spirituality, Medicine, and the Distortion of Christianity*. New York: Oxford University Press.

Sider, Ronald J. 2005. *Scandal of the Evangelical Conscience: Why Are Christians Living Just Like the Rest of the World?* Grand Rapids, MI: Baker.

Sieving, Renee E., Clea S. McNeely, and Robert William Blum. 2000. "Maternal Expectations, Mother-Child Connectedness, and Adolescent Sexual Debut." *Archives of Pediatrics and Adolescent Medicine* 154: 809–816.

Singh, Susheela, and Jacqueline E. Darroch. 2000. "Adolescent Pregnancy and Childbearing: Levels and Trends in Developed Countries." *Family Planning Perspectives* 32: 14–23.

Slade, Joseph W. 2001. *Pornography and Sexual Representation: A Reference Guide* (Vol. 1). Westport, CT: Greenwood.

Smedes, Lewis B. 1976. *Sex for Christians: The Limits and Liberties of Sexual Living*. Grand Rapids, MI: Eerdmans.

Smidt, Corwin (ed.). 2003. *Religion as Social Capital: Producing the Common Good*. Waco, TX: Baylor University Press.

Smith, Aaron. 2006. "Merck's Dance with the Religious Right." *CNNMoney.com*, May 16. Retrieved May 16, 2006, from http://money.cnn.com/2006/05/15/news/economy/merck/index.htm.

Smith, Christian. 1996. *Resisting Reagan: The U.S. Central America Peace Movement*. Chicago: University of Chicago Press.

———. 2003a. "Introduction: Rethinking the Secularization of American Public Life." Pp. 1–96 in *The Secular Revolution: Power, Interests, and Conflict in the Secularization of American Public Life*, edited by Christian Smith. Berkeley: University of California Press.

———. 2003b. *Moral, Believing Animals: Human Personhood and Culture*. New York: Oxford University Press.

———. 2003c. "Theorizing Religious Effects among American Adolescents." *Journal for the Scientific Study of Religion* 42(1): 17–30.

Smith, Christian, with Melinda Lundquist Denton. 2005. *Soul Searching: The Religious and Spiritual Lives of American Teenagers*. New York: Oxford University Press.

Smith, Christian, with Michael Emerson, Sally Gallagher, Paul Kennedy, and David Sikkink. 1998. *American Evangelicalism: Embattled and Thriving*. Chicago: University of Chicago Press.

Sonnenberg, Roger R. 1998. *Human Sexuality: A Christian Perspective*. St. Louis, MO: Concordia.

Stack, Steven, Ira Wasserman, and Roger Kern. 2004. "Adult Social Bonds and Use of Internet Pornography." *Social Science Quarterly* 85: 75–88.

Stark, Rodney. 1996. "Religion as Context: Hellfire and Delinquency One More Time." *Sociology of Religion* 57: 163–173.

———. 1997. *The Rise of Christianity: How the Obscure, Marginal Jesus Movement Became the Dominant Religious Force in the Western World in a Few Centuries*. San Francisco, CA: HarperSanFrancisco.

———. 2000. "Religious Effects: In Praise of 'Idealistic Humbug.'" *Review of Religious Research* 41: 289–310.

Stark, Rodney, and William Sims Bainbridge. 1996. *Religion, Deviance, and Social Control*. New York: Routledge.

Steensland, Brian, Jerry Park, Mark Regnerus, Lynn Robinson, Bradford Wilcox, and Robert Woodberry. 2000. "The Measure of American Religion: Toward Improving the State of the Art." *Social Forces* 79: 291–318.

Steinberg, Laurence, and Amanda Sheffield Morris. 2001. "Adolescent Development." *Annual Review of Psychology* 52: 83–110.

Steinman, Kenneth J., and Marc A. Zimmerman. 2004. "Religious Activity and Risk Behavior among African American Adolescents: Concurrent and Developmental Effects." *American Journal of Community Psychology* 33: 151–161.

Studer, Marlena, and Arland Thornton. 1987. "Adolescent Religiosity and Contraceptive Usage." *Journal of Marriage and the Family* 49: 117–128.

Swidler, Ann. 1986. "Culture in Action: Symbols and Strategies." *American Sociological Review* 51: 273–286.

Taris, Toon W., and Gün R. Semin. 1997. "Parent-Child Interaction during Adolescence, and the Adolescent's Sexual Experience: Control, Closeness, and Conflict." *Journal of Youth and Adolescence* 26: 373–398.

Taylor, Charles. 1991. *The Ethics of Authenticity*. Cambridge, MA: Harvard University Press.

Teitler, Julien O., and Christopher C. Weiss. 2000. "Effects of Neighborhood and School Environments on Transitions to First Sexual Intercourse." *Sociology of Education* 73: 112–132.

Thio, Alex. 2001. *Deviant Behavior*, 6th ed. Boston: Allyn and Bacon.

Thompson, Sharon. 1990. "Putting a Big Thing into a Little Hole: Teenage Girls' Accounts of Sexual Initiation." *Journal of Sex Research* 27: 341–361.

Thomson, Elizabeth. 1982. "Socialization for Sexual and Contraceptive Behavior: Moral Absolutes versus Relative Consequences." *Youth & Society* 14: 103–128.

Thornton, Arland. 1985. "Reciprocal Influences of Family and Religion in a Changing World." *Journal of Marriage and the Family* 47: 381–394.

Thornton, Arland, William G. Axinn, and Daniel H. Hill. 1992. "Reciprocal Effects of Religiosity, Cohabitation, and Marriage." *American Journal of Sociology* 98: 628–651.

Thornton, Arland, and Donald Camburn. 1989. "Religious Participation and Adolescent Sexual Behavior." *Journal of Marriage and the Family* 51: 641–653.

Torode, Sam, and Bethany Torode. 2002. *Open Embrace: A Protestant Couple Rethinks Contraception*. Grand Rapids, MI: Eerdmans.

Tourangeau, Roger, Lance J. Rips, and Kenneth A. Rasinski. 2000. *The Psychology of Survey Response*. Cambridge: Cambridge University Press.

Townsend, Nicholas W. 2002. *The Package Deal: Marriage, Work, and Fatherhood in Men's Lives*. Philadelphia, PA: Temple University Press.

Trimble, Douglas E. 1997. "The Religious Orientation Scale: Review and Meta-Analysis of Social Desirability Effects." *Educational and Psychological Measurement* 57: 970–986.

Udry, J. Richard and Peter Bearman. 1998. "New Methods for New Research on Adolescent Sexual Behavior." Pp. 241–269 in *New Perspectives on Adolescent Risk Behavior*, edited by R. Jessor. Cambridge: Cambridge University Press.

Uecker, Jeremy E., Nicole Angotti, and Mark D. Regnerus. 2006. "Going Most of the Way: Religion, Pledging, and Sexual 'Substitution' among Young Americans." University of Texas at Austin. Unpublished manuscript.

Uecker, Jeremy E., Mark D. Regnerus, and Margaret L. Vaaler. 2006. "Losing My Religion: The Social Sources of Religious Decline in Early Adulthood." University of Texas at Austin. Unpublished manuscript.

Upchurch, Dawn M., Carol S. Aneshensel, Clea A. Sucoff, and Lene Levy-Storms. 1999. "Neighborhood and Family Contexts of Adolescent Sexual Activity." *Journal of Marriage and the Family* 61: 920–933.

Van Biema, David, Julie Grace, and Emily Mitchell. 1999. "A Surge of Teen Spirit." *Time*, May 31, 58–59.

Waite, Linda J., and Kara Joyner. 2001. "Emotional Satisfaction and Physical Pleasure in Sexual Unions: Time Horizon, Sexual Behavior, and Sexual Exclusivity." *Journal of Marriage and the Family* 63: 247–264.

Wallace, John M., and David R. Williams. 1997. "Religion and Adolescent Health-Compromising Behavior." Pp. 444–468 in *Health Risks and Developmental Transitions during Adolescence*, edited by John Schulenberg, Jennifer Maggs, and Klaus Hurrelmann. New York: Cambridge University Press.

Watson, P. J., Ronald J. Morris, James E. Foster, and Ralph W. Hood, Jr. 1986. "Religiosity and Social Desirability." *Journal for the Scientific Study of Religion* 25: 215–232.

Wayment, Heidi A., Gail E. Wyatt, M. Belinda Tucker, Gloria J. Romero, Jennifer V. Carmona, Michael Newcomb, Beatriz M. Solis, Monika Riederle, and Claudia Mitchell-Kernan. 2003. "Predictors of Risky and Precautionary Sexual Behaviors among Single and Married White Women." *Journal of Applied Social Psychology* 33: 791–816.

Weigel, George. 1999. *Witness to Hope: The Biography of Pope John Paul II*. New York: HarperCollins.

Weinberger, Daniel R., Brita Elvevåg, and Jay N. Giedd. 2005. *The Adolescent Brain: A Work in Progress*. Washington, DC: National Campaign to Prevent Teen Pregnancy.

Werner-Wilson, Ronald Jay. 1998. "Are Virgins at Risk for Contracting HIV/AIDS?" *Journal of HIV/AIDS Prevention & Education for Adolescents & Children* 2: 63–71.

Wheat, Ed, and Gaye Wheat. 1981. *Intended for Pleasure: Sex Technique and Sexual Fulfillment in Christian Marriage*. Old Tappan, NJ: Revell.

Whitaker, Daniel J., and Kim S. Miller. 2000. "Parent-Adolescent Discussions about Sex and Condoms: Impact on Peer Influences of Sexual Risk Behavior." *Journal of Adolescent Research* 15: 251–273.

Whitaker, Daniel J., Kim S. Miller, and Leslie F. Clark. 2000. "Reconceptualizing Adolescent Sexual Behavior: Beyond Did They or Didn't They?" *Family Planning Perspectives* 32: 111–117.

Whitaker, Daniel J., Kim S. Miller, David C. May, and Martin L. Levin. 1999. "Teenage Partners' Communication about Sexual Risk and Condom Use: The Importance of Parent-Teenager Discussions." *Family Planning Perspectives* 31: 117–121.

White, Chris. 2004. *Group Suggestions for Introduction to True Love Waits.* Nashville, TN: LifeWay.

Wilcox, W. Bradford. 2002. "Religion, Convention, and Paternal Involvement." *Journal of Marriage and the Family* 64: 780–792.

———. 2004. *Soft Patriarchs, New Men: How Christianity Shapes Fathers and Husbands.* Chicago: University of Chicago Press.

Wiley, Juli Loesch. 2004. "The Delightful Secrets of Sex." *Touchstone Magazine*, January–February, 20–23.

Wimberley, Dale W. 1989. "Religion and Role-Identity: A Structural Symbolic Interactionist Conceptualization of Religiosity." *Sociological Quarterly* 30: 125–142.

Winner, Lauren F. 2005. *Real Sex: The Naked Truth about Chastity.* Grand Rapids, MI: Brazos.

Wojtyla, Karol (Pope John Paul II). *Love and Responsibility.* Trans. H. T. Willetts. 1981. San Francisco: Ignatius Press.

Woodsong, Cynthia, Michele Shedlin, and Helen Koo. 2004. "The 'Natural' Body, God and Contraceptive Use in the Southeastern United States." *Culture, Health & Sexuality* 6: 61–78.

Wuthnow, Robert. 1995. *Learning to Care: Elementary Kindness in an Age of Indifference.* New York: Oxford University Press.

———. 2004. "*The Religious Factor* Revisited." *Sociological Theory* 22: 205–218.

Wysocki, Diane K. 2001. "Let Your Fingers Do the Talking: Sex on an Adult Chat Line." Pp. 258–263 in *Readings in Deviant Behavior*, edited by Alex Thio and Thomas Calhoun. Boston: Allyn and Bacon.

Xu, Xiaohe, Clark D. Hudspeth, and John P. Bartkowski. 2005. "The Timing of First Marriage: Are There Religious Variations?" *Journal of Family Issues* 26: 584–618.

Yancey, Philip. 2003. *Rumors of Another World: What on Earth Are We Missing?* Grand Rapids, MI: Zondervan.

Yeung, W. Jean, Greg J. Duncan, and Martha S. Hill. 2000. "Putting Fathers Back in the Picture: Parental Activities and Children's Adult Outcomes." *Marriage and Family Review* 29: 97–113.

Young, Michael P. 2002. "Confessional Protest: The Religious Birth of U.S. National Social Movements." *American Sociological Review* 67: 660–688.

———. 2006. *Bearing Witness against Sin: The Evangelical Birth of the American Social Movement.* Chicago: University of Chicago Press.

Zelnik, Melvin, John F. Kantner, and Kathleen Ford. 1981. *Sex and Pregnancy in Adolescence.* Beverly Hills, CA: Sage.

# INDEX